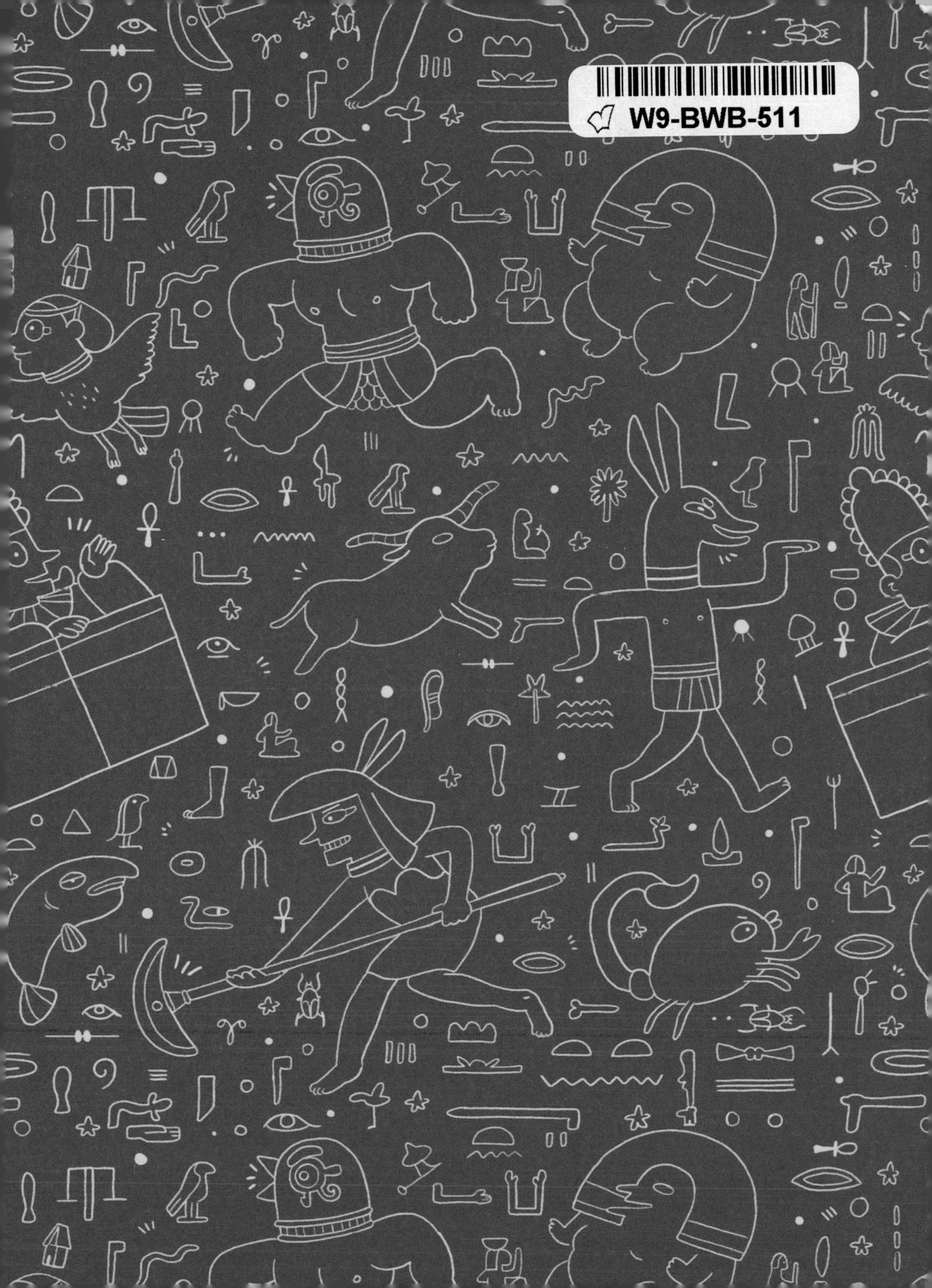

- PANTHEON -

ALL THE GODS OF A RELIGION
FROM GREEK PAN 'ALL' + THEOS 'GODS'

FOREWORD

* * * * * * *

THE CREATION TALES OF ANCIENT EGYPT DEVELOPED NOT ONLY THROUGHOUT THE CULTURE'S SIX THOUSAND YEAR HISTORY BUT ALSO GEOGRAPHICALLY, ACROSS THE ADMINISTRATIVE CENTRES OF THE NILE VALLEY, AND, IN SO DOING, SUBTLY DIFFERENT VARIATIONS OF THE NARRATIVES BECAME ESTABLISHED. CONSEQUENTLY, OUR MODERN UNDERSTANDING OF THESE FREQUENTLY COMPLEX POLITICO-RELIGIOUS TALES IS HAMPERED BY CONFLICTING VERSIONS AND BY THE FRAGMENTARY NATURE OF THEIR SURVIVAL.

IT IS, THEREFORE, A JOY TO ENCOUNTER HAMISH STEELE'S COMPREHENSIVE AND ESSENTIALLY LINEAR RETELLING, PRESENTED WITH VERVE, WIT, AND THE OCCASIONAL KNOWING WINK TO THE READER.

AT PANTHEON'S CORE SIT HORUS AND SET, TWO OF THE MOST ANCIENT AND RECOGNISABLE DEITIES OF EGYPTIAN RELIGION. THEIR ICONOGRAPHY REACHES FAR BACK INTO HISTORY, LONG BEFORE THE WRITTEN WORD, AND ALLUSIONS TO THEIR INTERMINABLE BATTLE ARE SCATTERED THROUGHOUT MUCH OF EGYPT'S ANCIENT ART AND LITERATURE. ARGUABLY, THE CONCEPTS OF THE MALIGN, REGICIDAL UNCLE AND THE WRONGED NEPHEW HAVE BECOME CULTURAL TROPES, IDENTIFIABLE IN THE LATER FOUNDATION MYTHS OF ANCIENT ROME, WILLIAM SHAKESPEARE'S HAMLET, AND EVEN DISNEY'S THE LION KING, WHILE ELEMENTS OF THE SEXUALLY AMBIVALENT SET MAY BE GLIMPSED IN PAUL LYNDE'S MISCHIEVOUS UNCLE ARTHUR FROM THE TELEVISION SITCOM, BEWITCHED.

IN PANTHEON, HOWEVER, HAMISH HAS SUCCEEDED IN REFASHIONING THESE VENERABLE FIGURES TO PROVIDE HIS OWN, UNIQUELY CONTEMPORARY INTERPRETATION, WHILE RETAINING APPROPRIATELY ANCIENT ECHOES.

— JOHN J JOHNSTON, EGYPTOLOGIST
JANUARY 2017

THE EGYPTIAN DEITIES

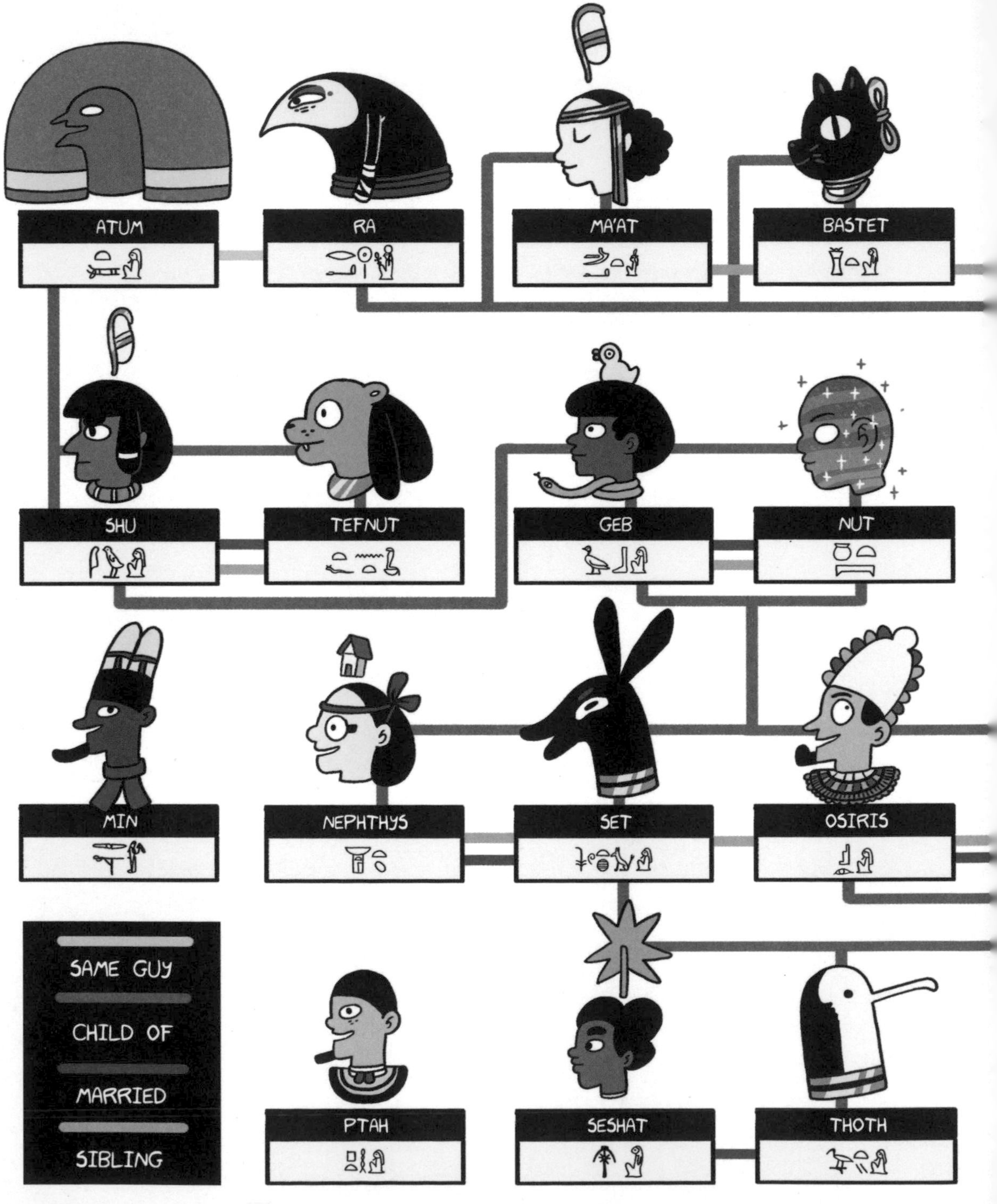
ATUM
RA
MA'AT
BASTET
SHU
TEFNUT
GEB
NUT
MIN
NEPHTHYS
SET
OSIRIS
SAME GUY
CHILD OF
MARRIED
SIBLING
PTAH
SESHAT
THOTH

THESE ARE SOME OF THE GODS AND GODDESSES FEATURED IN THE BOOK, BUT THIS IS BY NO MEANS A COMPLETE LIST. SPEND A NIGHT ON WIKIPEDIA! YOU MIGHT END UP DRAWING A WHOLE GRAPHIC NOVEL BECAUSE OF IT.

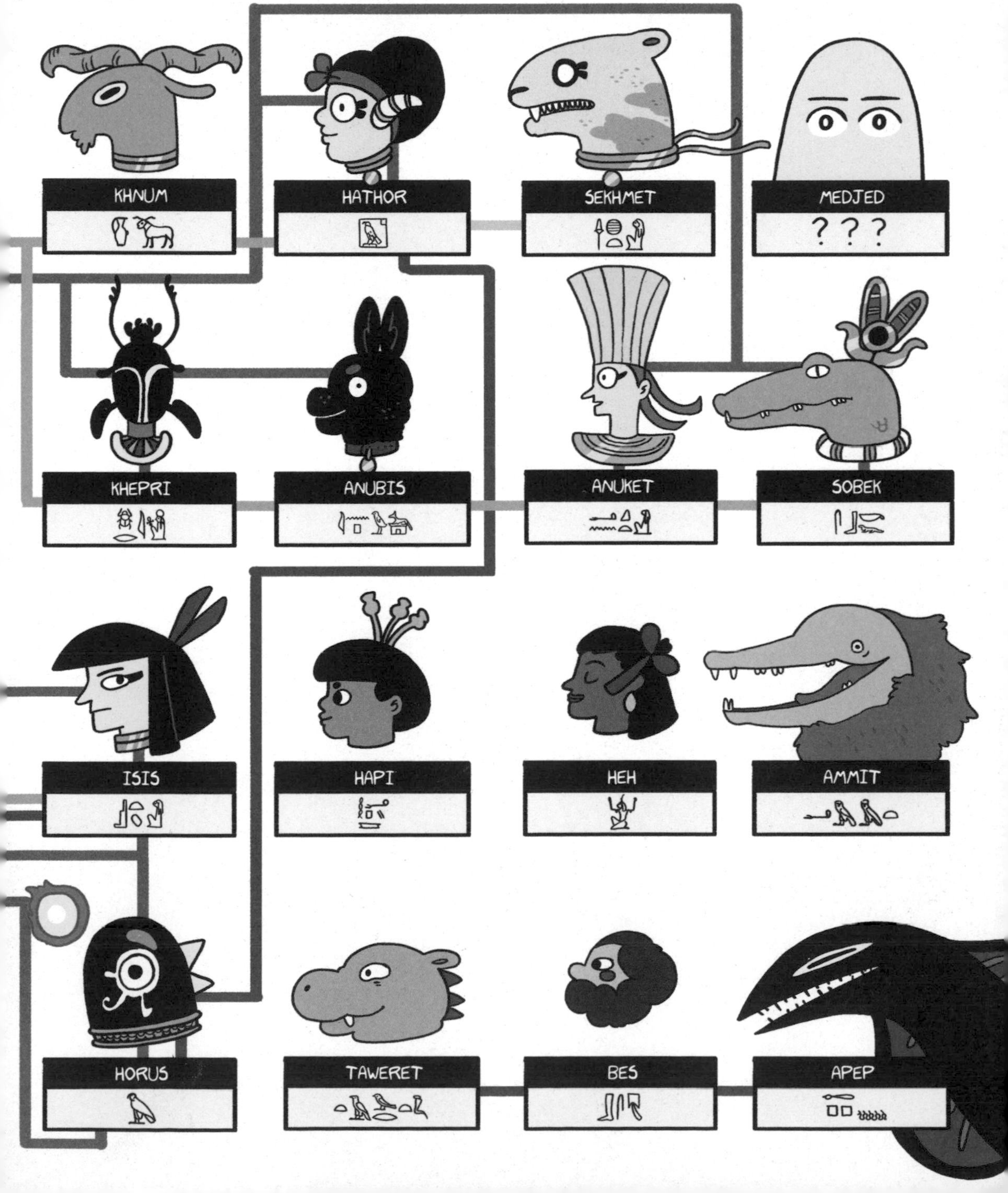
KHNUM
HATHOR
SEKHMET
MEDJED
???
KHEPRI
ANUBIS
ANUKET
SOBEK
ISIS
HAPI
HEH
AMMIT
HORUS
TAWERET
BES
APEP

THIS WAS THE FIRST EVENT.

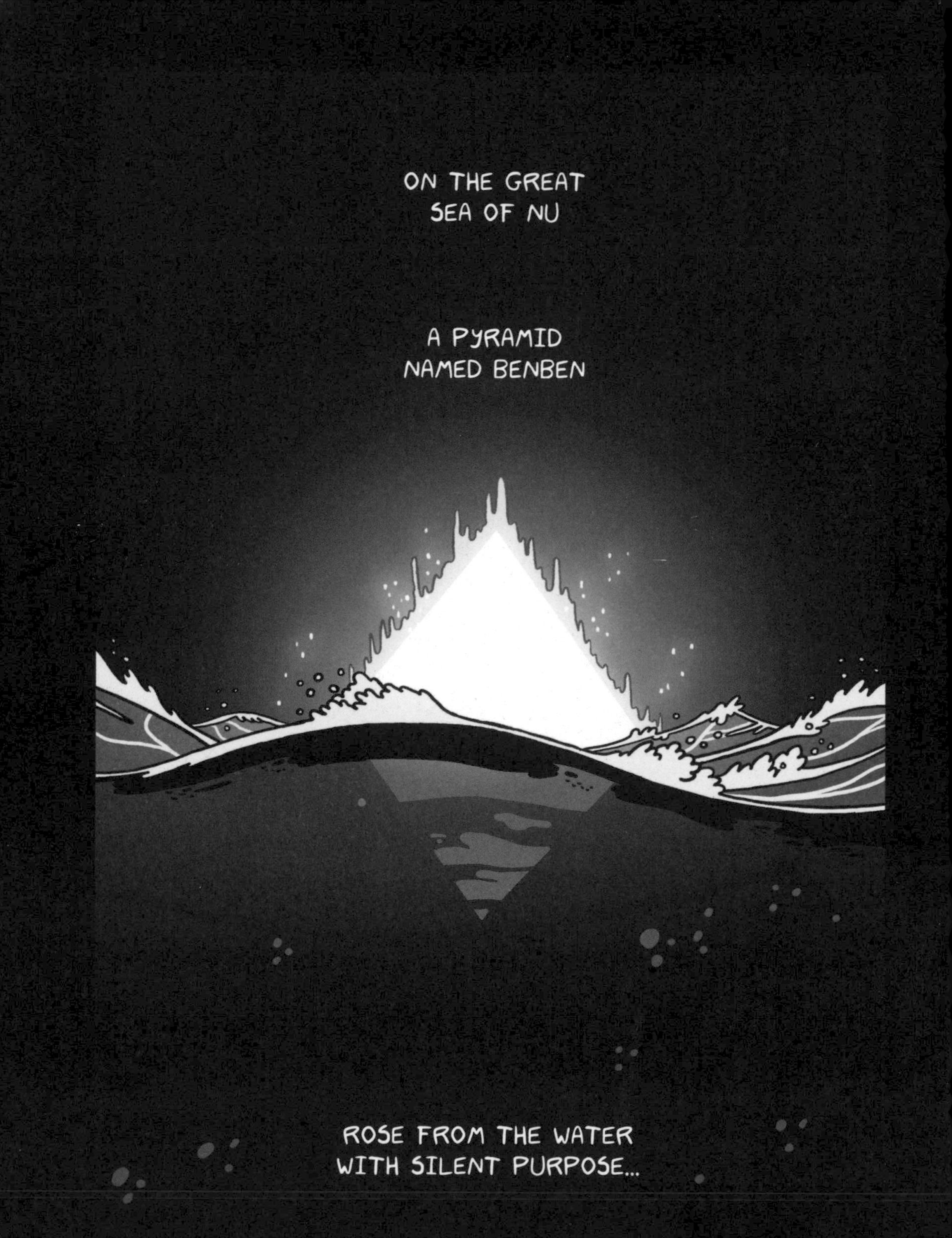
ON THE GREAT
SEA OF NU
A PYRAMID
NAMED BENBEN
ROSE FROM THE WATER
WITH SILENT PURPOSE...

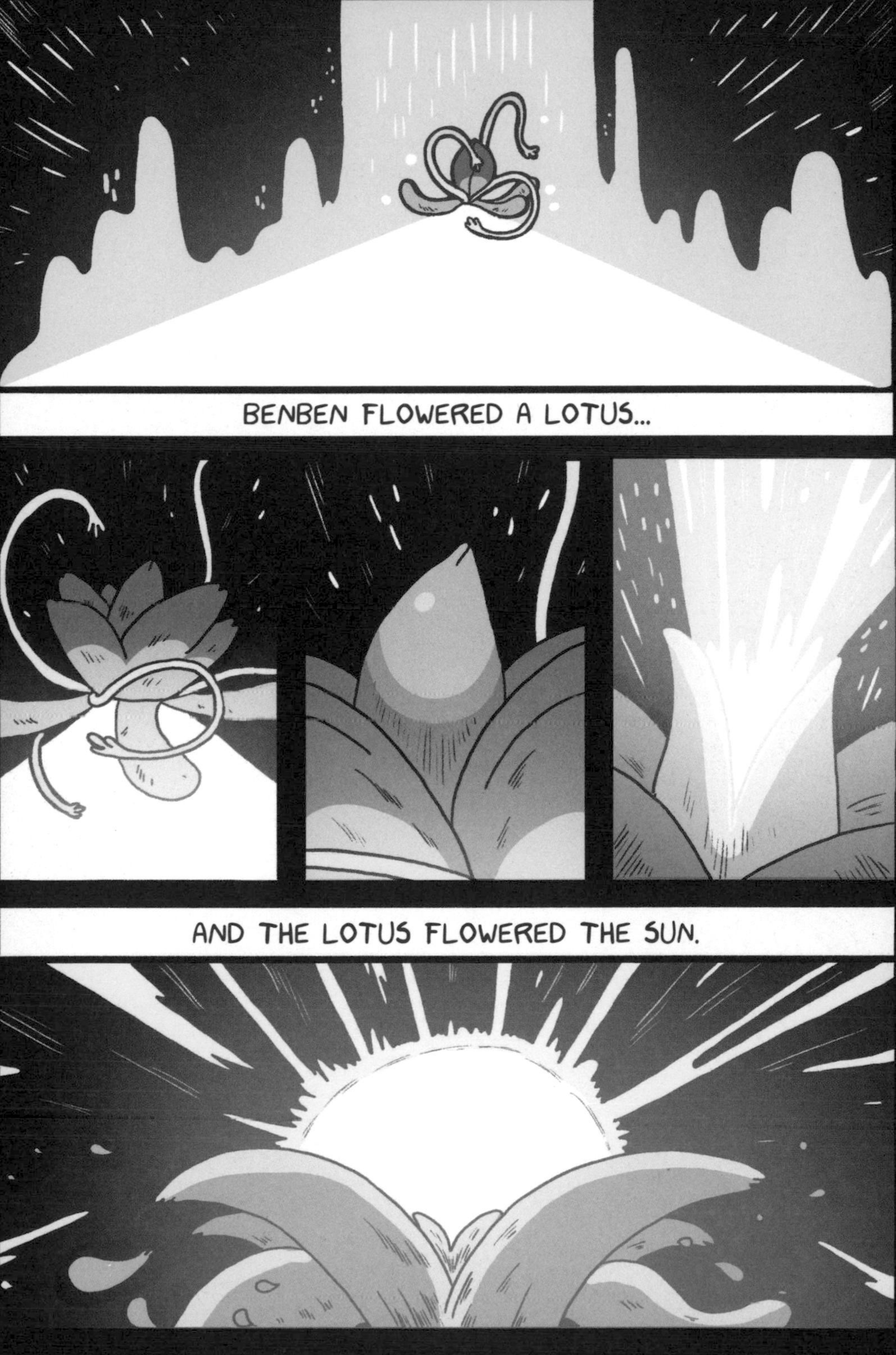
BENBEN FLOWERED A LOTUS...
AND THE LOTUS FLOWERED THE SUN.

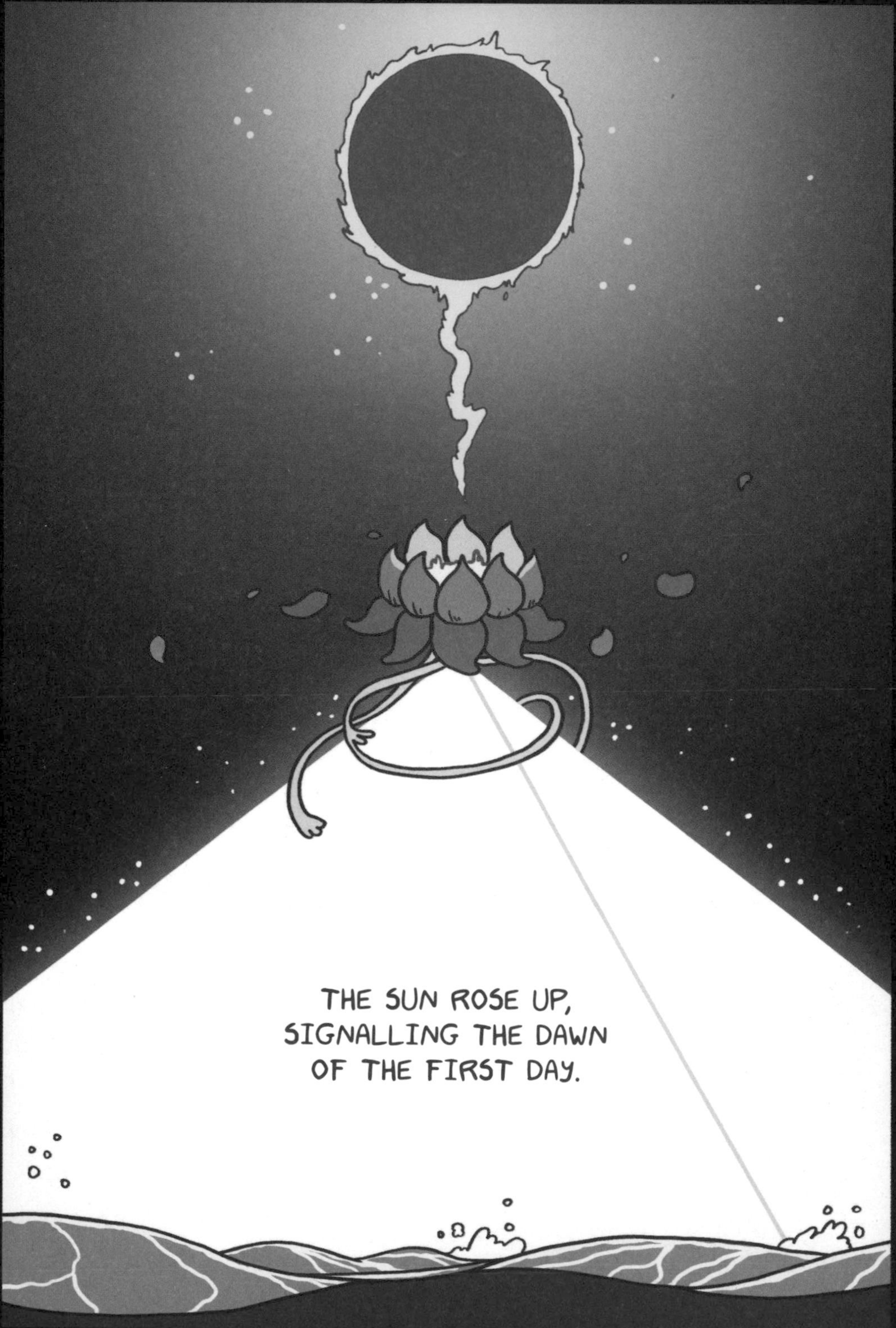
THE SUN ROSE UP, SIGNALLING THE DAWN OF THE FIRST DAY.

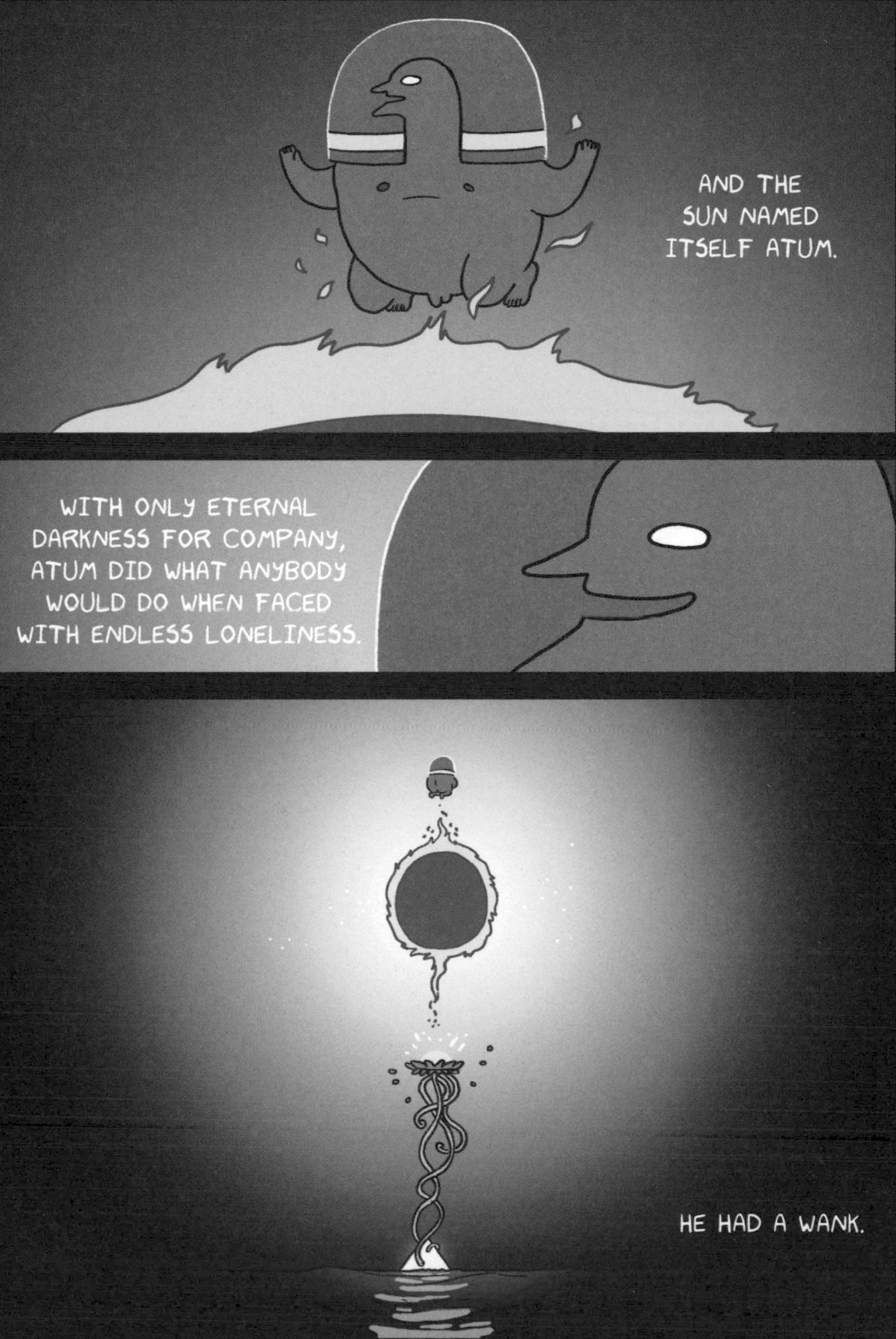
AND THE
SUN NAMED
ITSELF ATUM.
WITH ONLY ETERNAL
DARKNESS FOR COMPANY,
ATUM DID WHAT ANYBODY
WOULD DO WHEN FACED
WITH ENDLESS LONELINESS.
HE HAD A WANK.

HAMISH STEELE

PANT

NEON

THE TRUE STORY OF THE EGYPTIAN DEITIES

NOBROW
LONDON | NEW YORK

CHAPTER ONE

*** ASCENSION ***

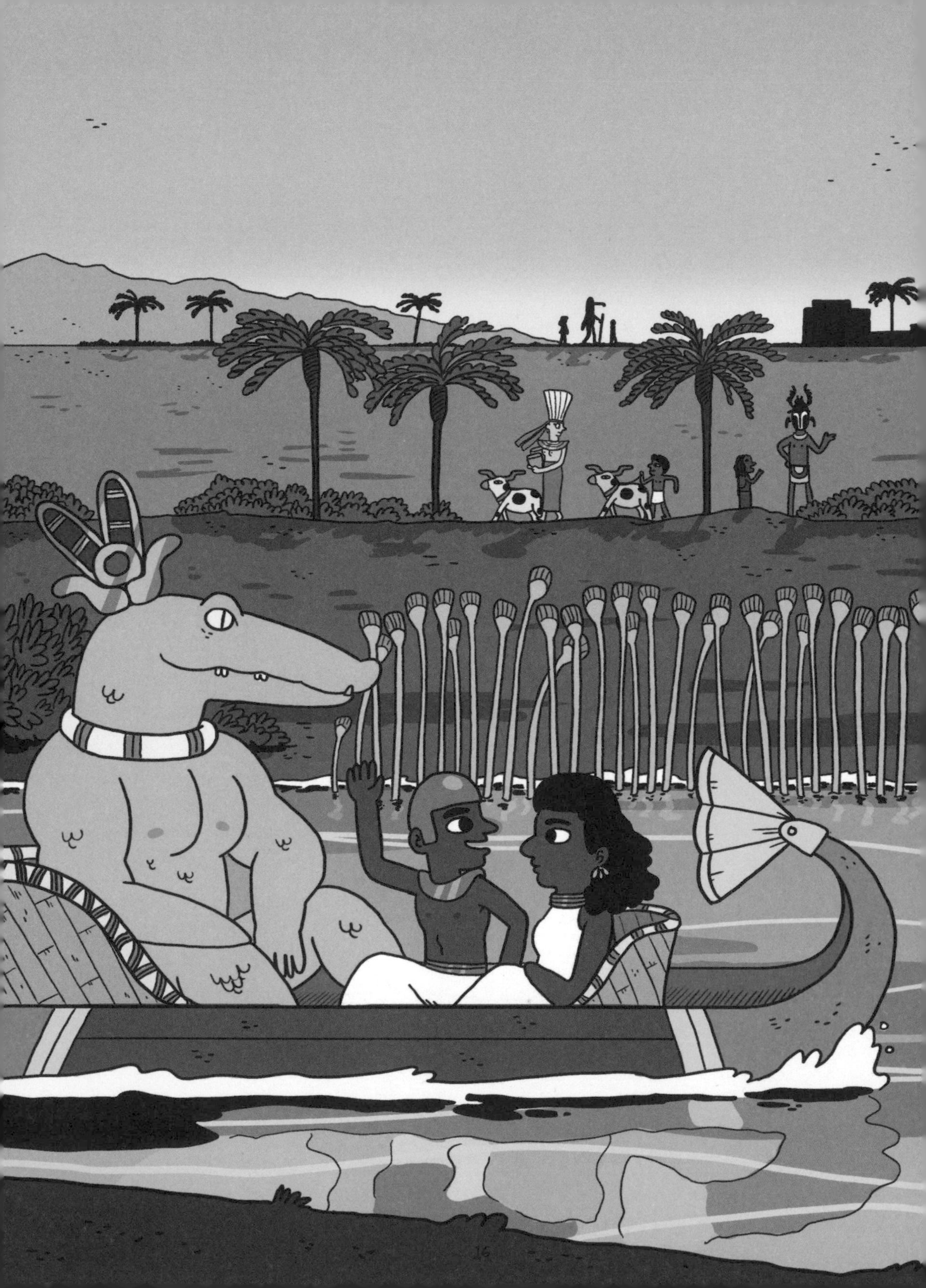

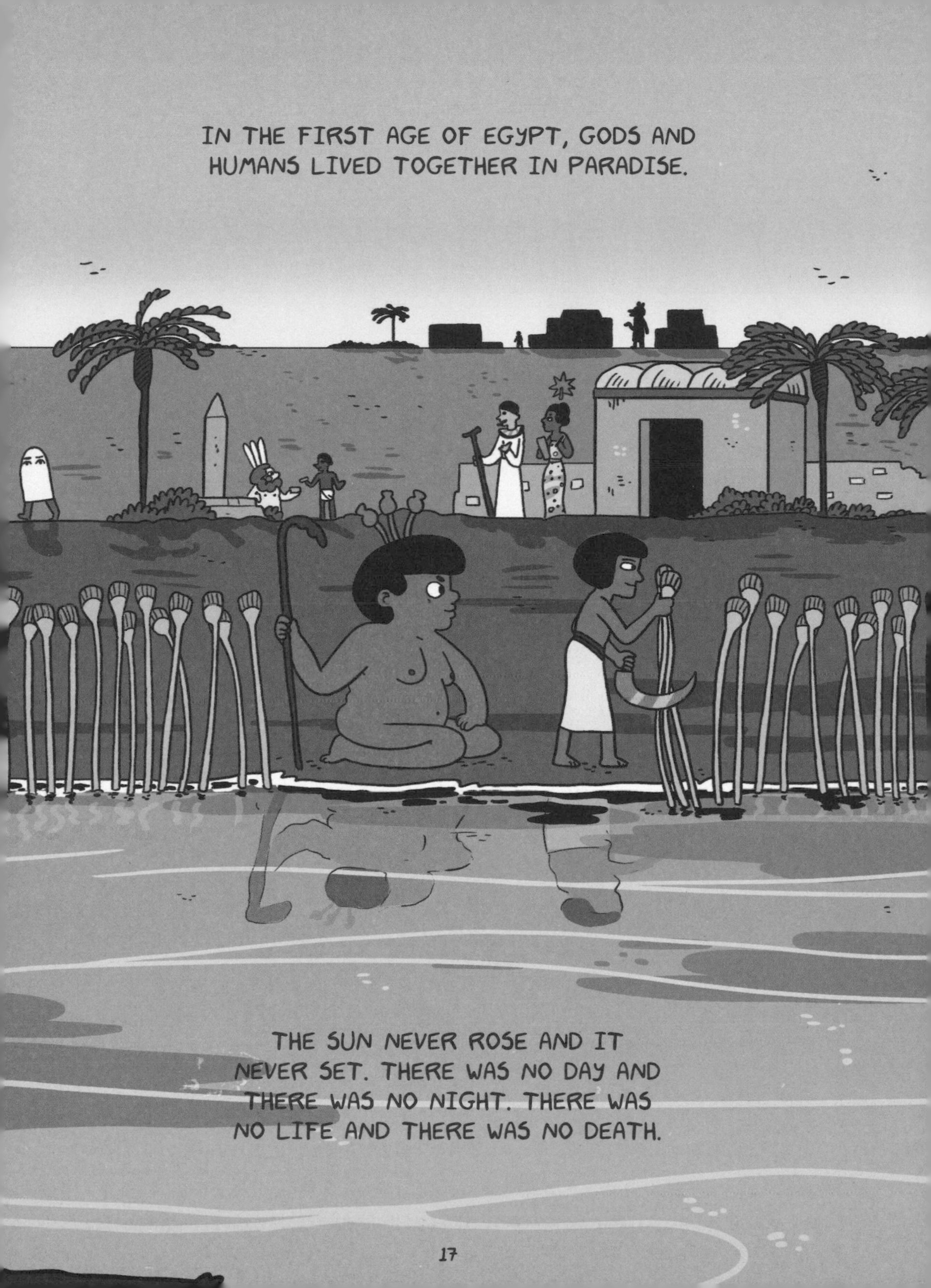
IN THE FIRST AGE OF EGYPT, GODS AND HUMANS LIVED TOGETHER IN PARADISE.
THE SUN NEVER ROSE AND IT NEVER SET. THERE WAS NO DAY AND THERE WAS NO NIGHT. THERE WAS NO LIFE AND THERE WAS NO DEATH.

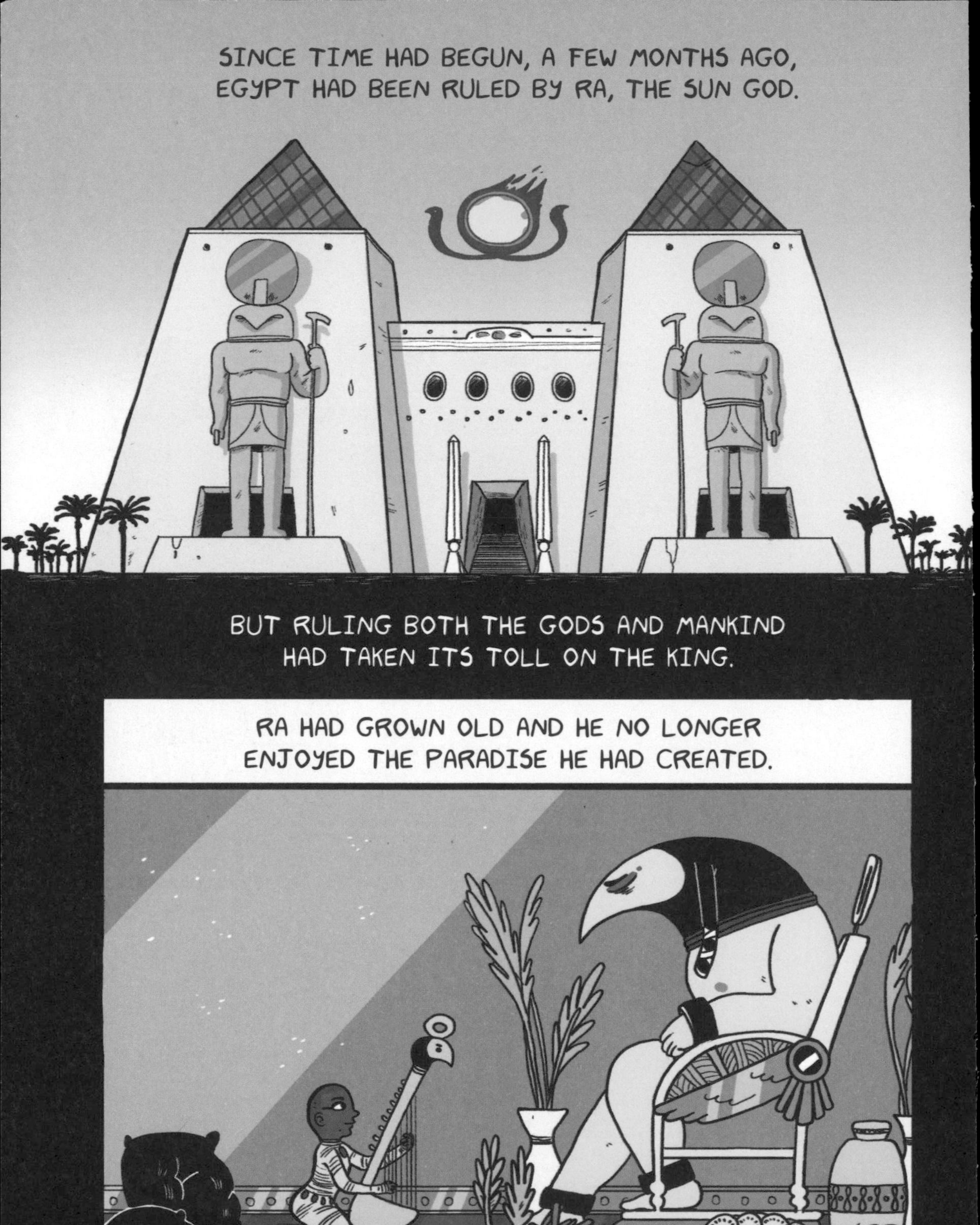
SINCE TIME HAD BEGUN, A FEW MONTHS AGO, EGYPT HAD BEEN RULED BY RA, THE SUN GOD.
BUT RULING BOTH THE GODS AND MANKIND HAD TAKEN ITS TOLL ON THE KING.
RA HAD GROWN OLD AND HE NO LONGER ENJOYED THE PARADISE HE HAD CREATED.

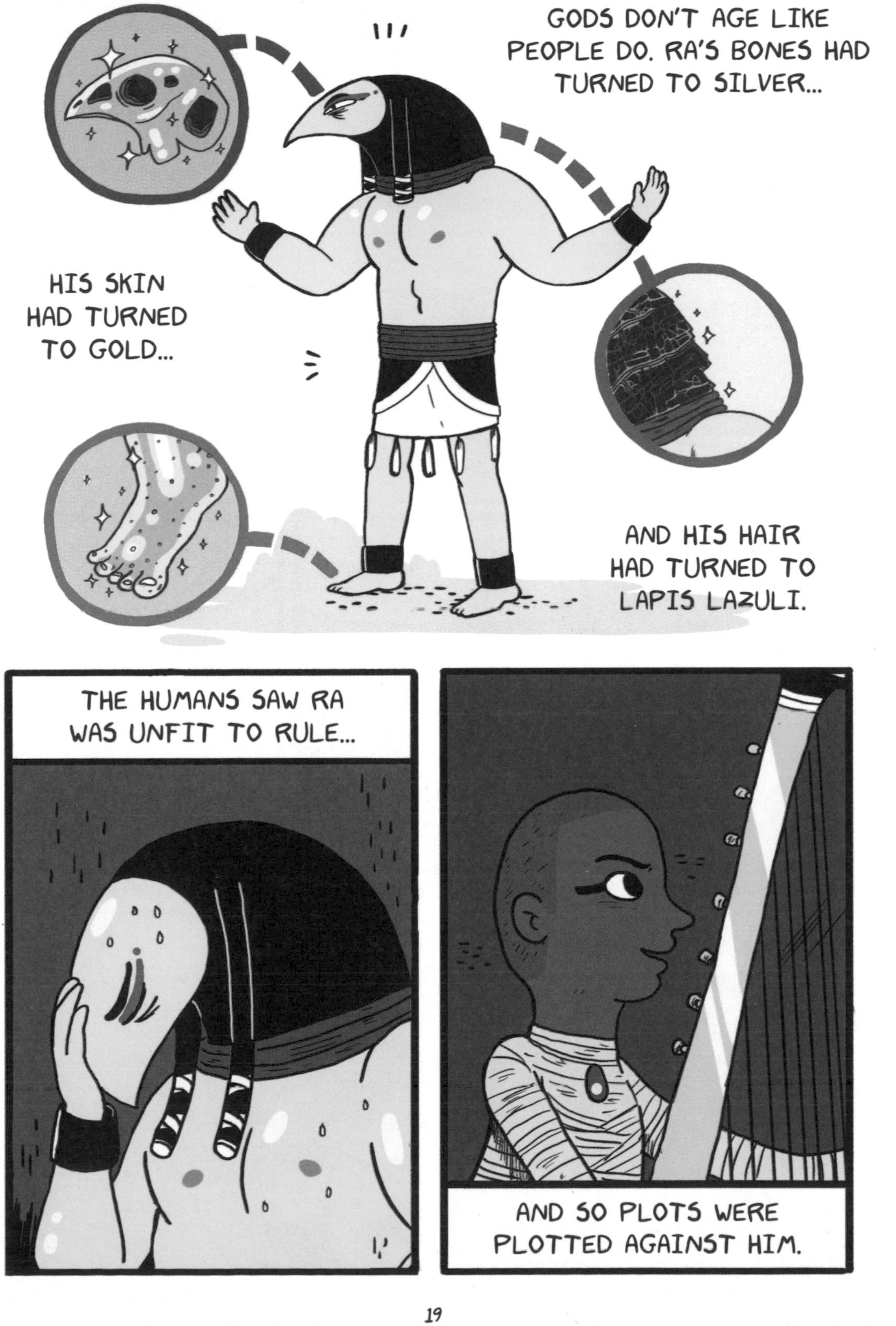
GODS DON'T AGE LIKE PEOPLE DO. RA'S BONES HAD TURNED TO SILVER...
HIS SKIN HAD TURNED TO GOLD...
AND HIS HAIR HAD TURNED TO LAPIS LAZULI.
THE HUMANS SAW RA WAS UNFIT TO RULE...
AND SO PLOTS WERE PLOTTED AGAINST HIM.

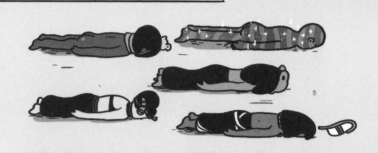

I'VE GATHERED YOU ON THE ROOF BECAUSE MY THRONE IS IN PERIL!

HUMANS WISH TO OVERTHROW THE GODS AND RULE THIS WORLD THEMSELVES!

I PROPOSE WE—

WAIT, WHY ARE YOU GUYS LYING DOWN?

OUT OF RESPECT! IT IS SOMETHING THE HUMANS HAVE LOST, RA!

BUT WE ARE EQUALS! I AM JUST ANOTHER GOD, LIKE YOU!

WE KNOW THAT IS NOT TRUE!

I HAVE A PLAN, BUT IT'S GONNA TAKE MORE THAN RESPECT!

I NEED SOMEONE WILLING TO DO SOME FREAKY SHIT!

I'M FREAKY!

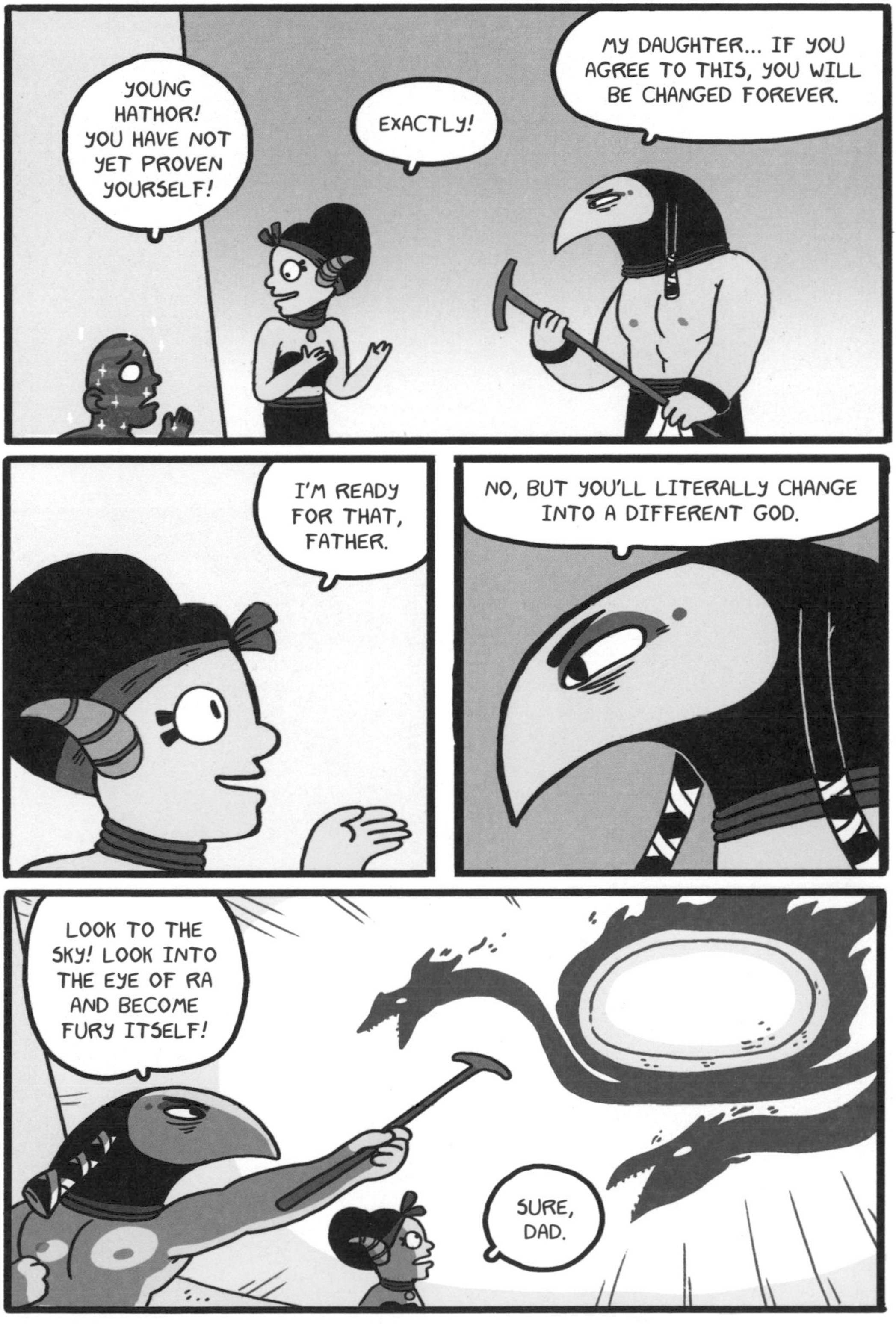
YOUNG HATHOR! YOU HAVE NOT YET PROVEN YOURSELF!
EXACTLY!
MY DAUGHTER... IF YOU AGREE TO THIS, YOU WILL BE CHANGED FOREVER.
I'M READY FOR THAT, FATHER.
NO, BUT YOU'LL LITERALLY CHANGE INTO A DIFFERENT GOD.
LOOK TO THE SKY! LOOK INTO THE EYE OF RA AND BECOME FURY ITSELF!
SURE, DAD.

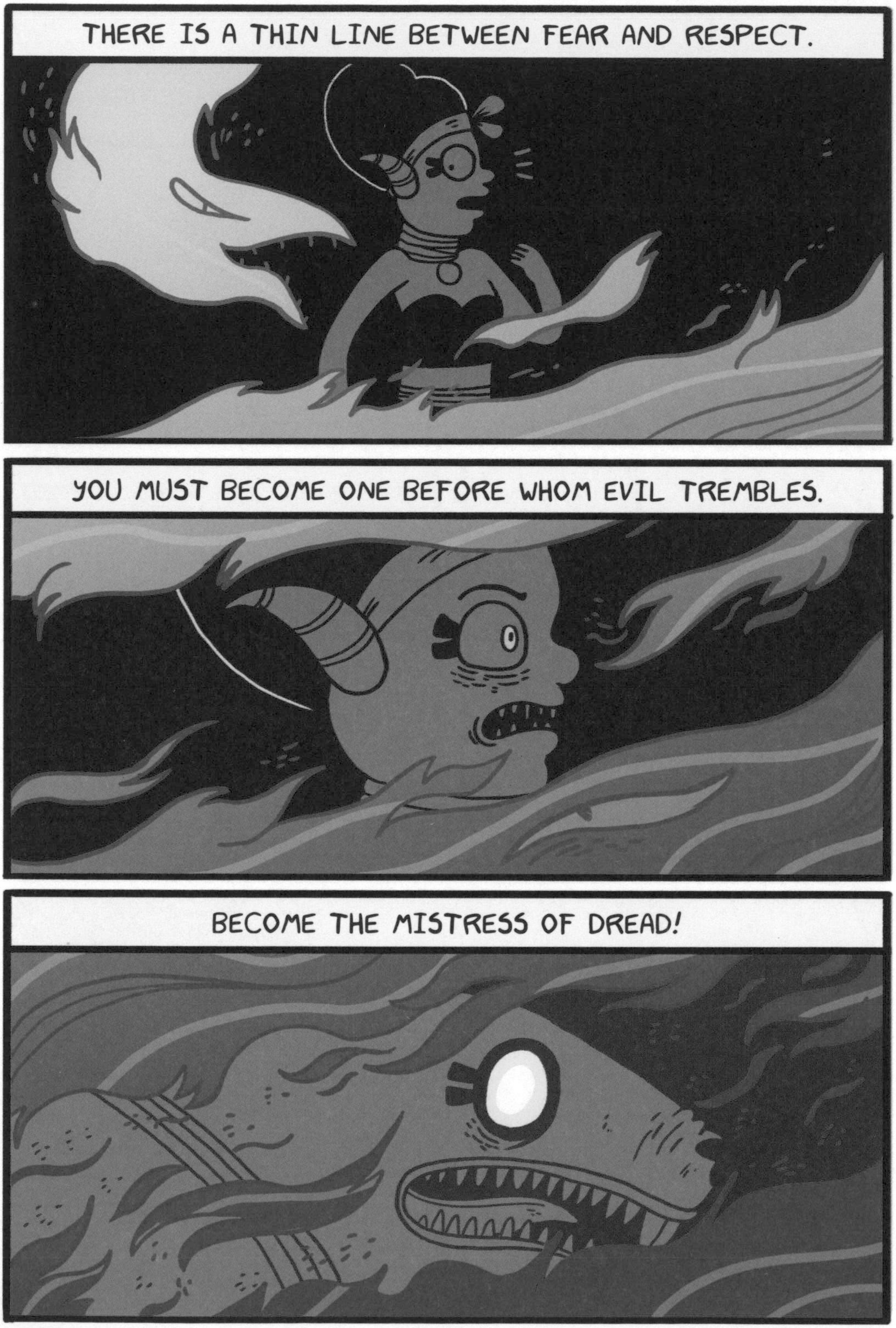
THERE IS A THIN LINE BETWEEN FEAR AND RESPECT.
YOU MUST BECOME ONE BEFORE WHOM EVIL TREMBLES.
BECOME THE MISTRESS OF DREAD!

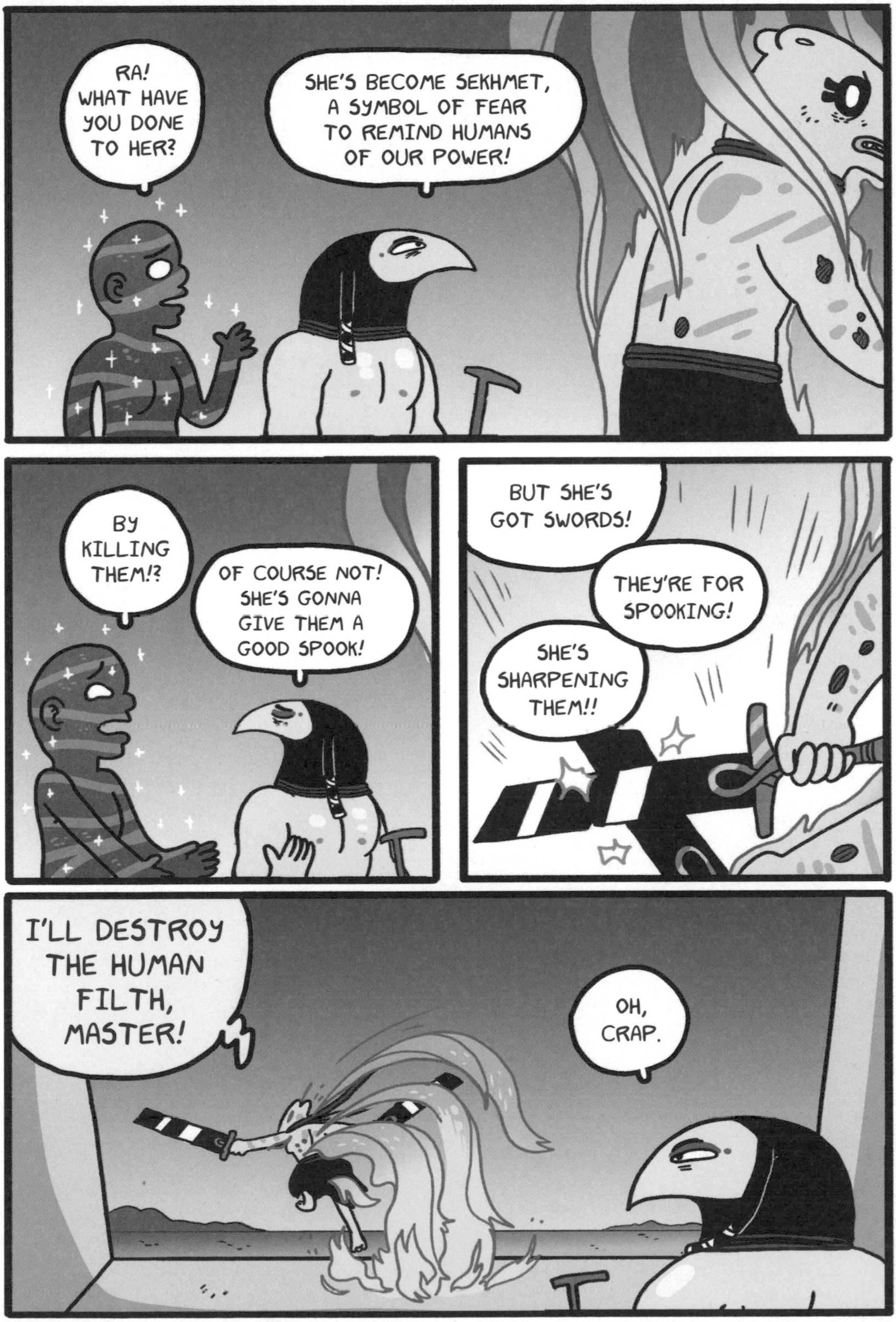
RA! WHAT HAVE YOU DONE TO HER?
SHE'S BECOME SEKHMET, A SYMBOL OF FEAR TO REMIND HUMANS OF OUR POWER!
BY KILLING THEM!?
OF COURSE NOT! SHE'S GONNA GIVE THEM A GOOD SPOOK!
BUT SHE'S GOT SWORDS!
THEY'RE FOR SPOOKING!
SHE'S SHARPENING THEM!!
I'LL DESTROY THE HUMAN FILTH, MASTER!
OH, CRAP.

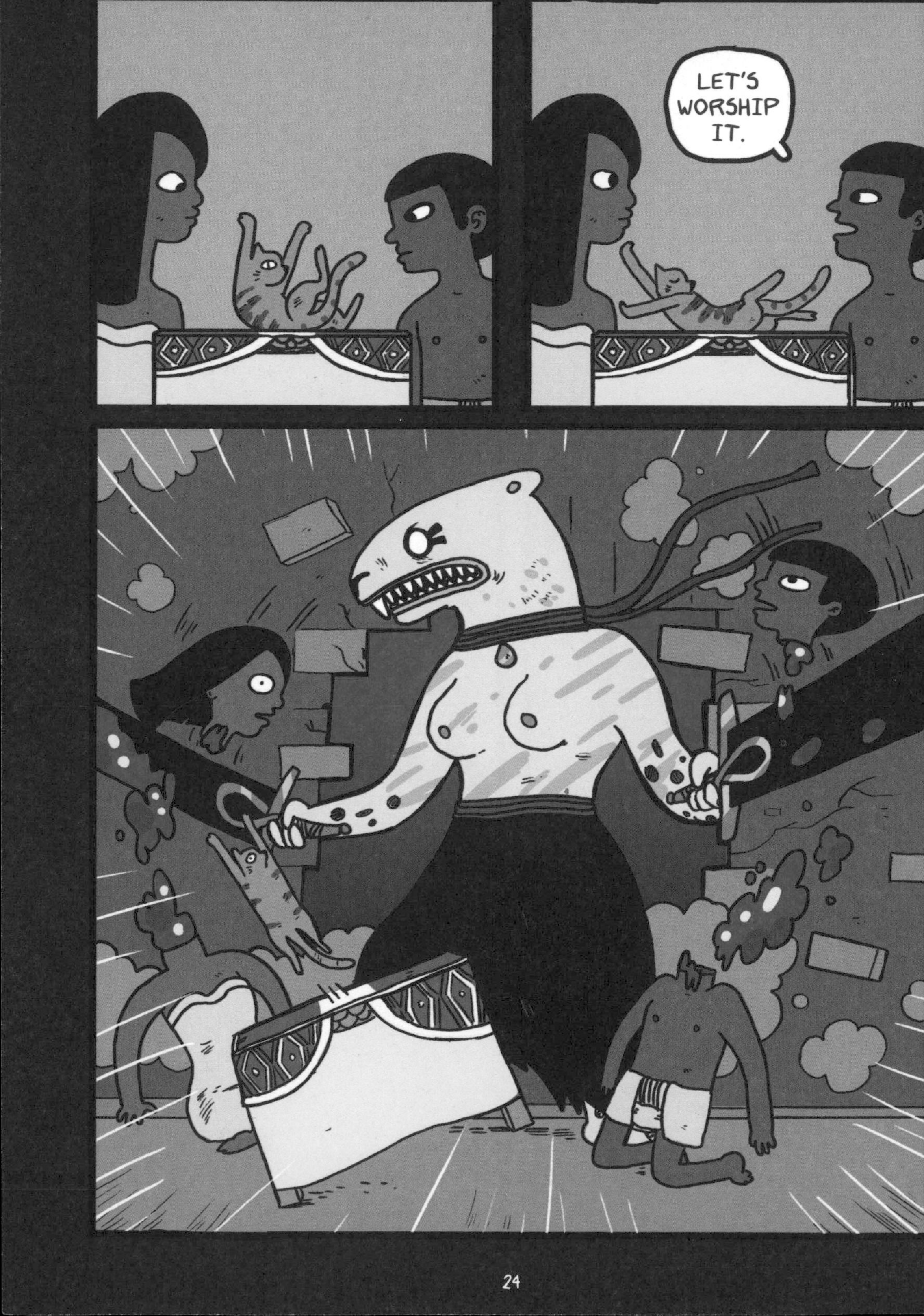
LET'S WORSHIP IT.

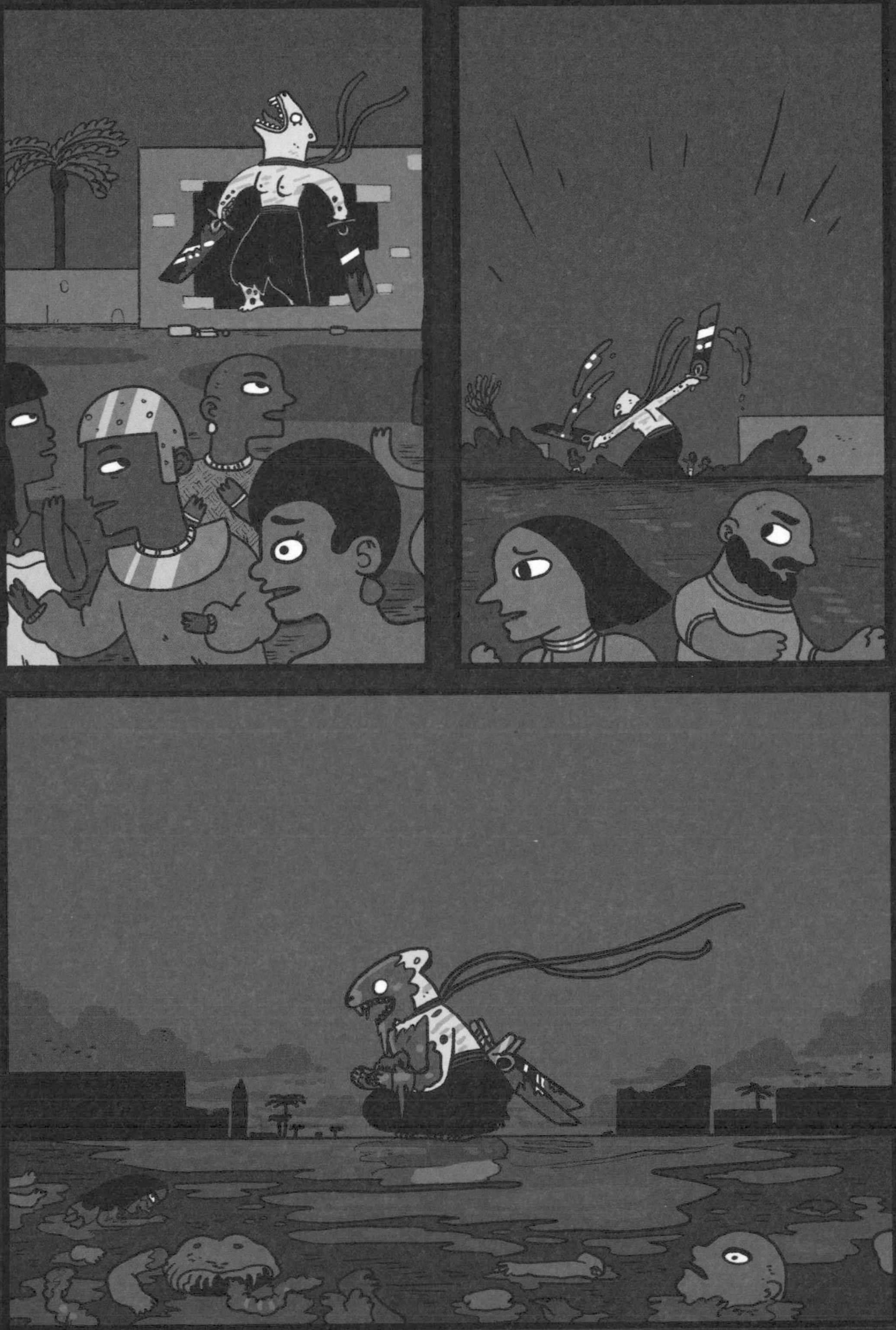

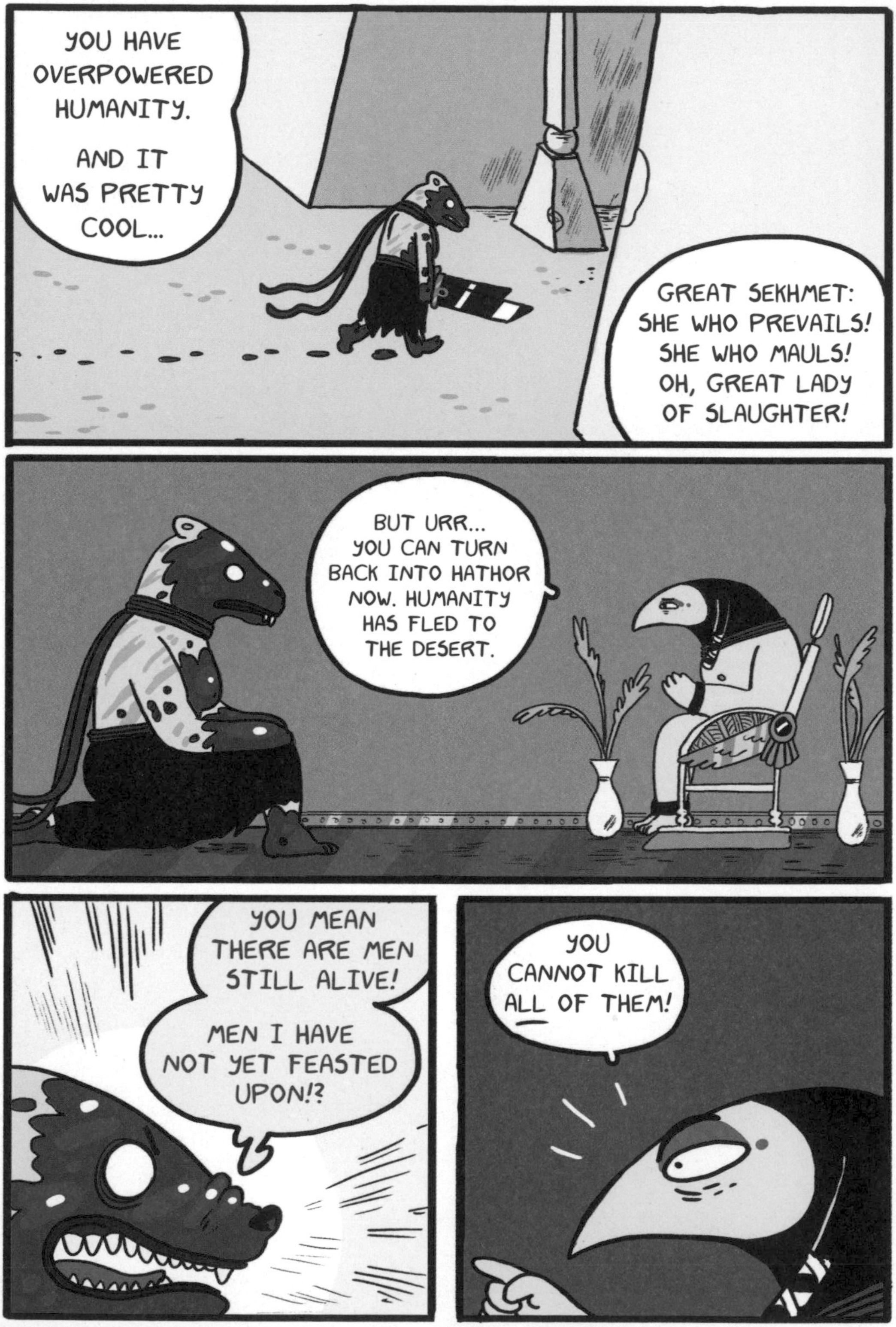
YOU HAVE OVERPOWERED HUMANITY.
AND IT WAS PRETTY COOL...
GREAT SEKHMET: SHE WHO PREVAILS! SHE WHO MAULS! OH, GREAT LADY OF SLAUGHTER!
BUT URR... YOU CAN TURN BACK INTO HATHOR NOW. HUMANITY HAS FLED TO THE DESERT.
YOU MEAN THERE ARE MEN STILL ALIVE!
MEN I HAVE NOT YET FEASTED UPON!?
YOU CANNOT KILL ALL OF THEM!

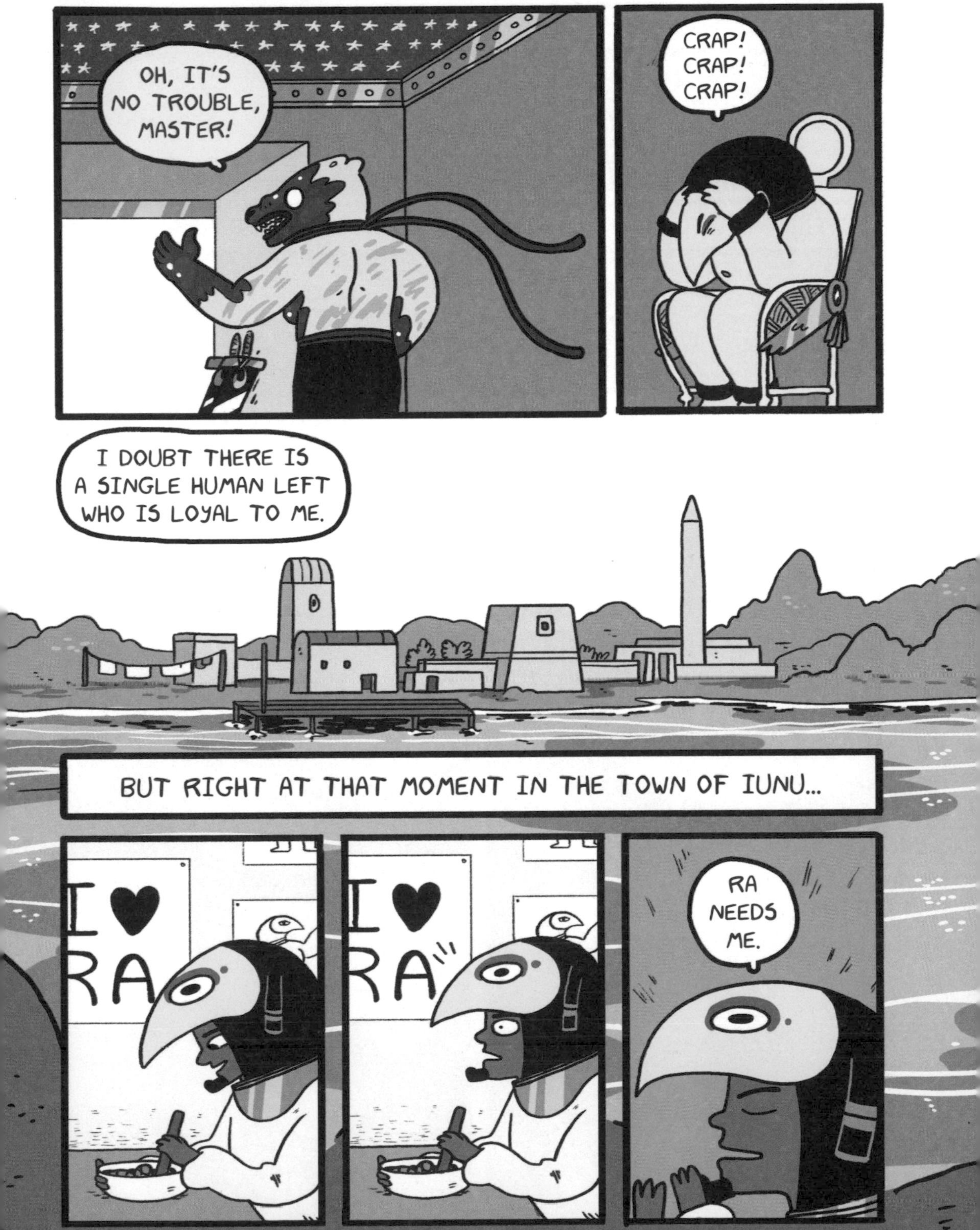
OH, IT'S NO TROUBLE, MASTER!
CRAP! CRAP! CRAP!
I DOUBT THERE IS A SINGLE HUMAN LEFT WHO IS LOYAL TO ME.
BUT RIGHT AT THAT MOMENT IN THE TOWN OF IUNU...
I ♥ RA
I ♥ RA
RA NEEDS ME.

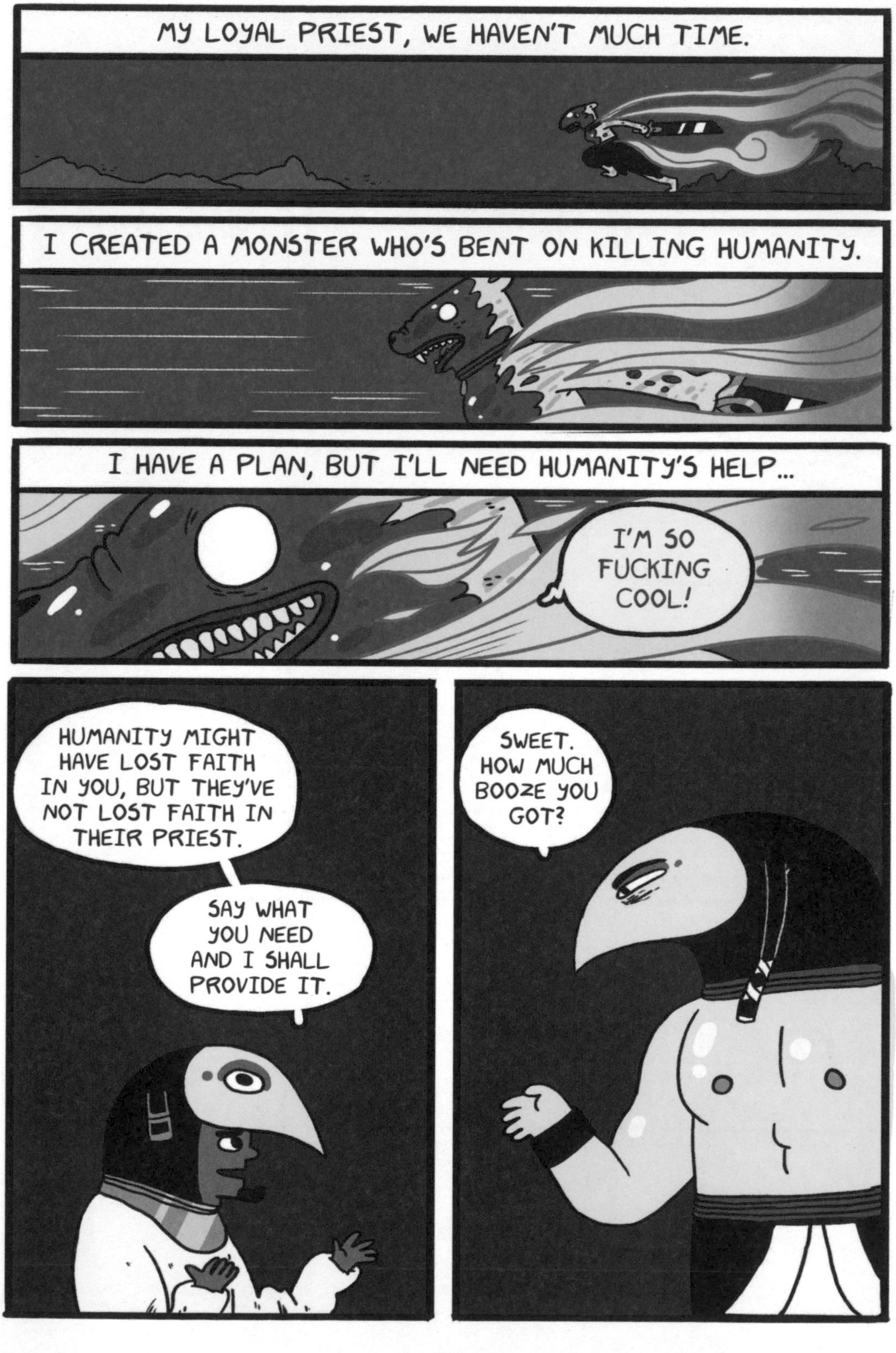
MY LOYAL PRIEST, WE HAVEN'T MUCH TIME.
I CREATED A MONSTER WHO'S BENT ON KILLING HUMANITY.
I HAVE A PLAN, BUT I'LL NEED HUMANITY'S HELP...
I'M SO FUCKING COOL!
HUMANITY MIGHT HAVE LOST FAITH IN YOU, BUT THEY'VE NOT LOST FAITH IN THEIR PRIEST.
SAY WHAT YOU NEED AND I SHALL PROVIDE IT.
SWEET. HOW MUCH BOOZE YOU GOT?

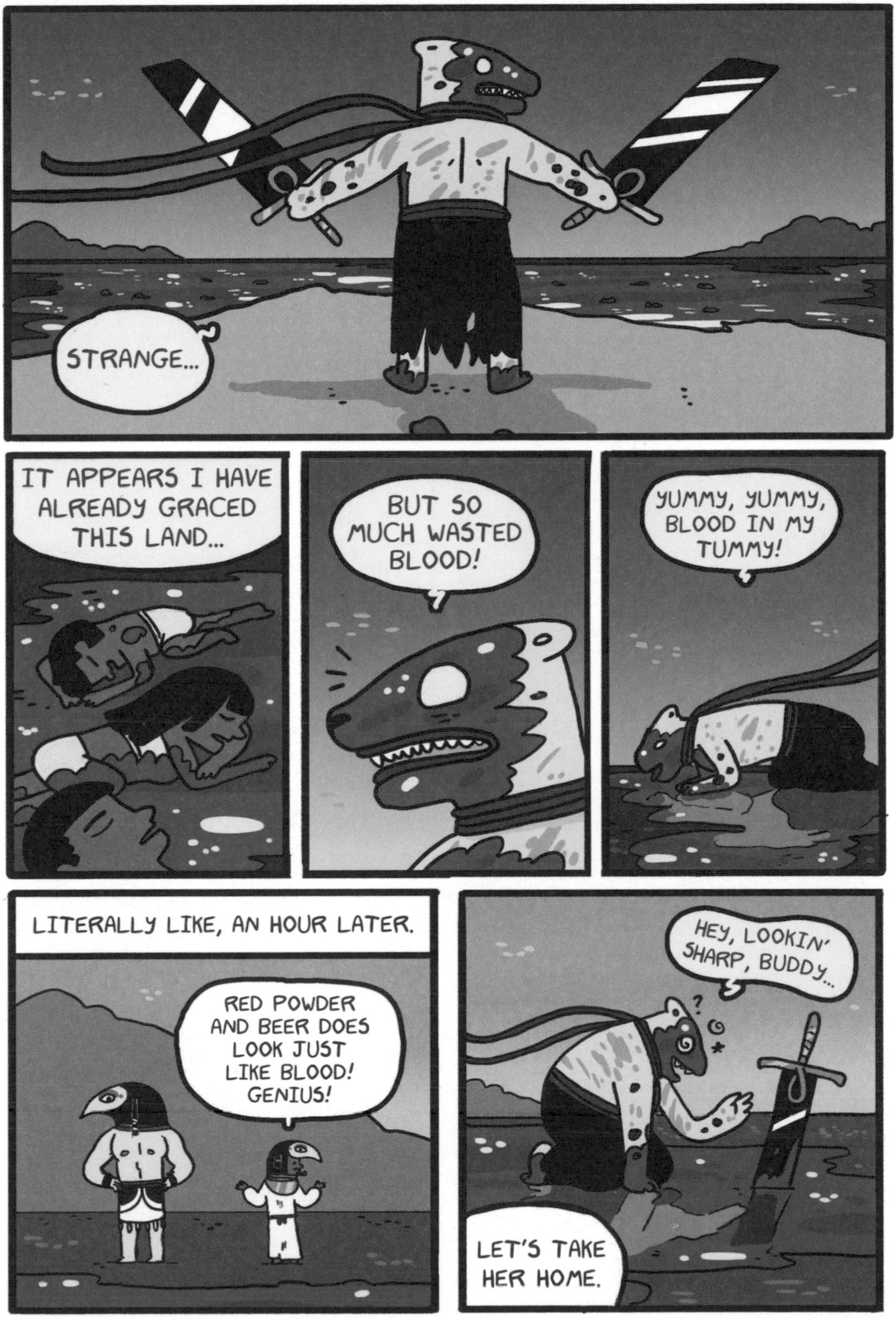
STRANGE...
IT APPEARS I HAVE ALREADY GRACED THIS LAND...
BUT SO MUCH WASTED BLOOD!
YUMMY, YUMMY, BLOOD IN MY TUMMY!
LITERALLY LIKE, AN HOUR LATER.
RED POWDER AND BEER DOES LOOK JUST LIKE BLOOD! GENIUS!
HEY, LOOKIN' SHARP, BUDDY...
LET'S TAKE HER HOME.

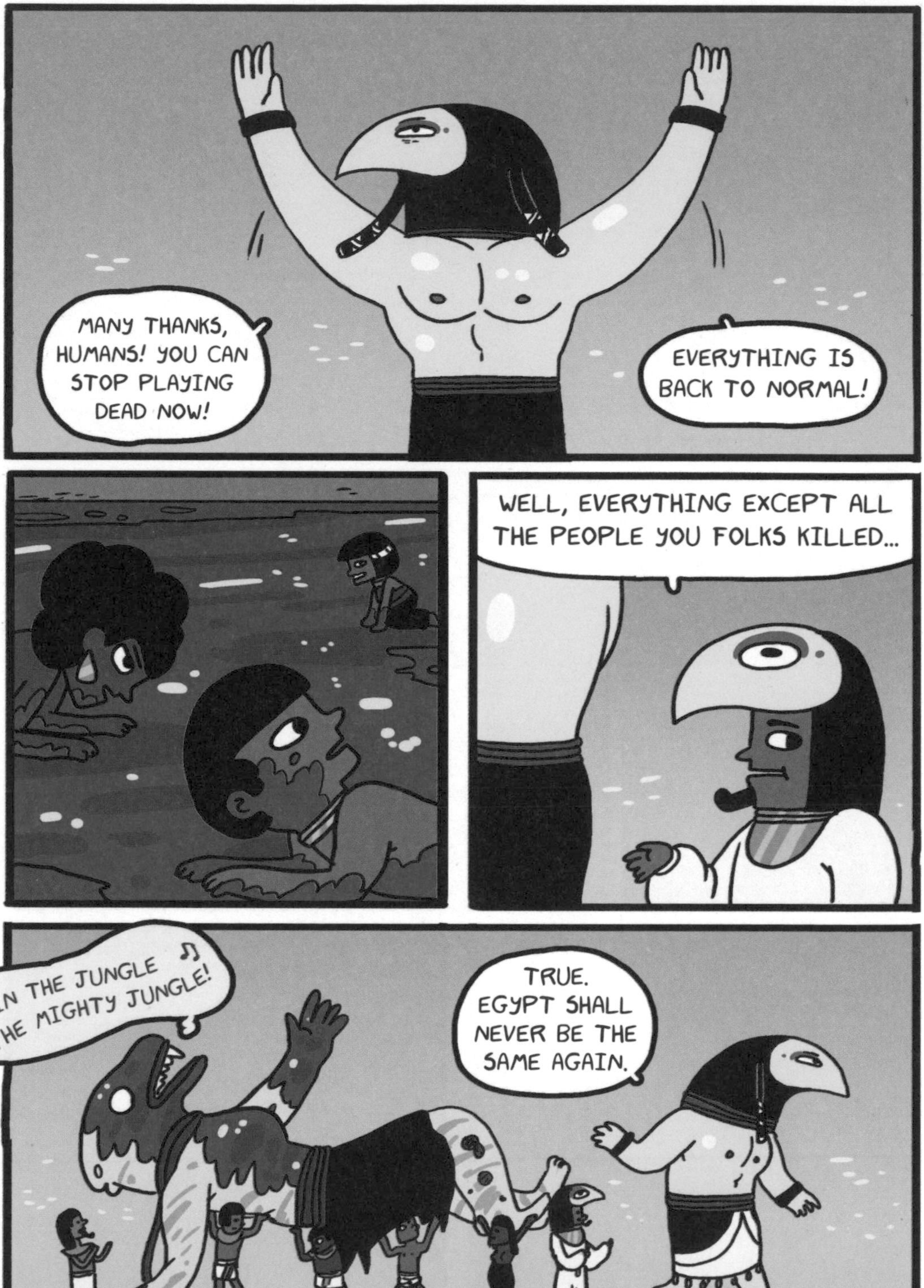
MANY THANKS, HUMANS! YOU CAN STOP PLAYING DEAD NOW!
EVERYTHING IS BACK TO NORMAL!
WELL, EVERYTHING EXCEPT ALL THE PEOPLE YOU FOLKS KILLED...
IN THE JUNGLE THE MIGHTY JUNGLE!
TRUE. EGYPT SHALL NEVER BE THE SAME AGAIN.

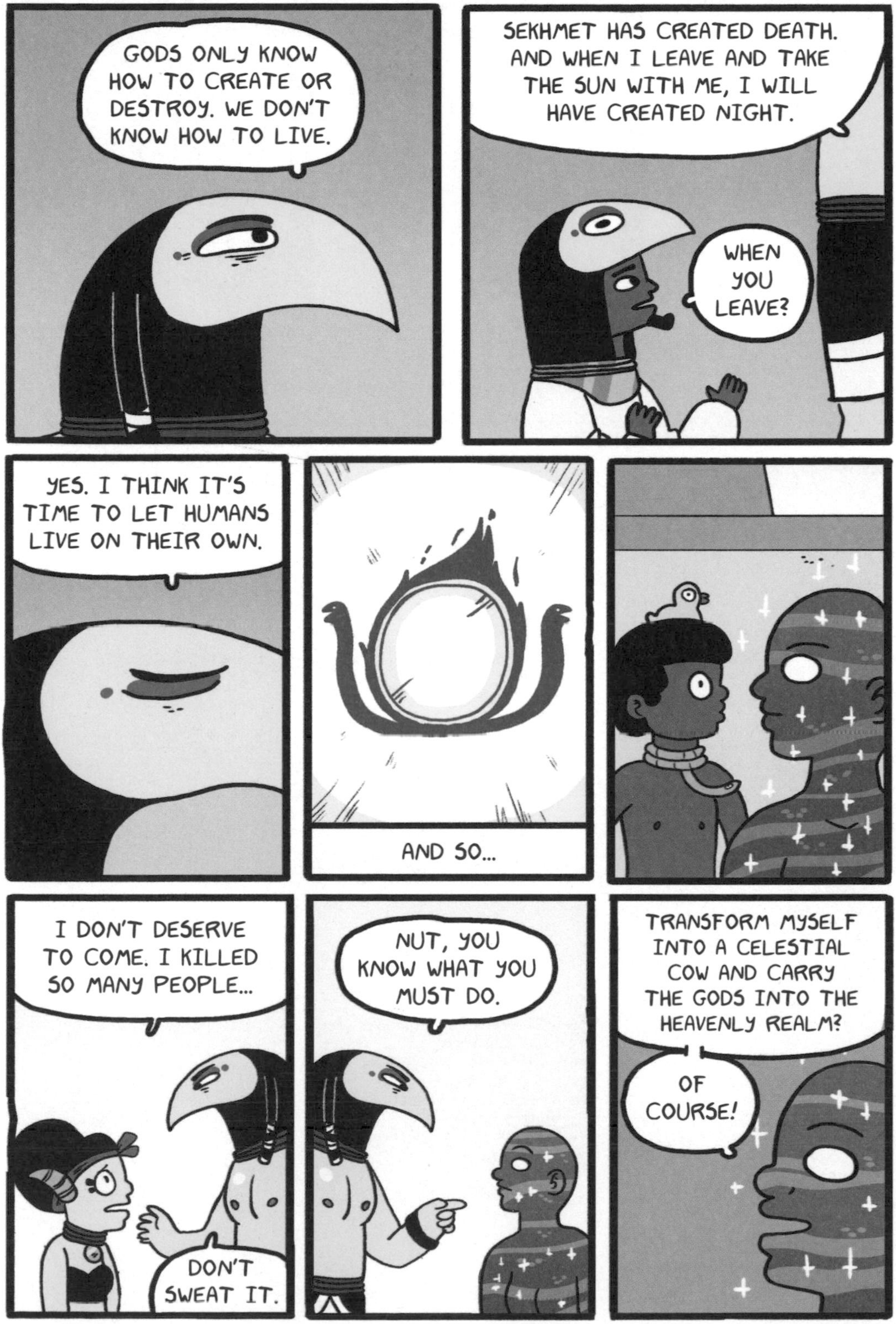

GODS ONLY KNOW HOW TO CREATE OR DESTROY. WE DON'T KNOW HOW TO LIVE.
SEKHMET HAS CREATED DEATH. AND WHEN I LEAVE AND TAKE THE SUN WITH ME, I WILL HAVE CREATED NIGHT.
WHEN YOU LEAVE?
YES. I THINK IT'S TIME TO LET HUMANS LIVE ON THEIR OWN.
AND SO...
I DON'T DESERVE TO COME. I KILLED SO MANY PEOPLE...
DON'T SWEAT IT.
NUT, YOU KNOW WHAT YOU MUST DO.
TRANSFORM MYSELF INTO A CELESTIAL COW AND CARRY THE GODS INTO THE HEAVENLY REALM?
OF COURSE!

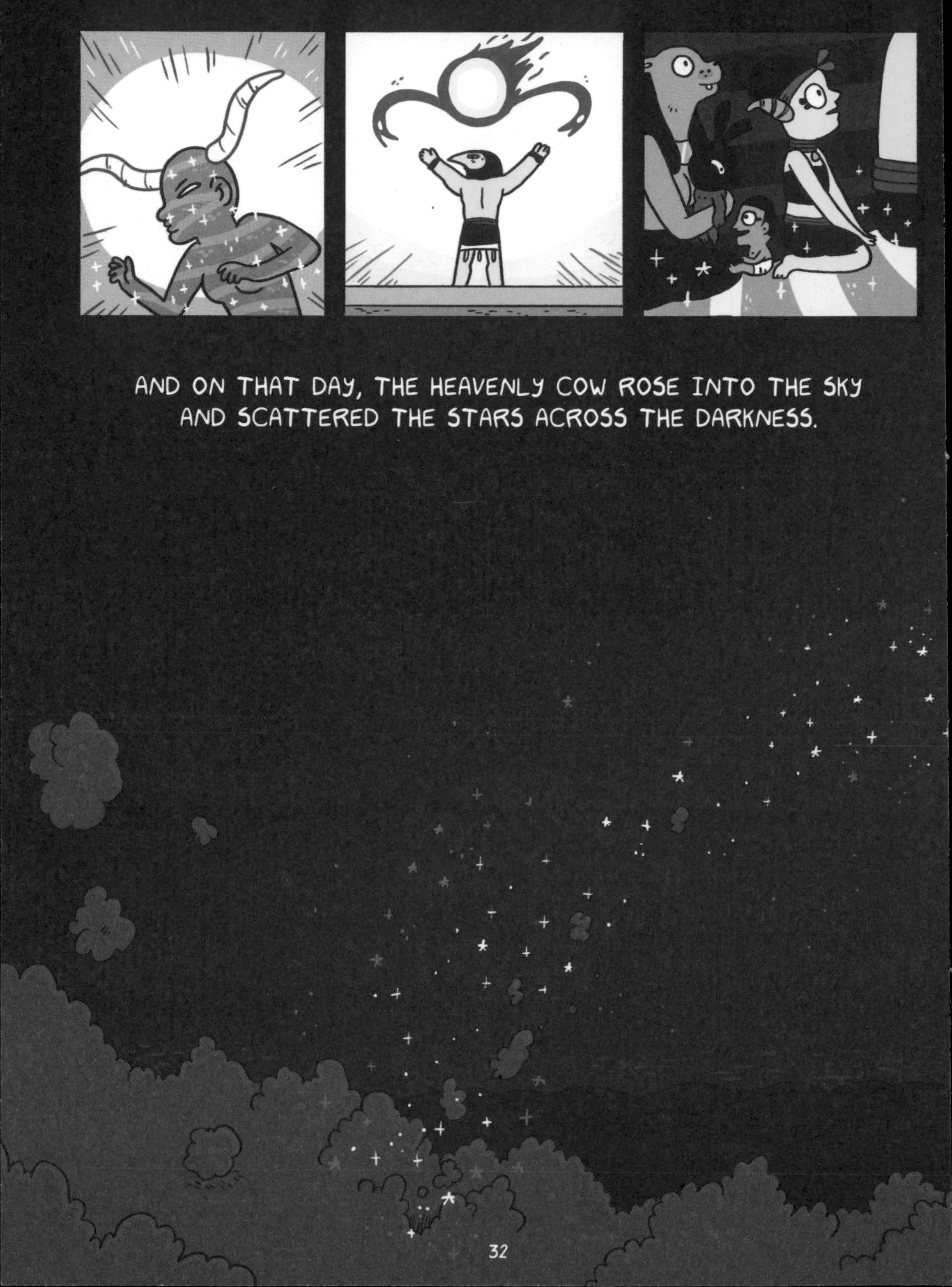
AND ON THAT DAY, THE HEAVENLY COW ROSE INTO THE SKY AND SCATTERED THE STARS ACROSS THE DARKNESS.

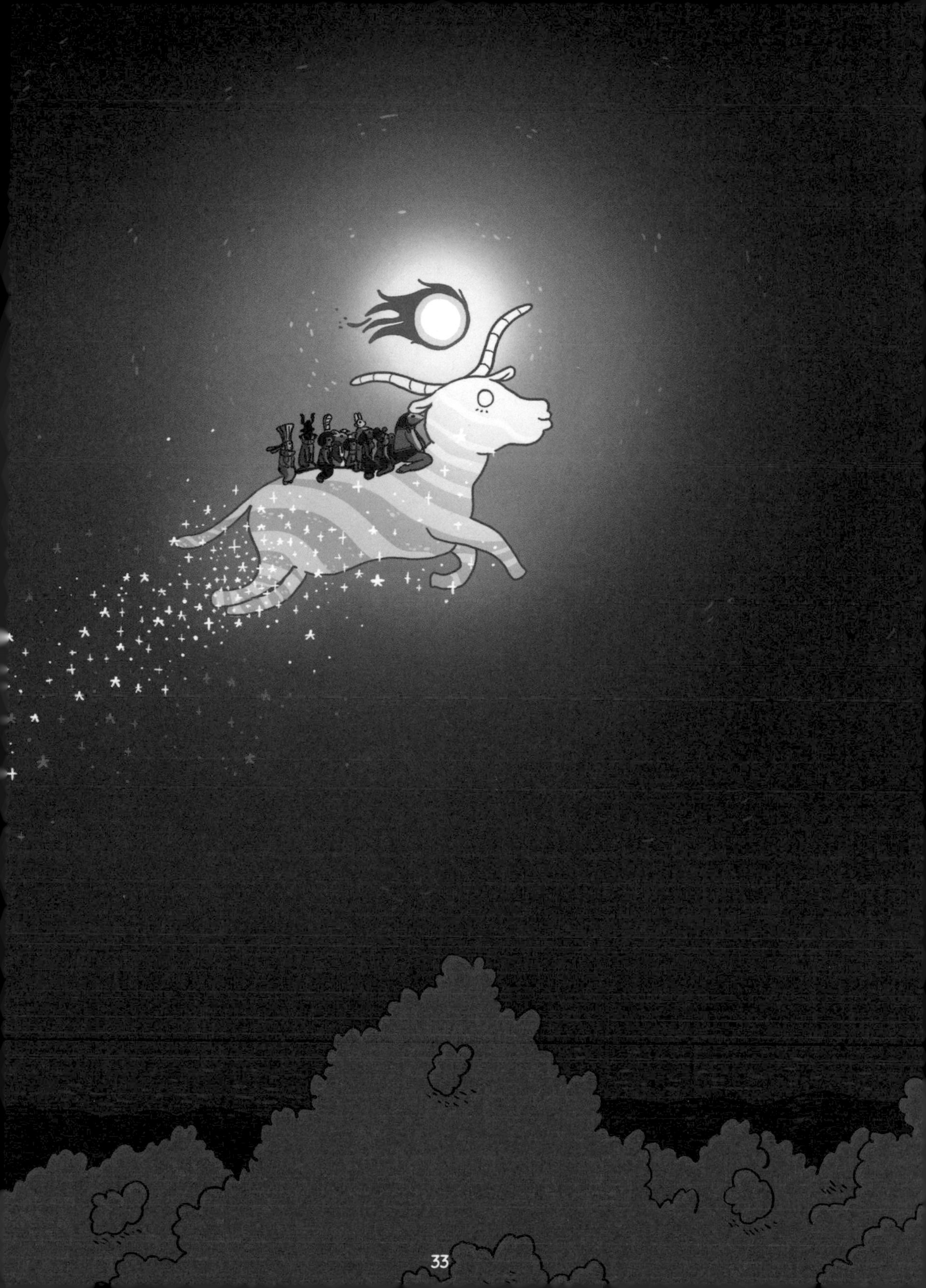

WHAT ARE WE GOING TO DO IN OUR NEW REALM, DAD?

Moo!

WELL, I'LL CREATE A FIELD OF ABUNDANCE FOR NUT TO GRAZE ON.

AND PERHAPS WE CAN STILL HAVE SOME CONTACT WITH THE HUMANS...

THE LIVING BELONG ON EARTH...

HOW?

BUT PERHAPS THE DEAD CAN JOIN US IN DUAT! I COULD GIVE THEM A FIELD OF THEIR OWN CALLED AARU.

HEY, IT'S ALL THE PEOPLE I KILLED! SORRY GUYS!

NO PROBS!

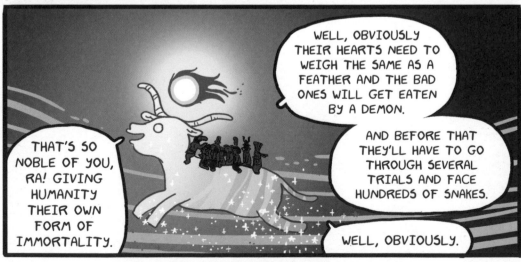

WELL, OBVIOUSLY THEIR HEARTS NEED TO WEIGH THE SAME AS A FEATHER AND THE BAD ONES WILL GET EATEN BY A DEMON.

AND BEFORE THAT THEY'LL HAVE TO GO THROUGH SEVERAL TRIALS AND FACE HUNDREDS OF SNAKES.

THAT'S SO NOBLE OF YOU, RA! GIVING HUMANITY THEIR OWN FORM OF IMMORTALITY.

WELL, OBVIOUSLY.

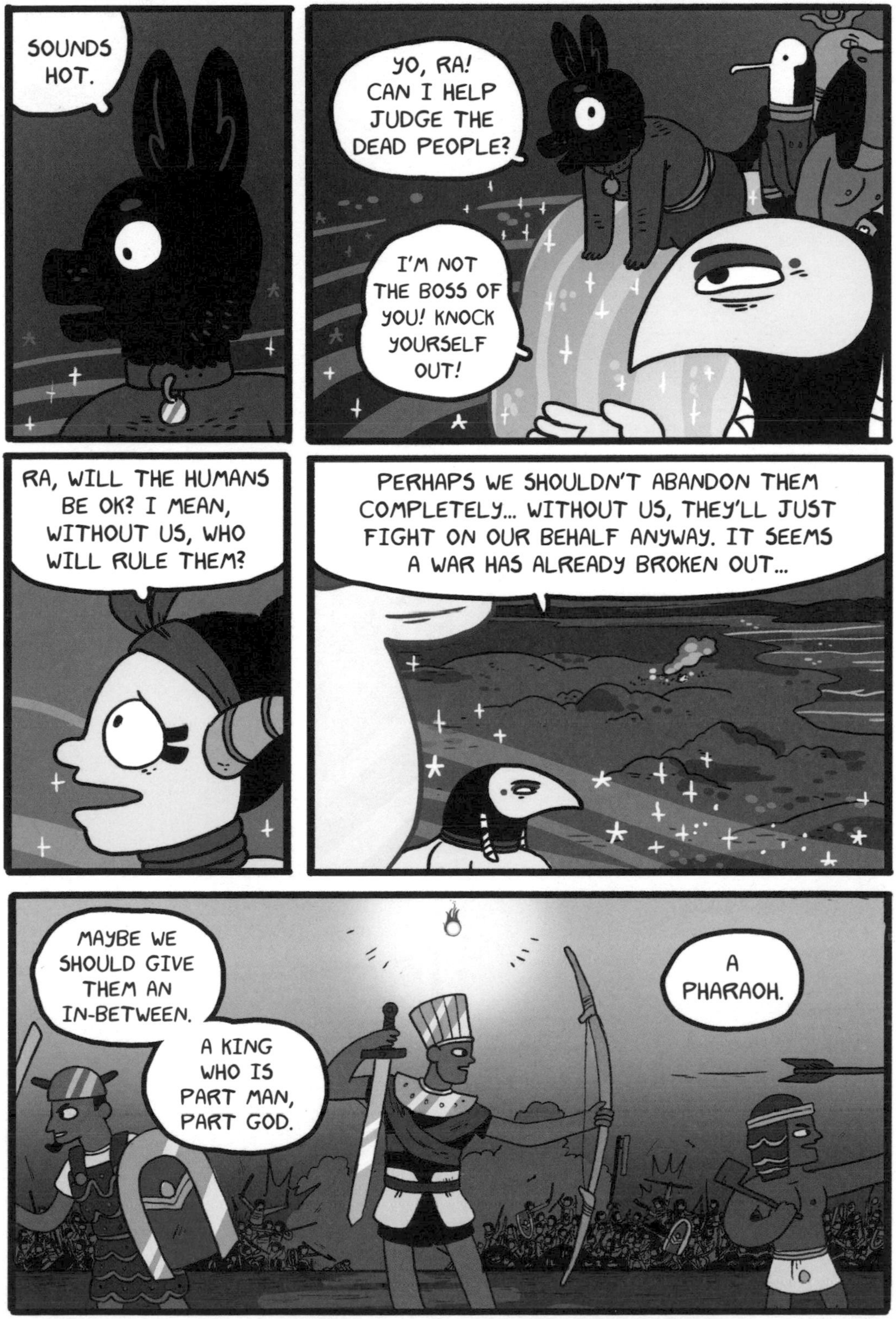
SOUNDS HOT.
YO, RA! CAN I HELP JUDGE THE DEAD PEOPLE?
I'M NOT THE BOSS OF YOU! KNOCK YOURSELF OUT!
RA, WILL THE HUMANS BE OK? I MEAN, WITHOUT US, WHO WILL RULE THEM?
PERHAPS WE SHOULDN'T ABANDON THEM COMPLETELY... WITHOUT US, THEY'LL JUST FIGHT ON OUR BEHALF ANYWAY. IT SEEMS A WAR HAS ALREADY BROKEN OUT...
MAYBE WE SHOULD GIVE THEM AN IN-BETWEEN.
A KING WHO IS PART MAN, PART GOD.
A PHARAOH.

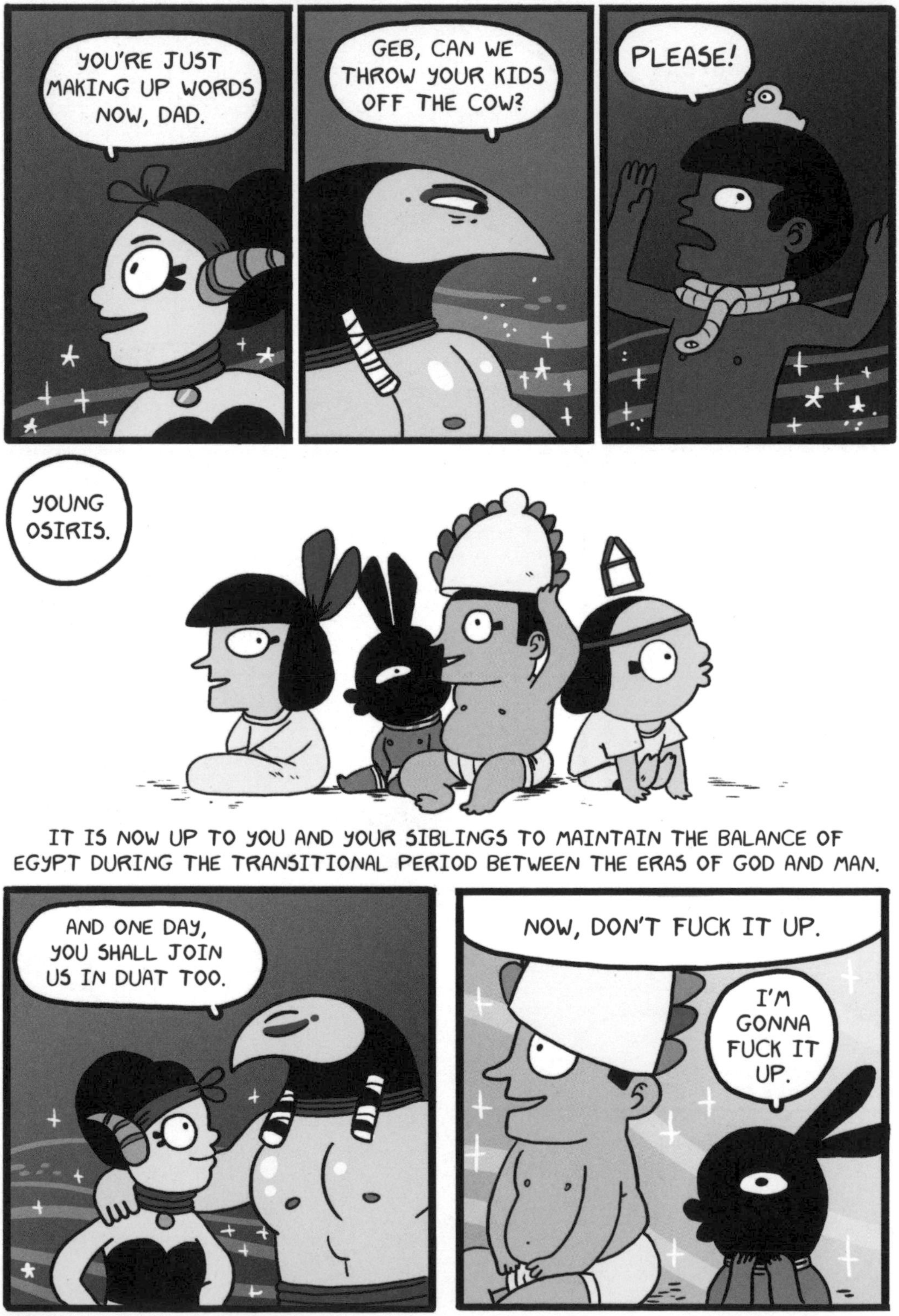
YOU'RE JUST MAKING UP WORDS NOW, DAD.
GEB, CAN WE THROW YOUR KIDS OFF THE COW?
PLEASE!
YOUNG OSIRIS.
IT IS NOW UP TO YOU AND YOUR SIBLINGS TO MAINTAIN THE BALANCE OF EGYPT DURING THE TRANSITIONAL PERIOD BETWEEN THE ERAS OF GOD AND MAN.
AND ONE DAY, YOU SHALL JOIN US IN DUAT TOO.
NOW, DON'T FUCK IT UP.
I'M GONNA FUCK IT UP.

CHAPTER TWO

★★★ USURPATION ★★★

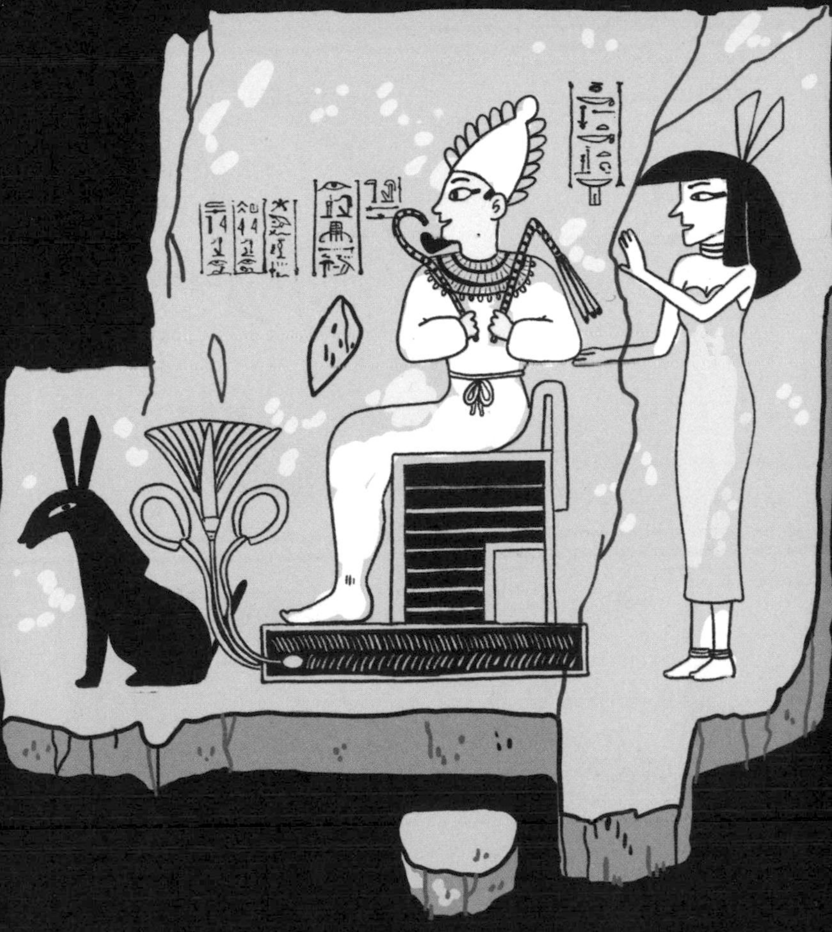

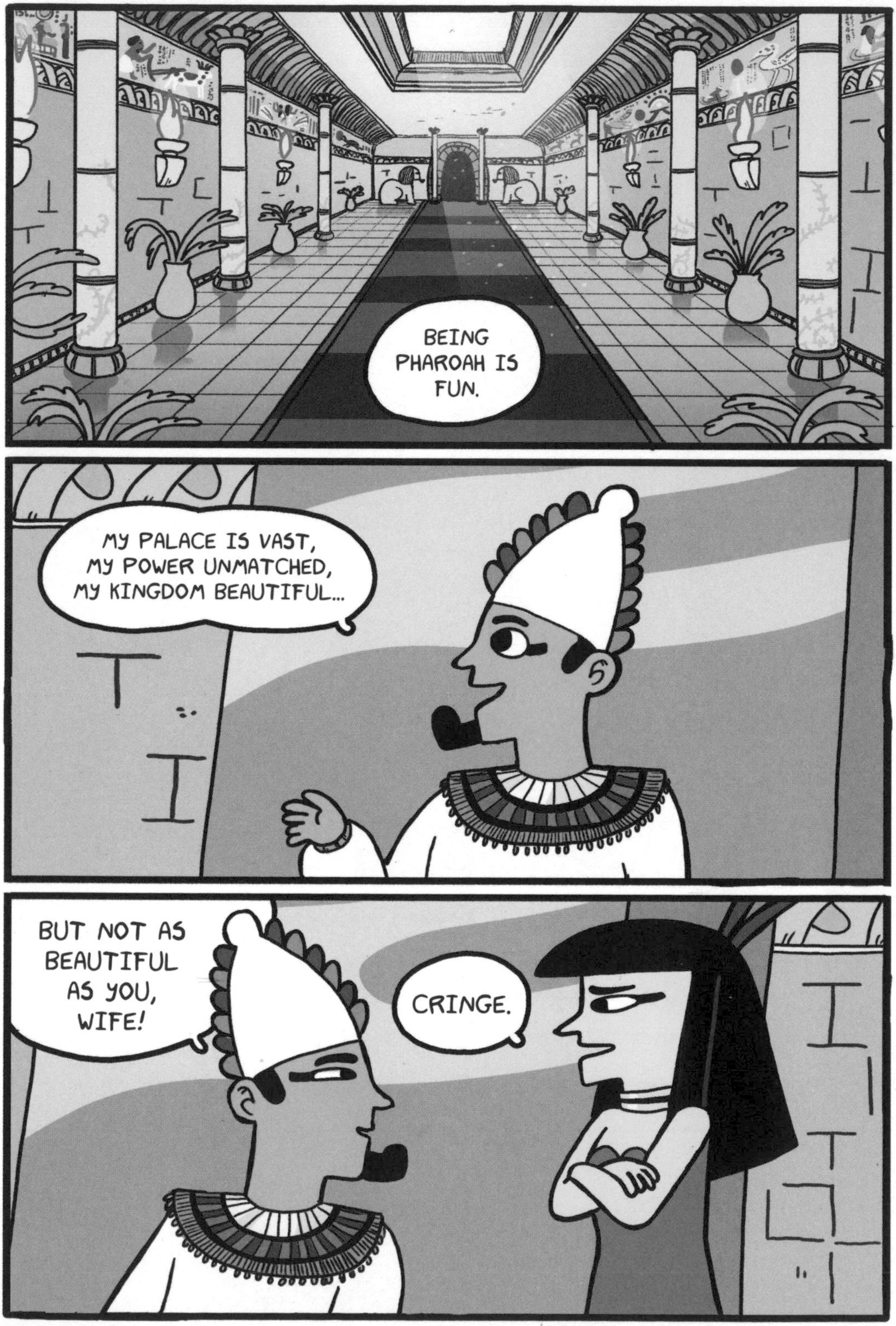
BEING PHAROAH IS FUN.
MY PALACE IS VAST, MY POWER UNMATCHED, MY KINGDOM BEAUTIFUL...
BUT NOT AS BEAUTIFUL AS YOU, WIFE!
CRINGE.

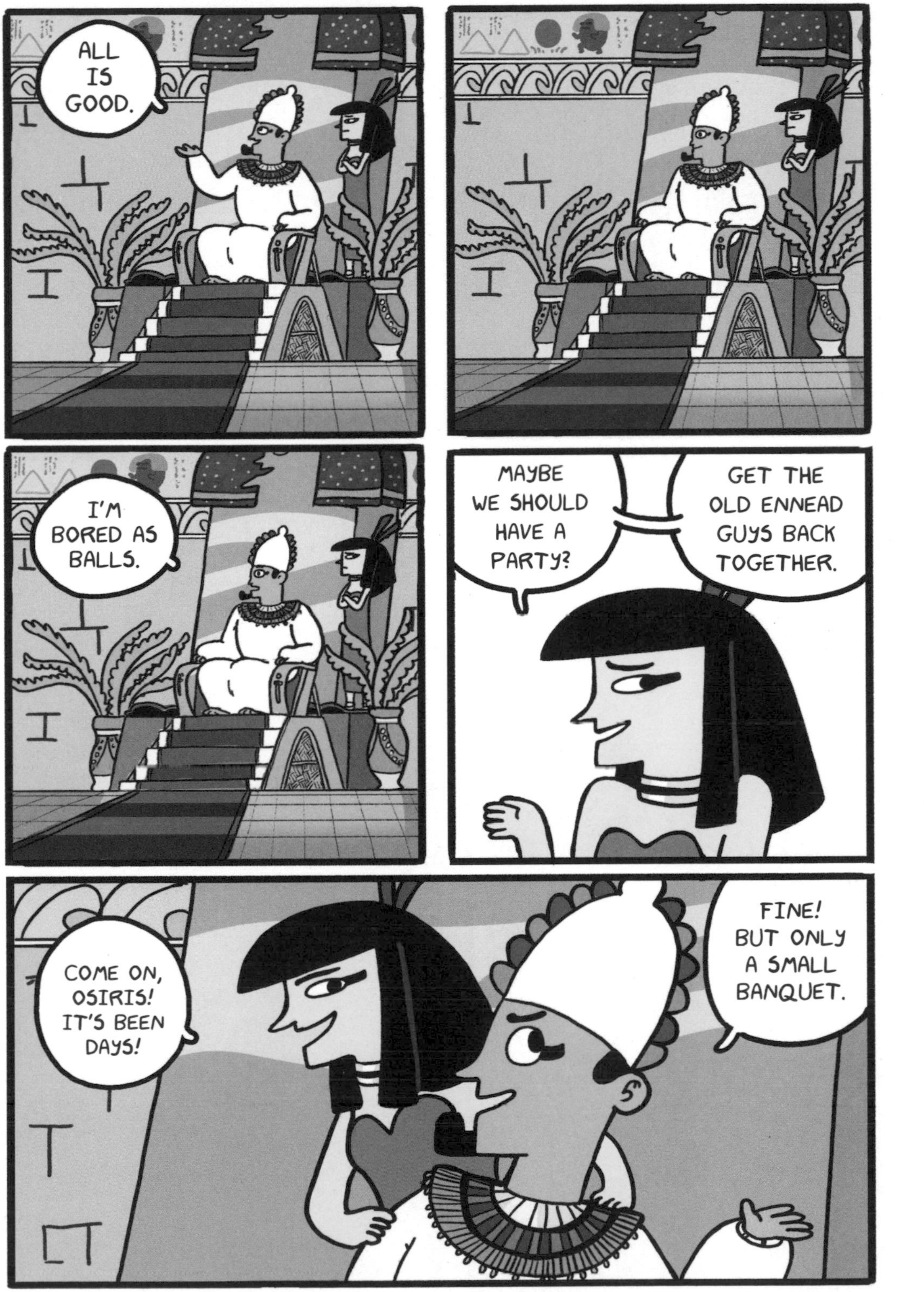
ALL IS GOOD.
I'M BORED AS BALLS.
MAYBE WE SHOULD HAVE A PARTY?
GET THE OLD ENNEAD GUYS BACK TOGETHER.
COME ON, OSIRIS! IT'S BEEN DAYS!
FINE! BUT ONLY A SMALL BANQUET.

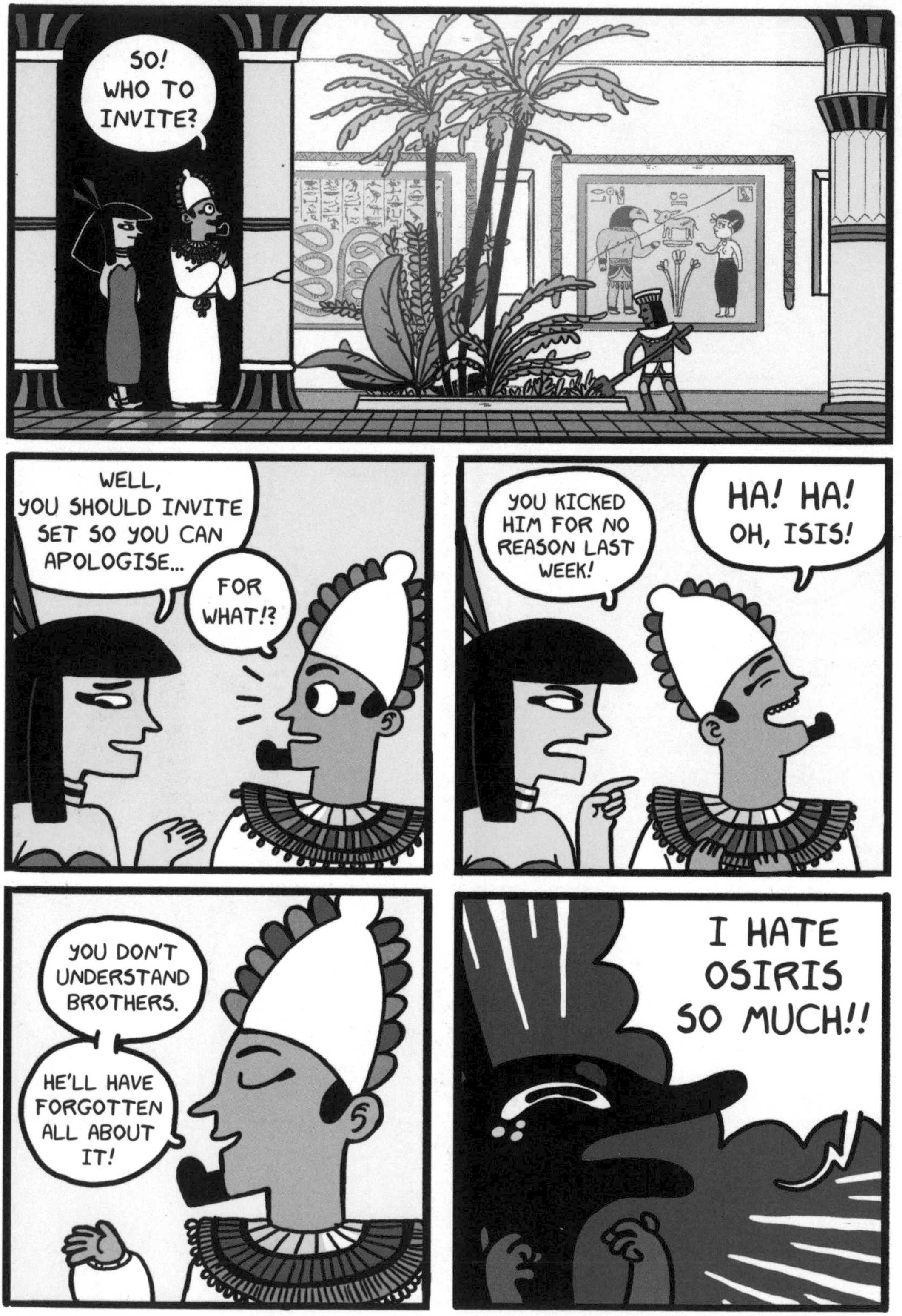
SO! WHO TO INVITE?
WELL, YOU SHOULD INVITE SET SO YOU CAN APOLOGISE...
FOR WHAT!?
YOU KICKED HIM FOR NO REASON LAST WEEK!
HA! HA! OH, ISIS!
YOU DON'T UNDERSTAND BROTHERS.
HE'LL HAVE FORGOTTEN ALL ABOUT IT!
I HATE OSIRIS SO MUCH!!

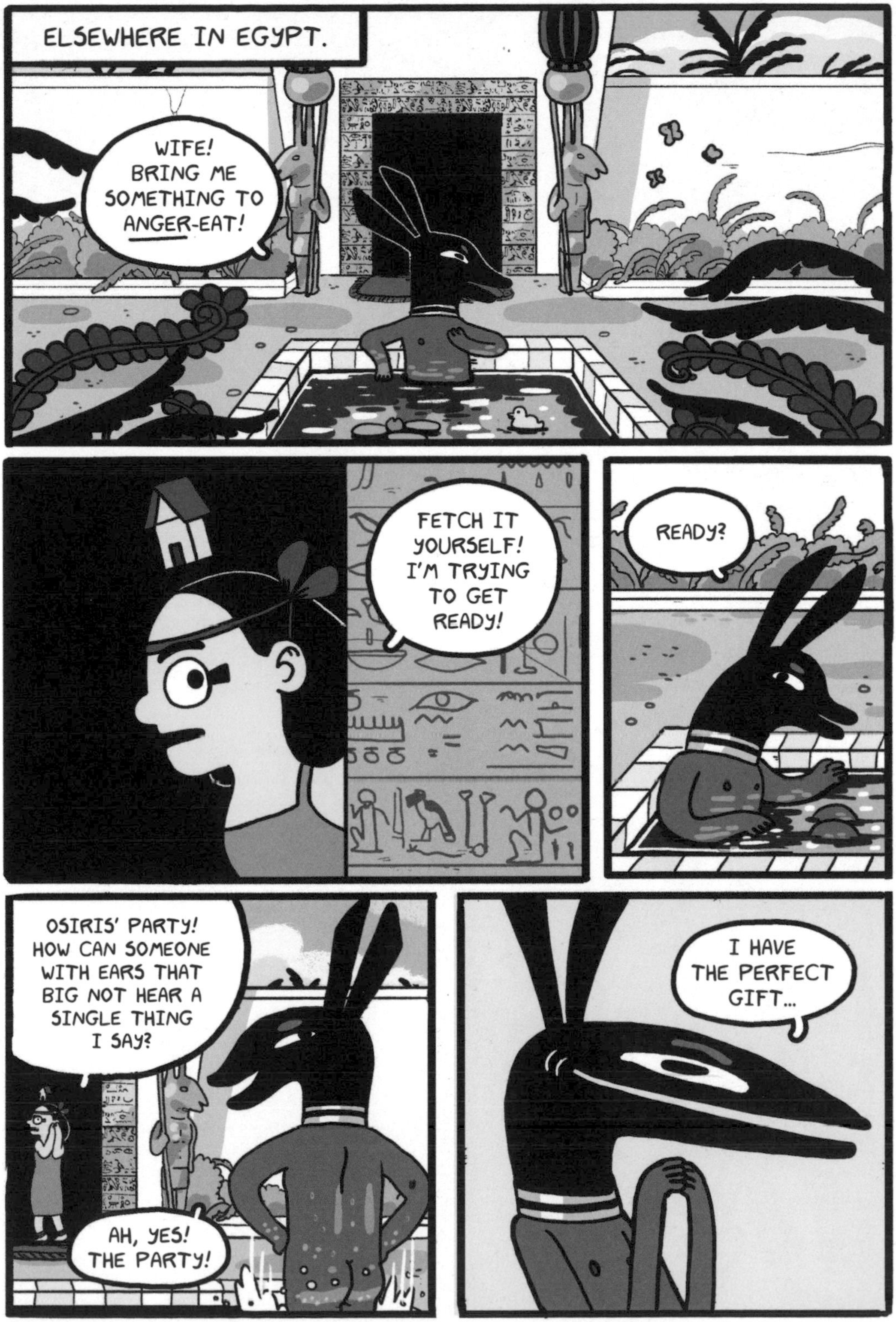

ELSEWHERE IN EGYPT.
WIFE! BRING ME SOMETHING TO ANGER-EAT!
FETCH IT YOURSELF! I'M TRYING TO GET READY!
READY?
OSIRIS' PARTY! HOW CAN SOMEONE WITH EARS THAT BIG NOT HEAR A SINGLE THING I SAY?
AH, YES! THE PARTY!
I HAVE THE PERFECT GIFT...

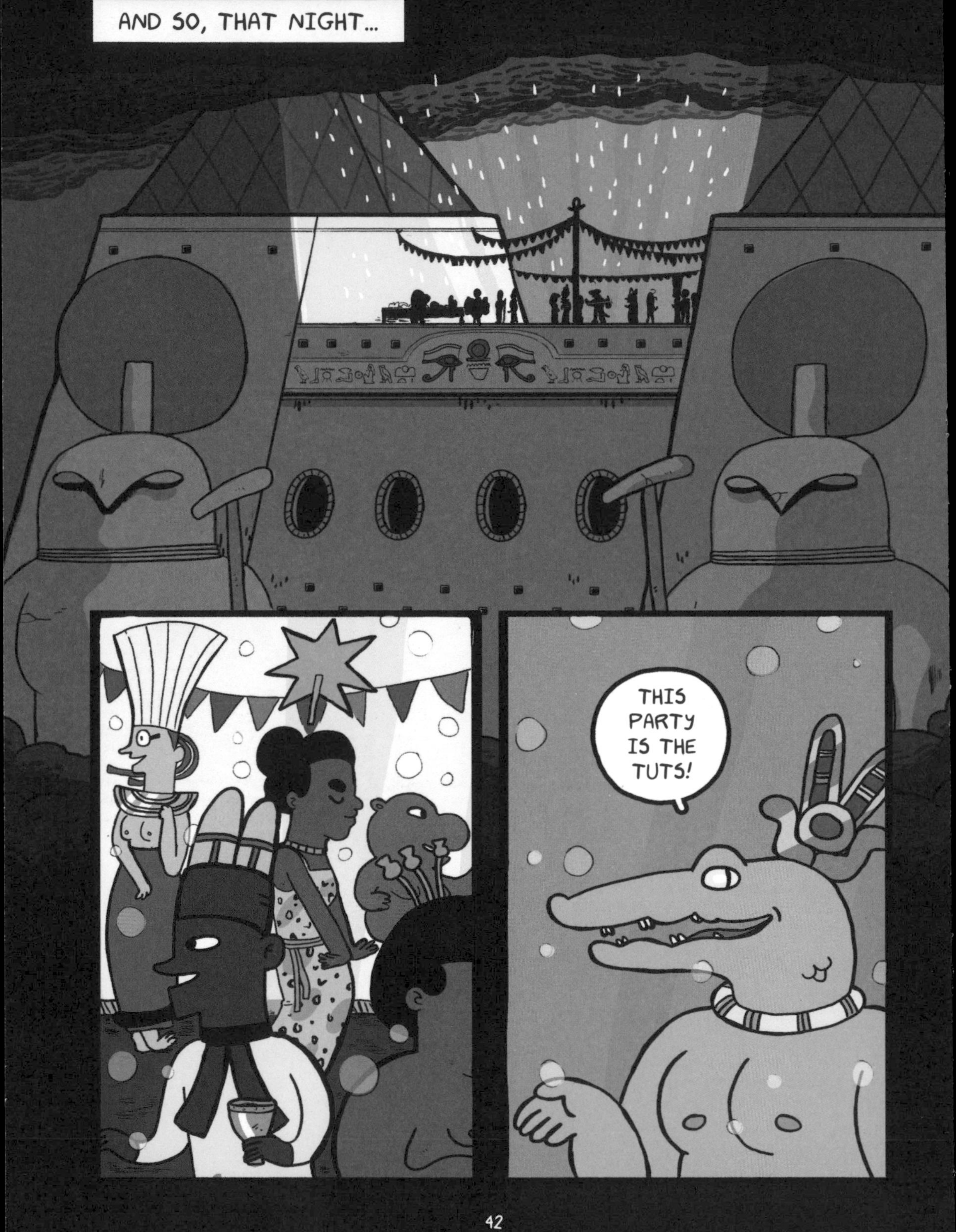
AND SO, THAT NIGHT...
THIS PARTY IS THE TUTS!

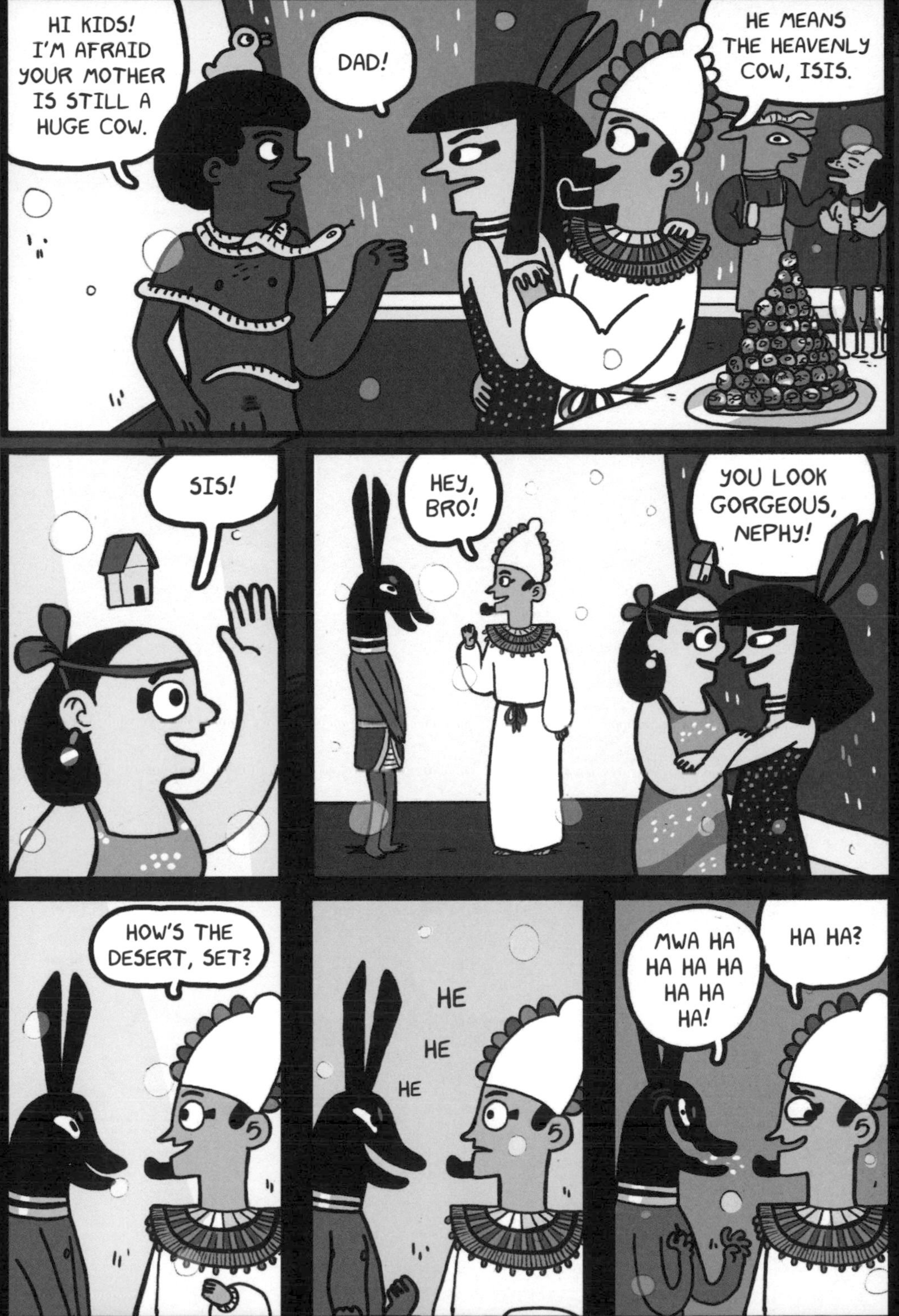
HI KIDS! I'M AFRAID YOUR MOTHER IS STILL A HUGE COW.
DAD!
HE MEANS THE HEAVENLY COW, ISIS.
SIS!
HEY, BRO!
YOU LOOK GORGEOUS, NEPHY!
HOW'S THE DESERT, SET?
HE HE HE
MWA HA HA HA HA HA HA HA!
HA HA?

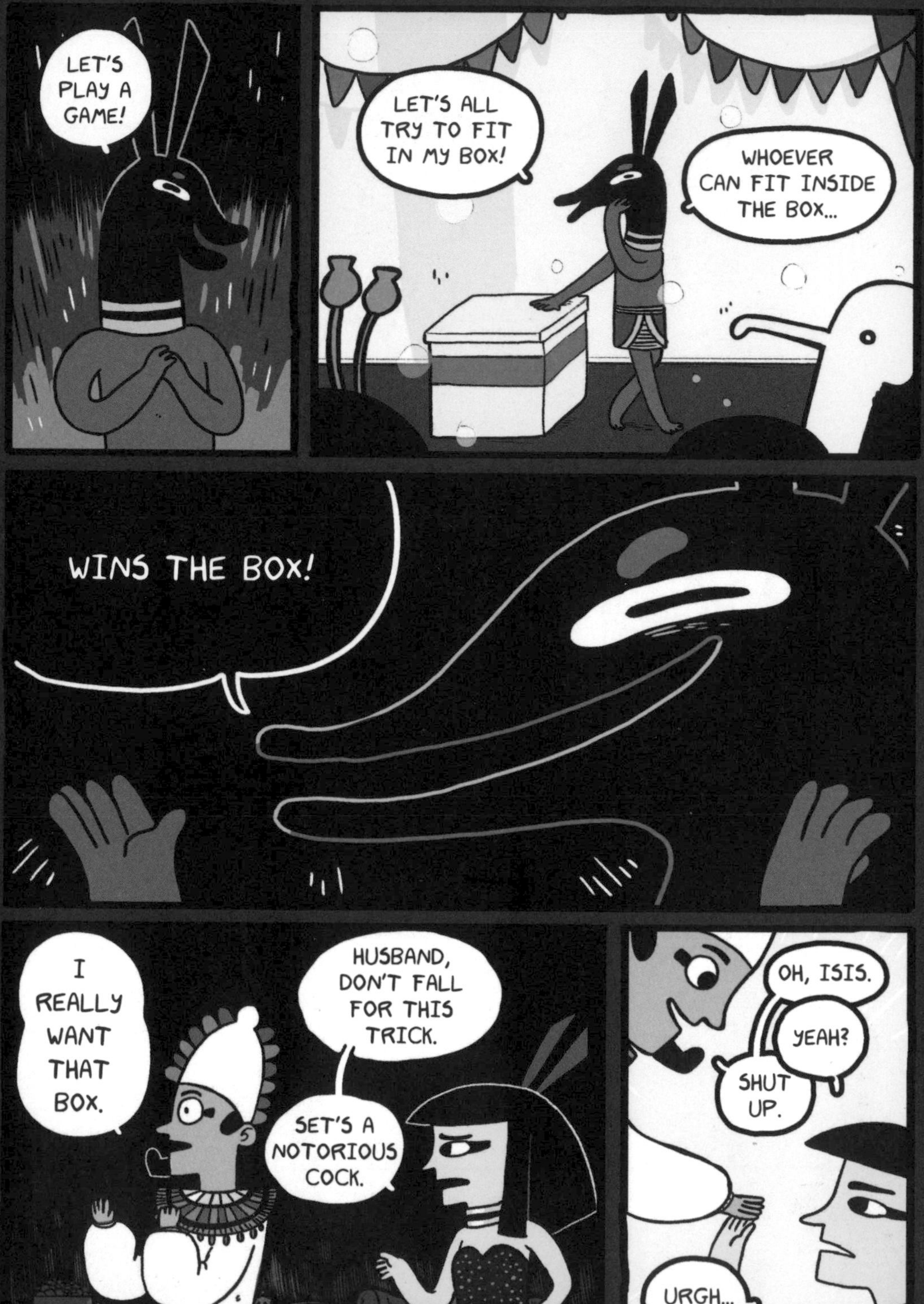
LET'S PLAY A GAME!
LET'S ALL TRY TO FIT IN MY BOX!
WHOEVER CAN FIT INSIDE THE BOX...
WINS THE BOX!
I REALLY WANT THAT BOX.
HUSBAND, DON'T FALL FOR THIS TRICK.
SET'S A NOTORIOUS COCK.
OH, ISIS.
YEAH?
SHUT UP.
URGH...

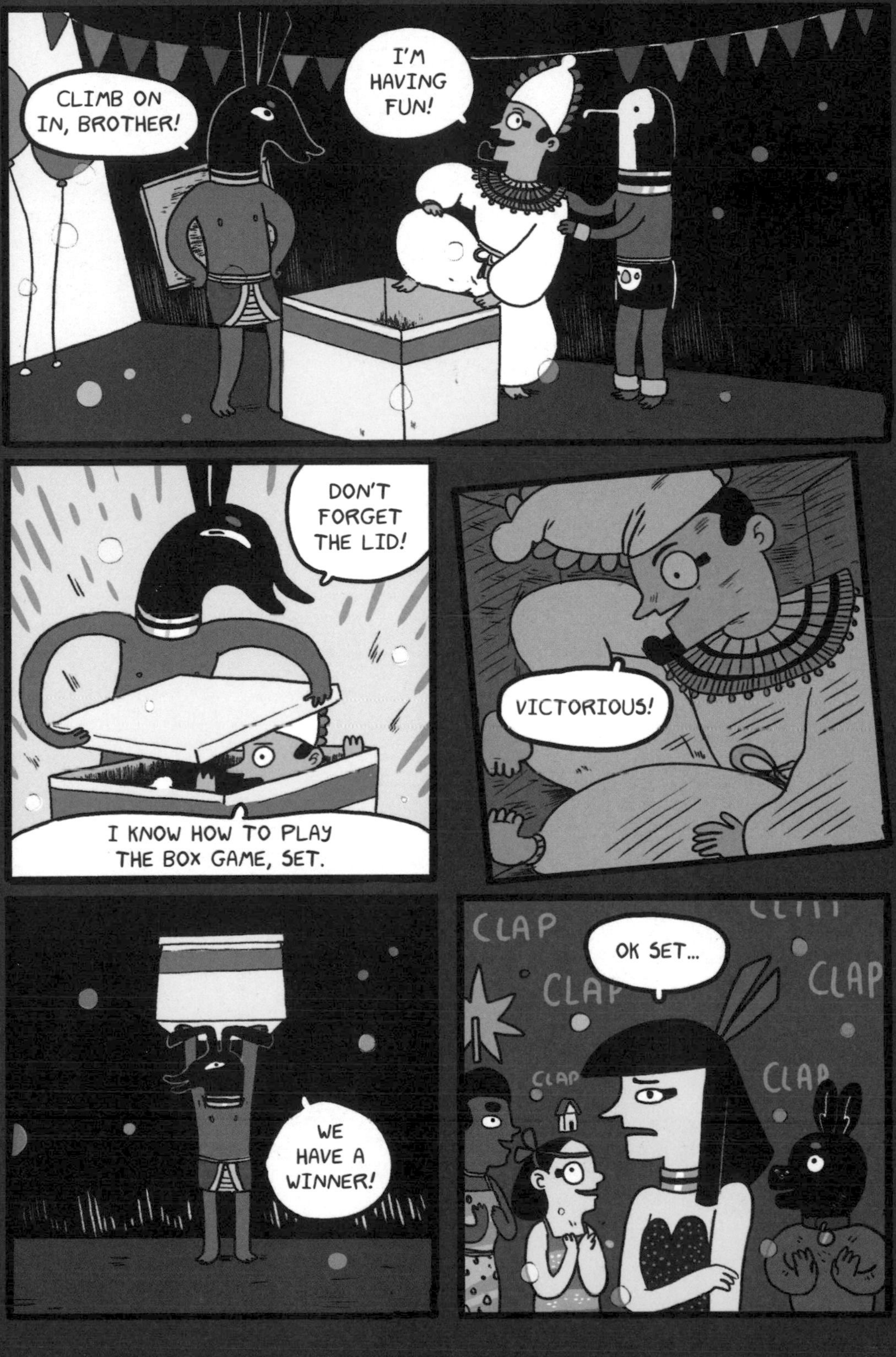

CLIMB ON IN, BROTHER!
I'M HAVING FUN!
DON'T FORGET THE LID!
I KNOW HOW TO PLAY THE BOX GAME, SET.
VICTORIOUS!
WE HAVE A WINNER!
CLAP
OK SET...
CLAP
CLAP
CLAP
CLAP

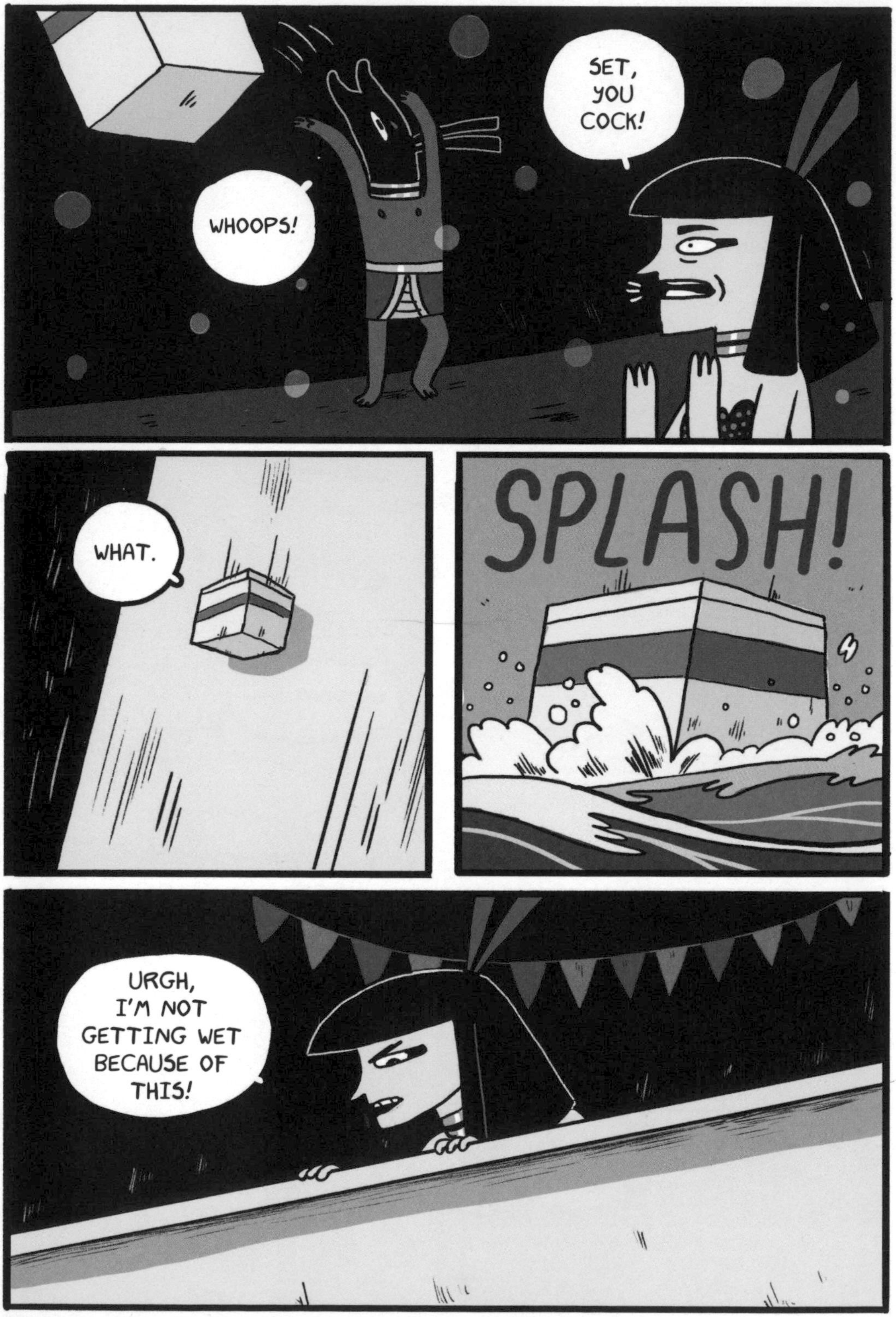
SET, YOU COCK!
WHOOPS!
WHAT.
SPLASH!
URGH, I'M NOT GETTING WET BECAUSE OF THIS!

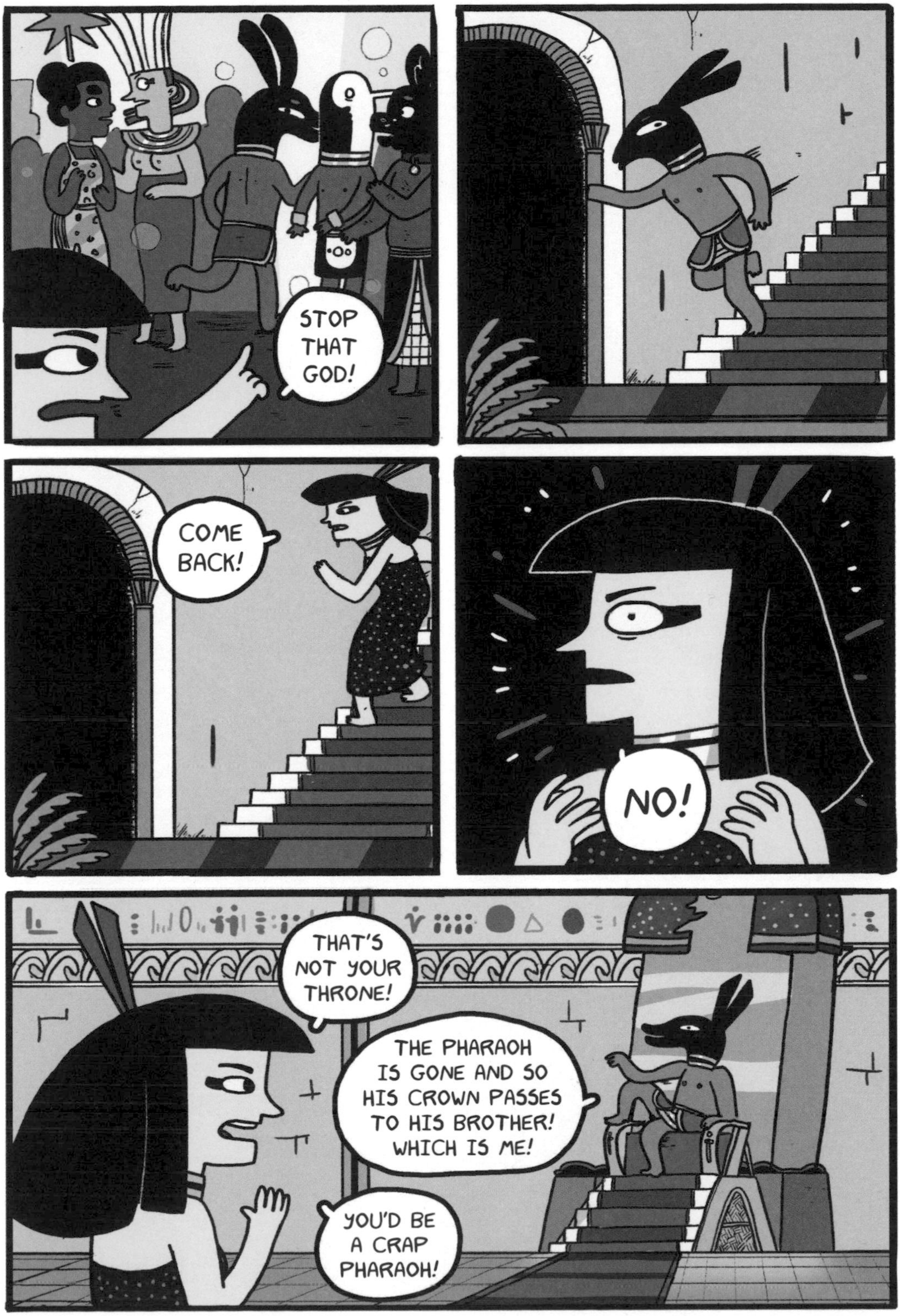

STOP THAT GOD!
COME BACK!
NO!
THAT'S NOT YOUR THRONE!
THE PHARAOH IS GONE AND SO HIS CROWN PASSES TO HIS BROTHER! WHICH IS ME!
YOU'D BE A CRAP PHARAOH!

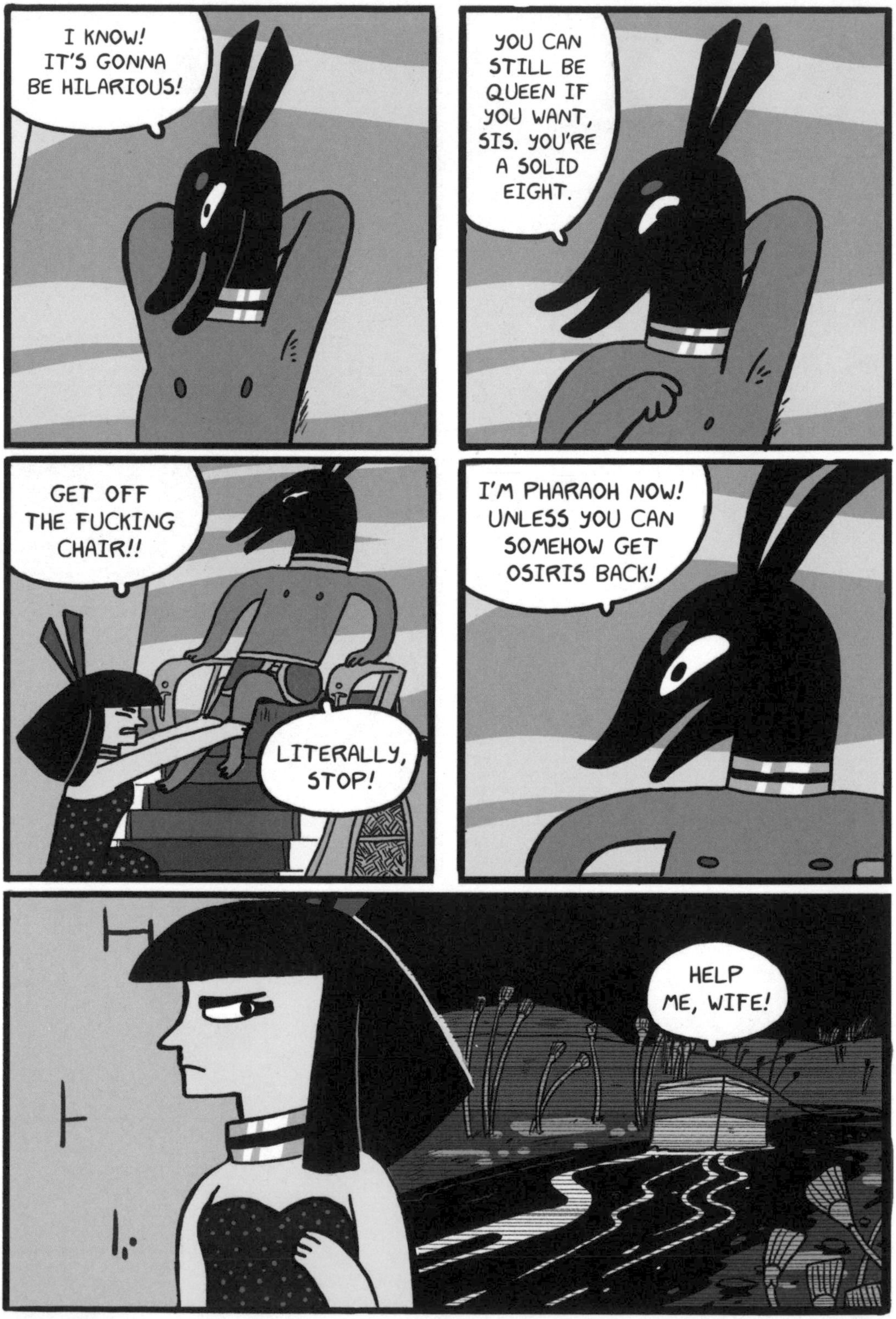
I KNOW! IT'S GONNA BE HILARIOUS!
YOU CAN STILL BE QUEEN IF YOU WANT, SIS. YOU'RE A SOLID EIGHT.
GET OFF THE FUCKING CHAIR!!
LITERALLY, STOP!
I'M PHARAOH NOW! UNLESS YOU CAN SOMEHOW GET OSIRIS BACK!
HELP ME, WIFE!

CHAPTER THREE

★★★ SEVERANCE ★★★

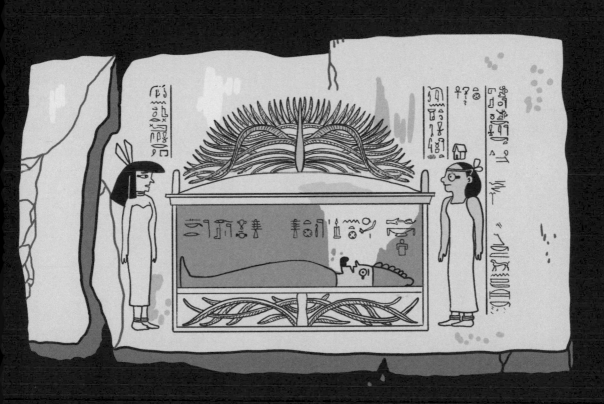

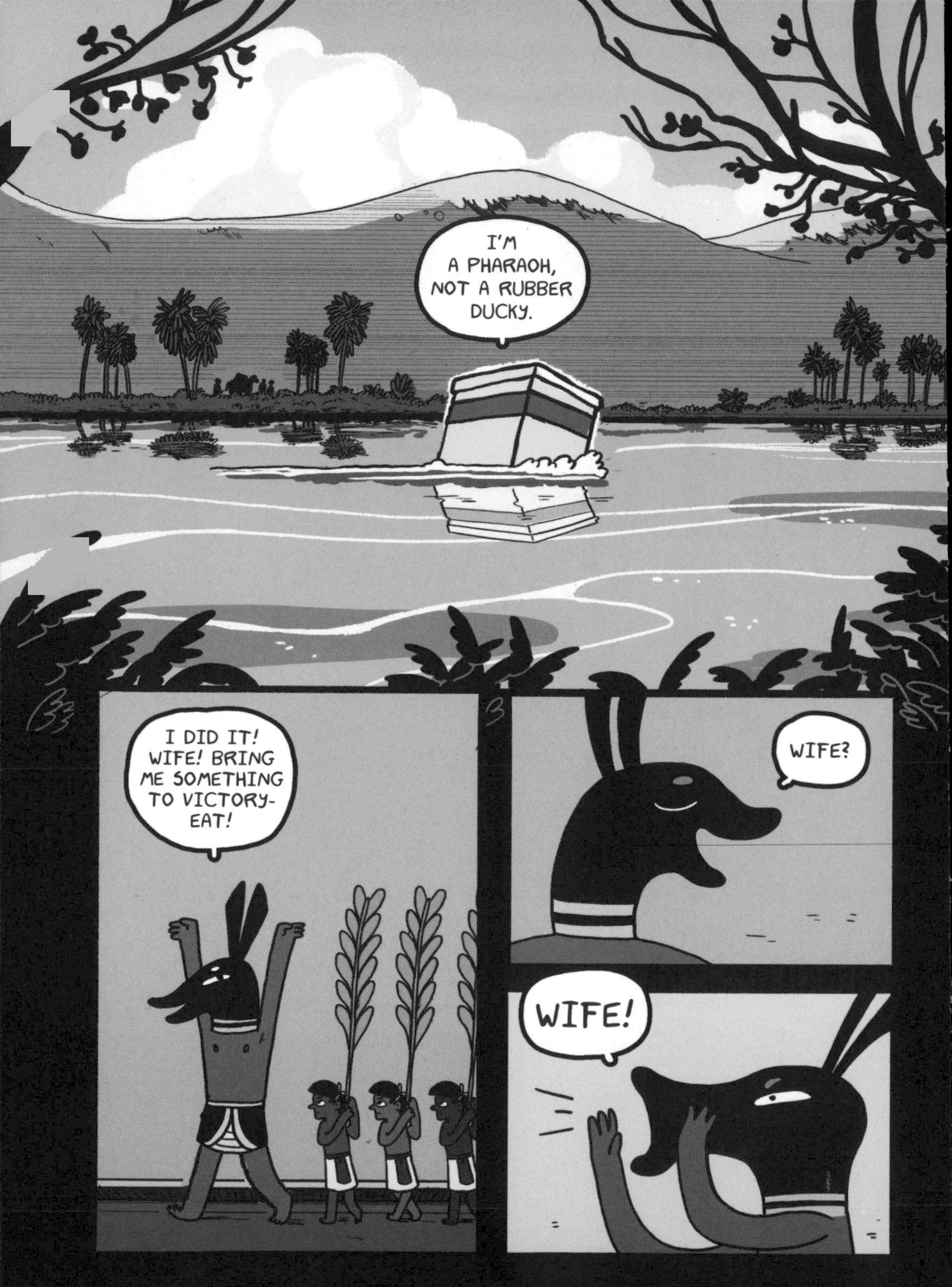
I'M A PHARAOH, NOT A RUBBER DUCKY.
I DID IT! WIFE! BRING ME SOMETHING TO VICTORY-EAT!
WIFE?
WIFE!

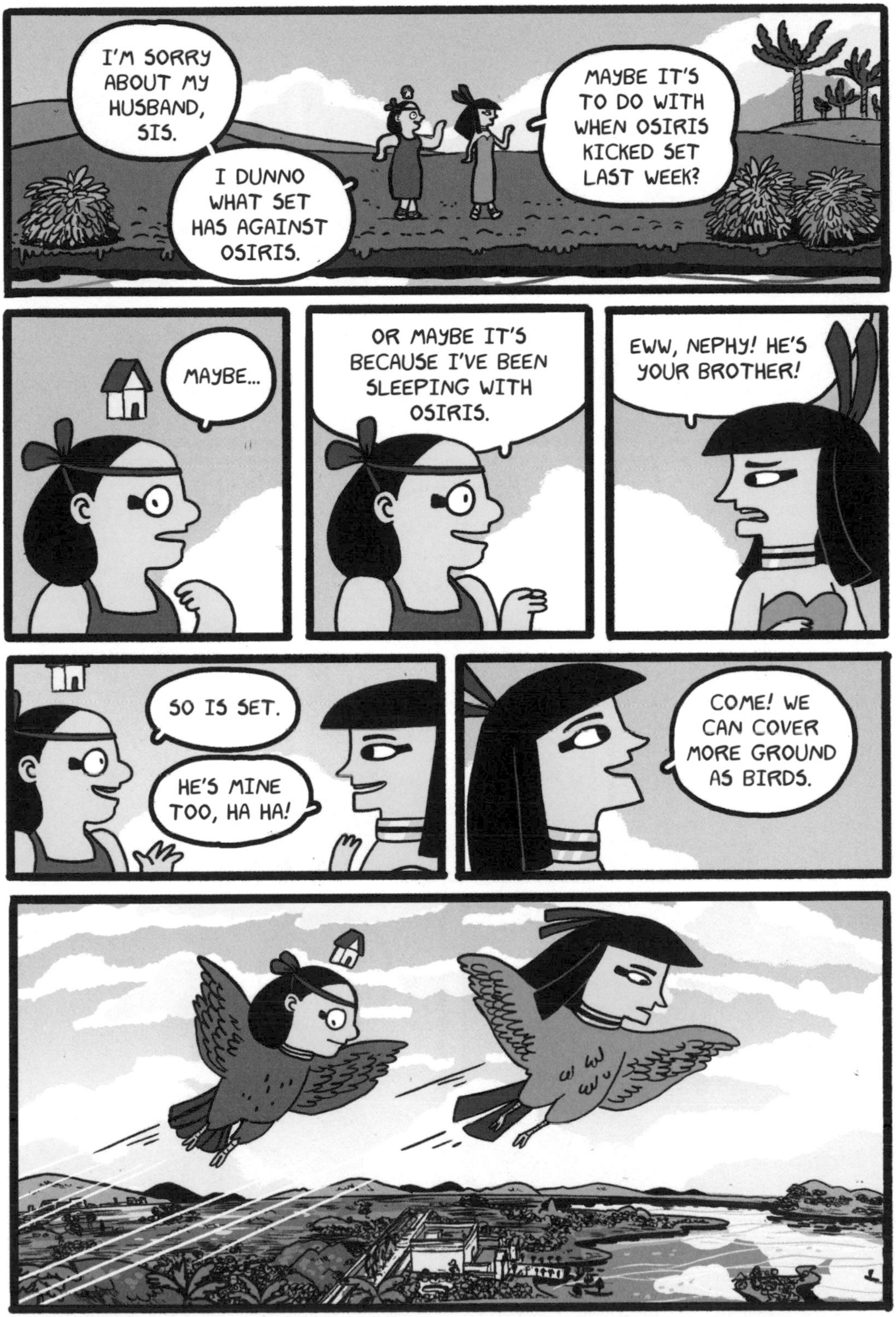
I'M SORRY ABOUT MY HUSBAND, SIS.
I DUNNO WHAT SET HAS AGAINST OSIRIS.
MAYBE IT'S TO DO WITH WHEN OSIRIS KICKED SET LAST WEEK?
MAYBE...
OR MAYBE IT'S BECAUSE I'VE BEEN SLEEPING WITH OSIRIS.
EWW, NEPHY! HE'S YOUR BROTHER!
SO IS SET.
HE'S MINE TOO, HA HA!
COME! WE CAN COVER MORE GROUND AS BIRDS.

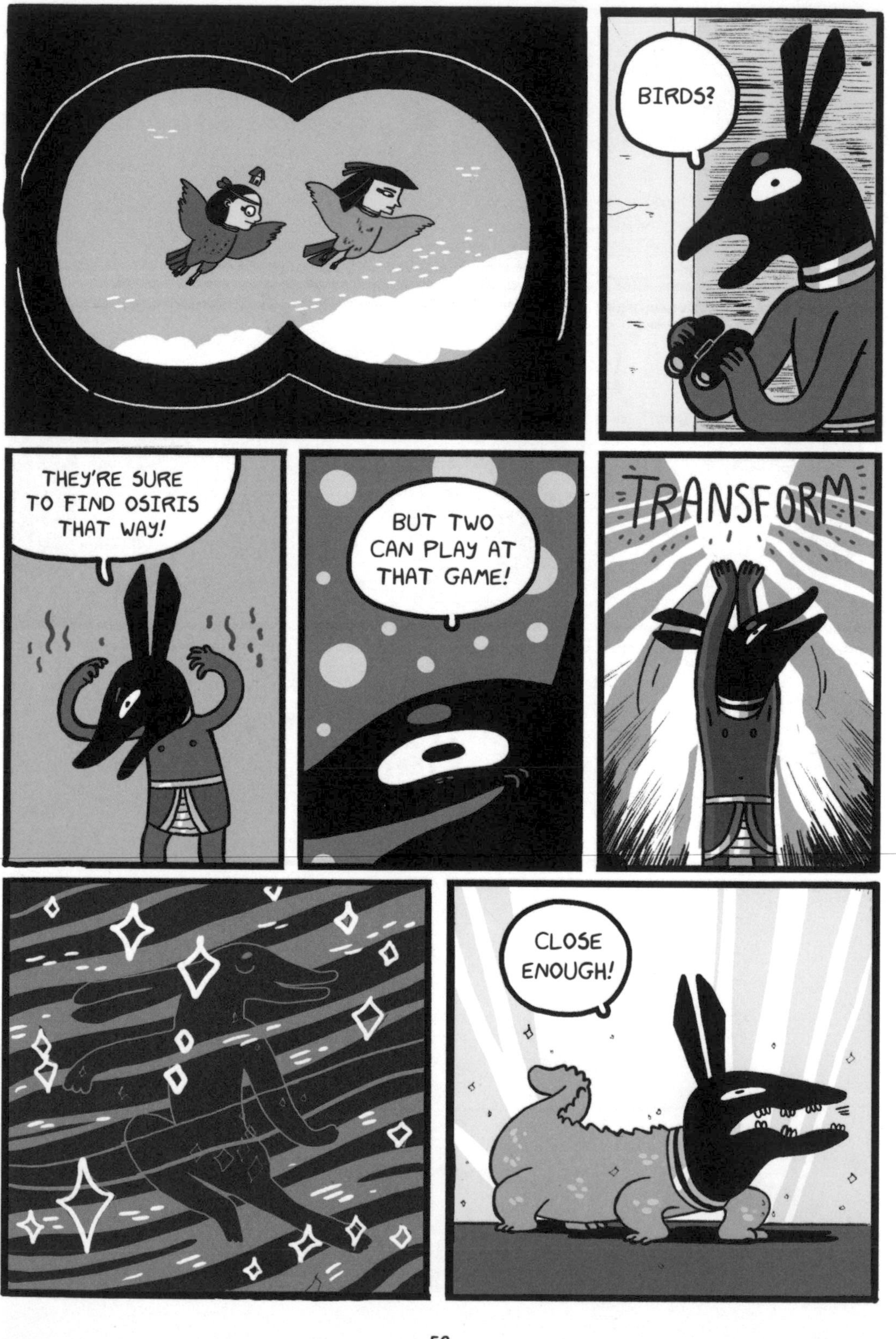
BIRDS?
THEY'RE SURE TO FIND OSIRIS THAT WAY!
BUT TWO CAN PLAY AT THAT GAME!
TRANSFORM
CLOSE ENOUGH!

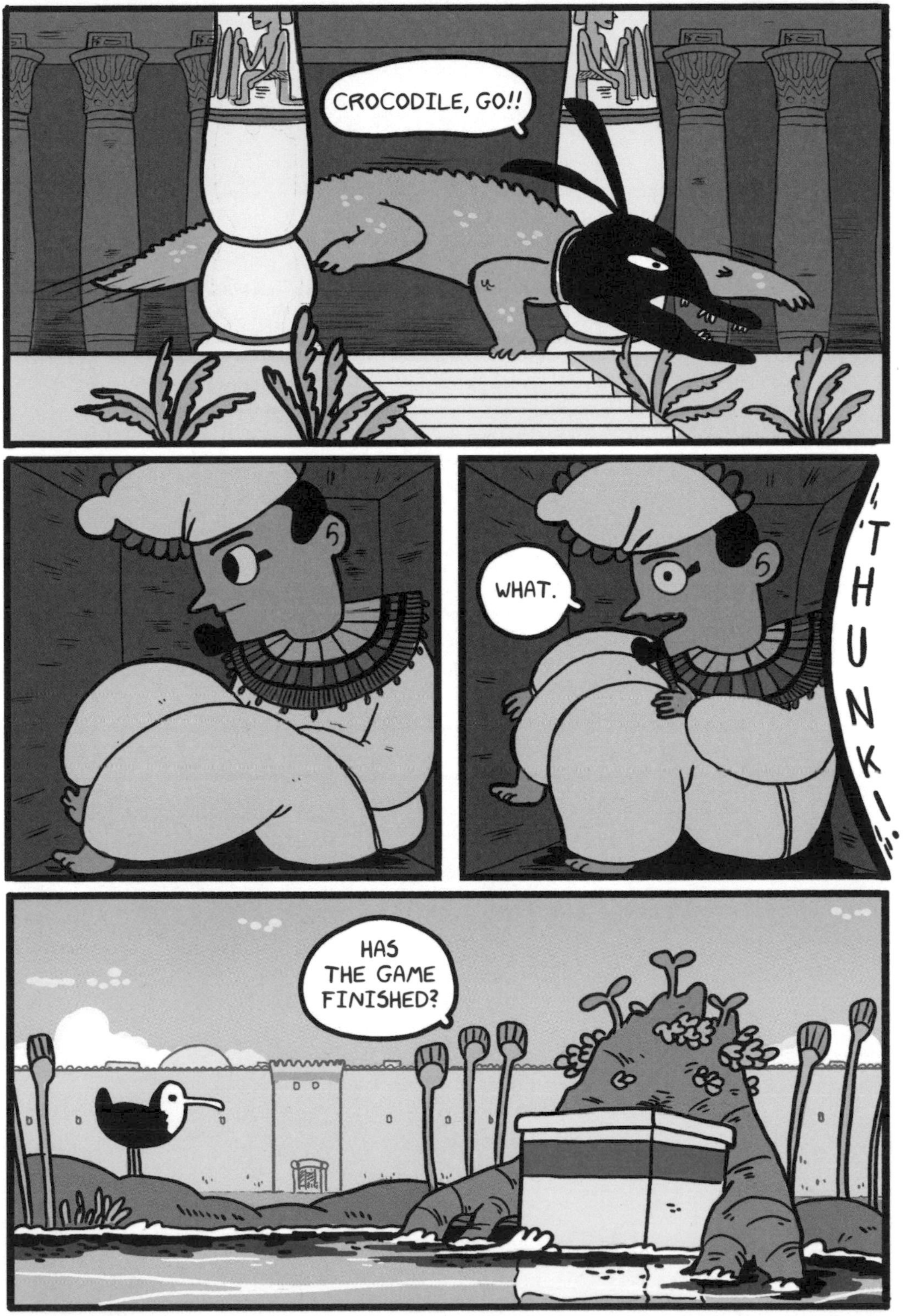
CROCODILE, GO!!
WHAT.
THUNK!
HAS THE GAME FINISHED?

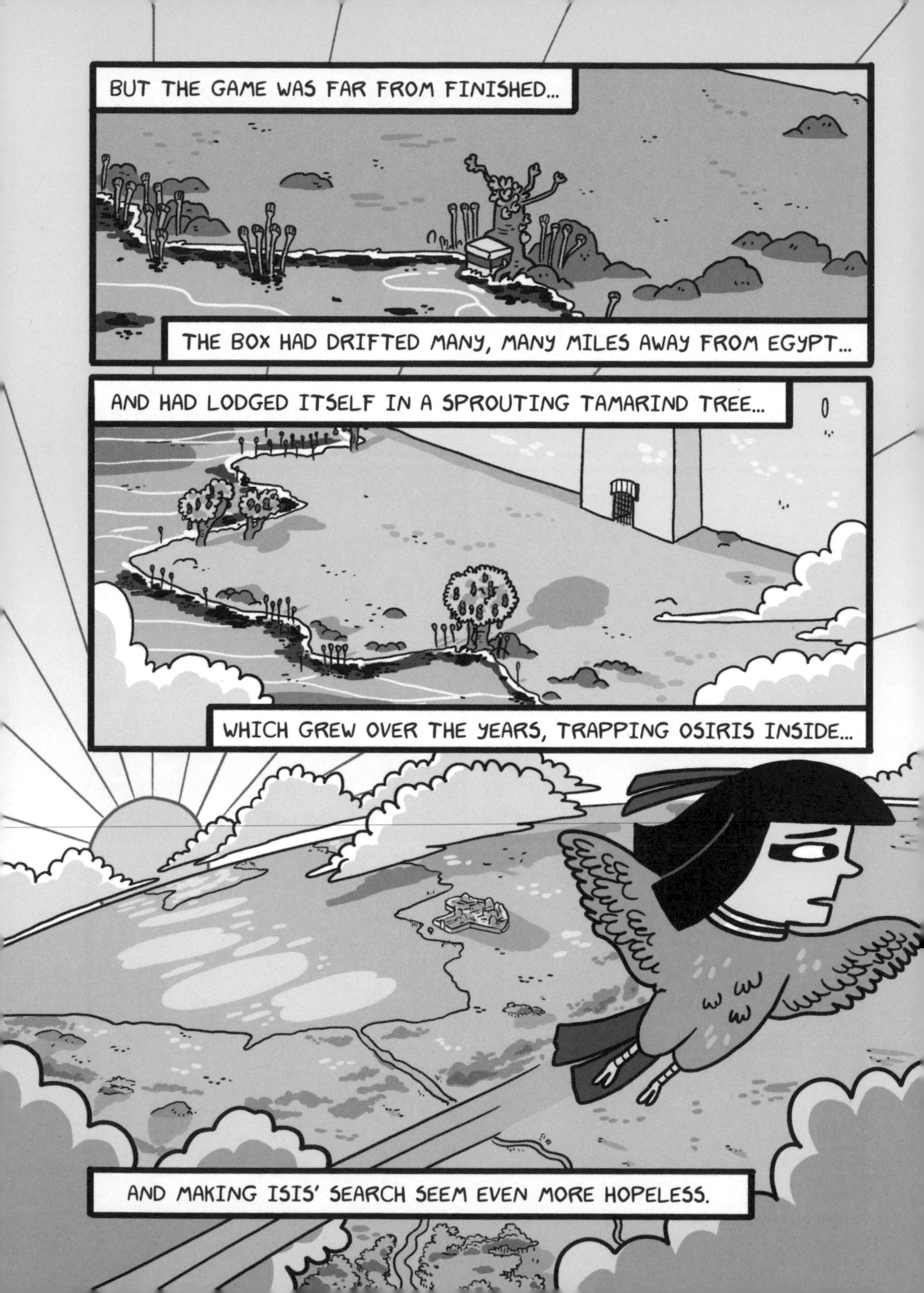
BUT THE GAME WAS FAR FROM FINISHED...
THE BOX HAD DRIFTED MANY, MANY MILES AWAY FROM EGYPT...
AND HAD LODGED ITSELF IN A SPROUTING TAMARIND TREE...
WHICH GREW OVER THE YEARS, TRAPPING OSIRIS INSIDE...
AND MAKING ISIS' SEARCH SEEM EVEN MORE HOPELESS.

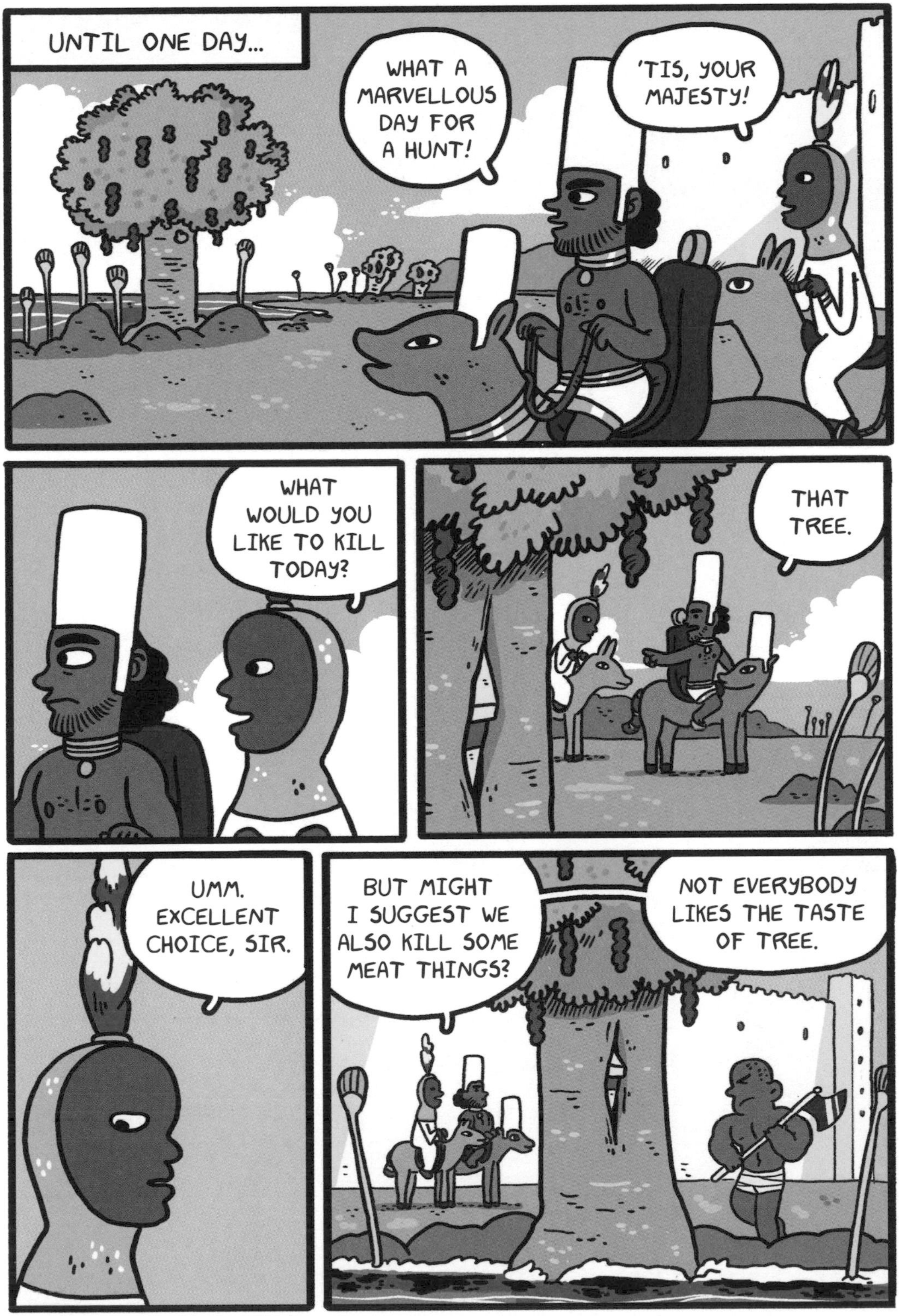
UNTIL ONE DAY...
WHAT A MARVELLOUS DAY FOR A HUNT!
'TIS, YOUR MAJESTY!
WHAT WOULD YOU LIKE TO KILL TODAY?
THAT TREE.
UMM. EXCELLENT CHOICE, SIR.
BUT MIGHT I SUGGEST WE ALSO KILL SOME MEAT THINGS?
NOT EVERYBODY LIKES THE TASTE OF TREE.

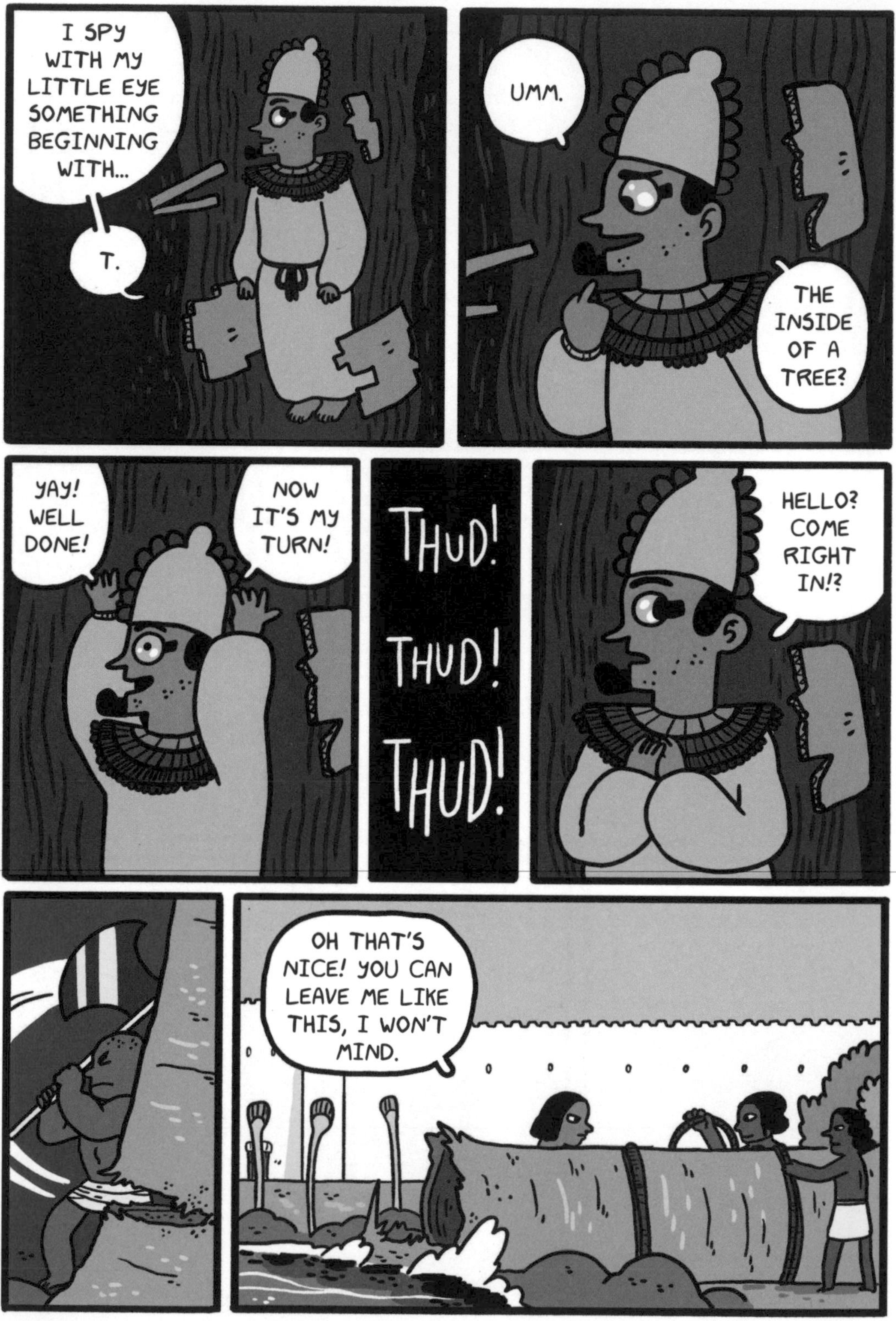
I SPY WITH MY LITTLE EYE SOMETHING BEGINNING WITH...
T.
UMM.
THE INSIDE OF A TREE?
YAY! WELL DONE!
NOW IT'S MY TURN!
THUD! THUD! THUD!
HELLO? COME RIGHT IN!?
OH THAT'S NICE! YOU CAN LEAVE ME LIKE THIS, I WON'T MIND.

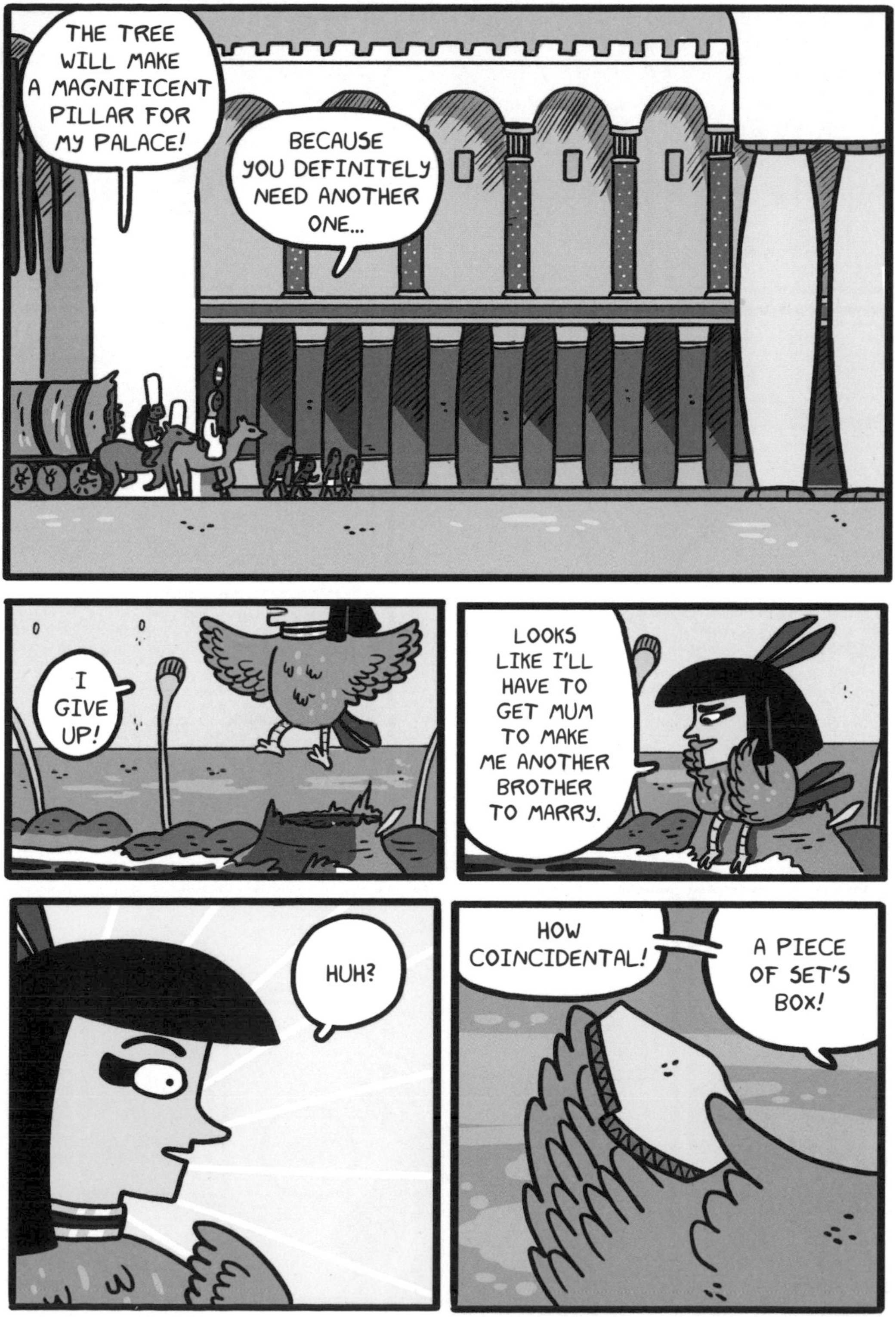
THE TREE WILL MAKE A MAGNIFICENT PILLAR FOR MY PALACE!
BECAUSE YOU DEFINITELY NEED ANOTHER ONE...
I GIVE UP!
LOOKS LIKE I'LL HAVE TO GET MUM TO MAKE ME ANOTHER BROTHER TO MARRY.
HUH?
HOW COINCIDENTAL!
A PIECE OF SET'S BOX!

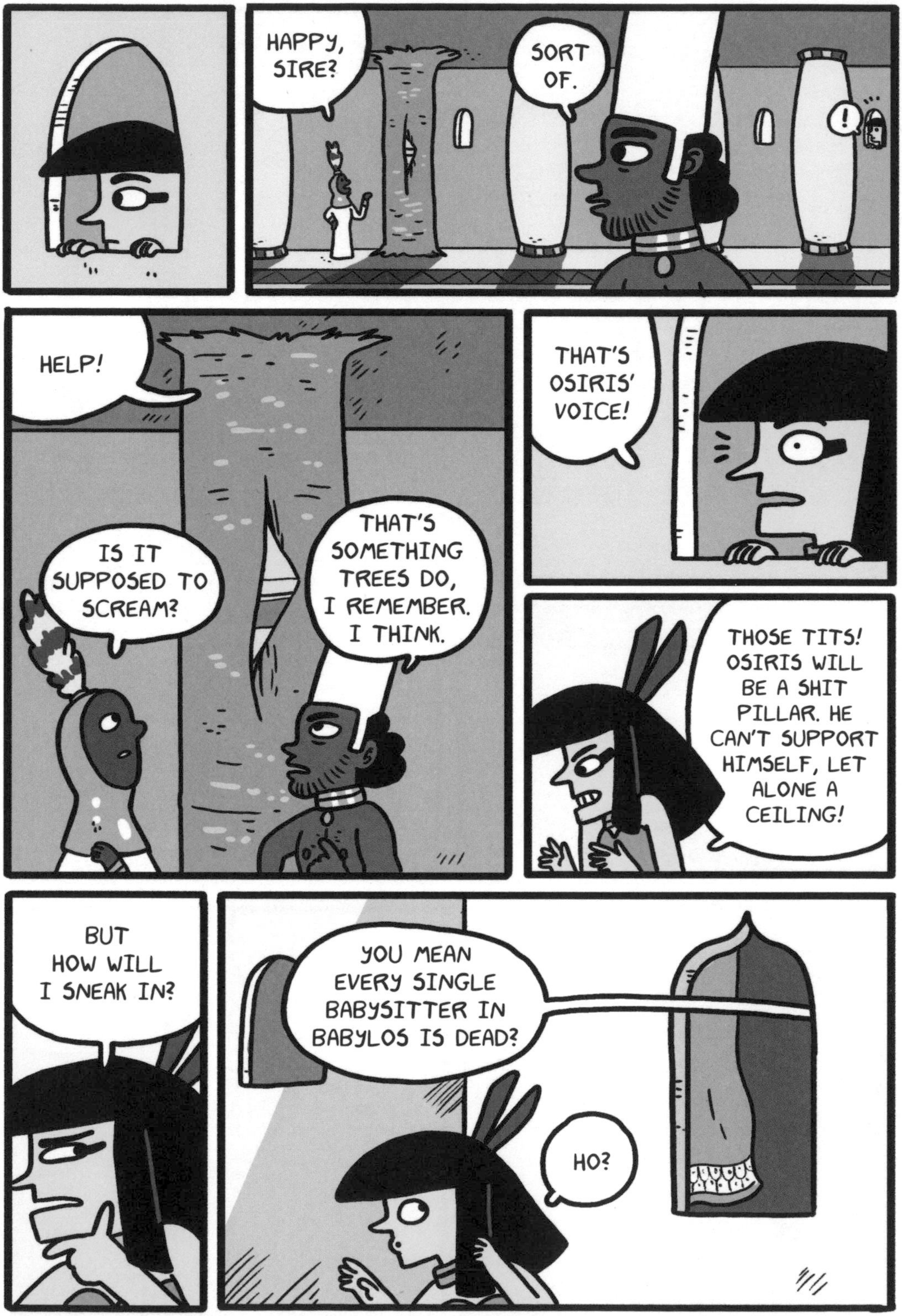
HAPPY, SIRE?
SORT OF.
!
HELP!
THAT'S OSIRIS' VOICE!
IS IT SUPPOSED TO SCREAM?
THAT'S SOMETHING TREES DO, I REMEMBER. I THINK.
THOSE TITS! OSIRIS WILL BE A SHIT PILLAR. HE CAN'T SUPPORT HIMSELF, LET ALONE A CEILING!
BUT HOW WILL I SNEAK IN?
YOU MEAN EVERY SINGLE BABYSITTER IN BABYLOS IS DEAD?
HO?

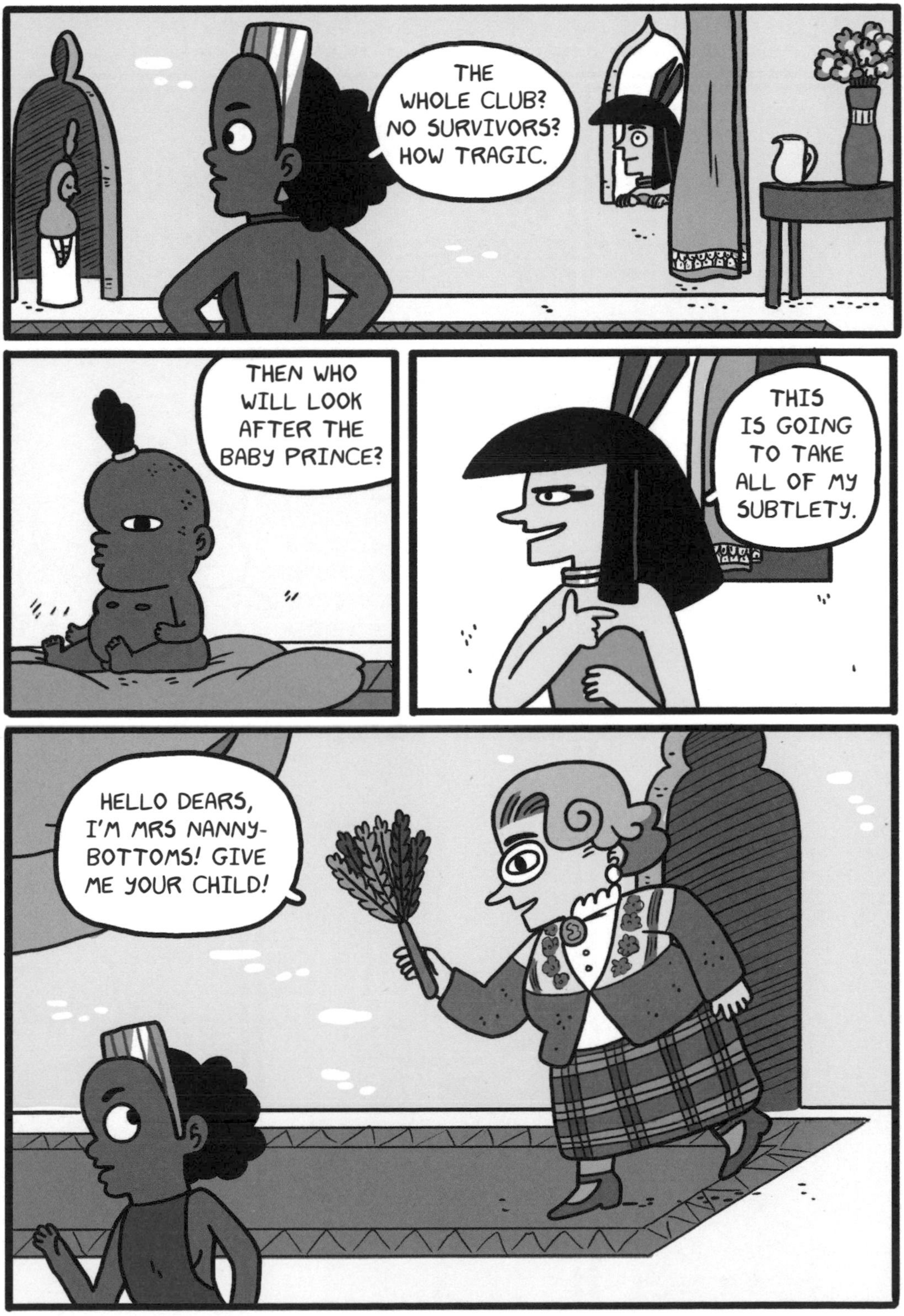
THE WHOLE CLUB? NO SURVIVORS? HOW TRAGIC.
THEN WHO WILL LOOK AFTER THE BABY PRINCE?
THIS IS GOING TO TAKE ALL OF MY SUBTLETY.
HELLO DEARS, I'M MRS NANNY-BOTTOMS! GIVE ME YOUR CHILD!

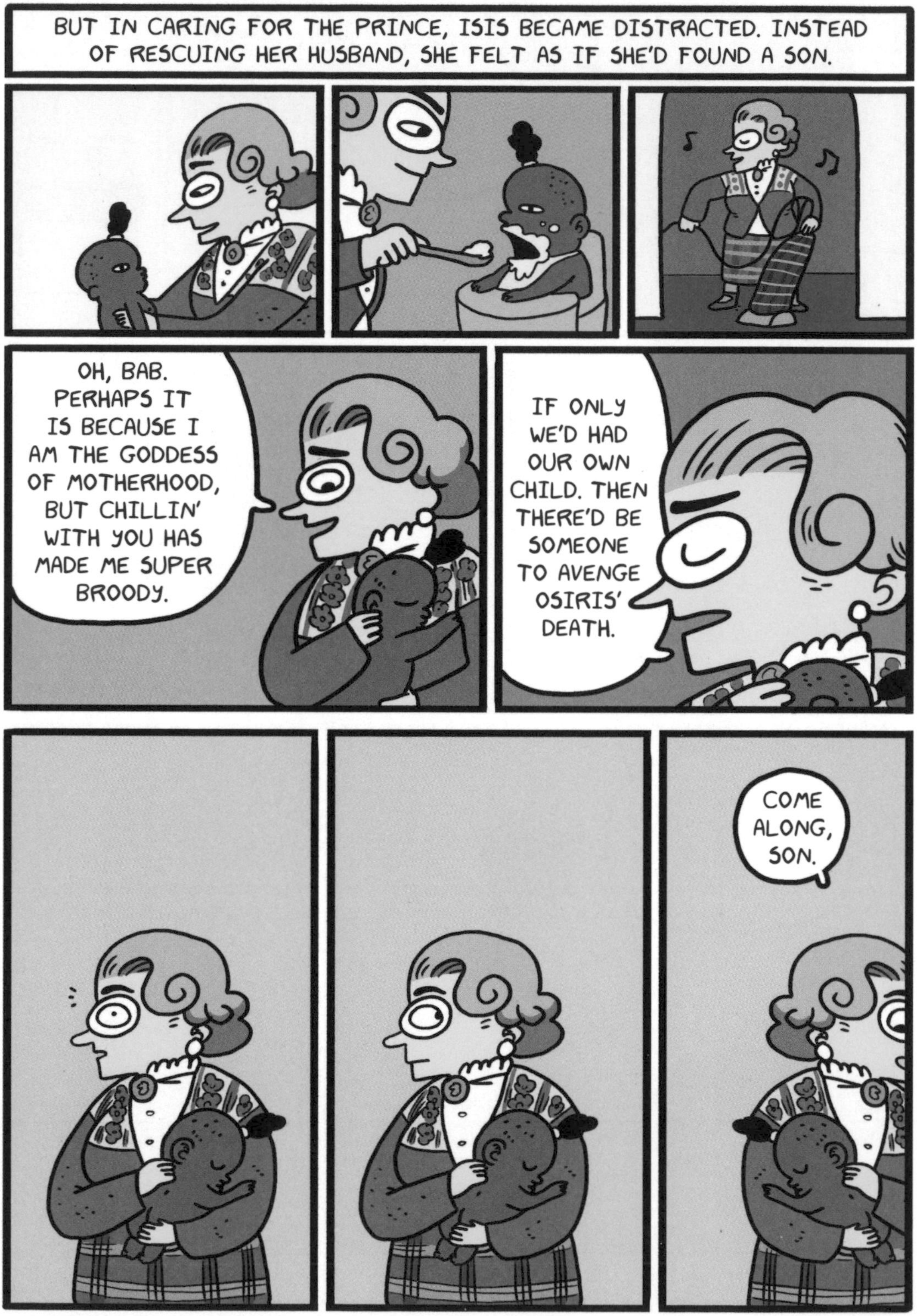
BUT IN CARING FOR THE PRINCE, ISIS BECAME DISTRACTED. INSTEAD OF RESCUING HER HUSBAND, SHE FELT AS IF SHE'D FOUND A SON.
OH, BAB. PERHAPS IT IS BECAUSE I AM THE GODDESS OF MOTHERHOOD, BUT CHILLIN' WITH YOU HAS MADE ME SUPER BROODY.
IF ONLY WE'D HAD OUR OWN CHILD. THEN THERE'D BE SOMEONE TO AVENGE OSIRIS' DEATH.
COME ALONG, SON.

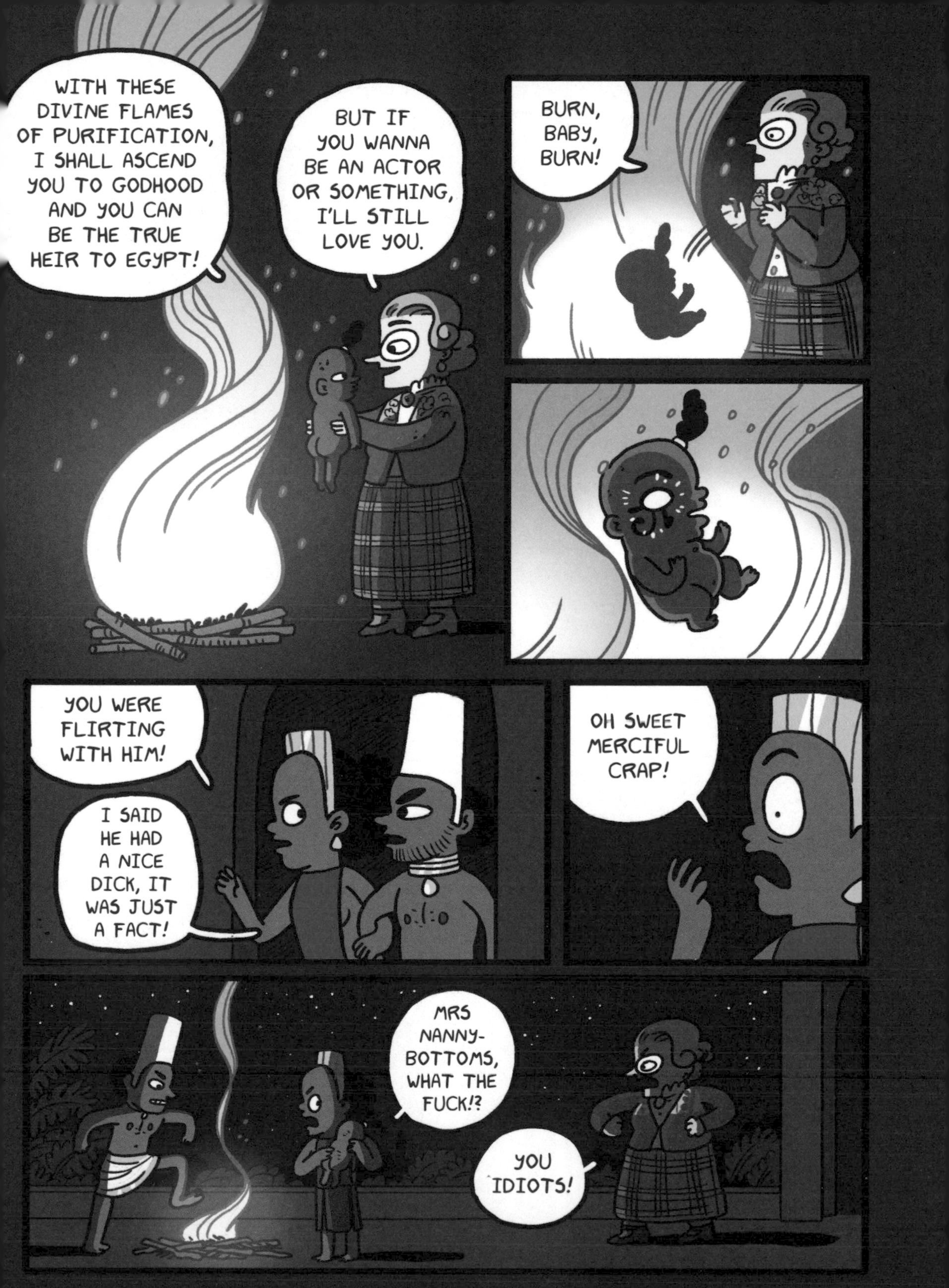
WITH THESE DIVINE FLAMES OF PURIFICATION, I SHALL ASCEND YOU TO GODHOOD AND YOU CAN BE THE TRUE HEIR TO EGYPT!
BUT IF YOU WANNA BE AN ACTOR OR SOMETHING, I'LL STILL LOVE YOU.
BURN, BABY, BURN!
YOU WERE FLIRTING WITH HIM!
I SAID HE HAD A NICE DICK, IT WAS JUST A FACT!
OH SWEET MERCIFUL CRAP!
MRS NANNY-BOTTOMS, WHAT THE FUCK!?
YOU IDIOTS!

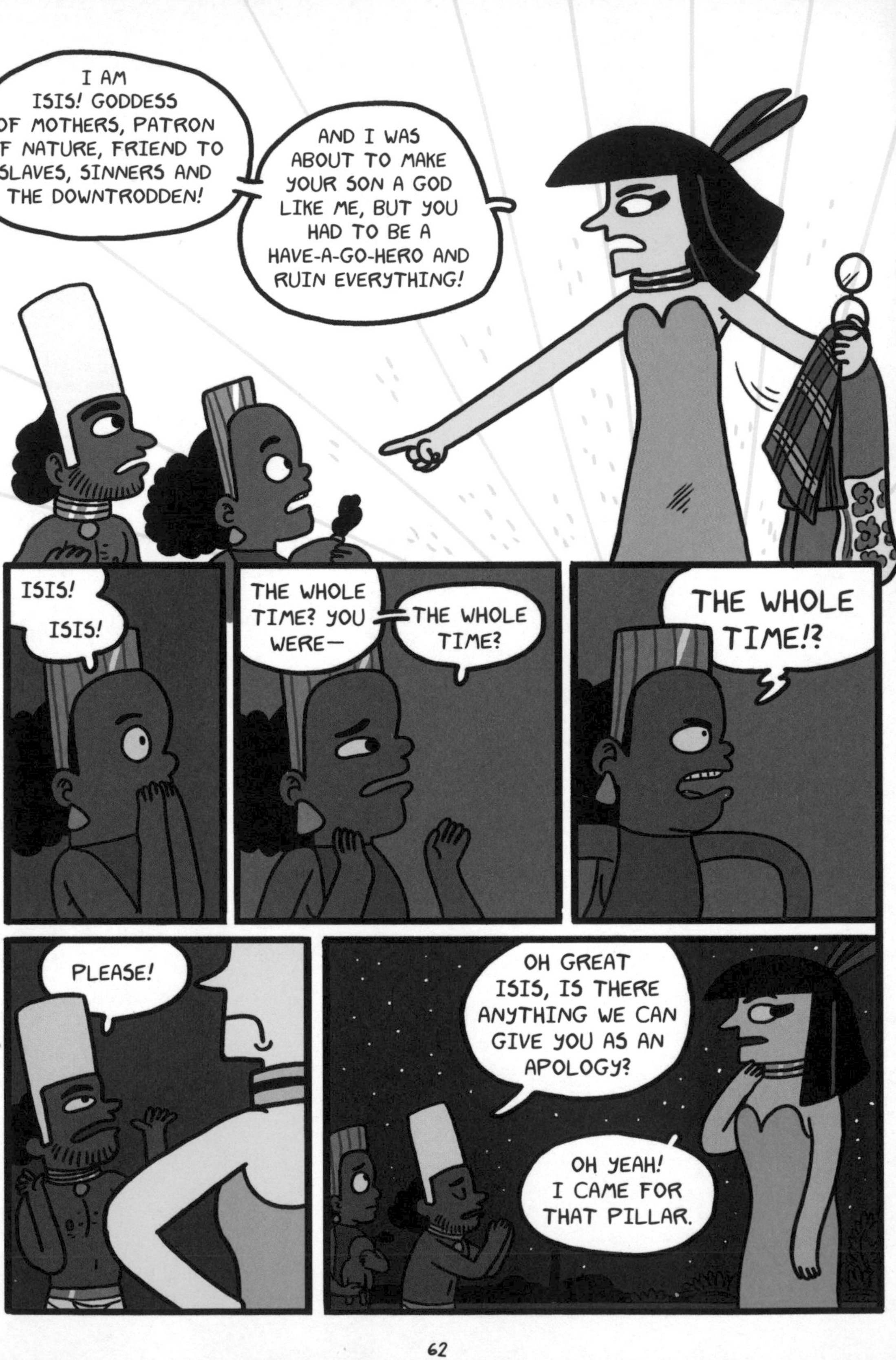
I AM ISIS! GODDESS OF MOTHERS, PATRON OF NATURE, FRIEND TO SLAVES, SINNERS AND THE DOWNTRODDEN!
AND I WAS ABOUT TO MAKE YOUR SON A GOD LIKE ME, BUT YOU HAD TO BE A HAVE-A-GO-HERO AND RUIN EVERYTHING!
ISIS!
ISIS!
THE WHOLE TIME? YOU WERE—
THE WHOLE TIME?
THE WHOLE TIME!?
PLEASE!
OH GREAT ISIS, IS THERE ANYTHING WE CAN GIVE YOU AS AN APOLOGY?
OH YEAH! I CAME FOR THAT PILLAR.

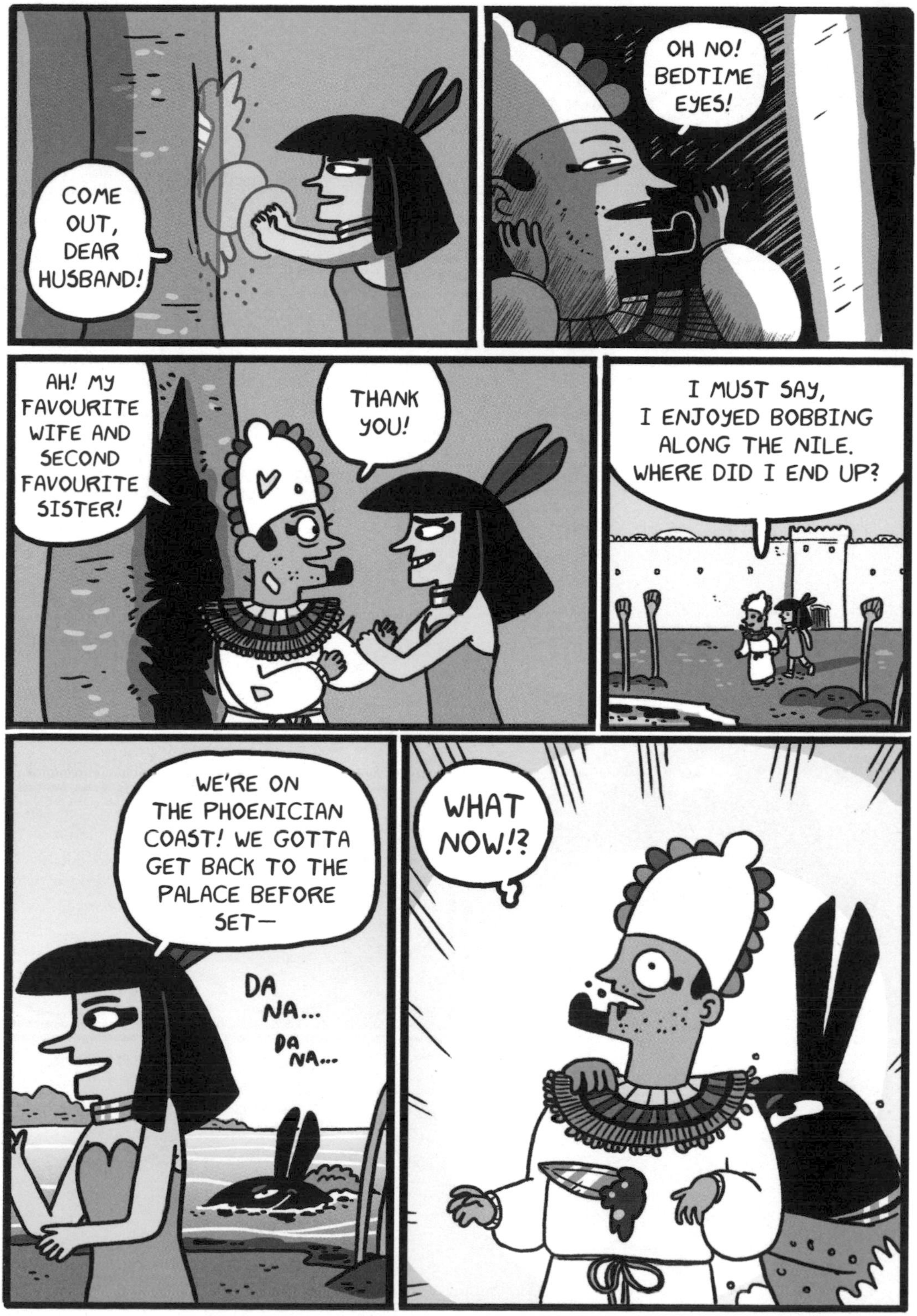
COME OUT, DEAR HUSBAND!
OH NO! BEDTIME EYES!
AH! MY FAVOURITE WIFE AND SECOND FAVOURITE SISTER!
THANK YOU!
I MUST SAY, I ENJOYED BOBBING ALONG THE NILE. WHERE DID I END UP?
WE'RE ON THE PHOENICIAN COAST! WE GOTTA GET BACK TO THE PALACE BEFORE SET—
DA NA...
DA NA...
WHAT NOW!?

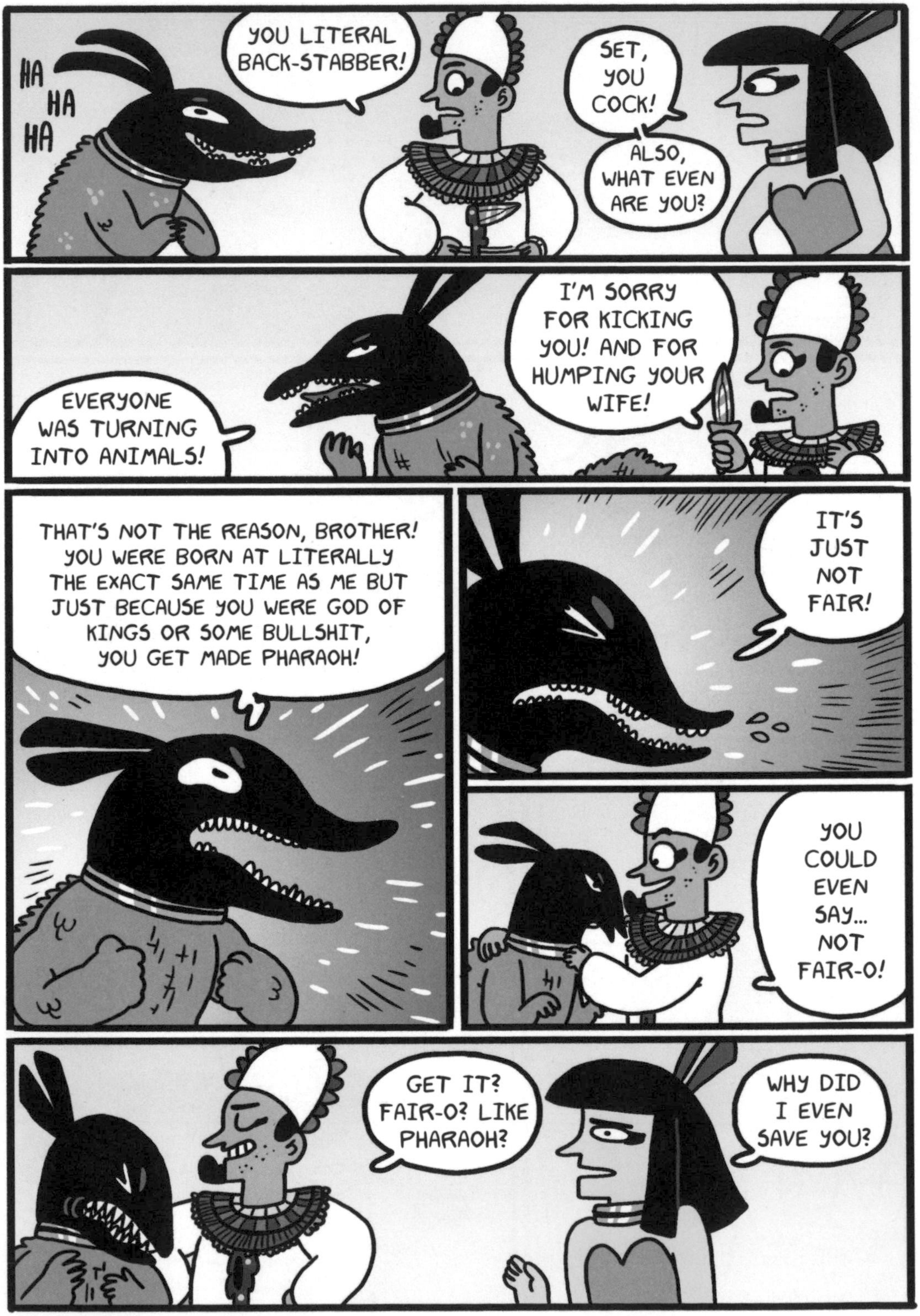
HA
HA
HA
YOU LITERAL BACK-STABBER!
SET, YOU COCK!
ALSO, WHAT EVEN ARE YOU?
I'M SORRY FOR KICKING YOU! AND FOR HUMPING YOUR WIFE!
EVERYONE WAS TURNING INTO ANIMALS!
THAT'S NOT THE REASON, BROTHER! YOU WERE BORN AT LITERALLY THE EXACT SAME TIME AS ME BUT JUST BECAUSE YOU WERE GOD OF KINGS OR SOME BULLSHIT, YOU GET MADE PHARAOH!
IT'S JUST NOT FAIR!
YOU COULD EVEN SAY... NOT FAIR-O!
GET IT? FAIR-O? LIKE PHARAOH?
WHY DID I EVEN SAVE YOU?

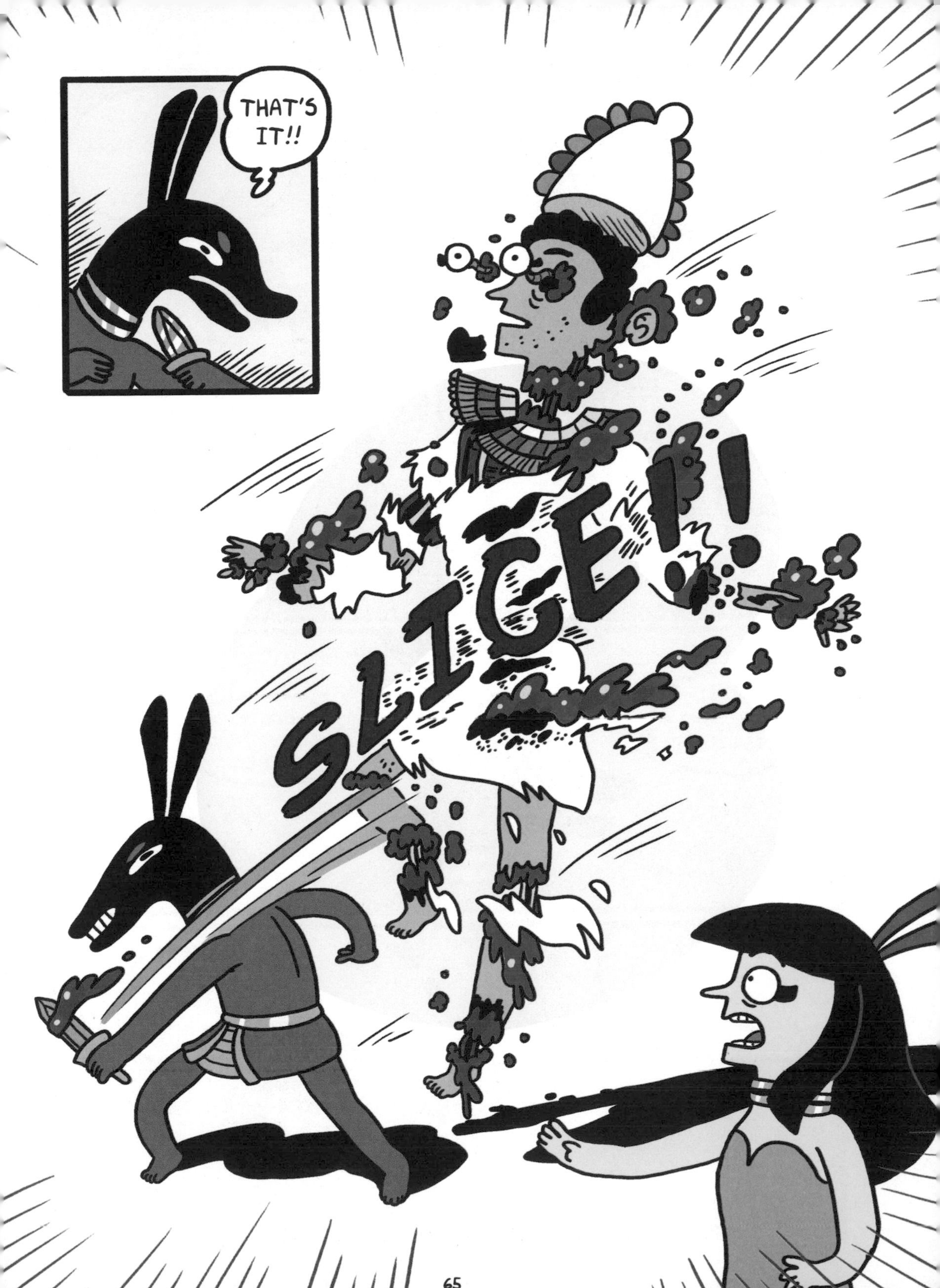
THAT'S IT!!
SLICE!!

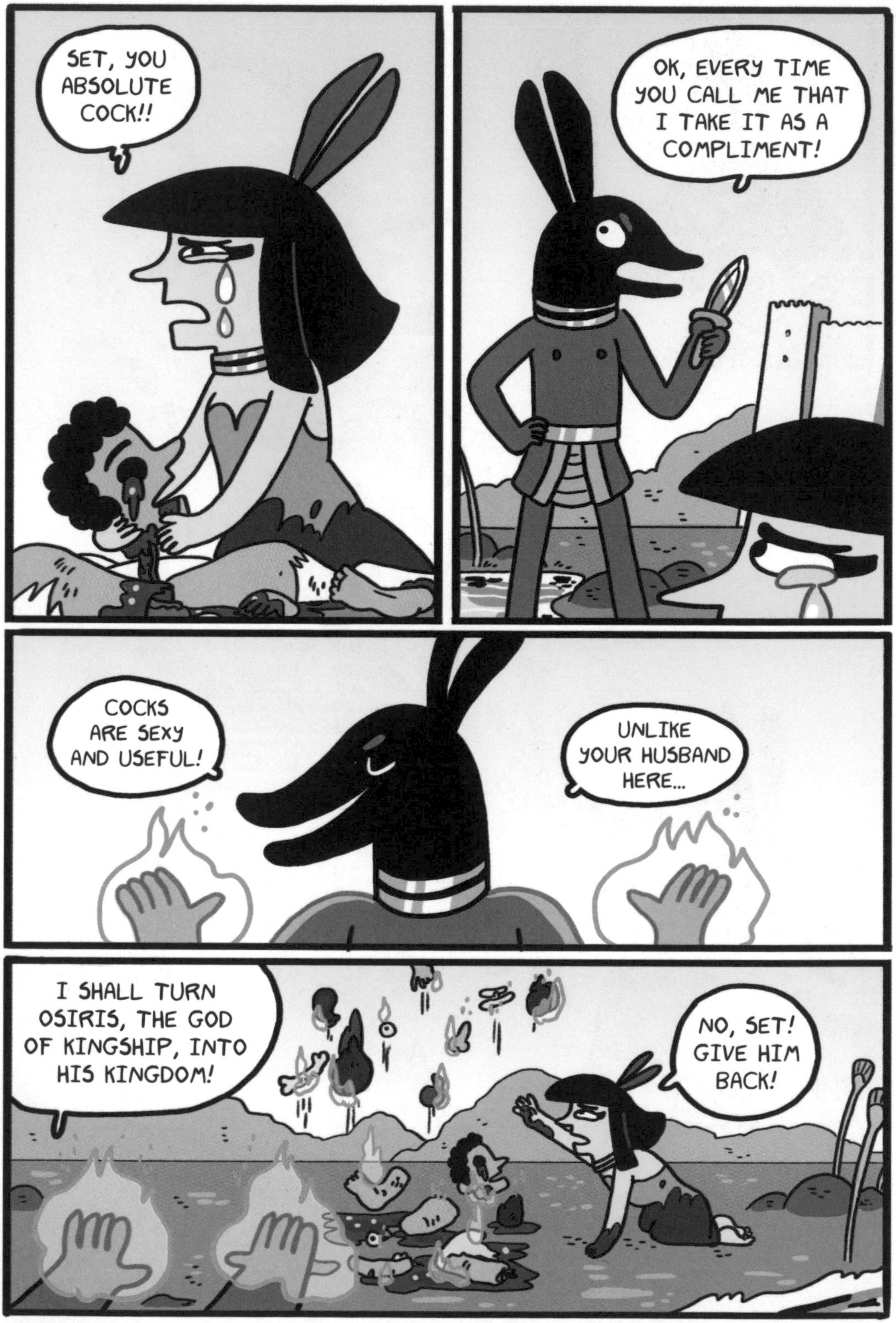
SET, YOU ABSOLUTE COCK!!
OK, EVERY TIME YOU CALL ME THAT I TAKE IT AS A COMPLIMENT!
COCKS ARE SEXY AND USEFUL!
UNLIKE YOUR HUSBAND HERE...
I SHALL TURN OSIRIS, THE GOD OF KINGSHIP, INTO HIS KINGDOM!
NO, SET! GIVE HIM BACK!

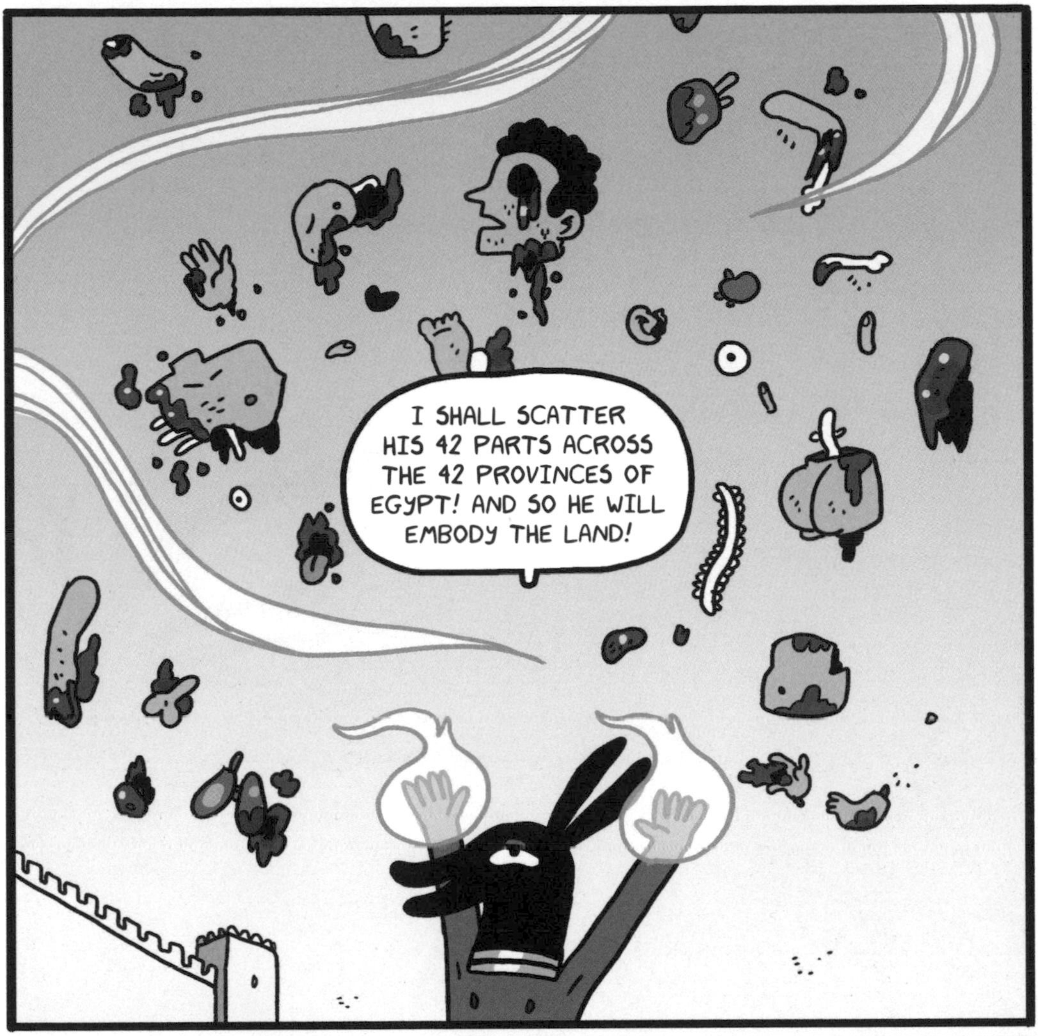
I SHALL SCATTER HIS 42 PARTS ACROSS THE 42 PROVINCES OF EGYPT! AND SO HE WILL EMBODY THE LAND!

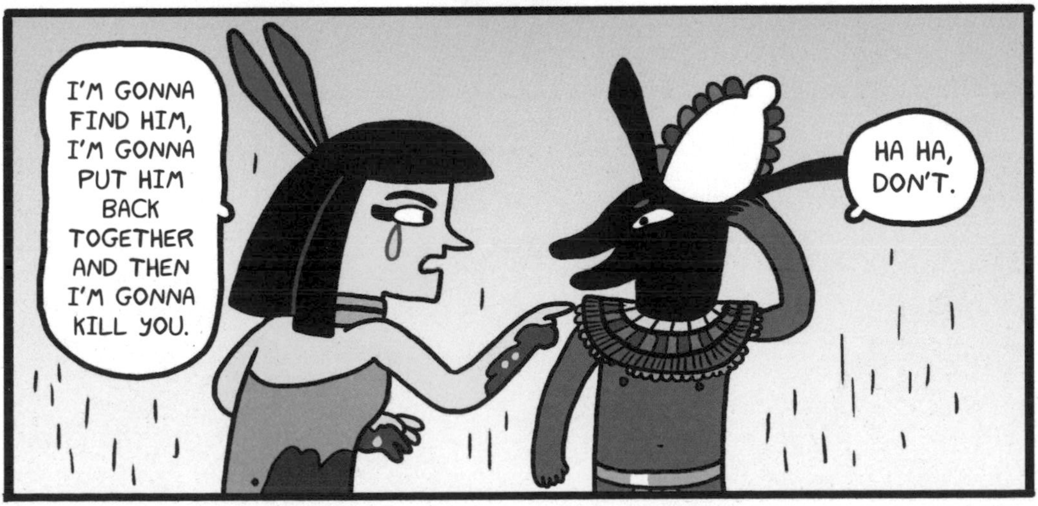
I'M GONNA FIND HIM, I'M GONNA PUT HIM BACK TOGETHER AND THEN I'M GONNA KILL YOU.
HA HA, DON'T.

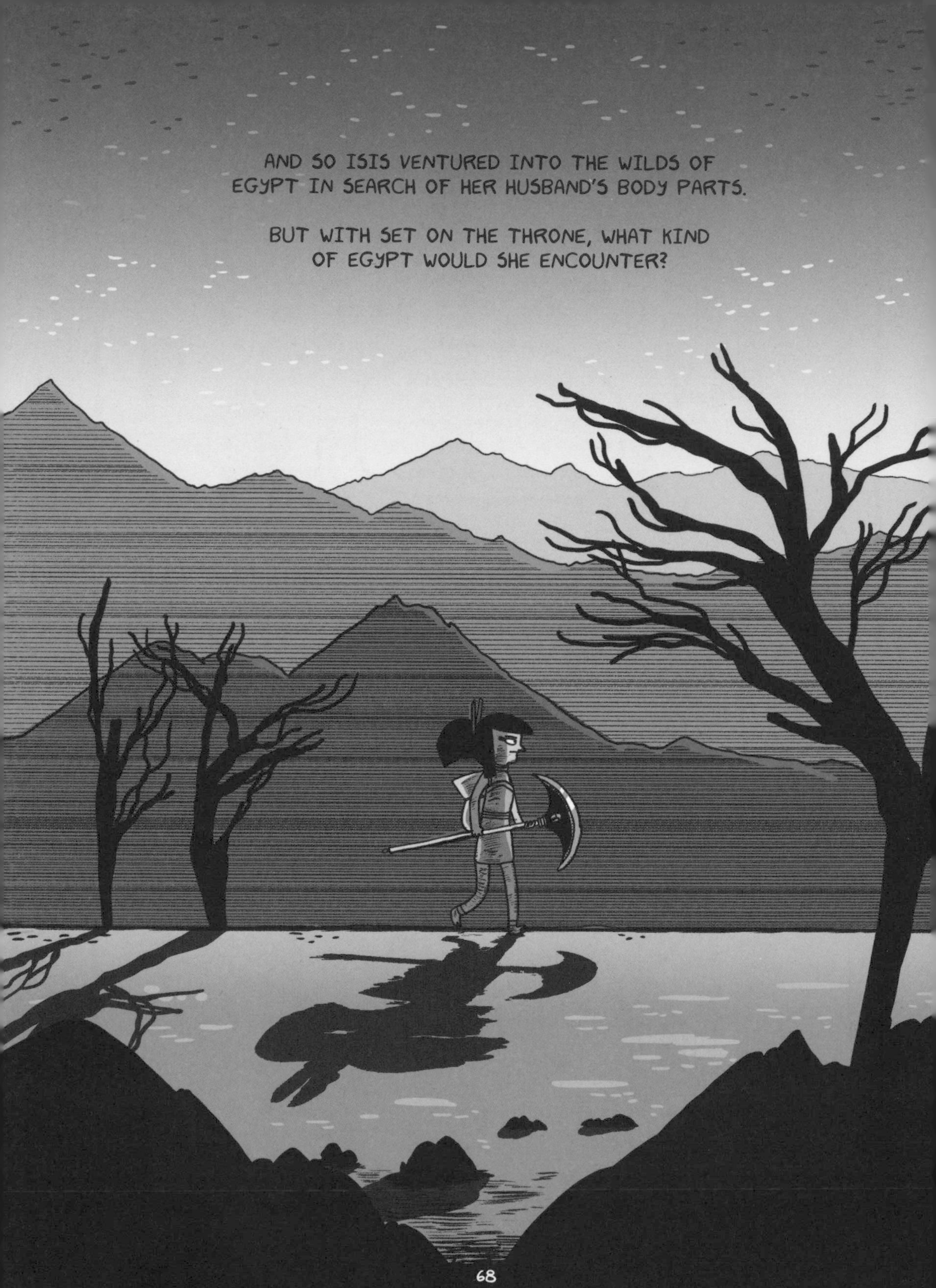
AND SO ISIS VENTURED INTO THE WILDS OF EGYPT IN SEARCH OF HER HUSBAND'S BODY PARTS.
BUT WITH SET ON THE THRONE, WHAT KIND OF EGYPT WOULD SHE ENCOUNTER?

CHAPTER FOUR

✷ ✷ ✷ JUDGEMENT ✷ ✷ ✷

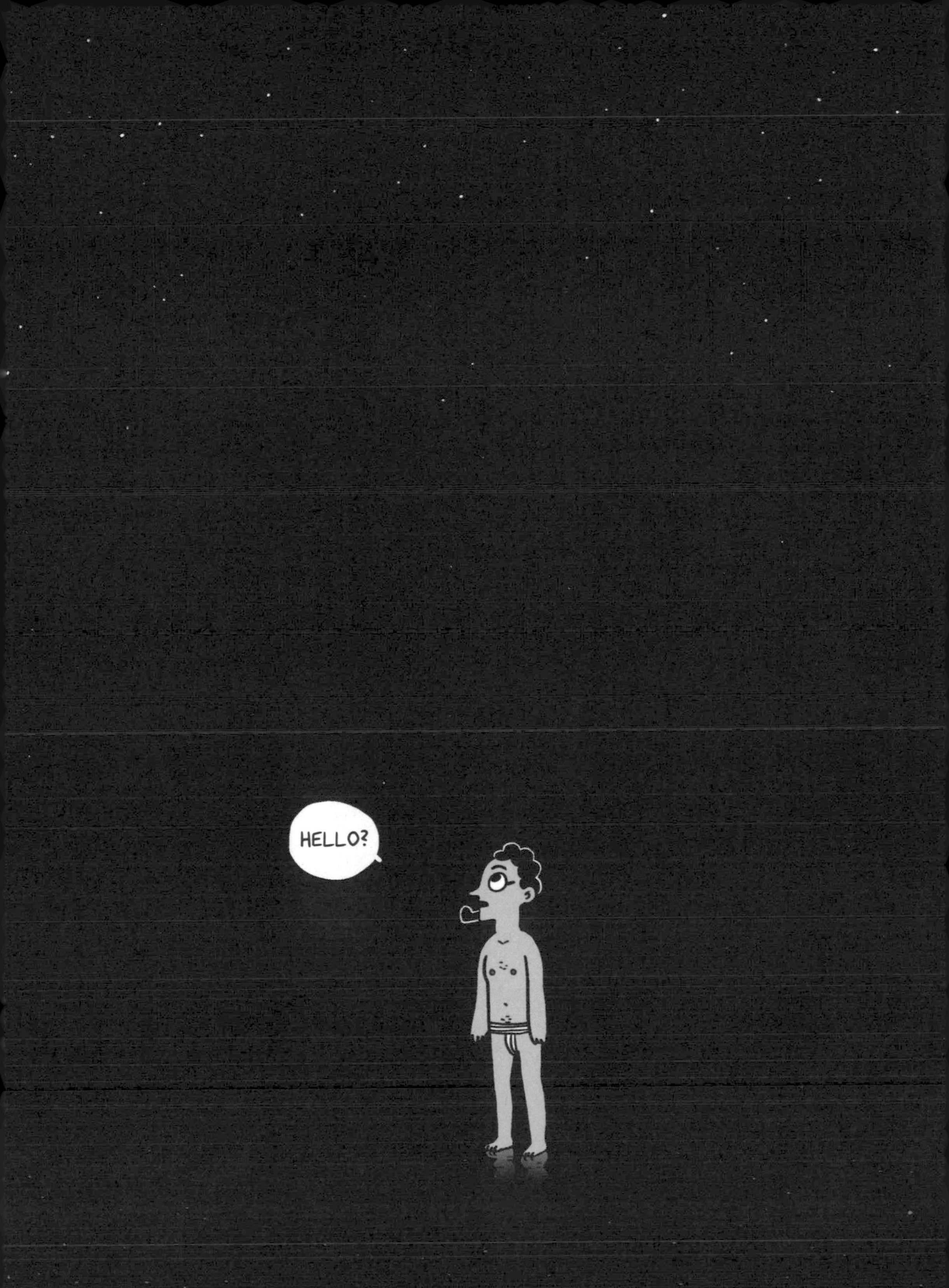
HELLO?

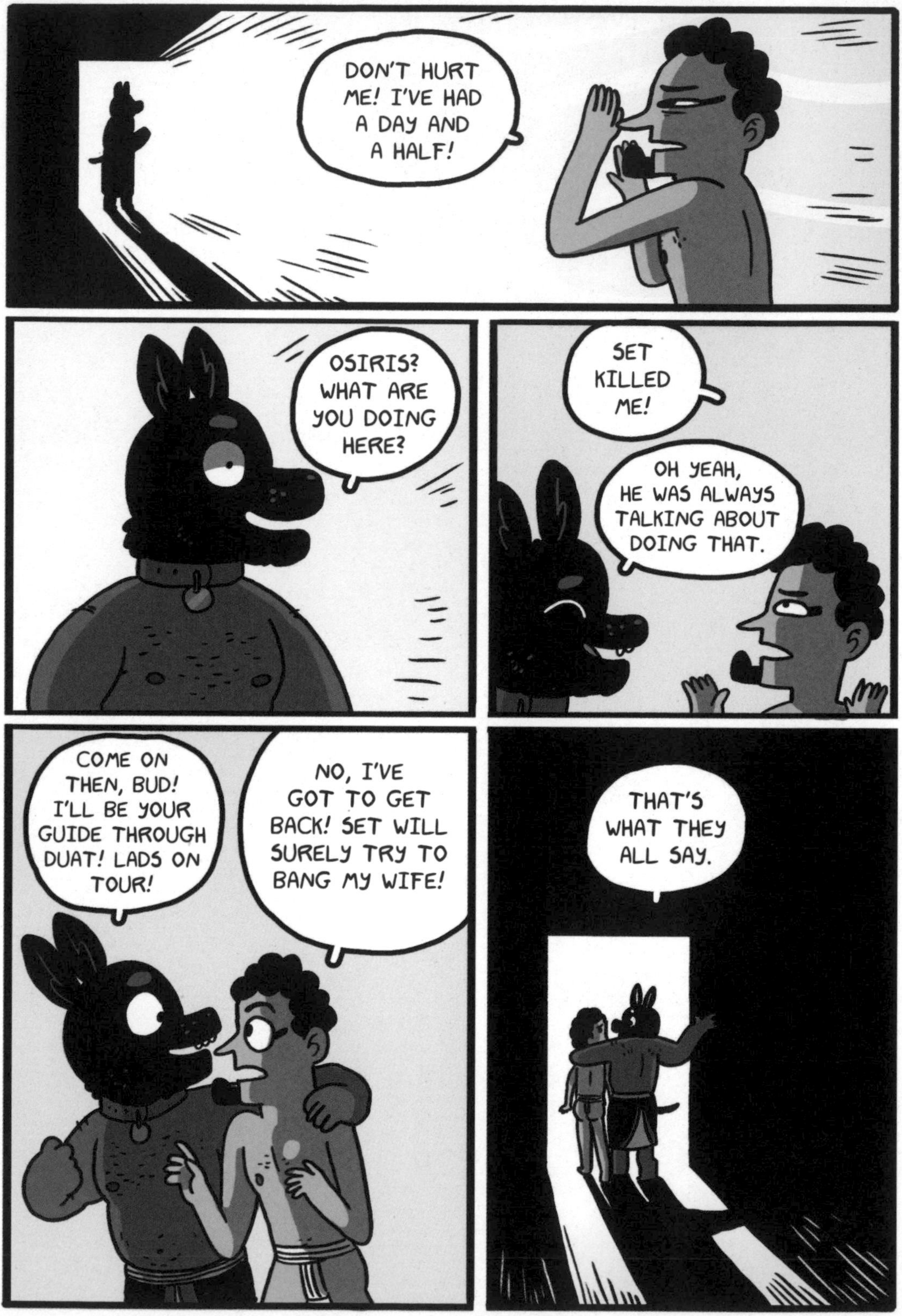
DON'T HURT ME! I'VE HAD A DAY AND A HALF!
OSIRIS? WHAT ARE YOU DOING HERE?
SET KILLED ME!
OH YEAH, HE WAS ALWAYS TALKING ABOUT DOING THAT.
COME ON THEN, BUD! I'LL BE YOUR GUIDE THROUGH DUAT! LADS ON TOUR!
NO, I'VE GOT TO GET BACK! SET WILL SURELY TRY TO BANG MY WIFE!
THAT'S WHAT THEY ALL SAY.

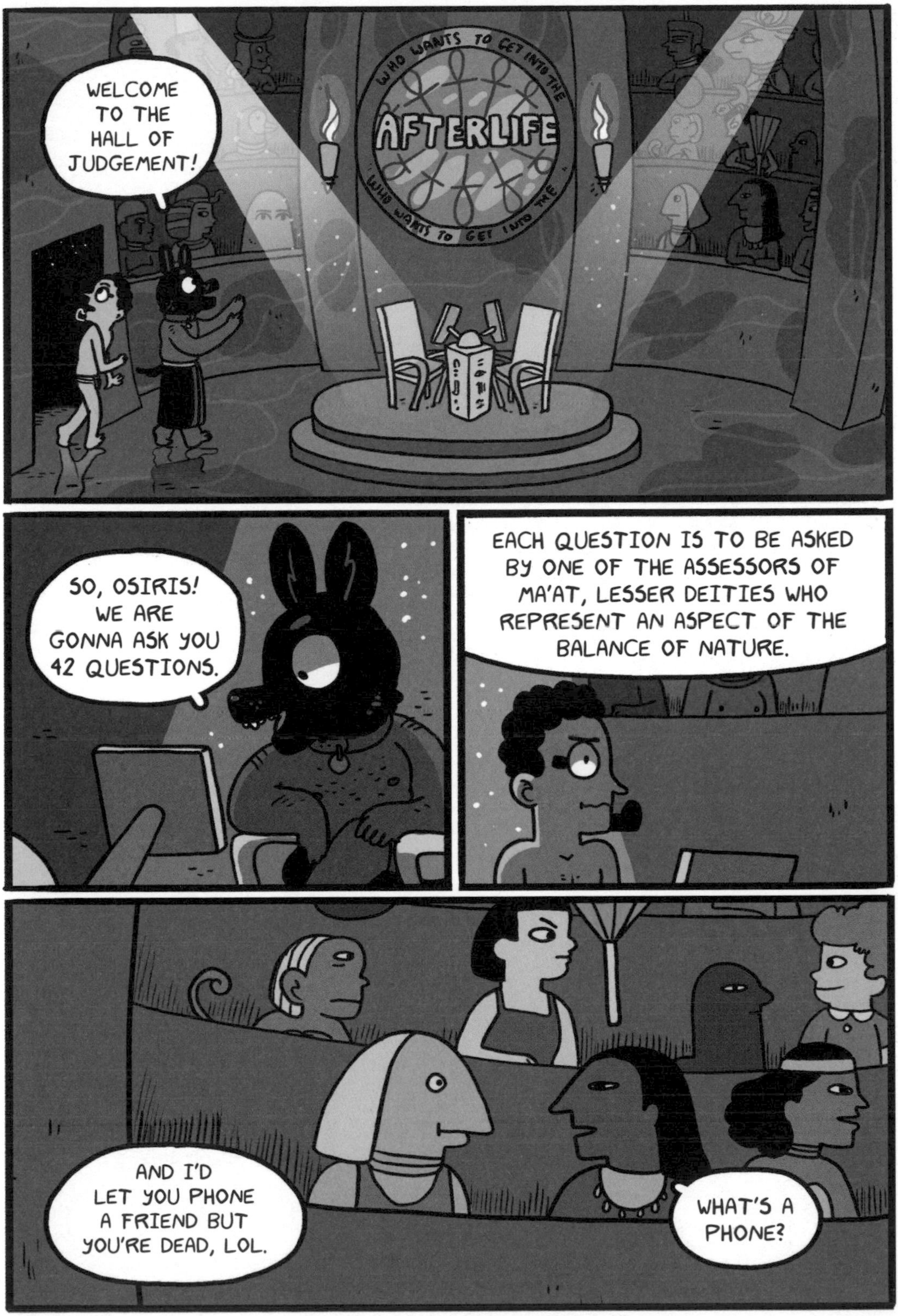
WHO WANTS TO GET INTO THE
AFTERLIFE
WHO WANTS TO GET INTO THE
WELCOME TO THE HALL OF JUDGEMENT!
SO, OSIRIS! WE ARE GONNA ASK YOU 42 QUESTIONS.
EACH QUESTION IS TO BE ASKED BY ONE OF THE ASSESSORS OF MA'AT, LESSER DEITIES WHO REPRESENT AN ASPECT OF THE BALANCE OF NATURE.
AND I'D LET YOU PHONE A FRIEND BUT YOU'RE DEAD, LOL.
WHAT'S A PHONE?

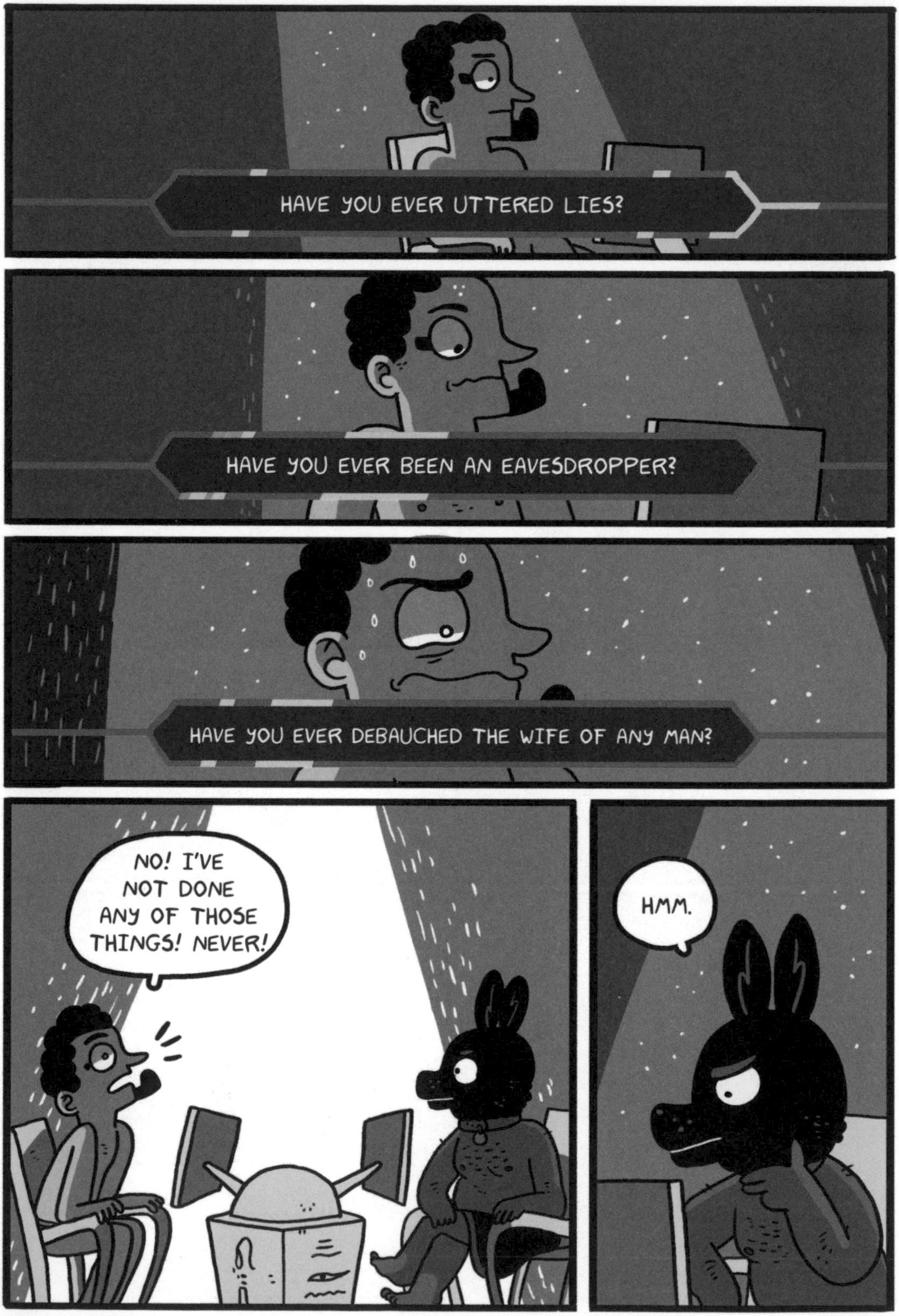
HAVE YOU EVER UTTERED LIES?
HAVE YOU EVER BEEN AN EAVESDROPPER?
HAVE YOU EVER DEBAUCHED THE WIFE OF ANY MAN?
NO! I'VE NOT DONE ANY OF THOSE THINGS! NEVER!
HMM.

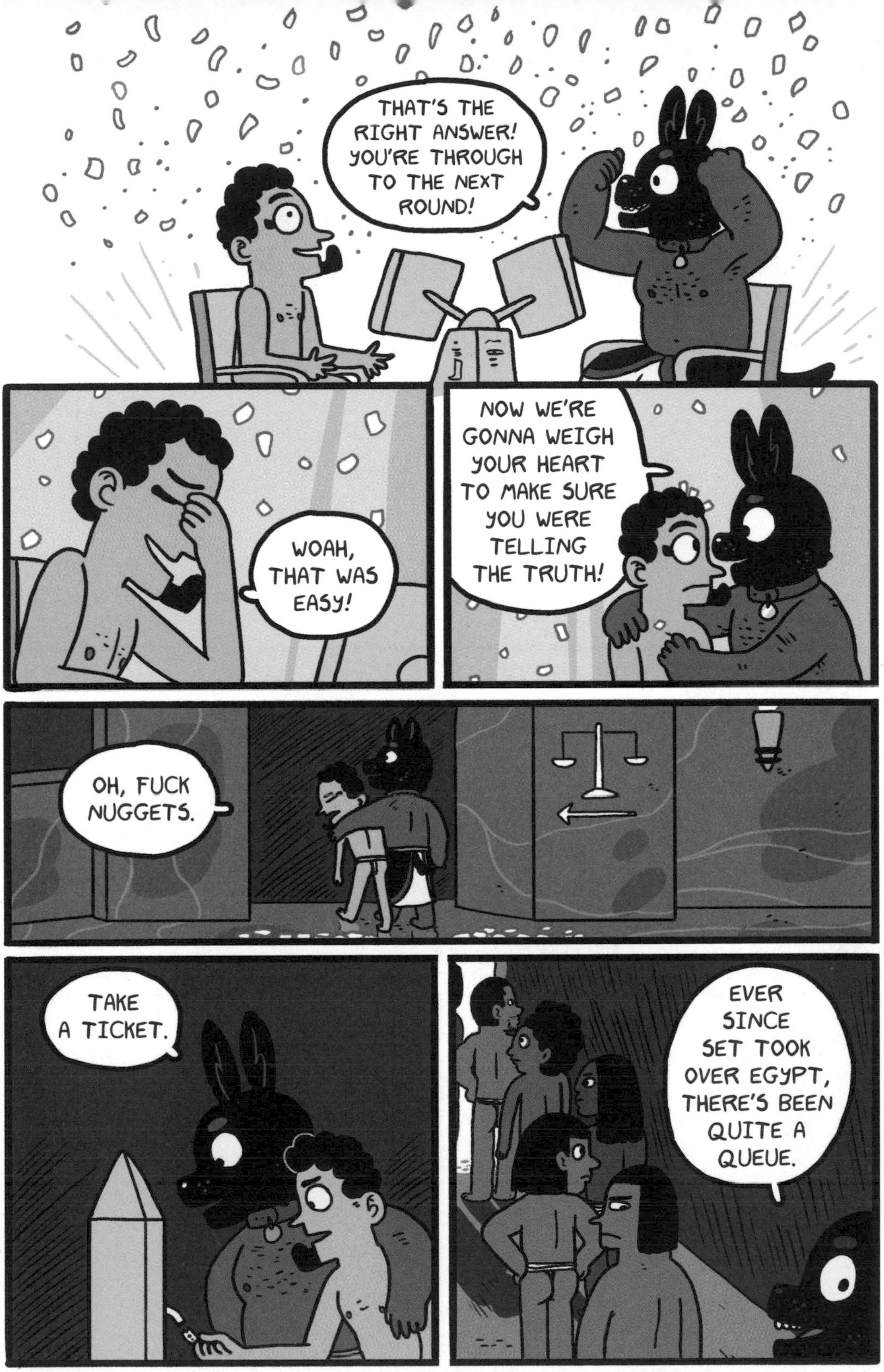
THAT'S THE RIGHT ANSWER! YOU'RE THROUGH TO THE NEXT ROUND!
WOAH, THAT WAS EASY!
NOW WE'RE GONNA WEIGH YOUR HEART TO MAKE SURE YOU WERE TELLING THE TRUTH!
OH, FUCK NUGGETS.
TAKE A TICKET.
EVER SINCE SET TOOK OVER EGYPT, THERE'S BEEN QUITE A QUEUE.

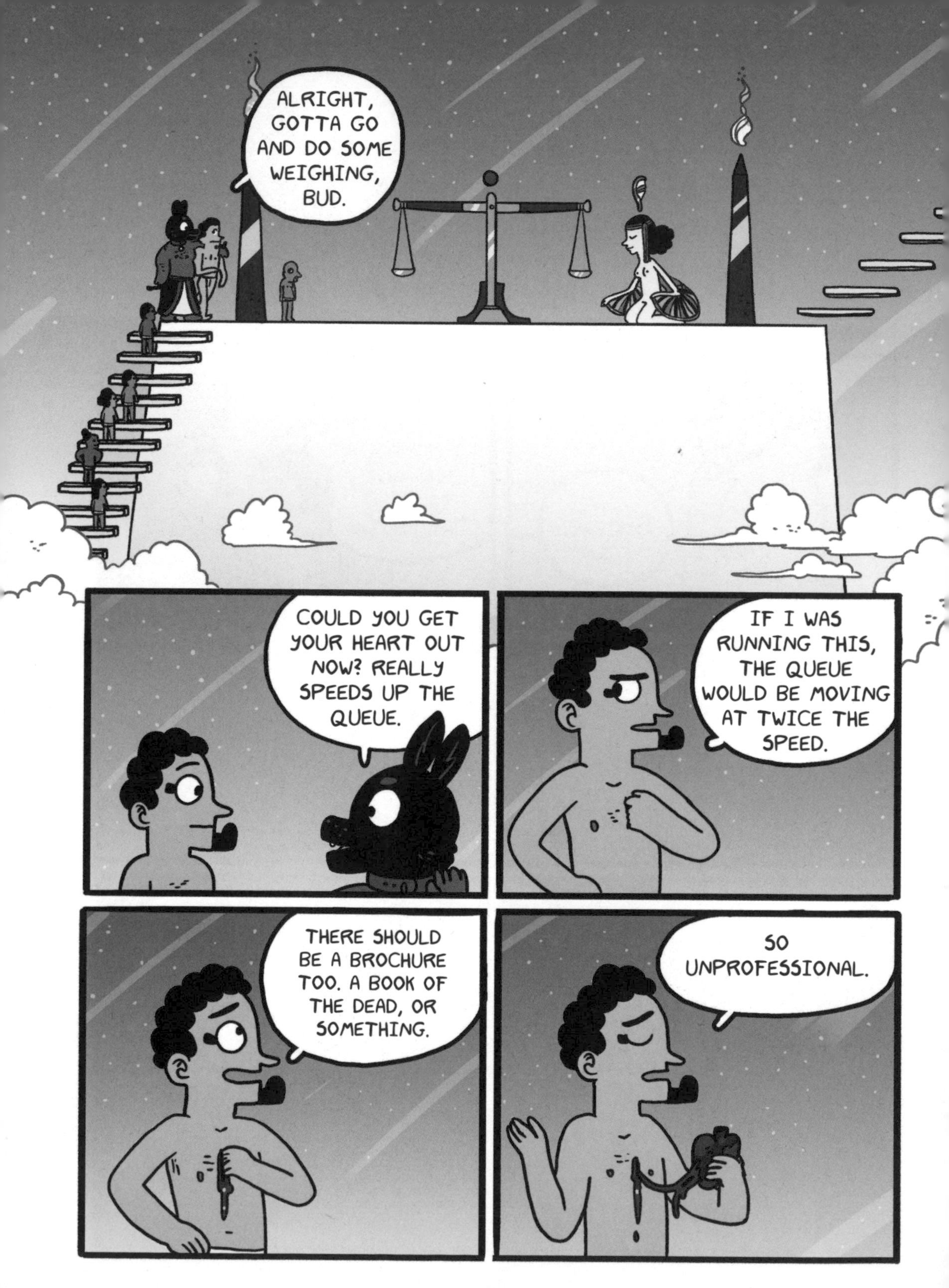
ALRIGHT, GOTTA GO AND DO SOME WEIGHING, BUD.
COULD YOU GET YOUR HEART OUT NOW? REALLY SPEEDS UP THE QUEUE.
IF I WAS RUNNING THIS, THE QUEUE WOULD BE MOVING AT TWICE THE SPEED.
THERE SHOULD BE A BROCHURE TOO. A BOOK OF THE DEAD, OR SOMETHING.
SO UNPROFESSIONAL.

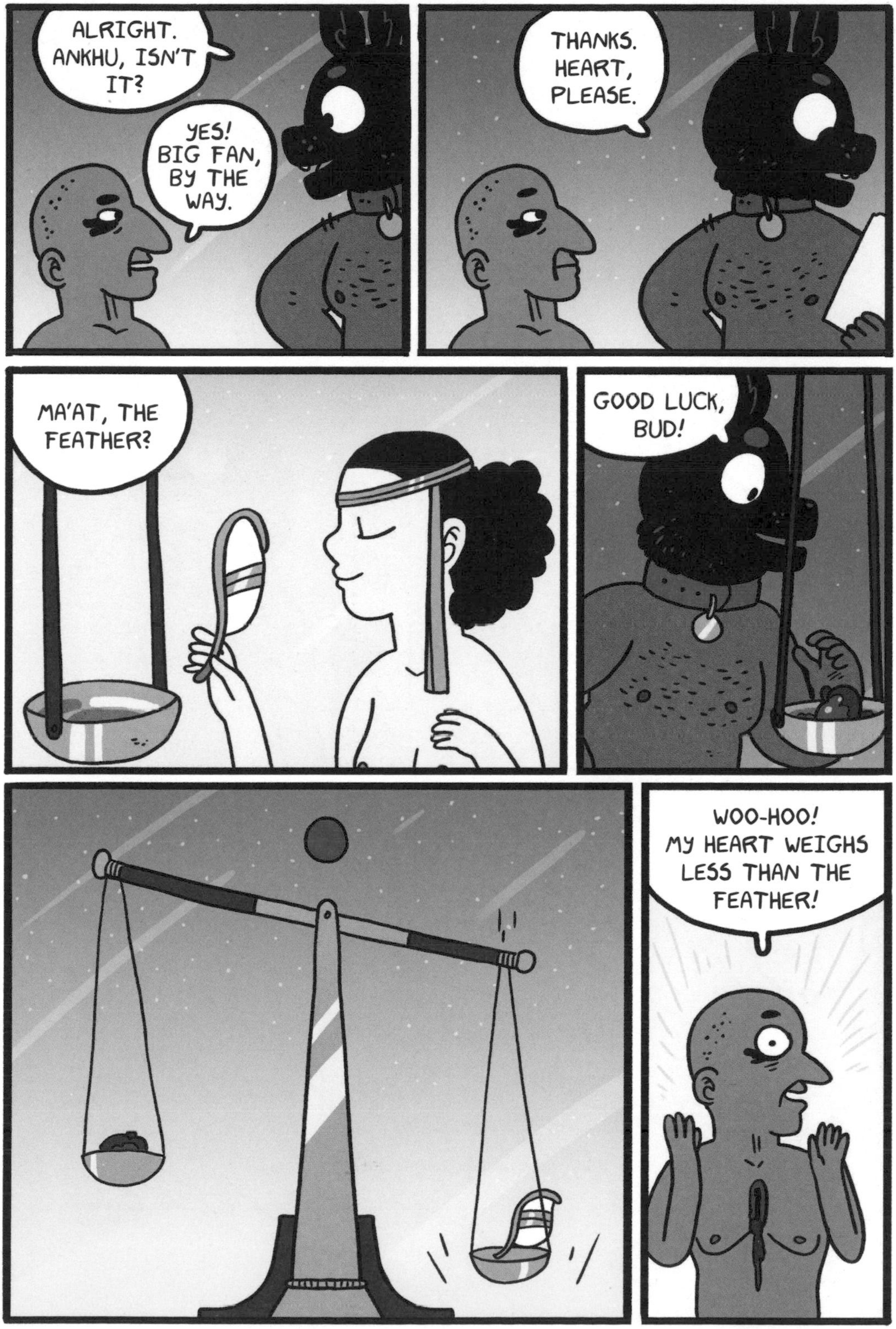
ALRIGHT. ANKHU, ISN'T IT?
YES! BIG FAN, BY THE WAY.
THANKS. HEART, PLEASE.
MA'AT, THE FEATHER?
GOOD LUCK, BUD!
WOO-HOO! MY HEART WEIGHS LESS THAN THE FEATHER!

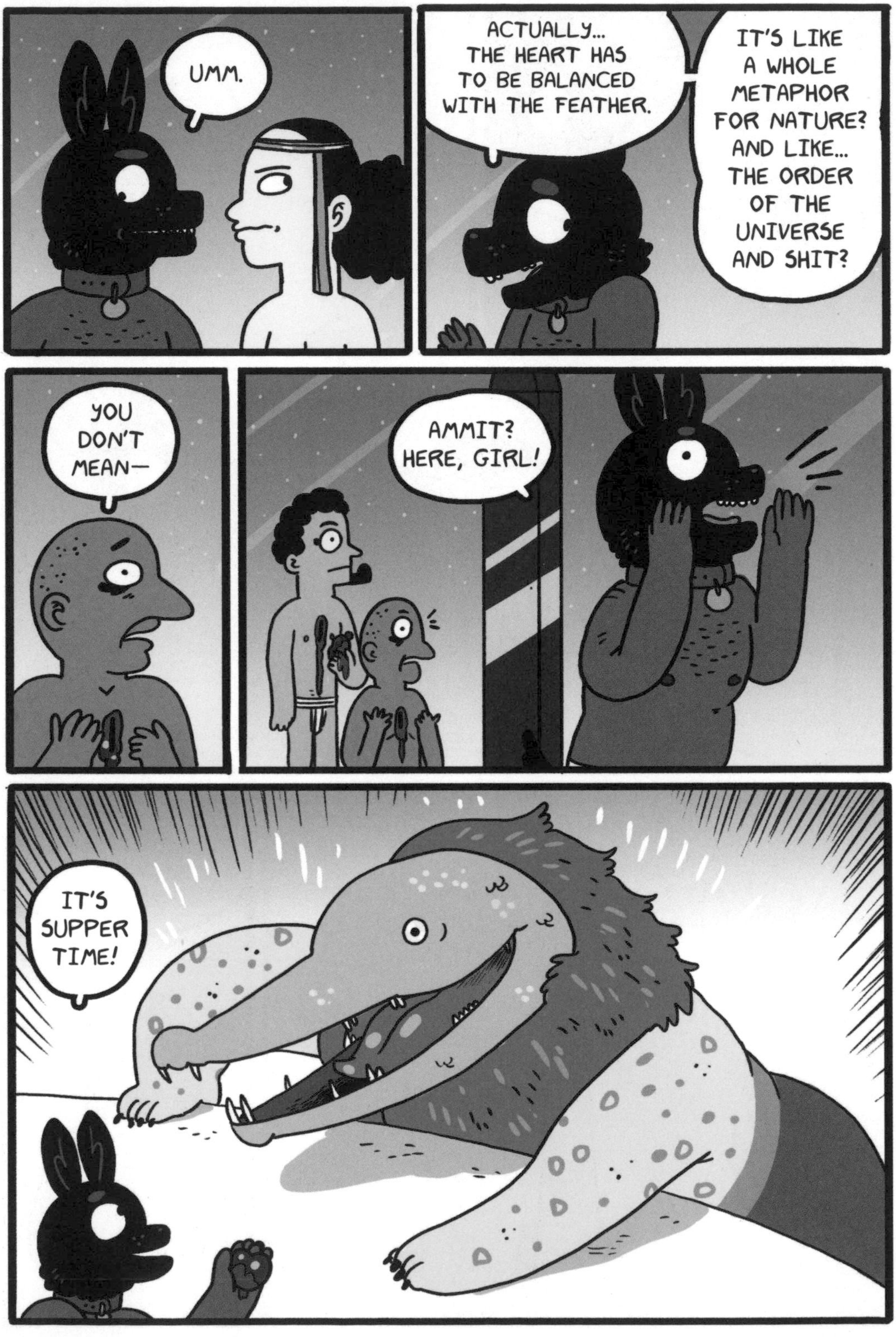
UMM.
ACTUALLY... THE HEART HAS TO BE BALANCED WITH THE FEATHER.
IT'S LIKE A WHOLE METAPHOR FOR NATURE? AND LIKE... THE ORDER OF THE UNIVERSE AND SHIT?
YOU DON'T MEAN—
AMMIT? HERE, GIRL!
IT'S SUPPER TIME!

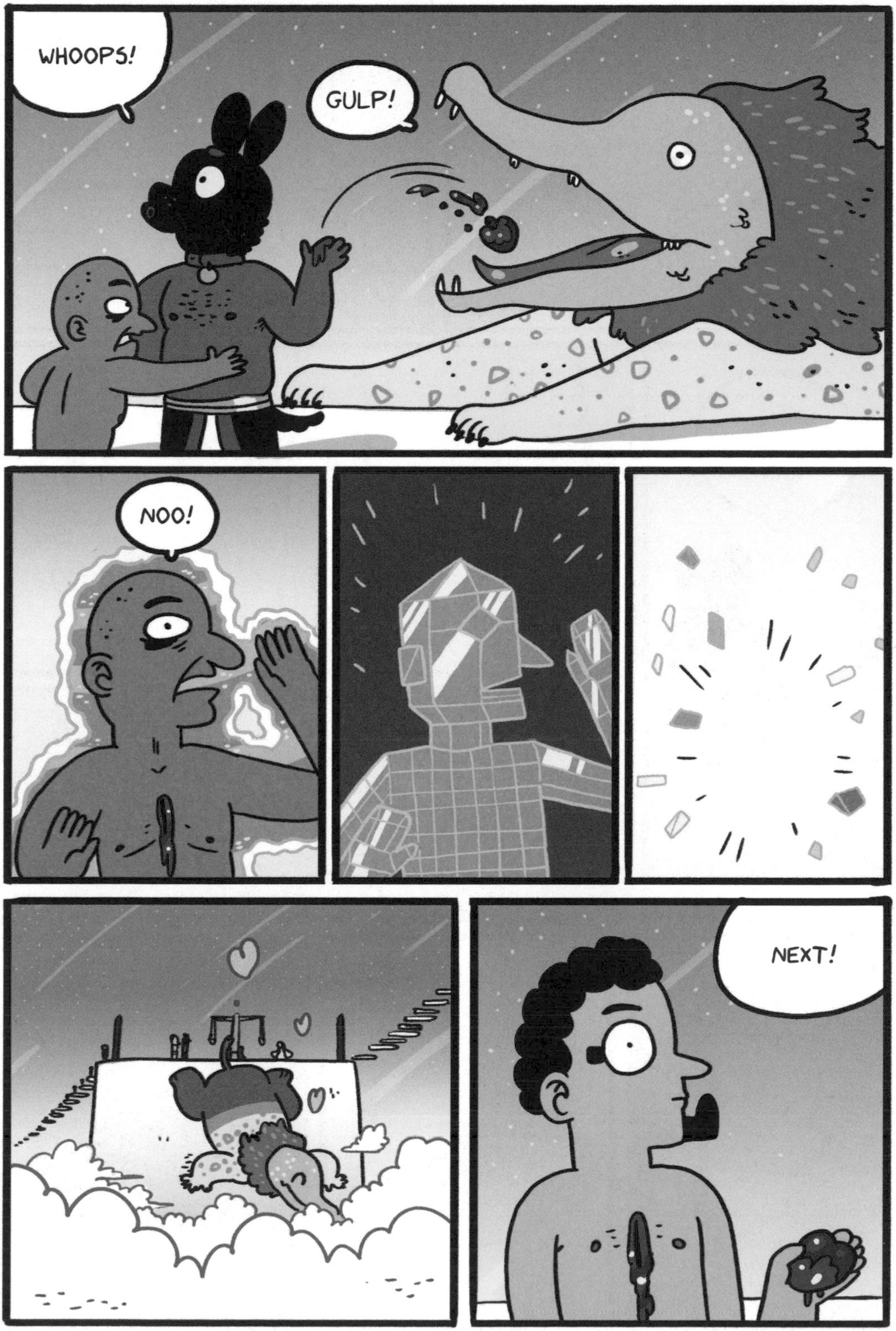
WHOOPS!
GULP!
NOO!
NEXT!

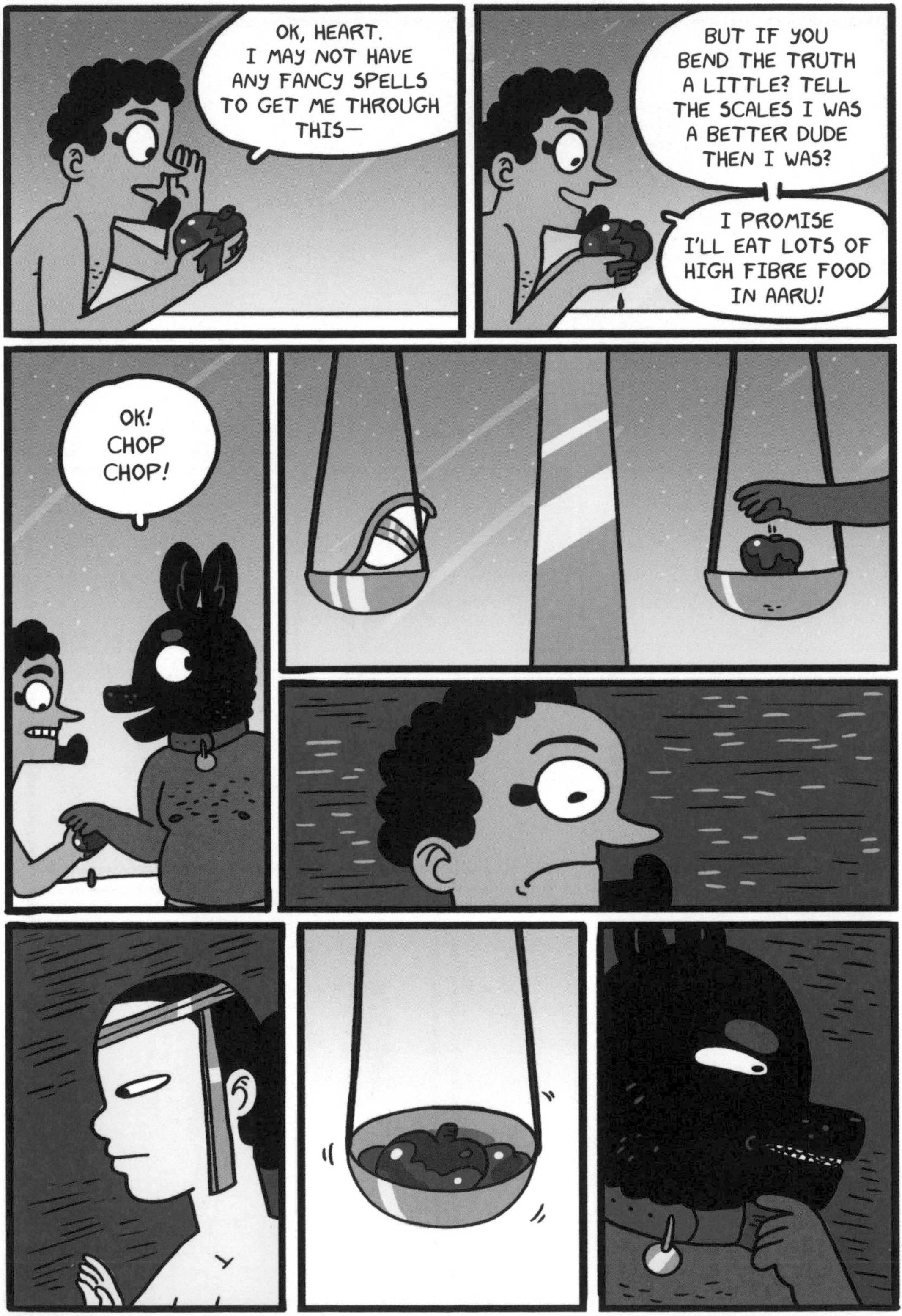
OK, HEART. I MAY NOT HAVE ANY FANCY SPELLS TO GET ME THROUGH THIS—
BUT IF YOU BEND THE TRUTH A LITTLE? TELL THE SCALES I WAS A BETTER DUDE THEN I WAS?
I PROMISE I'LL EAT LOTS OF HIGH FIBRE FOOD IN AARU!
OK! CHOP CHOP!

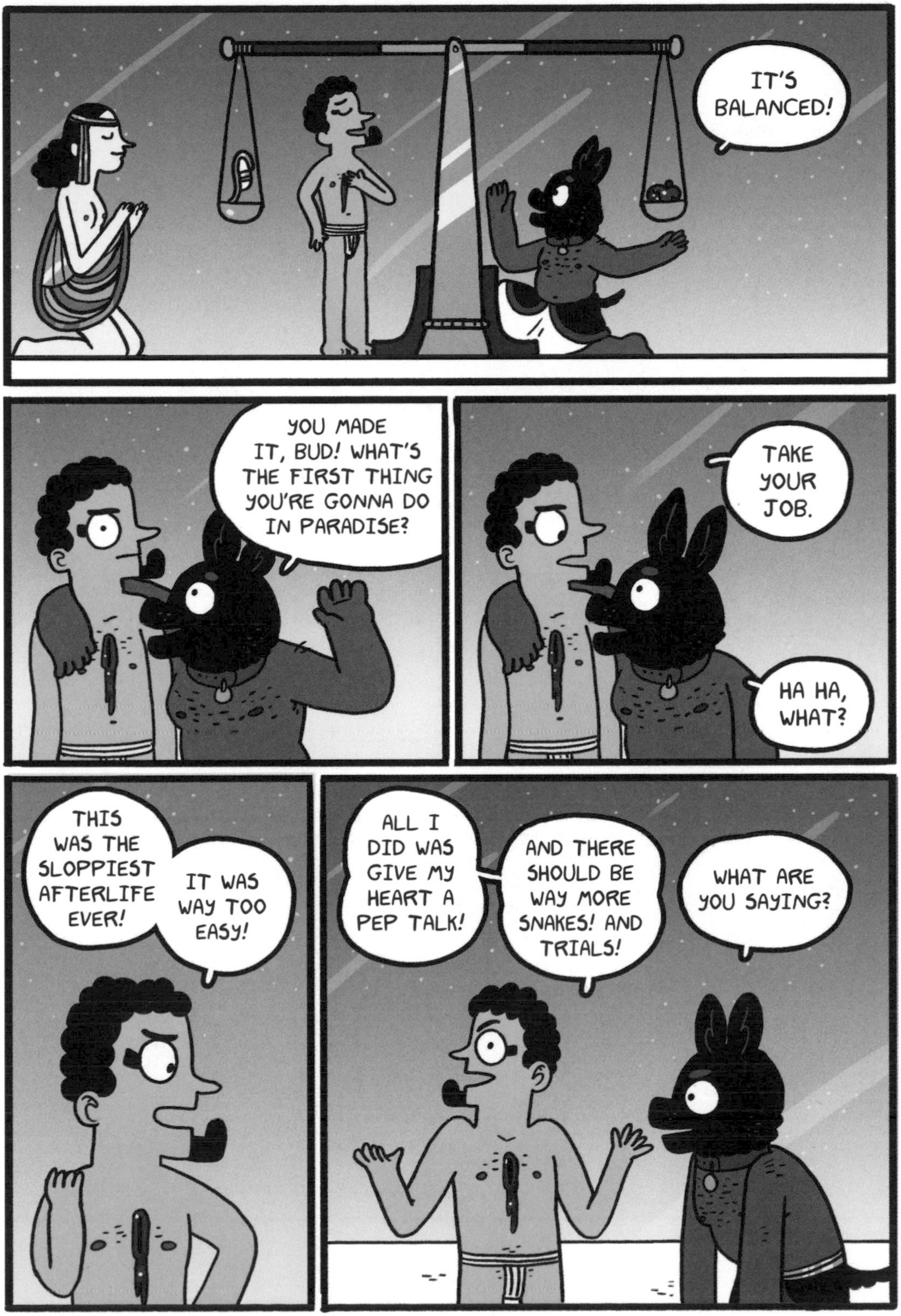
IT'S BALANCED!
YOU MADE IT, BUD! WHAT'S THE FIRST THING YOU'RE GONNA DO IN PARADISE?
TAKE YOUR JOB.
HA HA, WHAT?
THIS WAS THE SLOPPIEST AFTERLIFE EVER!
IT WAS WAY TOO EASY!
ALL I DID WAS GIVE MY HEART A PEP TALK!
AND THERE SHOULD BE WAY MORE SNAKES! AND TRIALS!
WHAT ARE YOU SAYING?

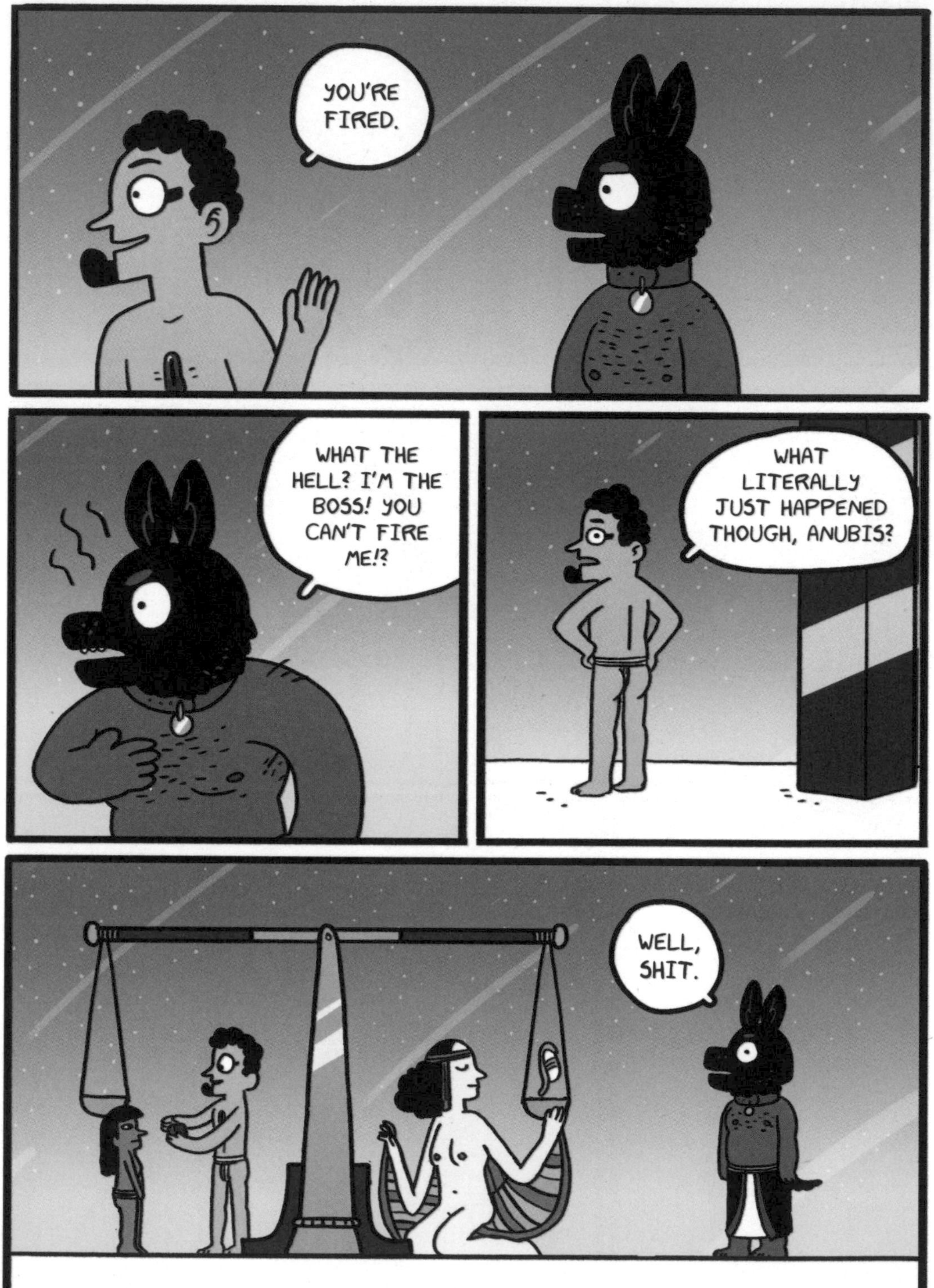
YOU'RE FIRED.
WHAT THE HELL? I'M THE BOSS! YOU CAN'T FIRE ME!?
WHAT LITERALLY JUST HAPPENED THOUGH, ANUBIS?
WELL, SHIT.

CHAPTER FIVE

★ ★ ★ COLLECTION ★ ★ ★

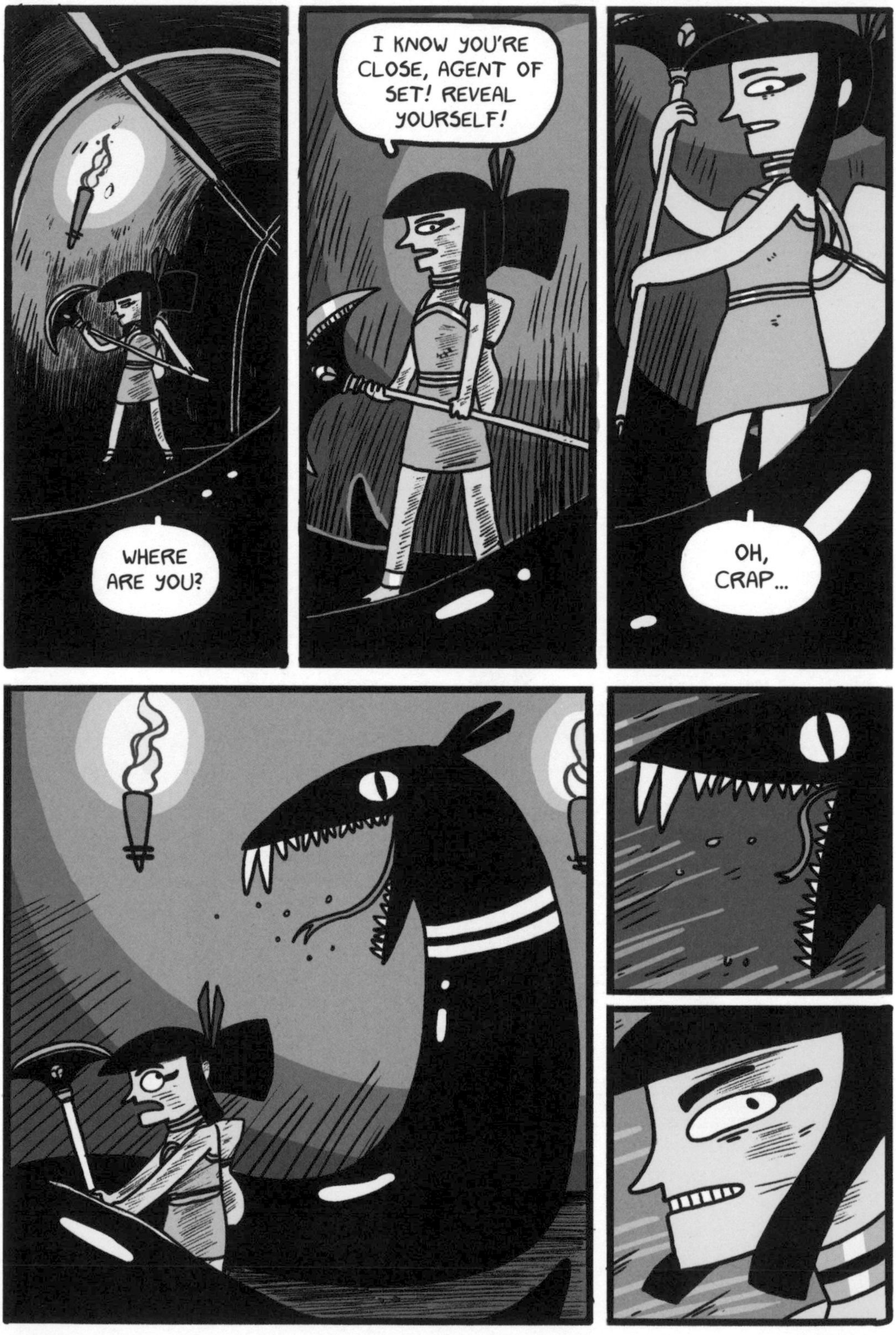
WHERE ARE YOU?
I KNOW YOU'RE CLOSE, AGENT OF SET! REVEAL YOURSELF!
OH, CRAP...

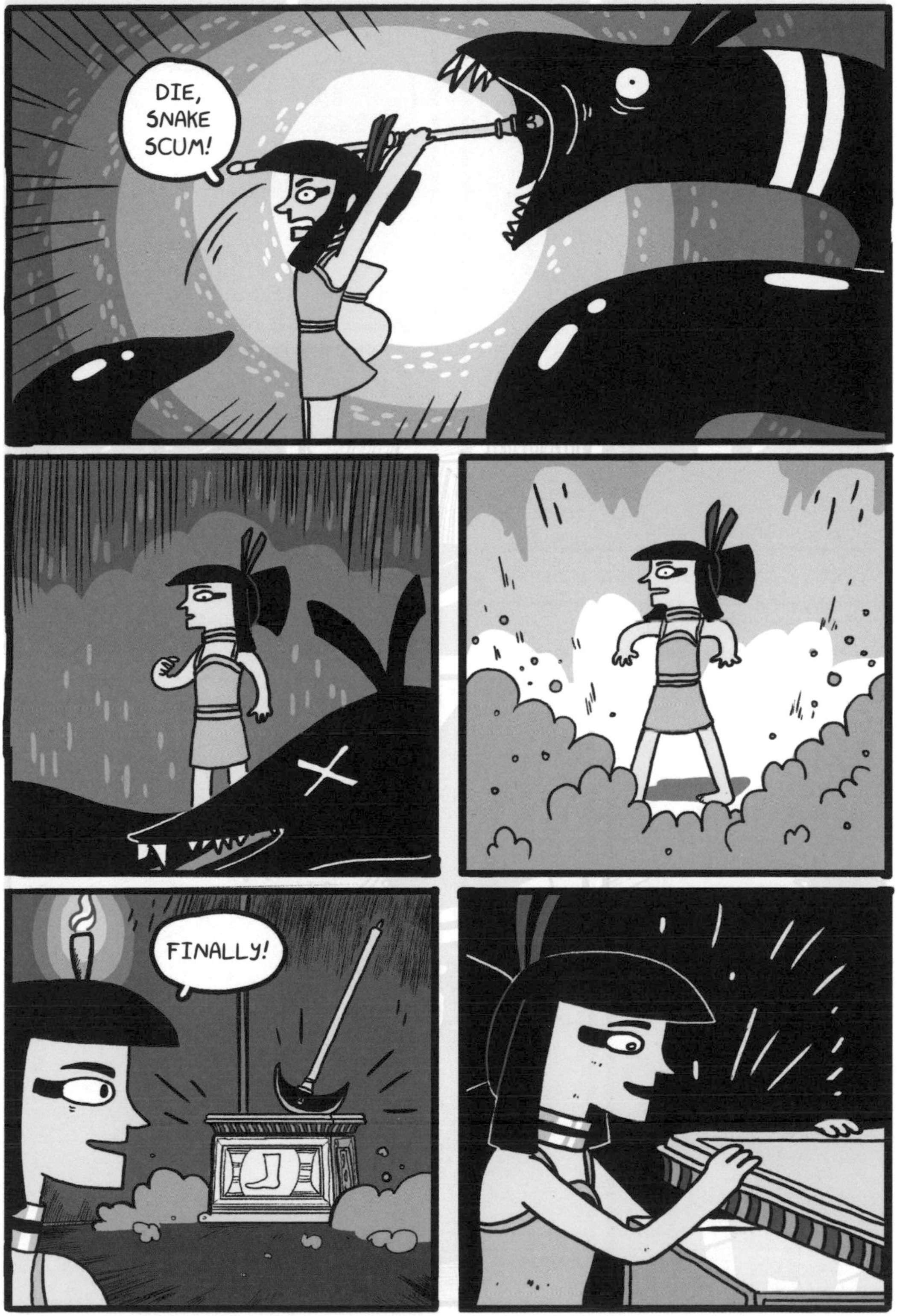
DIE, SNAKE SCUM!
FINALLY!

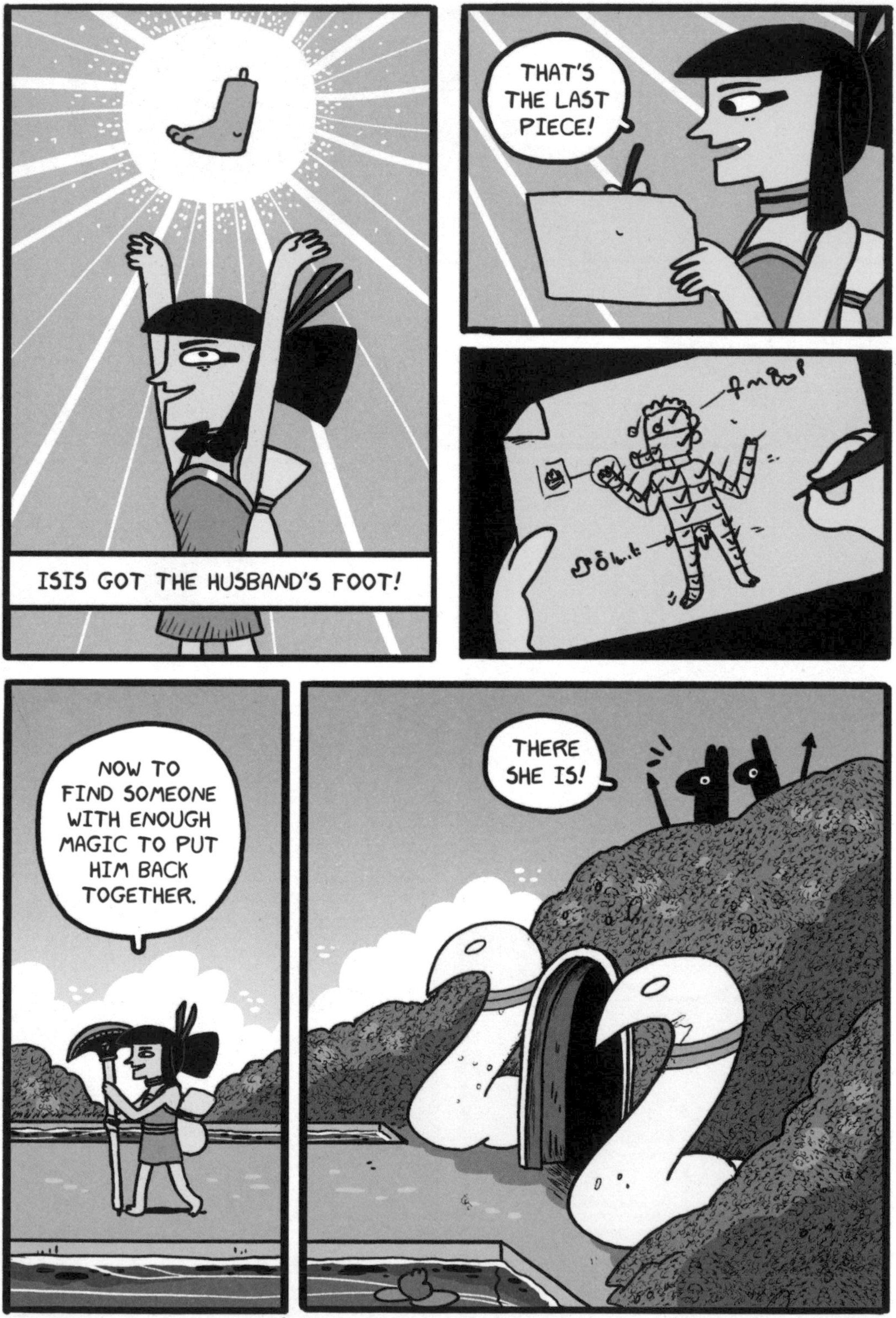
ISIS GOT THE HUSBAND'S FOOT!
THAT'S THE LAST PIECE!
NOW TO FIND SOMEONE WITH ENOUGH MAGIC TO PUT HIM BACK TOGETHER.
THERE SHE IS!

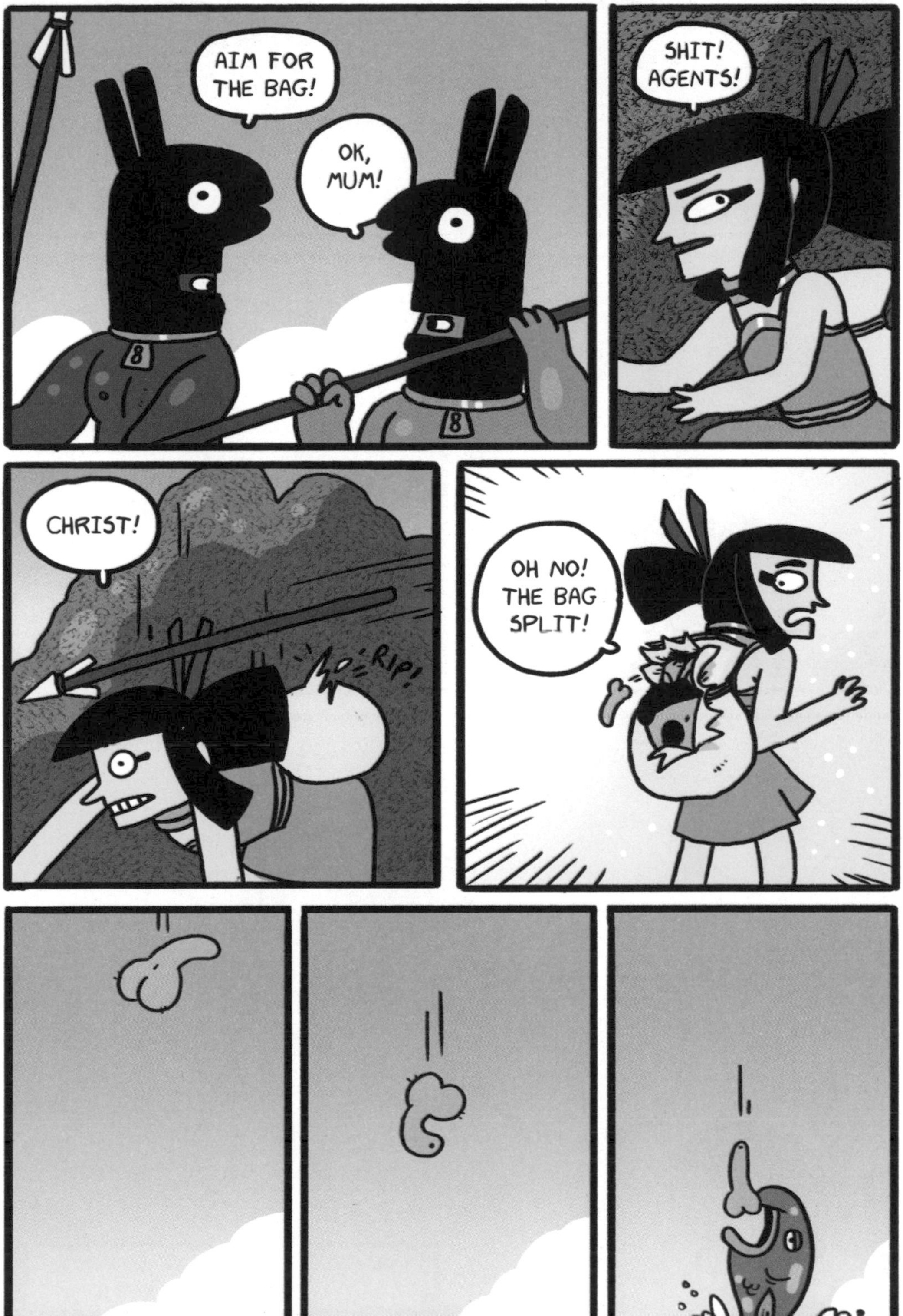
AIM FOR THE BAG!
OK, MUM!
SHIT! AGENTS!
CHRIST!
RIP!
OH NO! THE BAG SPLIT!

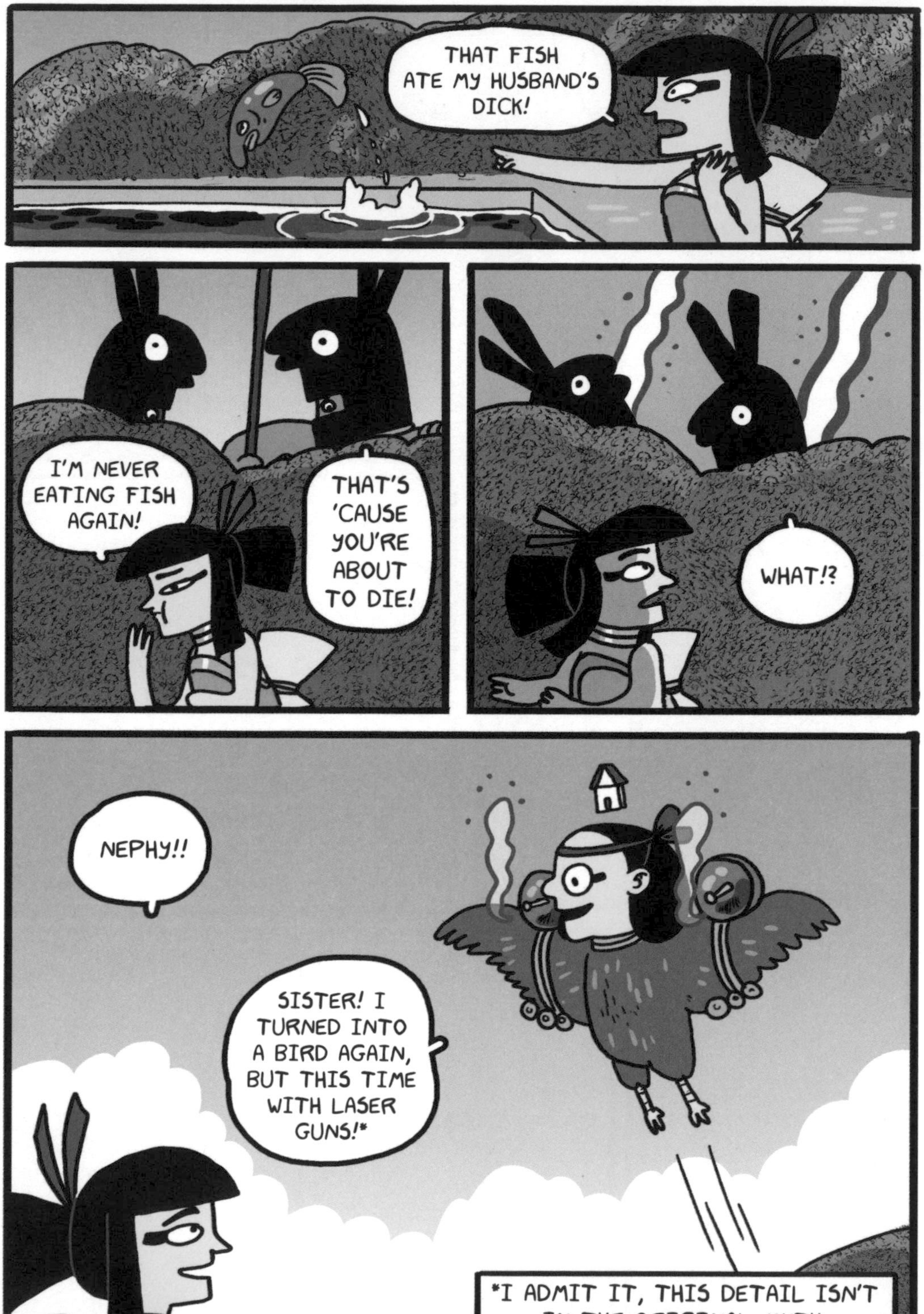
THAT FISH ATE MY HUSBAND'S DICK!
I'M NEVER EATING FISH AGAIN!
THAT'S 'CAUSE YOU'RE ABOUT TO DIE!
WHAT!?
NEPHY!!
SISTER! I TURNED INTO A BIRD AGAIN, BUT THIS TIME WITH LASER GUNS!*
*I ADMIT IT, THIS DETAIL ISN'T IN THE ORIGINAL MYTH.

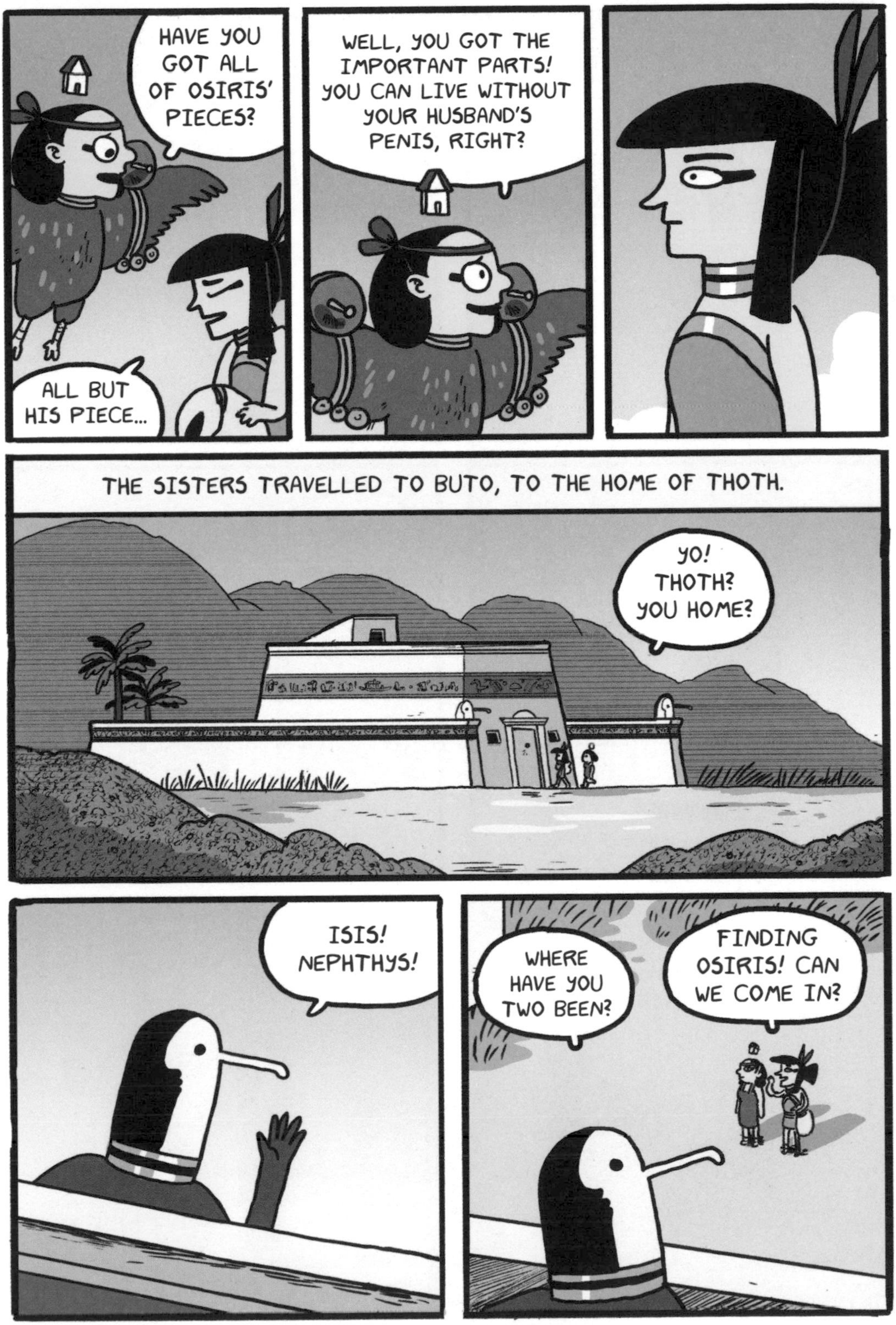

HAVE YOU GOT ALL OF OSIRIS' PIECES?
ALL BUT HIS PIECE...
WELL, YOU GOT THE IMPORTANT PARTS! YOU CAN LIVE WITHOUT YOUR HUSBAND'S PENIS, RIGHT?
THE SISTERS TRAVELLED TO BUTO, TO THE HOME OF THOTH.
YO! THOTH? YOU HOME?
ISIS! NEPHTHYS!
WHERE HAVE YOU TWO BEEN?
FINDING OSIRIS! CAN WE COME IN?

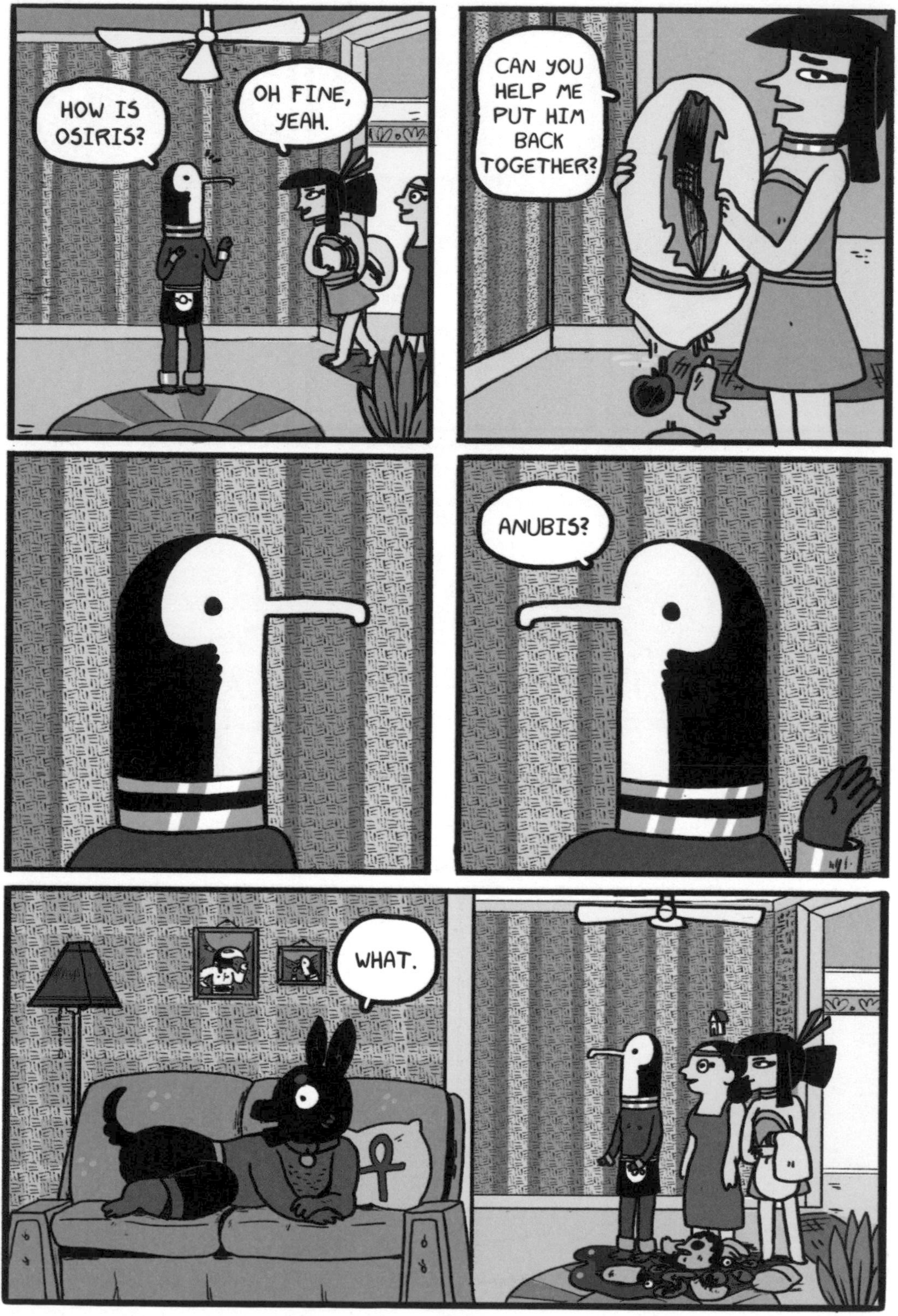
HOW IS OSIRIS?
OH FINE, YEAH.
CAN YOU HELP ME PUT HIM BACK TOGETHER?
ANUBIS?
WHAT.

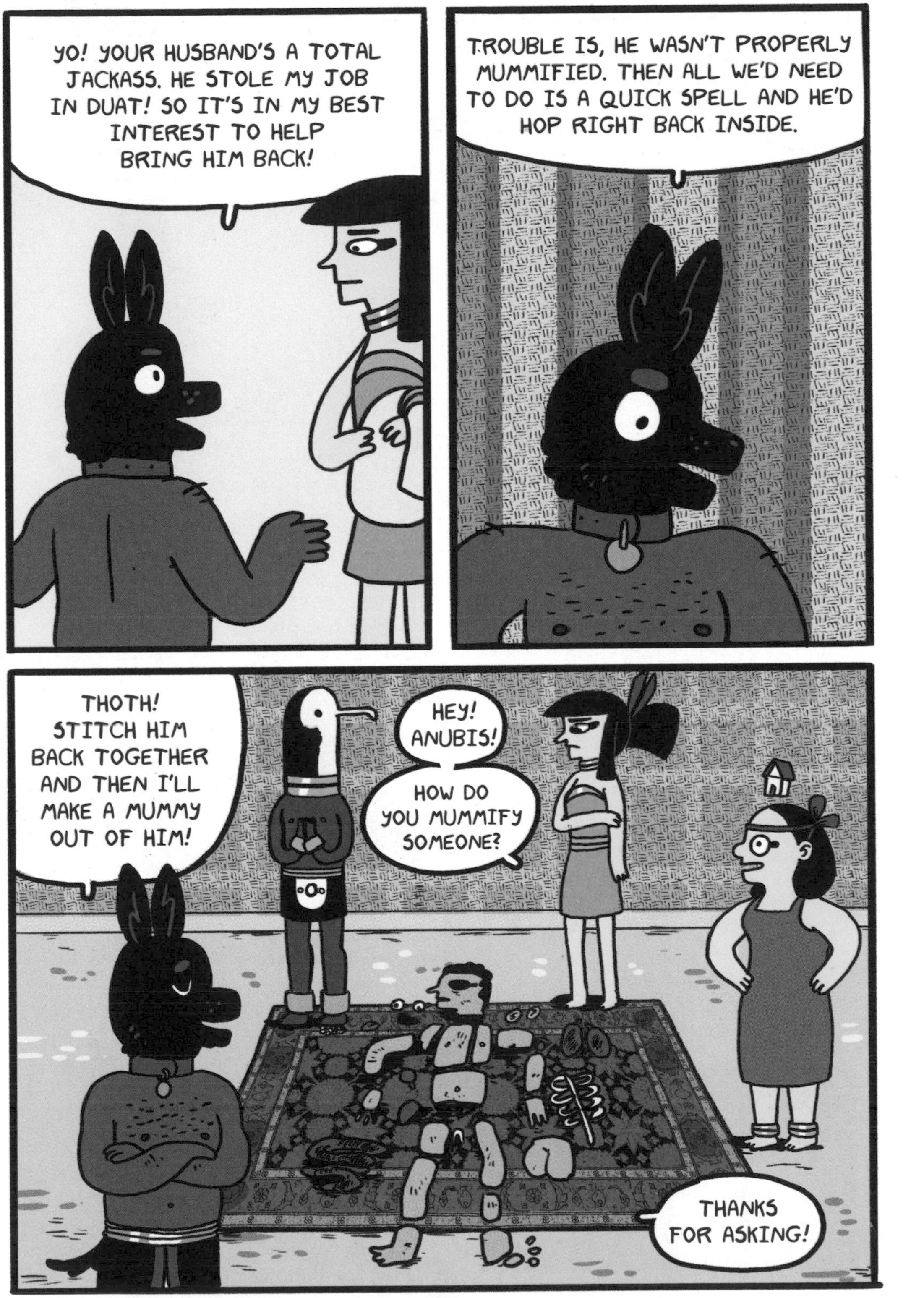

YO! YOUR HUSBAND'S A TOTAL JACKASS. HE STOLE MY JOB IN DUAT! SO IT'S IN MY BEST INTEREST TO HELP BRING HIM BACK!
TROUBLE IS, HE WASN'T PROPERLY MUMMIFIED. THEN ALL WE'D NEED TO DO IS A QUICK SPELL AND HE'D HOP RIGHT BACK INSIDE.
THOTH! STITCH HIM BACK TOGETHER AND THEN I'LL MAKE A MUMMY OUT OF HIM!
HEY! ANUBIS!
HOW DO YOU MUMMIFY SOMEONE?
THANKS FOR ASKING!

HOW TO MUMMIFY YOUR FRIENDS

WITH ANUBIS

WHAT YOU WILL NEED:

- DEAD FRIEND
- CANOPIC JARS
- LINENS
- CLOTH
- A COFFIN (OPTIONAL)
- SALT
- RESIN
- TIME AND PATIENCE
- A WILLINGNESS TO HAVE FUN!

1.

FIRSTLY, MAKE SURE YOUR FRIEND IS DEFINITELY DEAD (AND CLEAN!)

THIS IS ONE I WASHED EARLIER (IT'S OSIRIS!)

2. NOW, THIS IS MY FAVOURITE KIND OF SCRAMBLING HOOK. JUST SLIDE IT UP THE NOSTRILS AND MASH THE BRAIN UP SO IT POURS OUT NICE AND SMOOTHLY. IF YOU DON'T HAVE ONE, A LONG PENCIL OR STICK CAN BE JUST AS GOOD, BUT IT MIGHT TAKE A BIT LONGER!

3. THEN WE REMOVE THE ORGANS (EXCEPT THE HEART - HE'LL NEED THAT FOR HIS JUDGEMENT). I LIKE TO PUT THEM IN THESE CUTE LITTLE JARS, THAT THEY CAN CARRY WITH THEM TO DUAT. BUT ORDINARY TUPPERWARE WORKS!

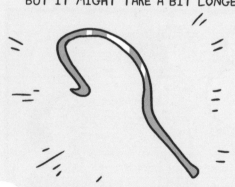

4. YOUR FRIEND MIGHT BE LOOKING A LITTLE DEFLATED, SO STUFF THE EMPTY BODY WITH CLOTH! THIS IS ALSO A GOOD TIME TO COVER THE CORPSE WITH WINE, SPICES AND YOUR PREFERRED SALT (I USE NATRON!)

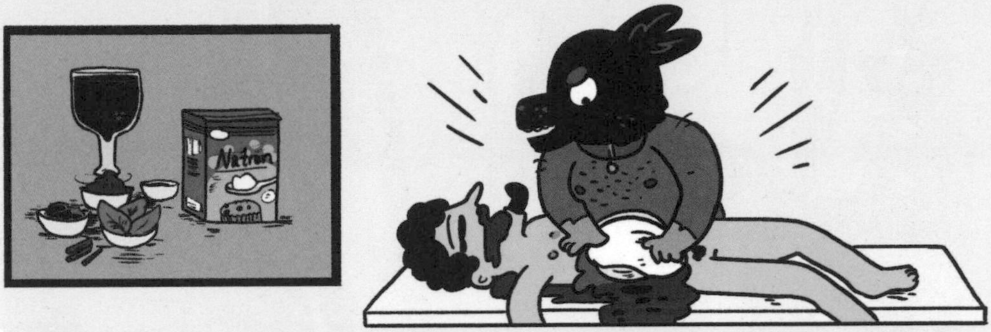
Natron

5. THEN, LEAVE THE BODY TO HANG FOR ABOUT 70 DAYS TO LET IT WORK UP A NICE LEATHER. REMEMBER TO REPLACE THE STUFFING WITH SAND ON THE 40TH DAY, THOUGH!

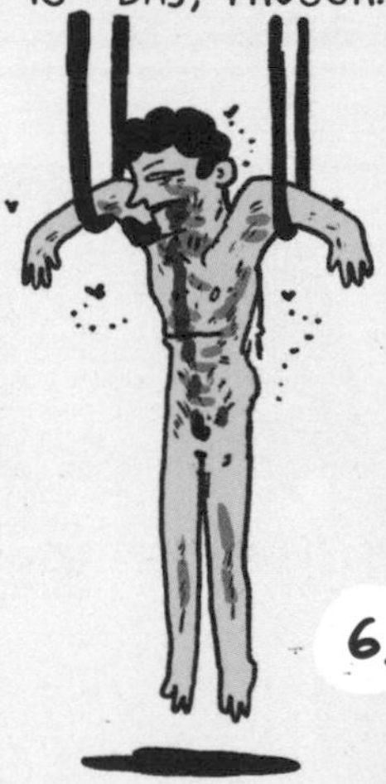

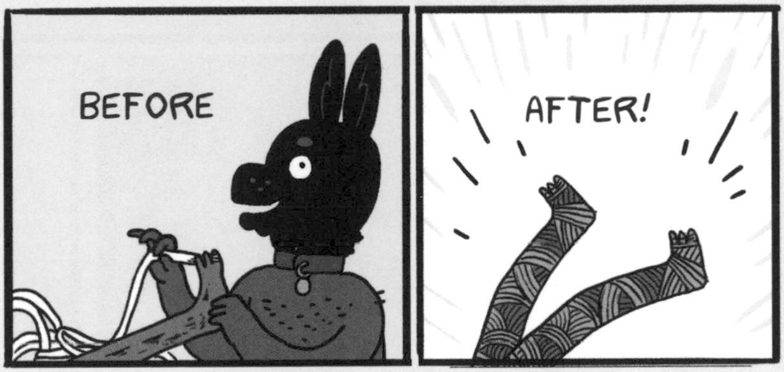
BEFORE
AFTER!

6. NOW WE CAN START THE FUN BIT! THE WRAPPING OF THE LINEN! START WITH THE TOES AND FINGERS, AND MOVE ON TO THE REST OF THE BODY, PLACING SOME GOLD IN THE LAYERS AS A NICE TREAT FOR WHEN HE WAKES UP!

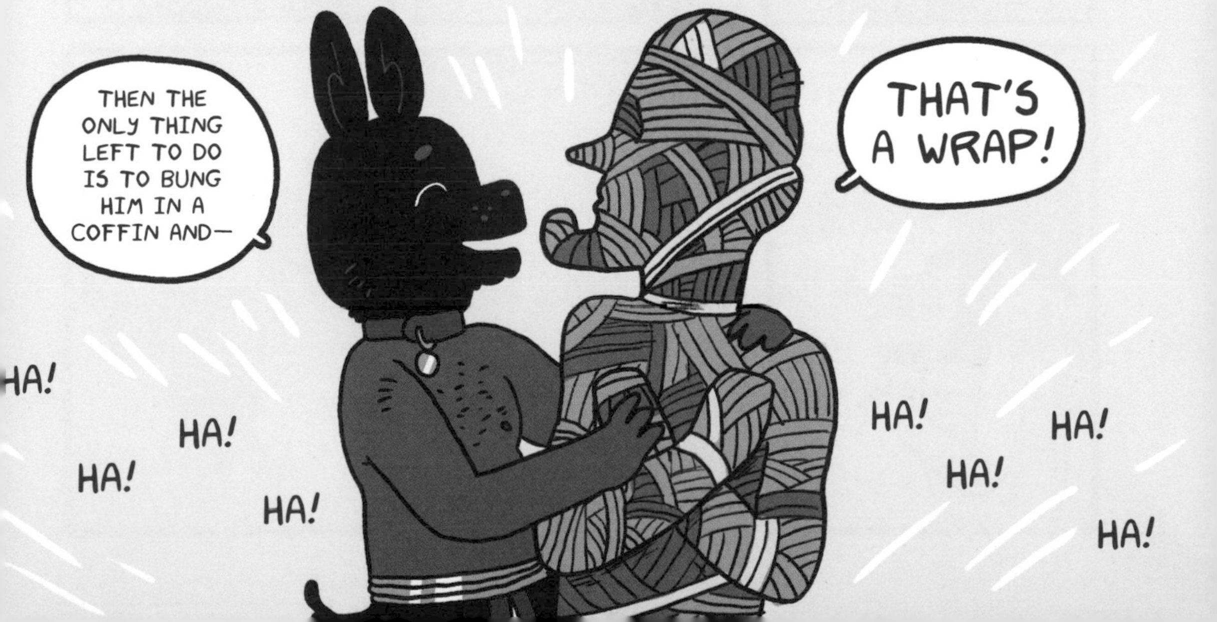
THEN THE ONLY THING LEFT TO DO IS TO BUNG HIM IN A COFFIN AND—
THAT'S A WRAP!
HA! HA! HA! HA! HA! HA! HA! HA! HA!

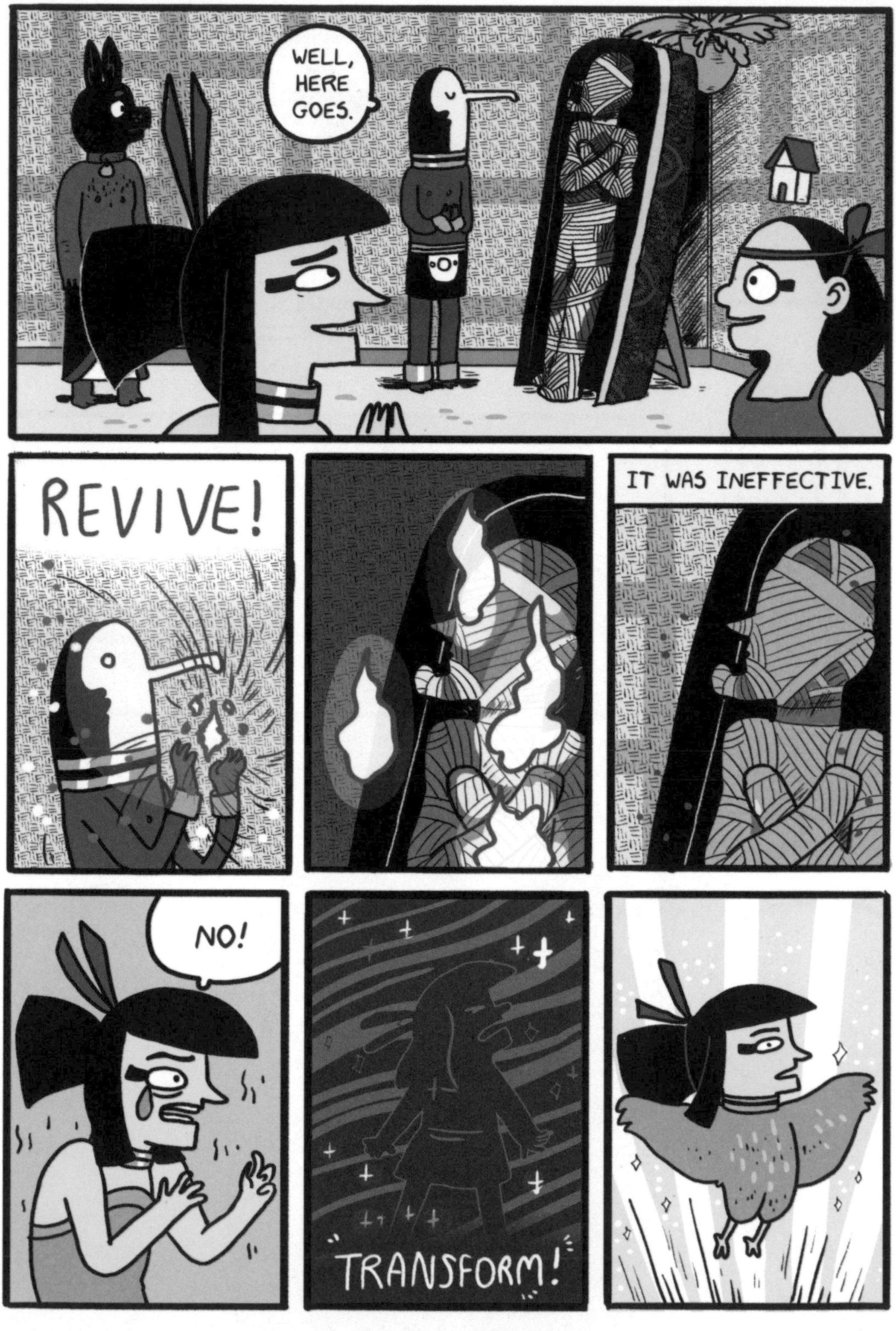
WELL, HERE GOES.
REVIVE!
IT WAS INEFFECTIVE.
NO!
TRANSFORM!

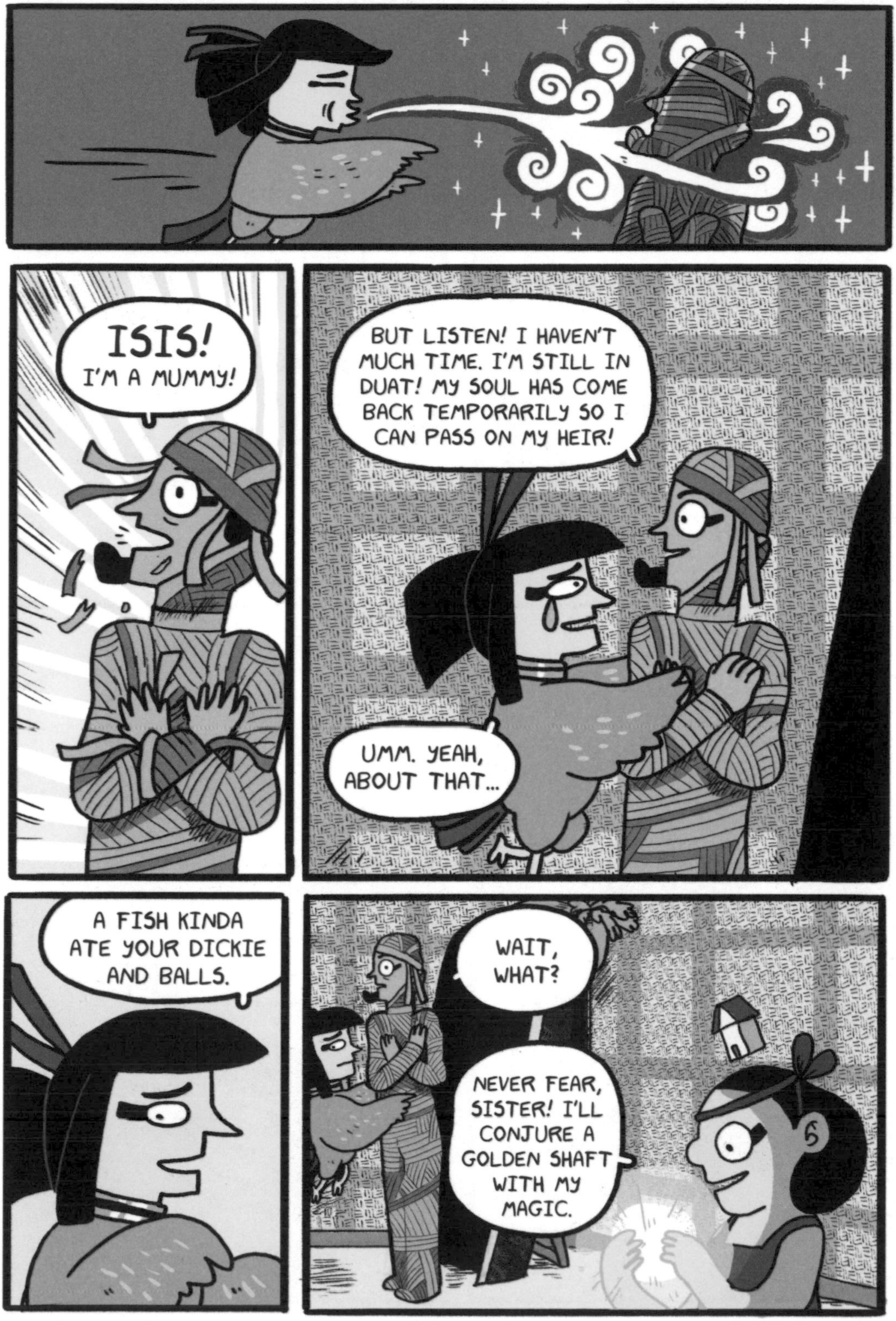
ISIS! I'M A MUMMY!
BUT LISTEN! I HAVEN'T MUCH TIME. I'M STILL IN DUAT! MY SOUL HAS COME BACK TEMPORARILY SO I CAN PASS ON MY HEIR!
UMM. YEAH, ABOUT THAT...
A FISH KINDA ATE YOUR DICKIE AND BALLS.
WAIT, WHAT?
NEVER FEAR, SISTER! I'LL CONJURE A GOLDEN SHAFT WITH MY MAGIC.

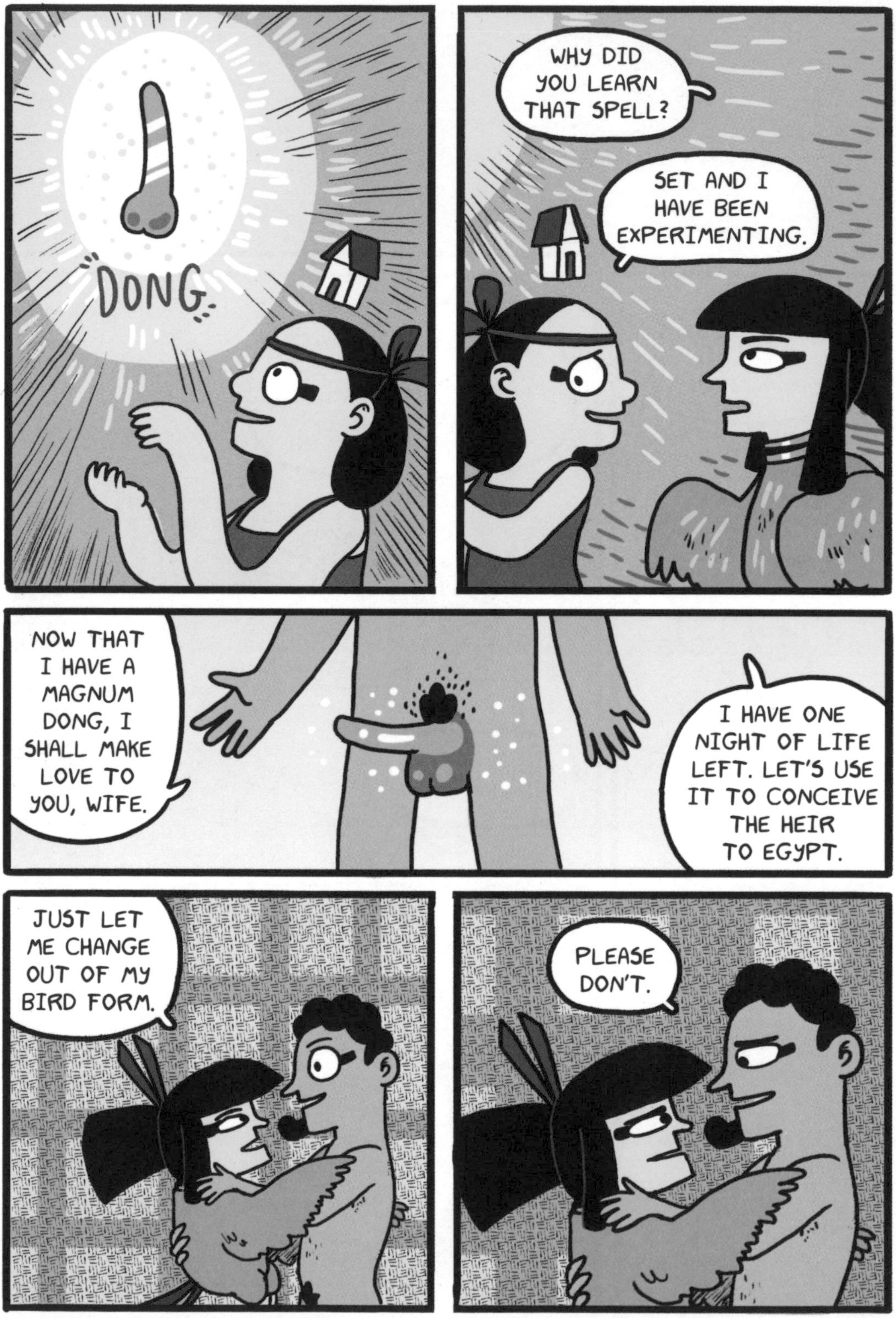
DONG
WHY DID YOU LEARN THAT SPELL?
SET AND I HAVE BEEN EXPERIMENTING.
NOW THAT I HAVE A MAGNUM DONG, I SHALL MAKE LOVE TO YOU, WIFE.
I HAVE ONE NIGHT OF LIFE LEFT. LET'S USE IT TO CONCEIVE THE HEIR TO EGYPT.
JUST LET ME CHANGE OUT OF MY BIRD FORM.
PLEASE DON'T.

CHAPTER SIX

★★★ BIRTH ★★★

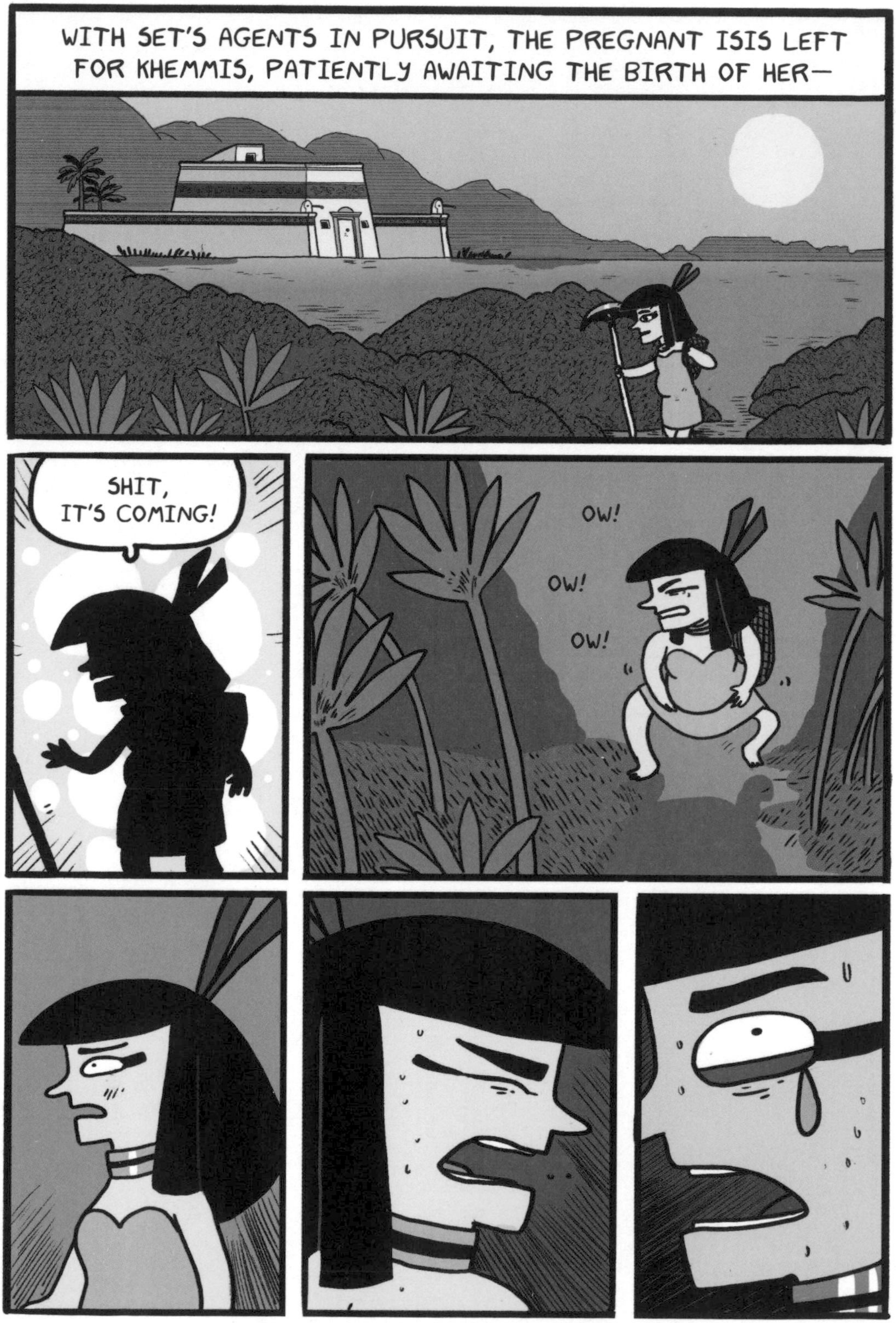
WITH SET'S AGENTS IN PURSUIT, THE PREGNANT ISIS LEFT FOR KHEMMIS, PATIENTLY AWAITING THE BIRTH OF HER—
SHIT, IT'S COMING!
OW!
OW!
OW!

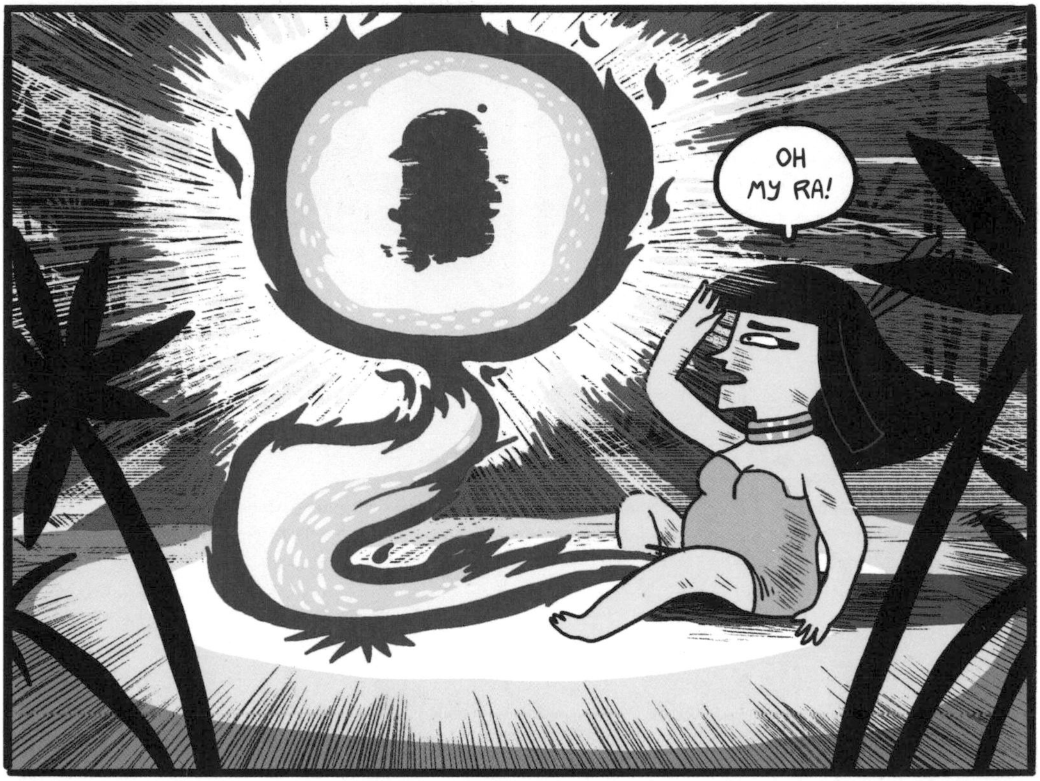
OH
MY RA!

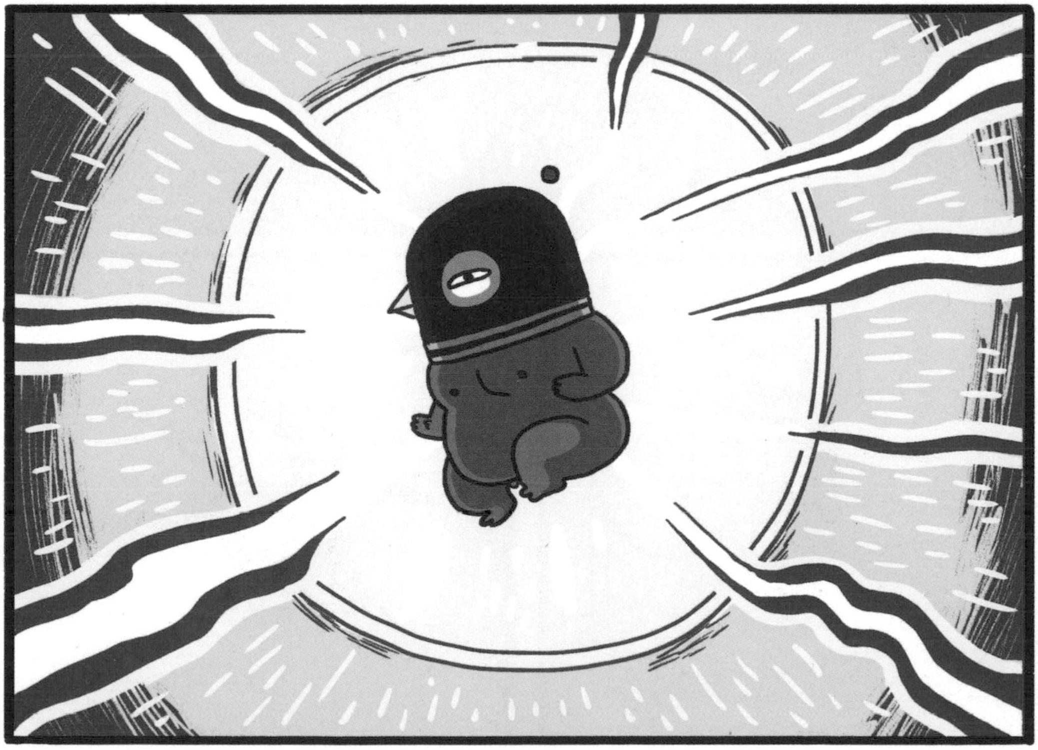

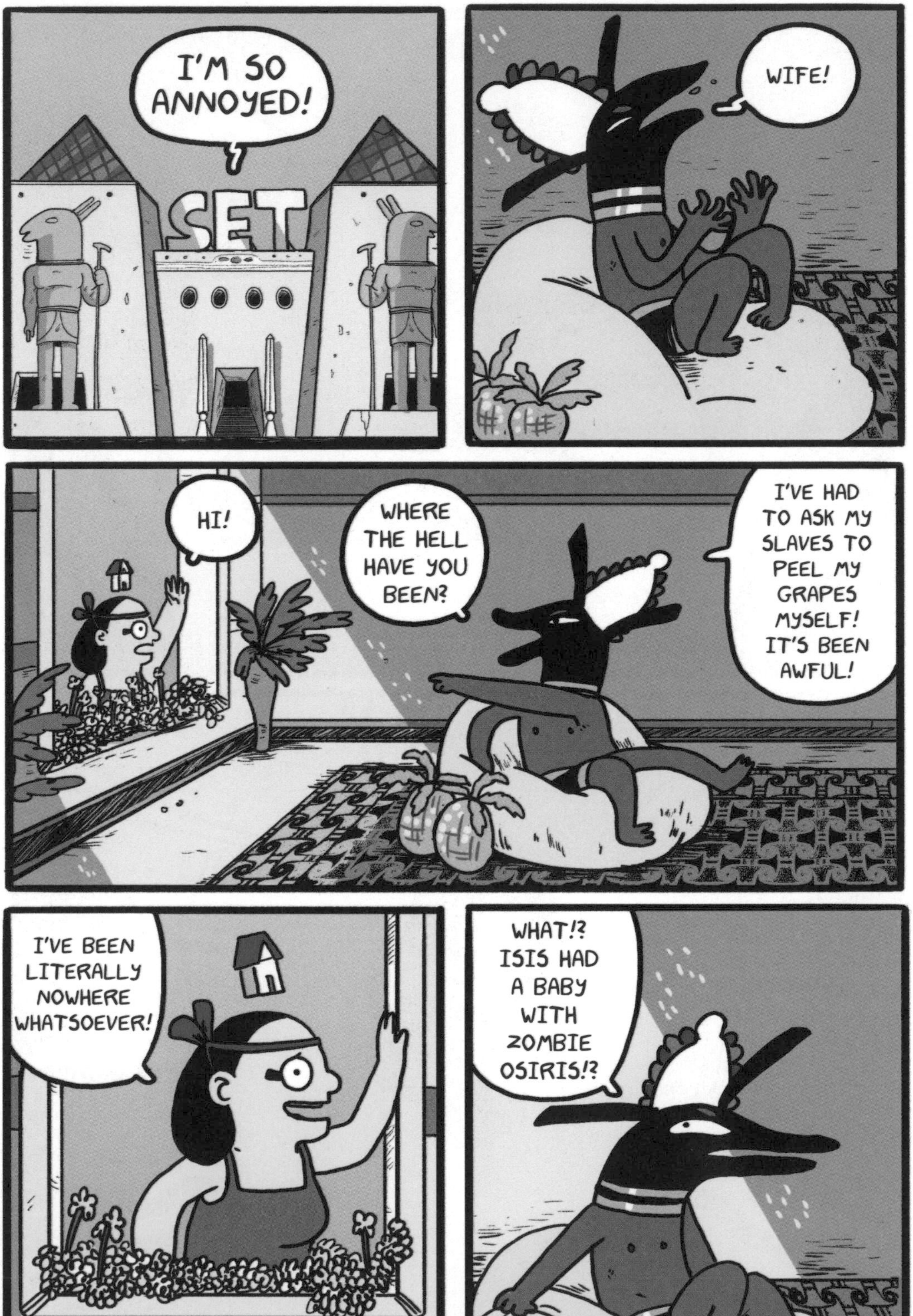

I'M SO ANNOYED!
SET
WIFE!
HI!
WHERE THE HELL HAVE YOU BEEN?
I'VE HAD TO ASK MY SLAVES TO PEEL MY GRAPES MYSELF! IT'S BEEN AWFUL!
I'VE BEEN LITERALLY NOWHERE WHATSOEVER!
WHAT!? ISIS HAD A BABY WITH ZOMBIE OSIRIS!?

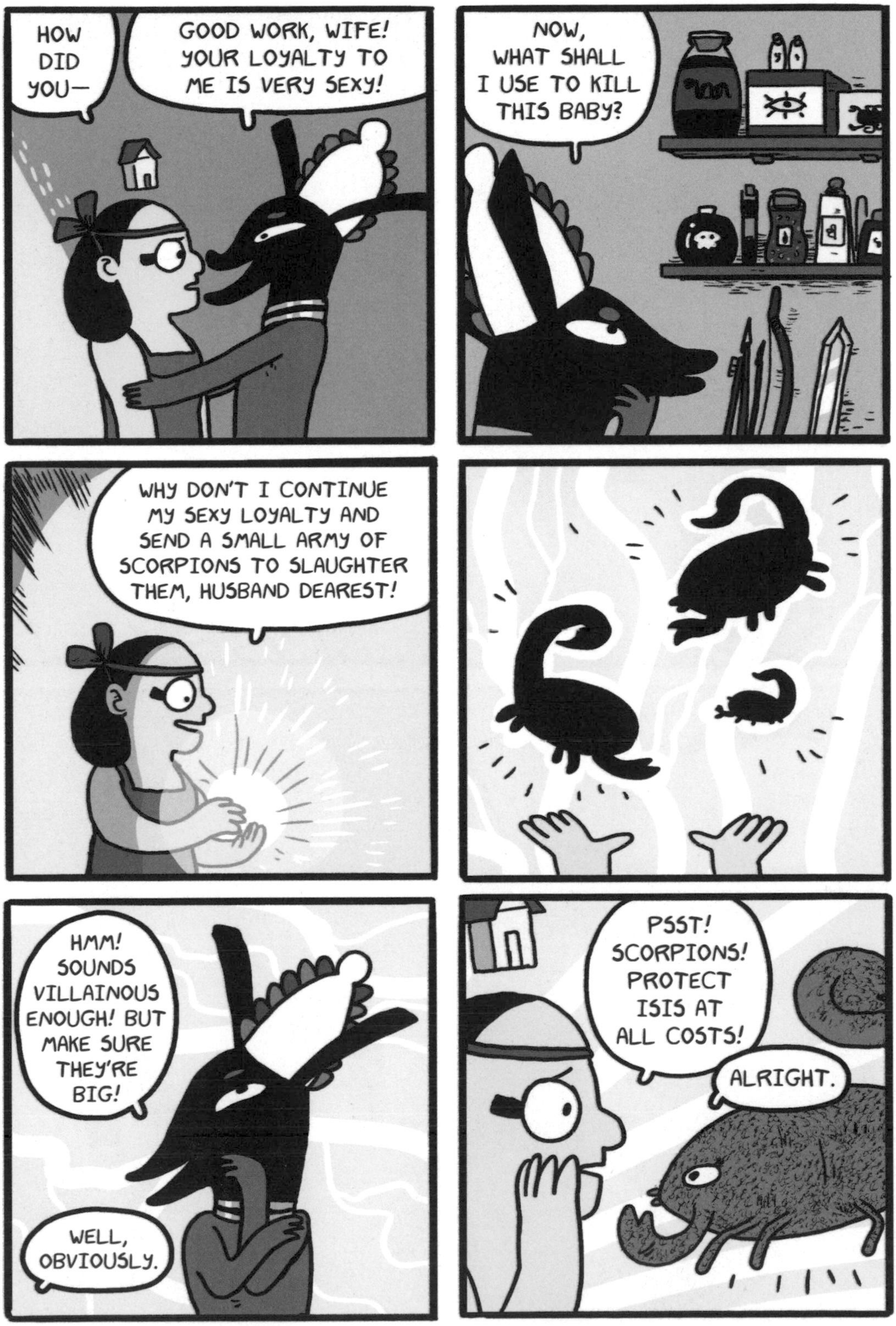
HOW DID YOU—
GOOD WORK, WIFE! YOUR LOYALTY TO ME IS VERY SEXY!
NOW, WHAT SHALL I USE TO KILL THIS BABY?
WHY DON'T I CONTINUE MY SEXY LOYALTY AND SEND A SMALL ARMY OF SCORPIONS TO SLAUGHTER THEM, HUSBAND DEAREST!
HMM! SOUNDS VILLAINOUS ENOUGH! BUT MAKE SURE THEY'RE BIG!
WELL, OBVIOUSLY.
PSST! SCORPIONS! PROTECT ISIS AT ALL COSTS!
ALRIGHT.

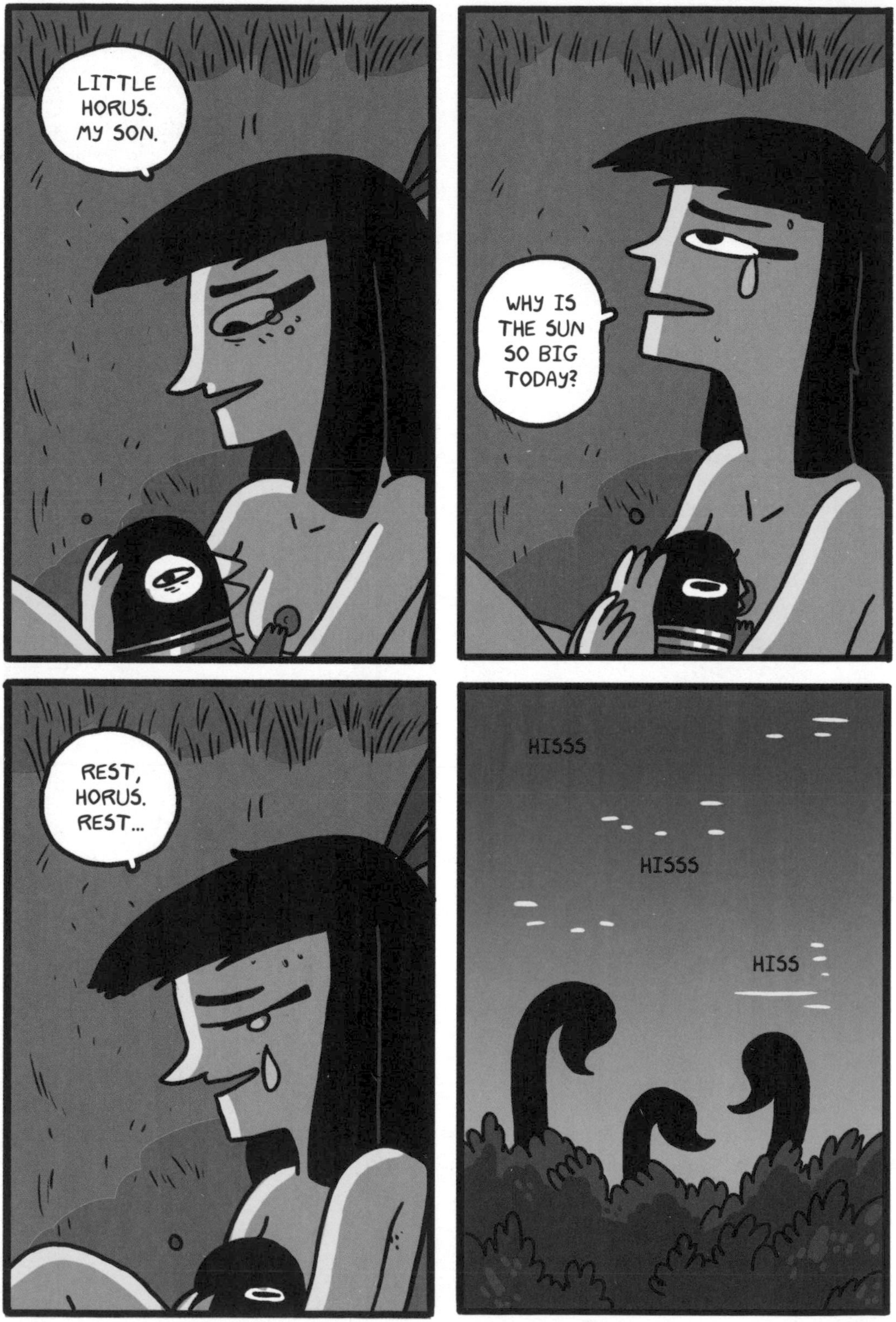
LITTLE HORUS. MY SON.
WHY IS THE SUN SO BIG TODAY?
REST, HORUS. REST...
HISSS
HISSS
HISS

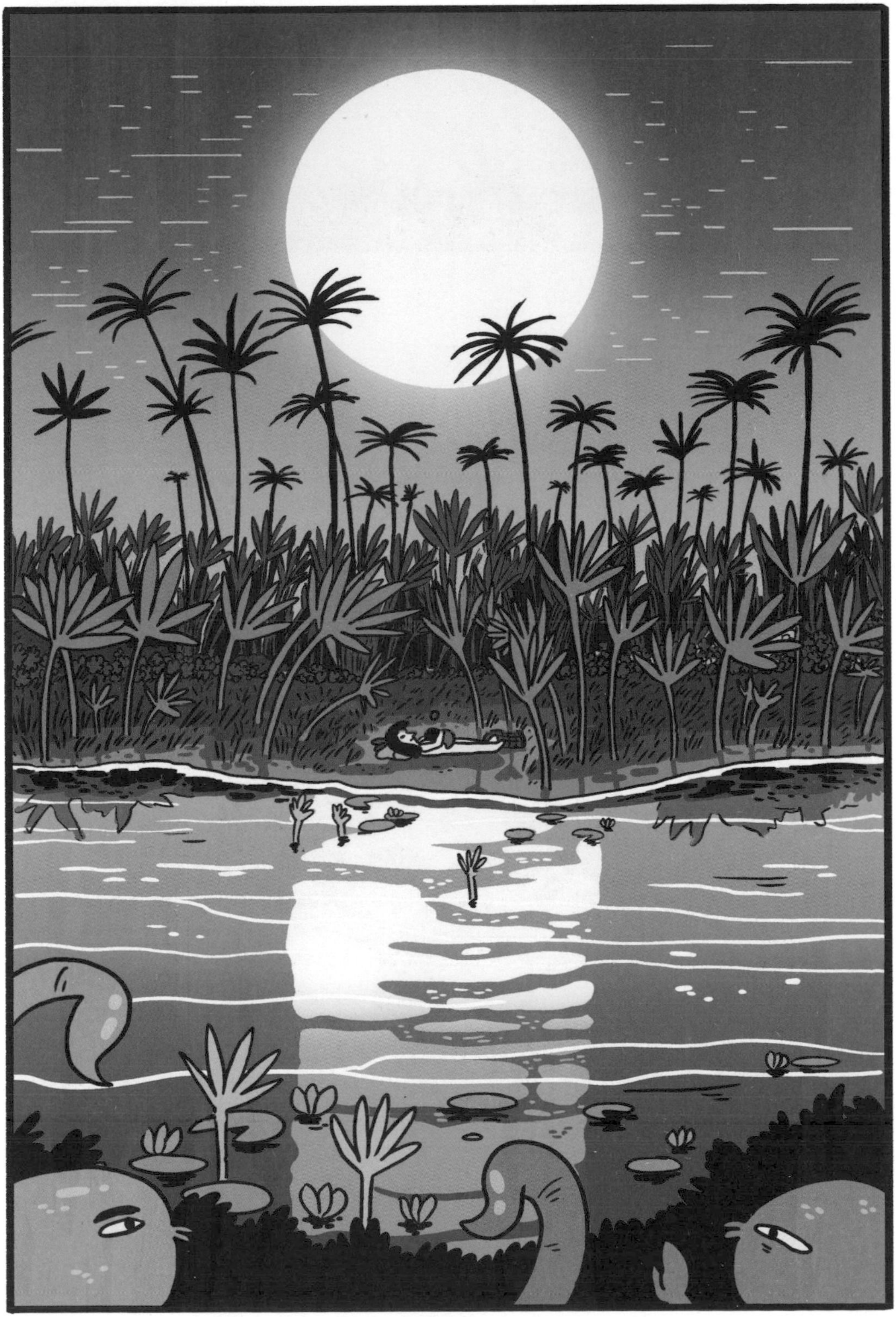

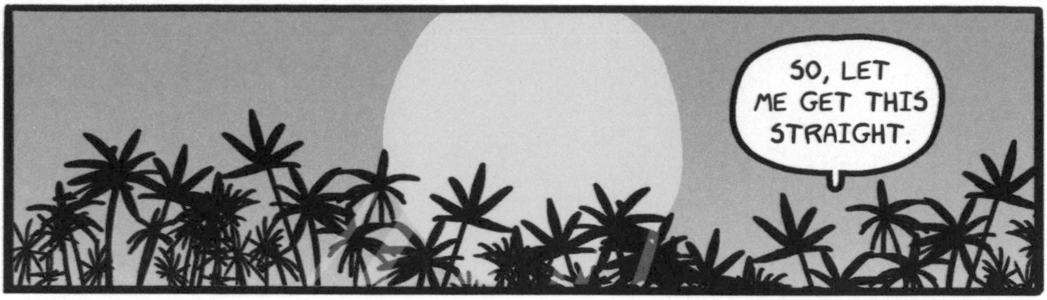
SO, LET ME GET THIS STRAIGHT.

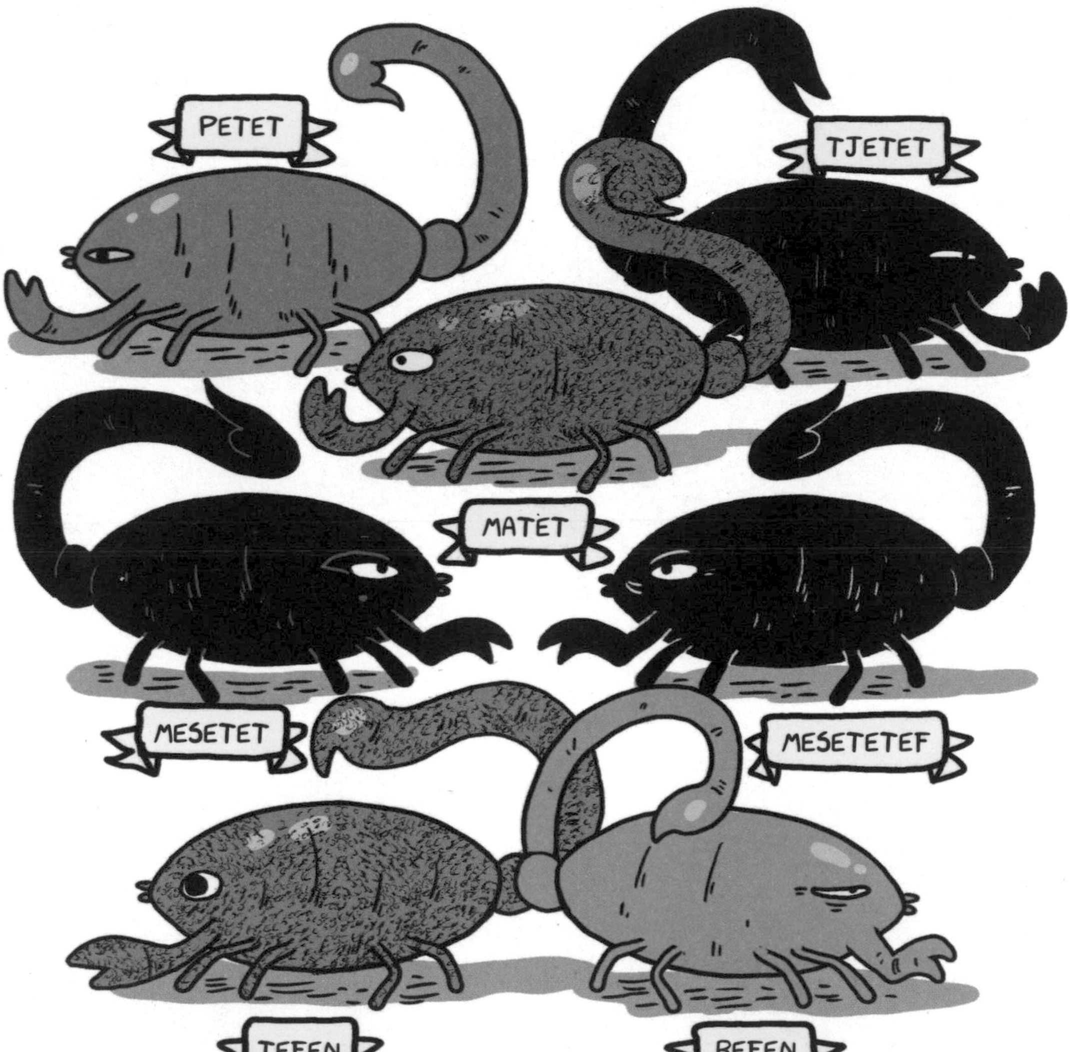
PETET
TJETET
MATET
MESETET
MESETETEF
TEFEN
BEFEN

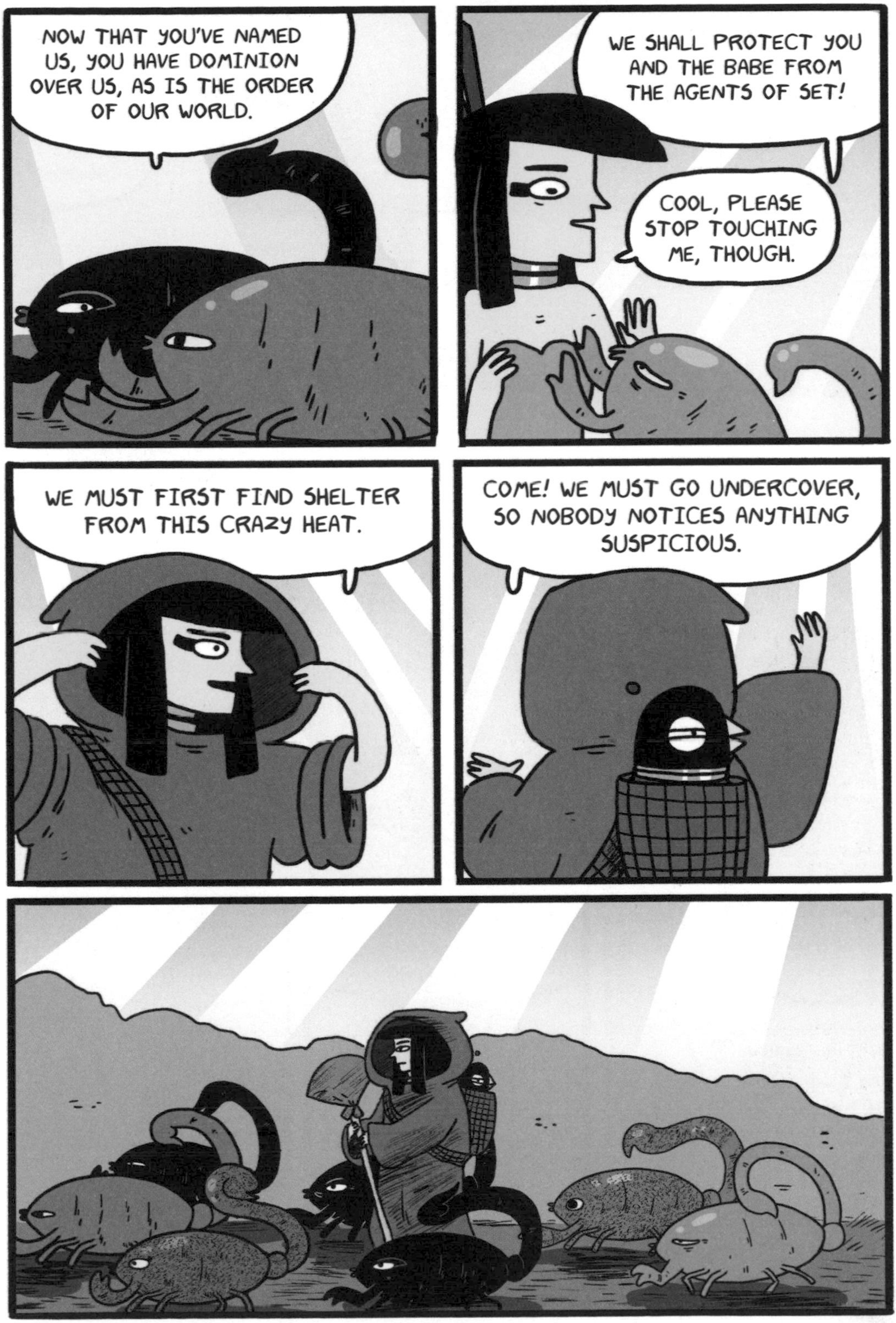
NOW THAT YOU'VE NAMED US, YOU HAVE DOMINION OVER US, AS IS THE ORDER OF OUR WORLD.
WE SHALL PROTECT YOU AND THE BABE FROM THE AGENTS OF SET!
COOL, PLEASE STOP TOUCHING ME, THOUGH.
WE MUST FIRST FIND SHELTER FROM THIS CRAZY HEAT.
COME! WE MUST GO UNDERCOVER, SO NOBODY NOTICES ANYTHING SUSPICIOUS.

THE TOWN OF THE TWIN SISTERS.

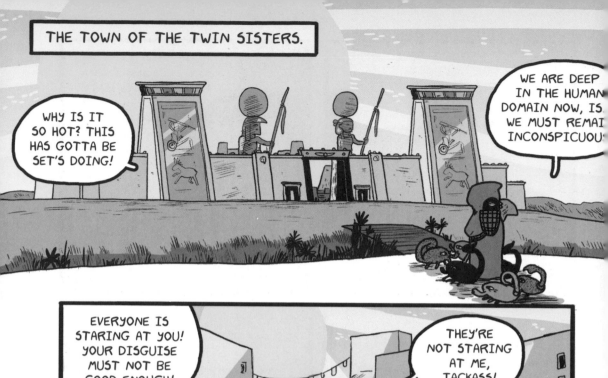

WHY IS IT SO HOT? THIS HAS GOTTA BE SET'S DOING!

WE ARE DEEP IN THE HUMAN DOMAIN NOW, IS. WE MUST REMAI INCONSPICUOU

EVERYONE IS STARING AT YOU! YOUR DISGUISE MUST NOT BE GOOD ENOUGH!

THEY'RE NOT STARING AT ME, JACKASS!

HELLO, MA'AM.

WE ARE LOOKING FOR SHELTER. MAY YOU OFFER ANY?

UMM. WELL, WE'RE SORT OF—

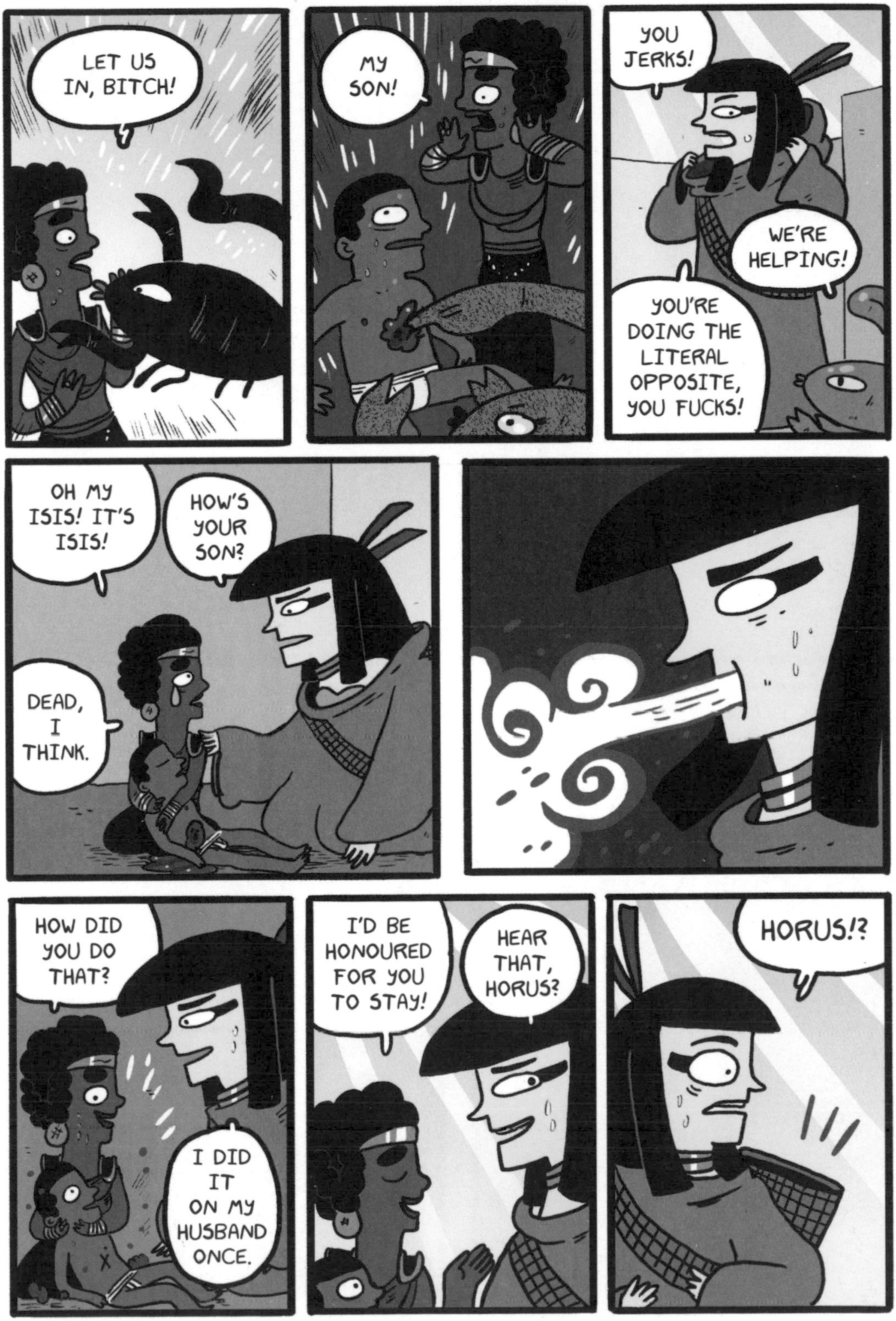
LET US IN, BITCH!
MY SON!
YOU JERKS!
WE'RE HELPING!
YOU'RE DOING THE LITERAL OPPOSITE, YOU FUCKS!
OH MY ISIS! IT'S ISIS!
HOW'S YOUR SON?
DEAD, I THINK.
HOW DID YOU DO THAT?
I DID IT ON MY HUSBAND ONCE.
I'D BE HONOURED FOR YOU TO STAY!
HEAR THAT, HORUS?
HORUS!?

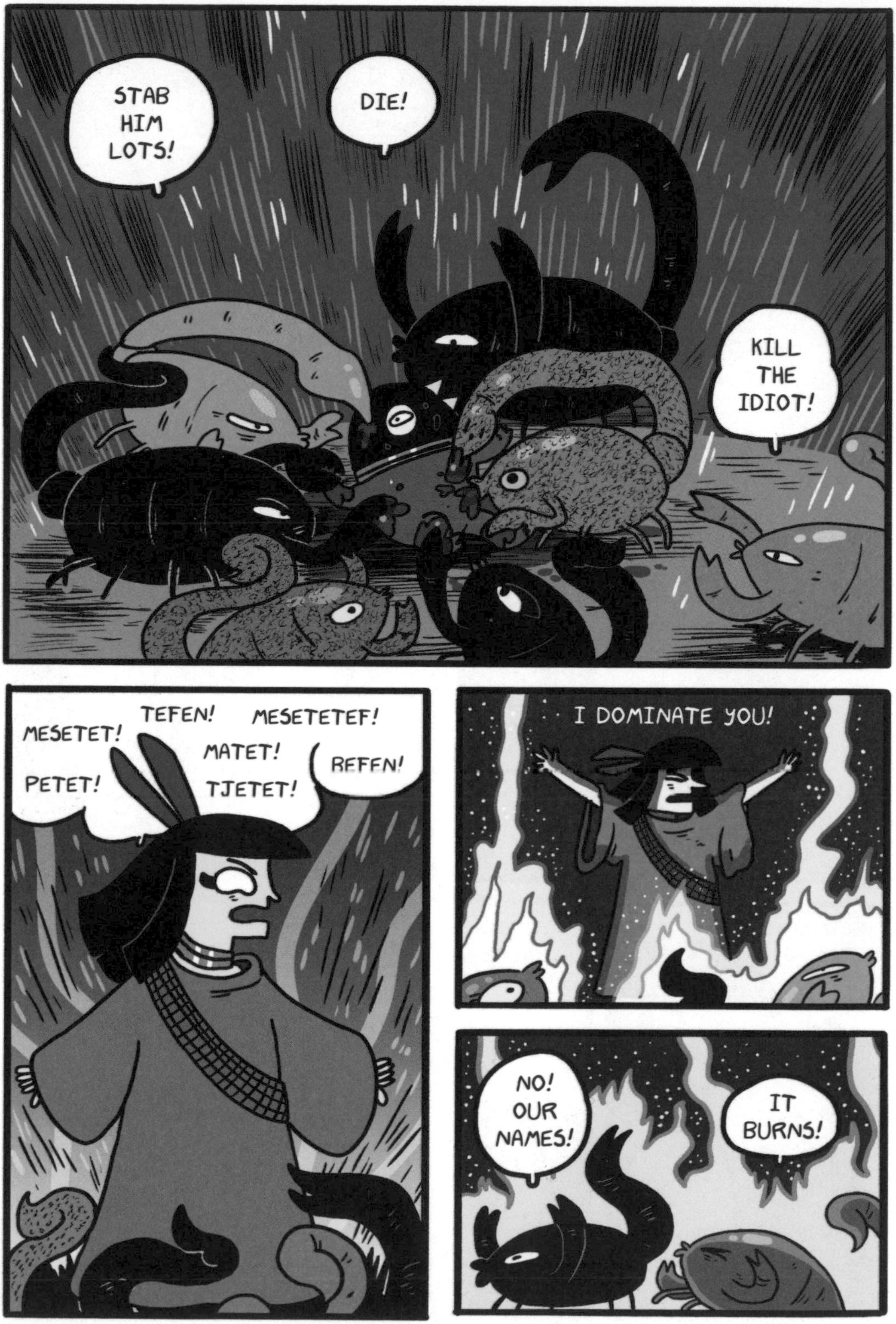
STAB HIM LOTS!
DIE!
KILL THE IDIOT!
MESETET!
TEFEN!
MESETETEF!
MATET!
PETET!
TJETET!
REFEN!
I DOMINATE YOU!
NO! OUR NAMES!
IT BURNS!

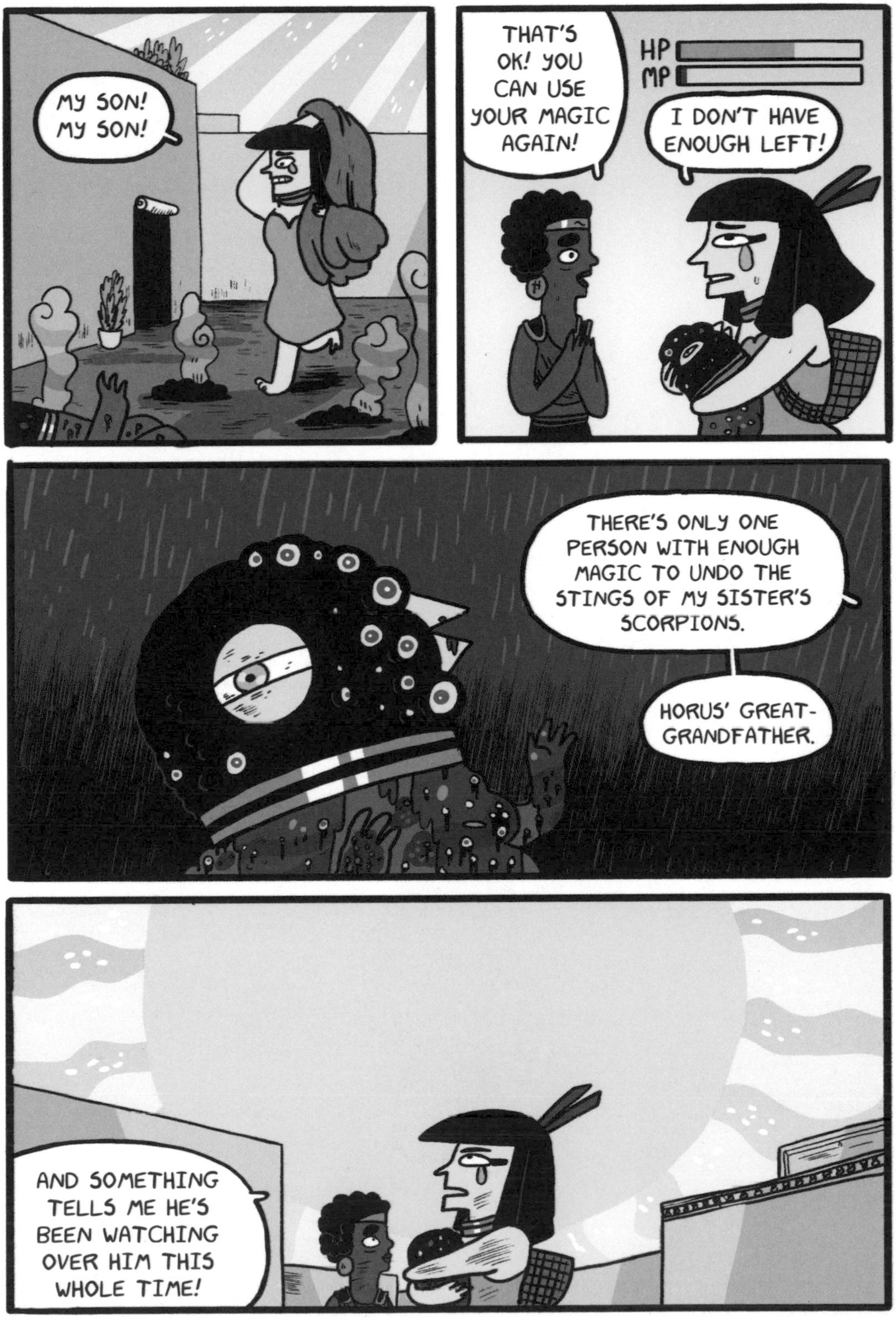

MY SON! MY SON!
THAT'S OK! YOU CAN USE YOUR MAGIC AGAIN!
HP
MP
I DON'T HAVE ENOUGH LEFT!
THERE'S ONLY ONE PERSON WITH ENOUGH MAGIC TO UNDO THE STINGS OF MY SISTER'S SCORPIONS.
HORUS' GREAT-GRANDFATHER.
AND SOMETHING TELLS ME HE'S BEEN WATCHING OVER HIM THIS WHOLE TIME!

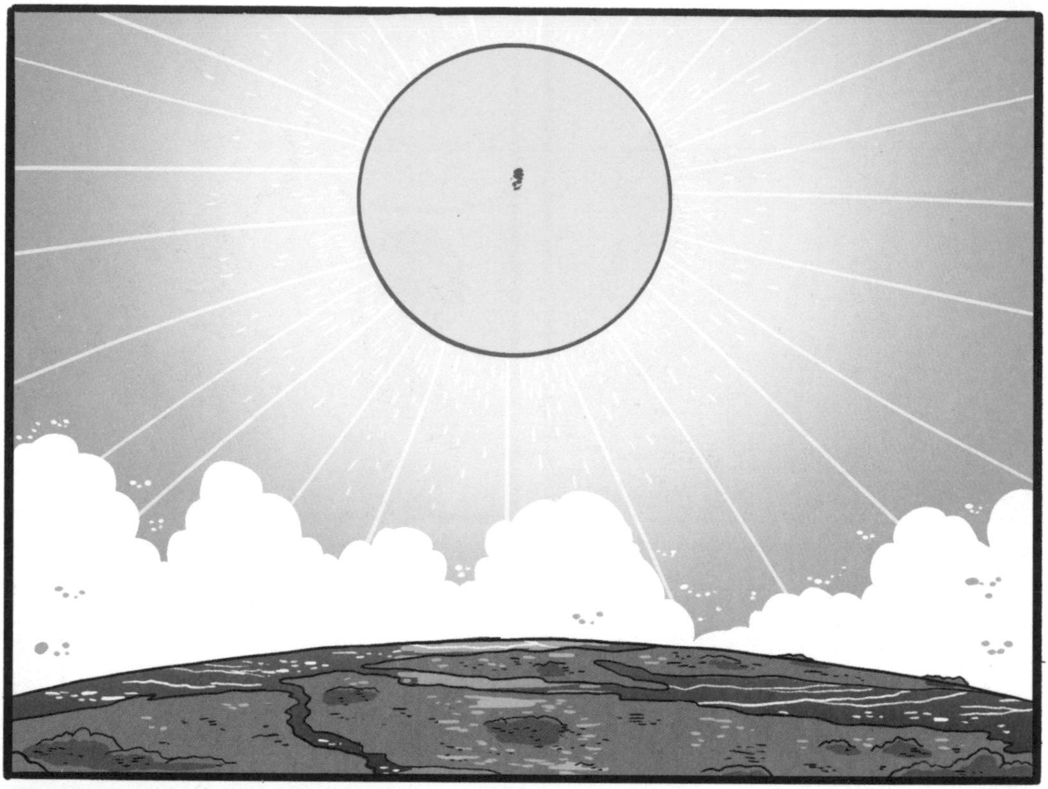

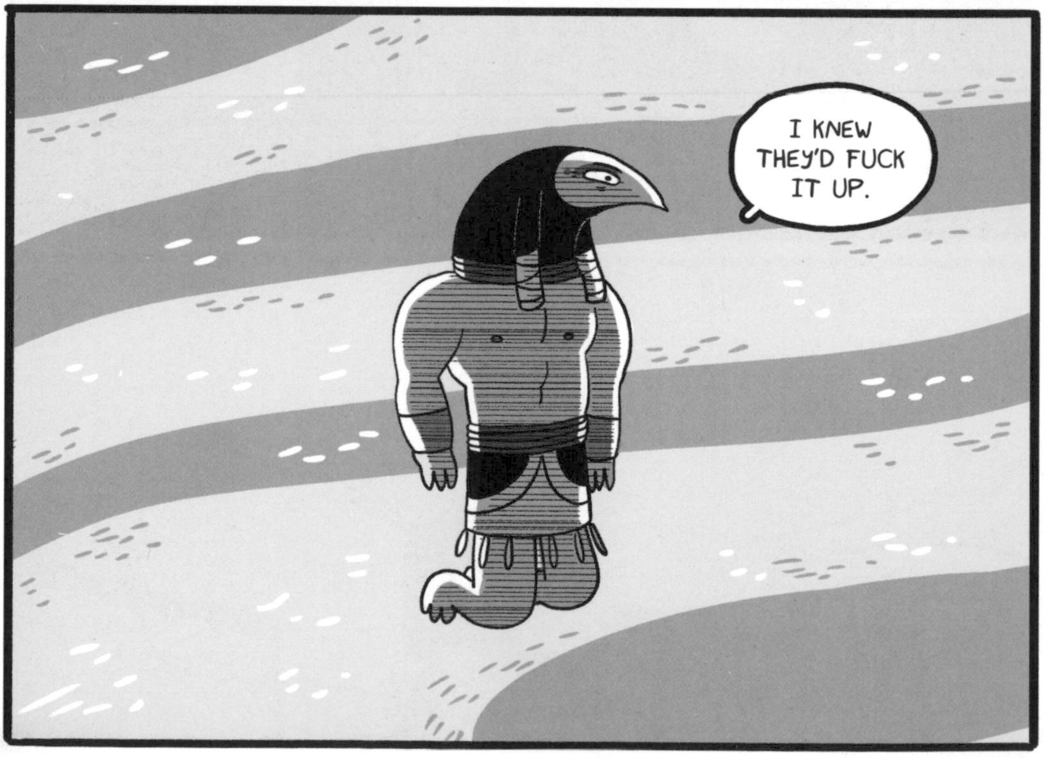
I KNEW THEY'D FUCK IT UP.

CHAPTER SEVEN

★★★ REVELATION ★★★

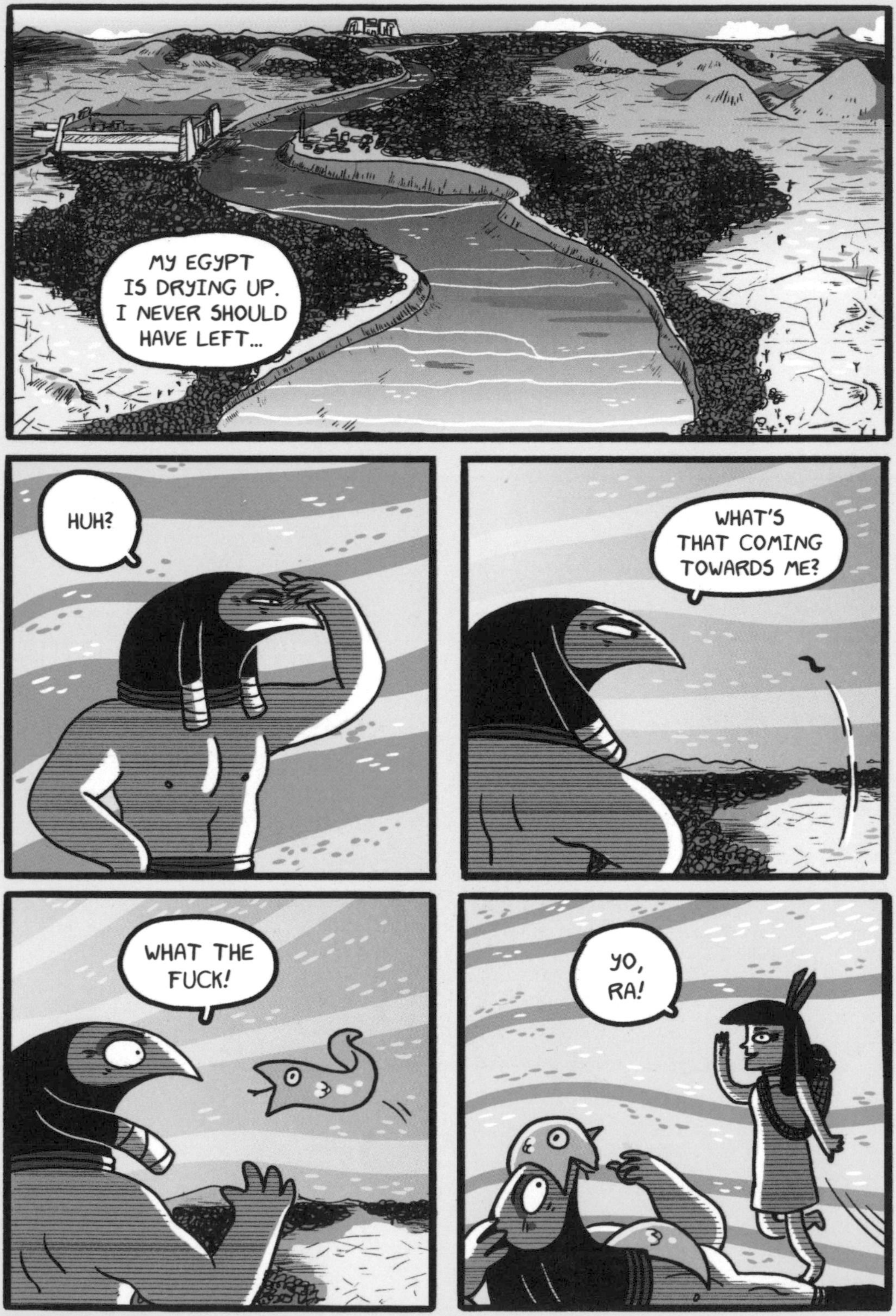
MY EGYPT IS DRYING UP. I NEVER SHOULD HAVE LEFT...
HUH?
WHAT'S THAT COMING TOWARDS ME?
WHAT THE FUCK!
YO, RA!

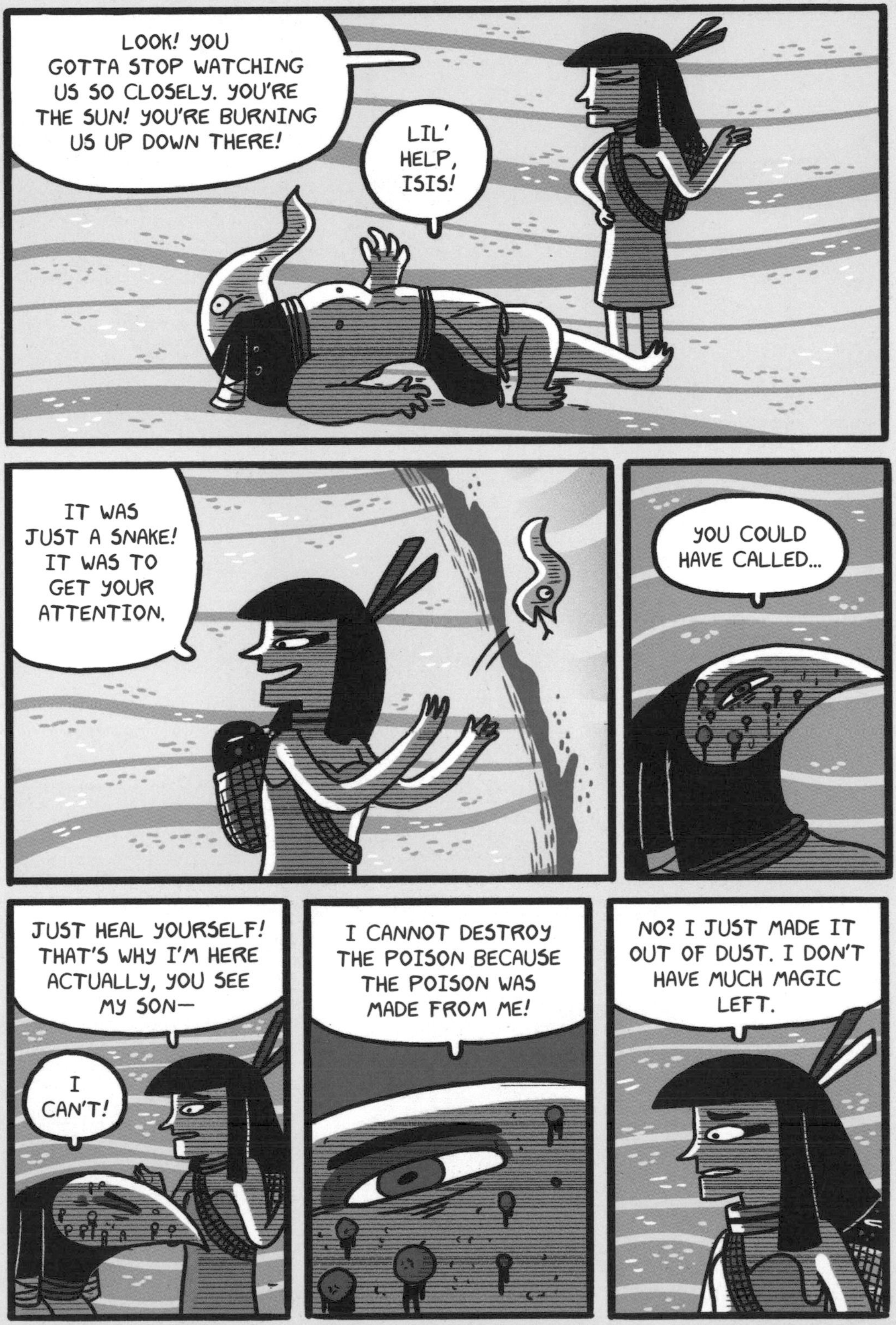
LOOK! YOU GOTTA STOP WATCHING US SO CLOSELY. YOU'RE THE SUN! YOU'RE BURNING US UP DOWN THERE!
LIL' HELP, ISIS!
IT WAS JUST A SNAKE! IT WAS TO GET YOUR ATTENTION.
YOU COULD HAVE CALLED...
JUST HEAL YOURSELF! THAT'S WHY I'M HERE ACTUALLY, YOU SEE MY SON—
I CAN'T!
I CANNOT DESTROY THE POISON BECAUSE THE POISON WAS MADE FROM ME!
NO? I JUST MADE IT OUT OF DUST. I DON'T HAVE MUCH MAGIC LEFT.

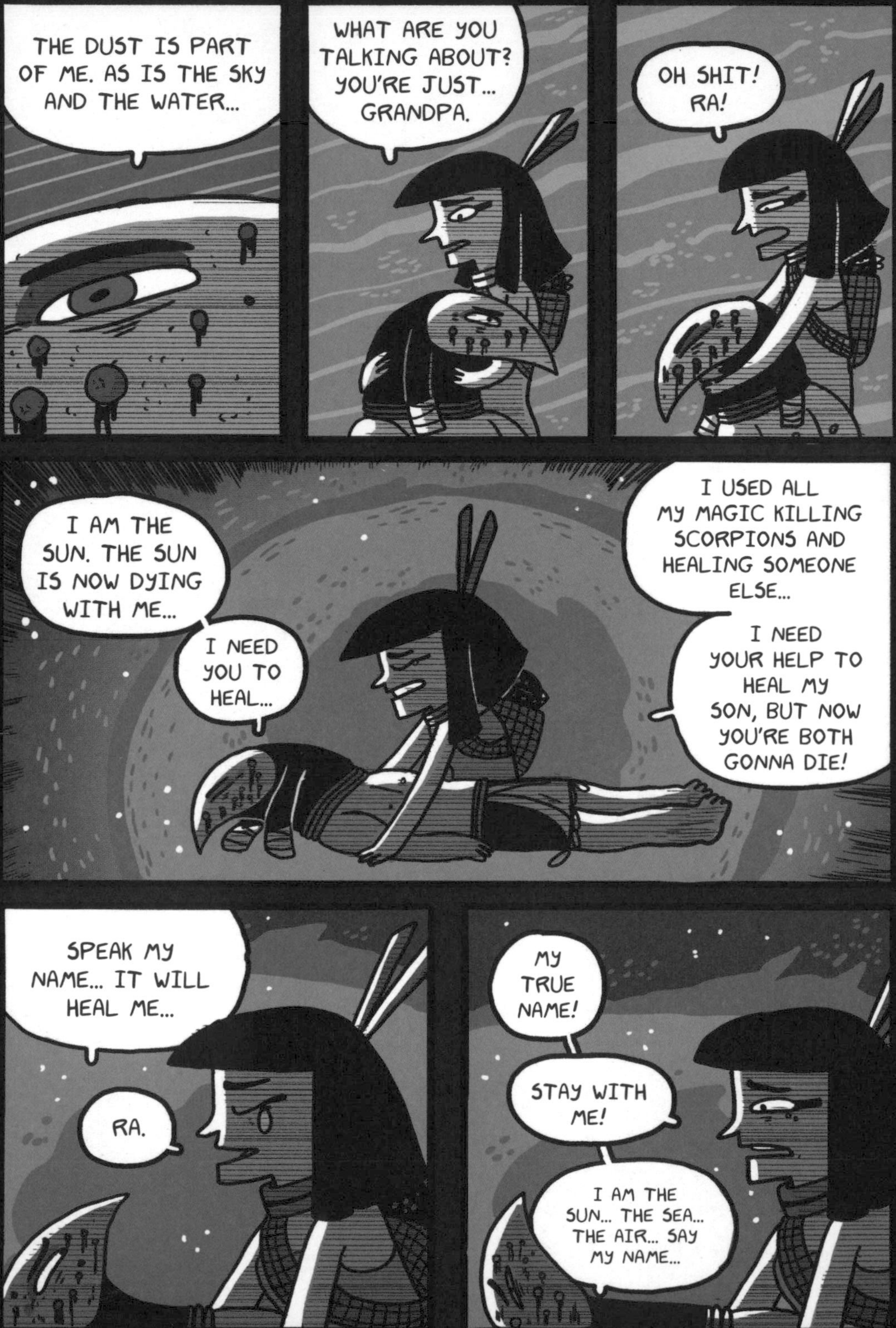
THE DUST IS PART OF ME. AS IS THE SKY AND THE WATER...
WHAT ARE YOU TALKING ABOUT? YOU'RE JUST... GRANDPA.
OH SHIT! RA!
I AM THE SUN. THE SUN IS NOW DYING WITH ME...
I NEED YOU TO HEAL...
I USED ALL MY MAGIC KILLING SCORPIONS AND HEALING SOMEONE ELSE...
I NEED YOUR HELP TO HEAL MY SON, BUT NOW YOU'RE BOTH GONNA DIE!
SPEAK MY NAME... IT WILL HEAL ME...
RA.
MY TRUE NAME!
STAY WITH ME!
I AM THE SUN... THE SEA... THE AIR... SAY MY NAME...

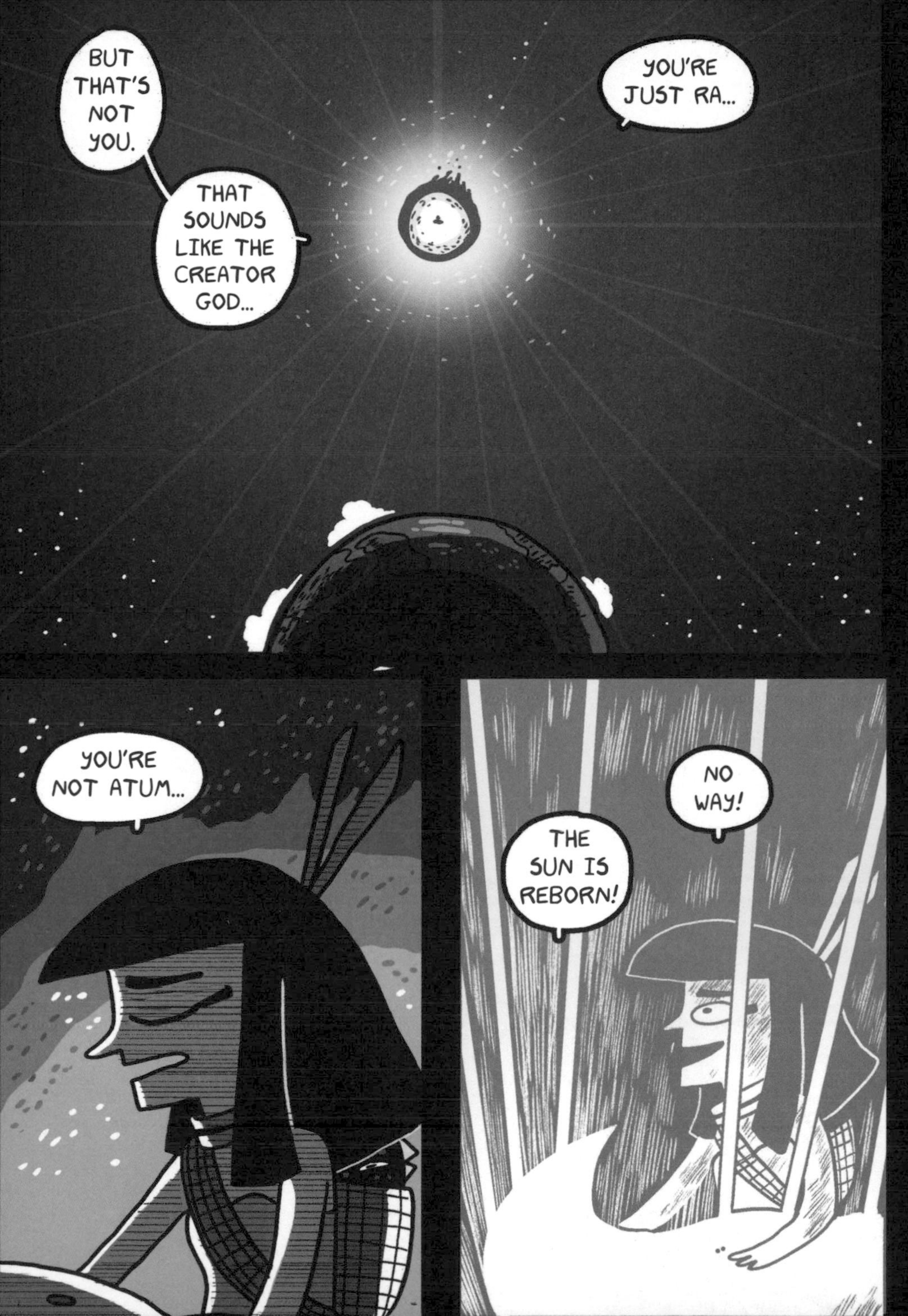
BUT THAT'S NOT YOU.
THAT SOUNDS LIKE THE CREATOR GOD...
YOU'RE JUST RA...
YOU'RE NOT ATUM...
NO WAY!
THE SUN IS REBORN!

THANK YOU FOR SAVING MY LIFE, ISIS.

FROM THE SNAKE YOU ATTACKED ME WITH.

I'M SORRY FOR COMING BACK. I PROMISE TO LEAVE EGYPT THIS TIME! NO GOOD COMES FROM ME BEING DOWN HERE.

BUT LOOK AT SET! WE'RE NOT DOING SO HOT OURSELVES.

I HAD HOPED THAT HORUS WOULD DESTROY SET AND BRING BALANCE BACK TO EGYPT...

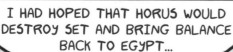

BUT HE'S SUCH A SICKLY THING.

BALANCE? MAYBE. BUT THAT CANNOT BE ACHIEVED THROUGH DESTRUCTION OF PART OF THE PANTHEON.

ATUM EJACULATED OUT SHU AND TEFNUT, WHO WALKED
THE EARTH AND SOWED THE AIR AND RAIN.

ATUM TURNED INTO ME, A SUN GOD, TO LIGHT THEIR WAY.

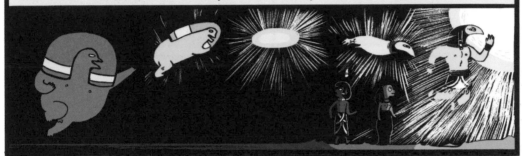

EVENTUALLY, SHU AND TEFNUT HAD NUT AND
GEB, WHO HAD YOU, OSIRIS, SET, AND NEPHTHYS.

DO YOU SEE?
YOU COULD GIVE HORUS ALL
THE POWER IN THE WORLD AND
HE COULD NOT STOP SET.
WE ARE ALL ASPECTS OF THE
SAME BEING. WE ARE ALL ATUM.
IT WILL TAKE CUNNING AND
TEAMWORK TO STOP A GOD...
I HAVE LEARNED THIS THE
HARD WAY.

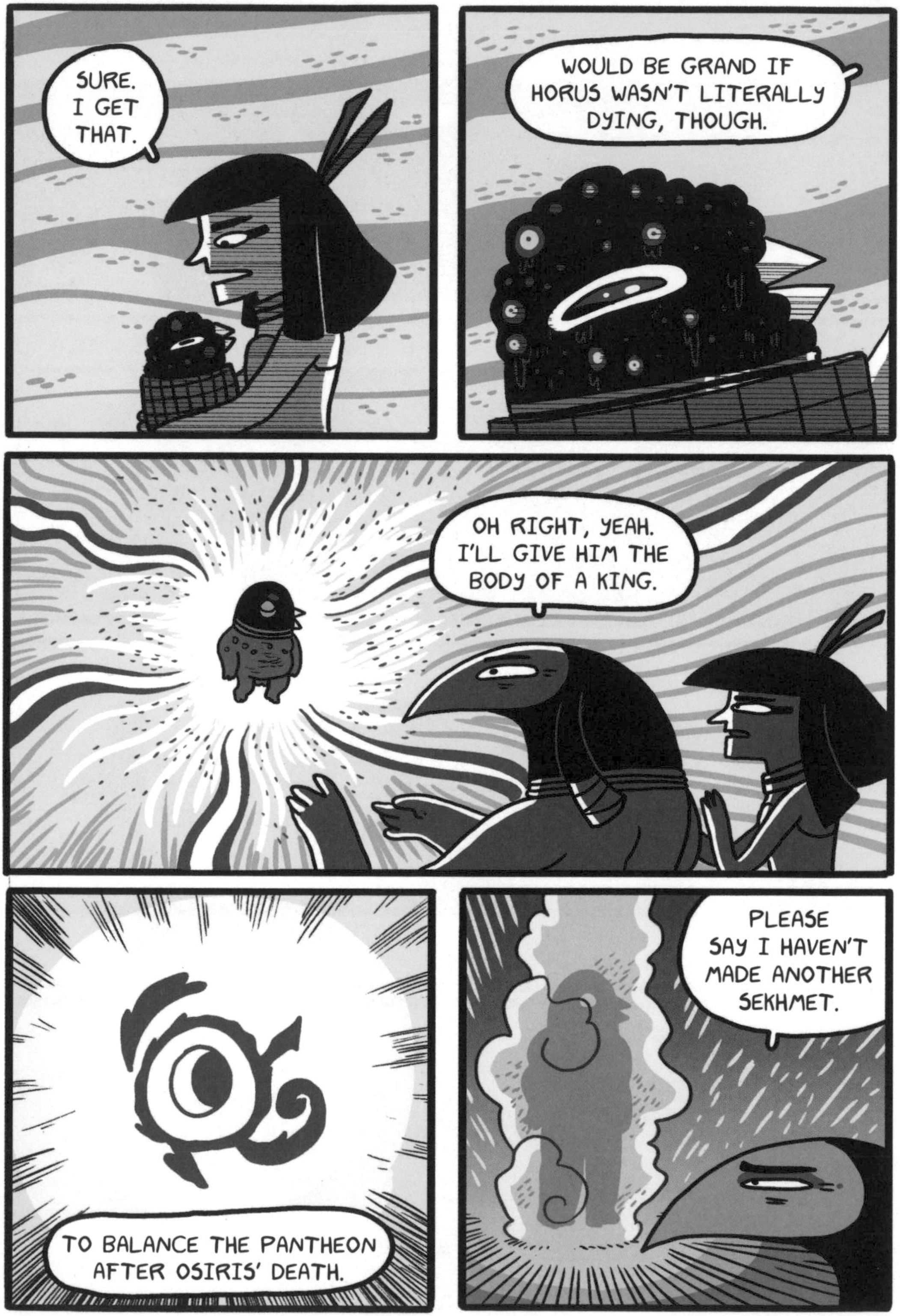
SURE. I GET THAT.
WOULD BE GRAND IF HORUS WASN'T LITERALLY DYING, THOUGH.
OH RIGHT, YEAH. I'LL GIVE HIM THE BODY OF A KING.
TO BALANCE THE PANTHEON AFTER OSIRIS' DEATH.
PLEASE SAY I HAVEN'T MADE ANOTHER SEKHMET.

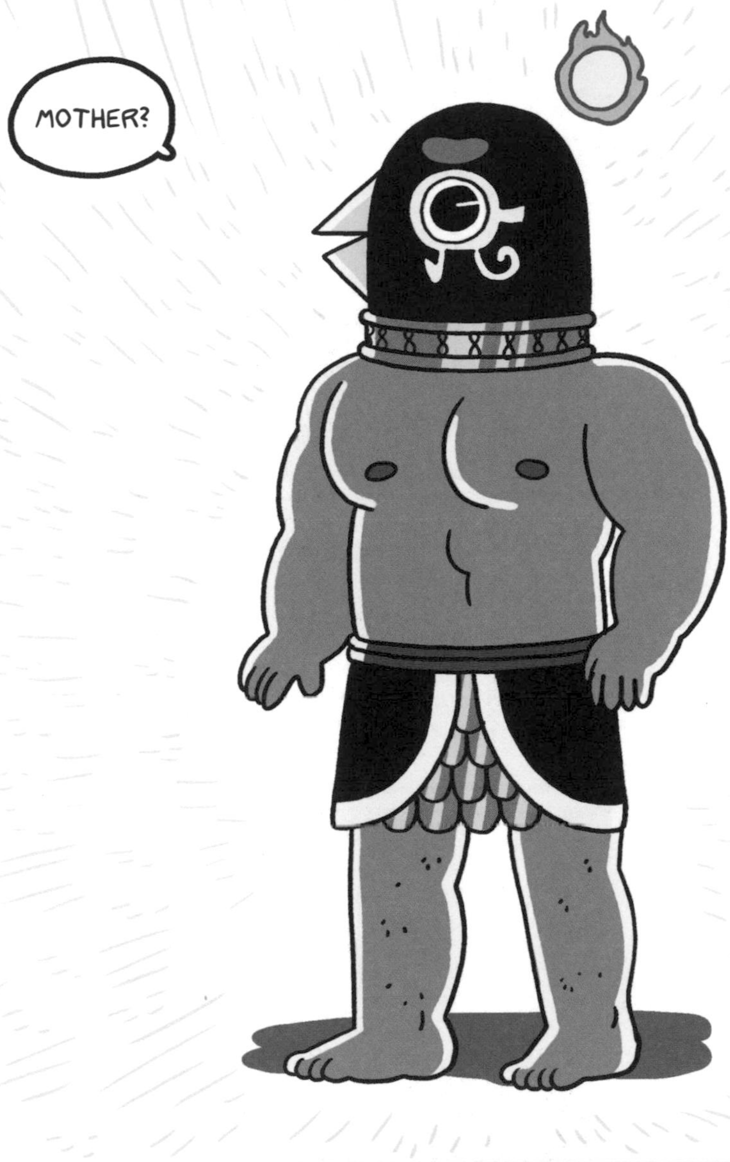
MOTHER?

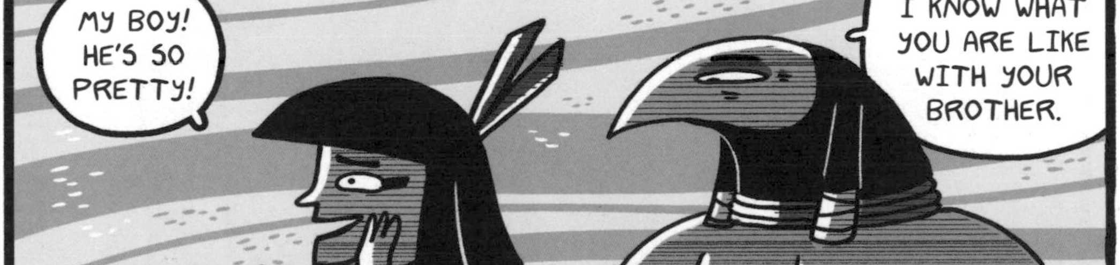
MY BOY! HE'S SO PRETTY!
EASY, ISIS. I KNOW WHAT YOU ARE LIKE WITH YOUR BROTHER.

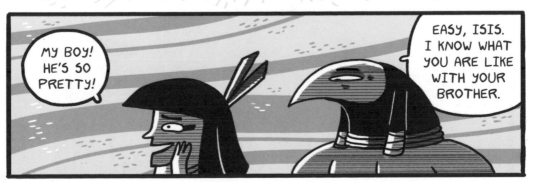

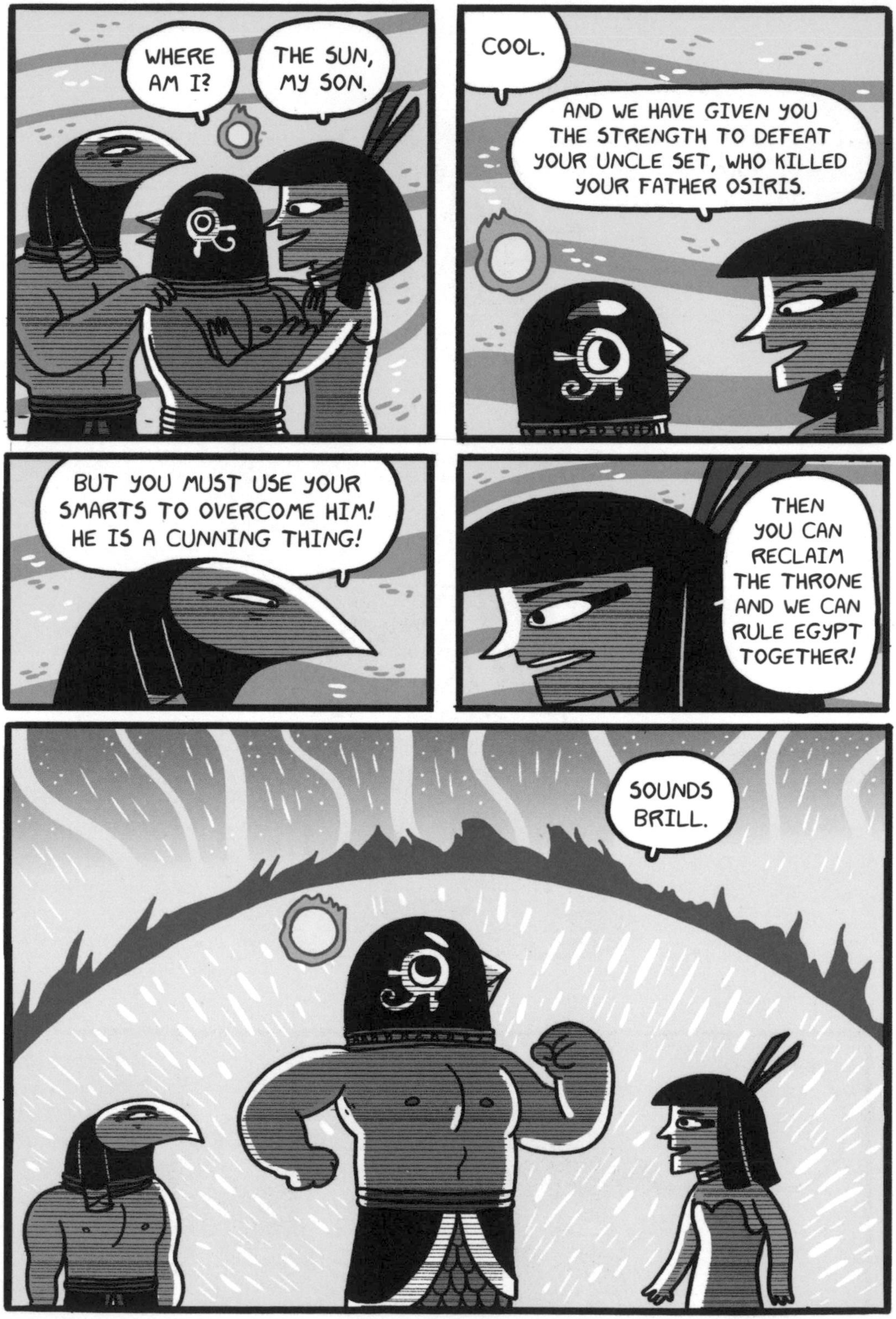
WHERE AM I?
THE SUN, MY SON.
COOL.
AND WE HAVE GIVEN YOU THE STRENGTH TO DEFEAT YOUR UNCLE SET, WHO KILLED YOUR FATHER OSIRIS.
BUT YOU MUST USE YOUR SMARTS TO OVERCOME HIM! HE IS A CUNNING THING!
THEN YOU CAN RECLAIM THE THRONE AND WE CAN RULE EGYPT TOGETHER!
SOUNDS BRILL.

CHAPTER EIGHT

✶✶✶ SEDUCTION ✶✶✶

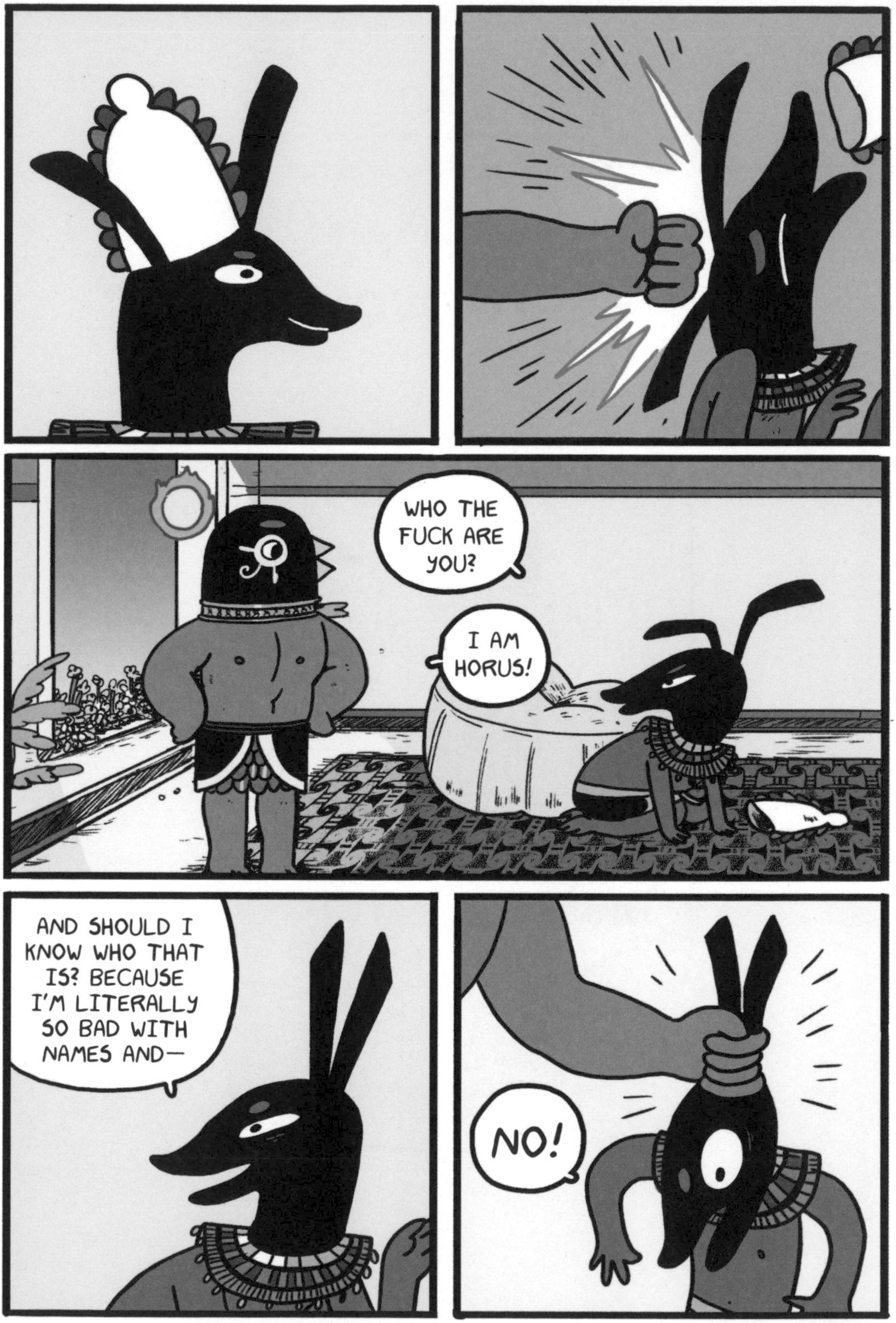
WHO THE FUCK ARE YOU?
I AM HORUS!
AND SHOULD I KNOW WHO THAT IS? BECAUSE I'M LITERALLY SO BAD WITH NAMES AND—
NO!

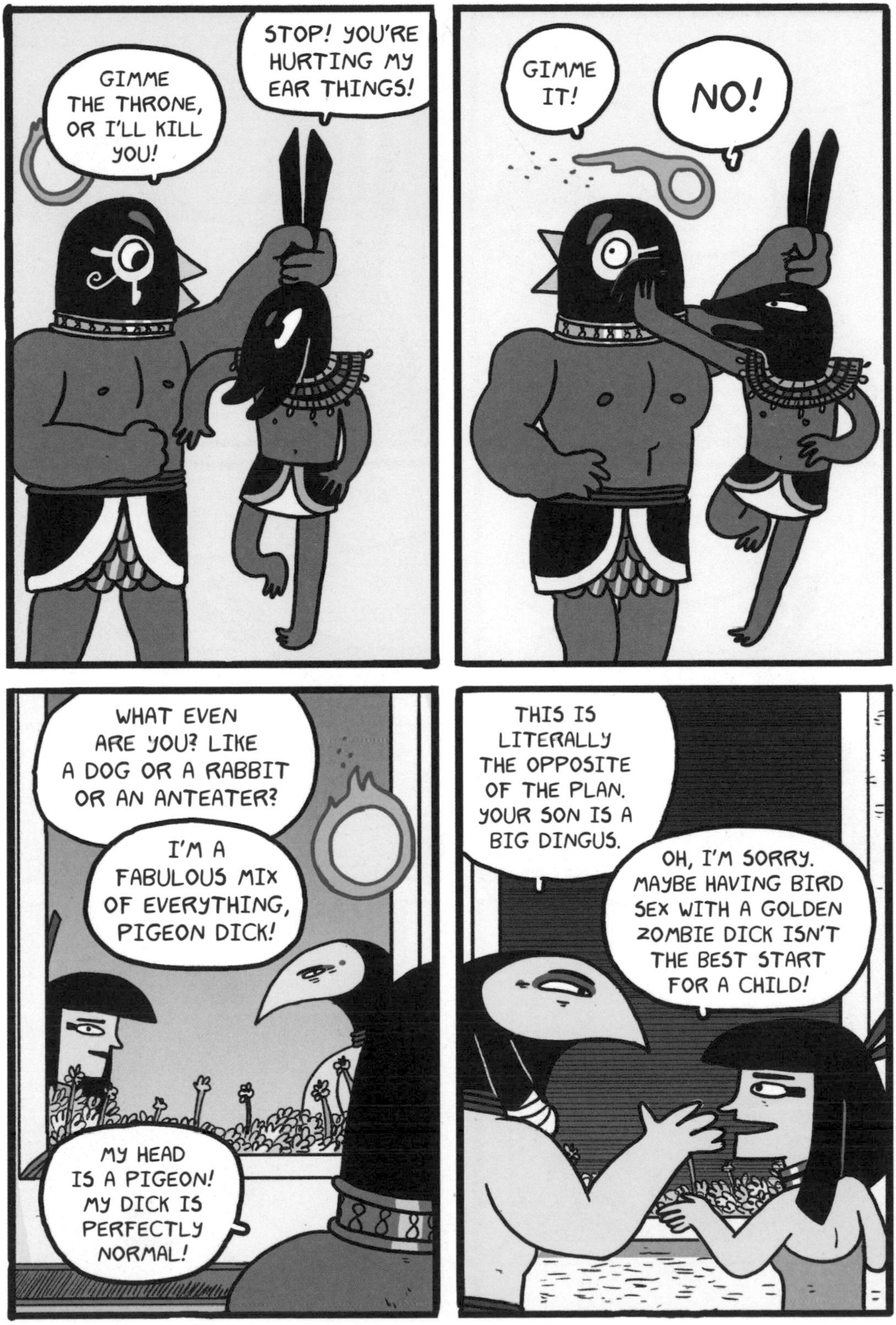
STOP! YOU'RE HURTING MY EAR THINGS!
GIMME THE THRONE, OR I'LL KILL YOU!
GIMME IT!
NO!
WHAT EVEN ARE YOU? LIKE A DOG OR A RABBIT OR AN ANTEATER?
I'M A FABULOUS MIX OF EVERYTHING, PIGEON DICK!
MY HEAD IS A PIGEON! MY DICK IS PERFECTLY NORMAL!
THIS IS LITERALLY THE OPPOSITE OF THE PLAN. YOUR SON IS A BIG DINGUS.
OH, I'M SORRY. MAYBE HAVING BIRD SEX WITH A GOLDEN ZOMBIE DICK ISN'T THE BEST START FOR A CHILD!

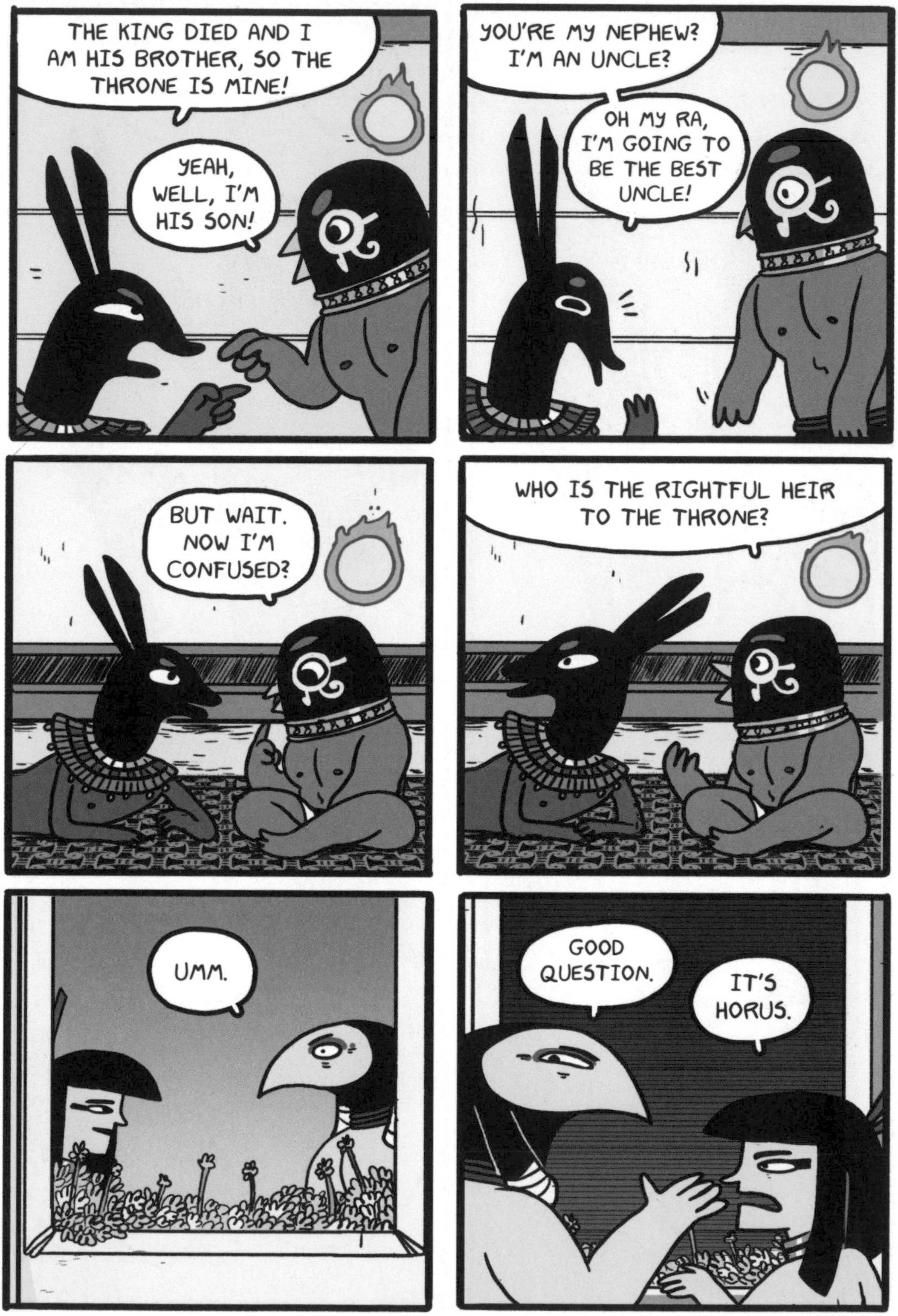
THE KING DIED AND I AM HIS BROTHER, SO THE THRONE IS MINE!
YEAH, WELL, I'M HIS SON!
YOU'RE MY NEPHEW? I'M AN UNCLE?
OH MY RA, I'M GOING TO BE THE BEST UNCLE!
BUT WAIT. NOW I'M CONFUSED?
WHO IS THE RIGHTFUL HEIR TO THE THRONE?
UMM.
GOOD QUESTION.
IT'S HORUS.

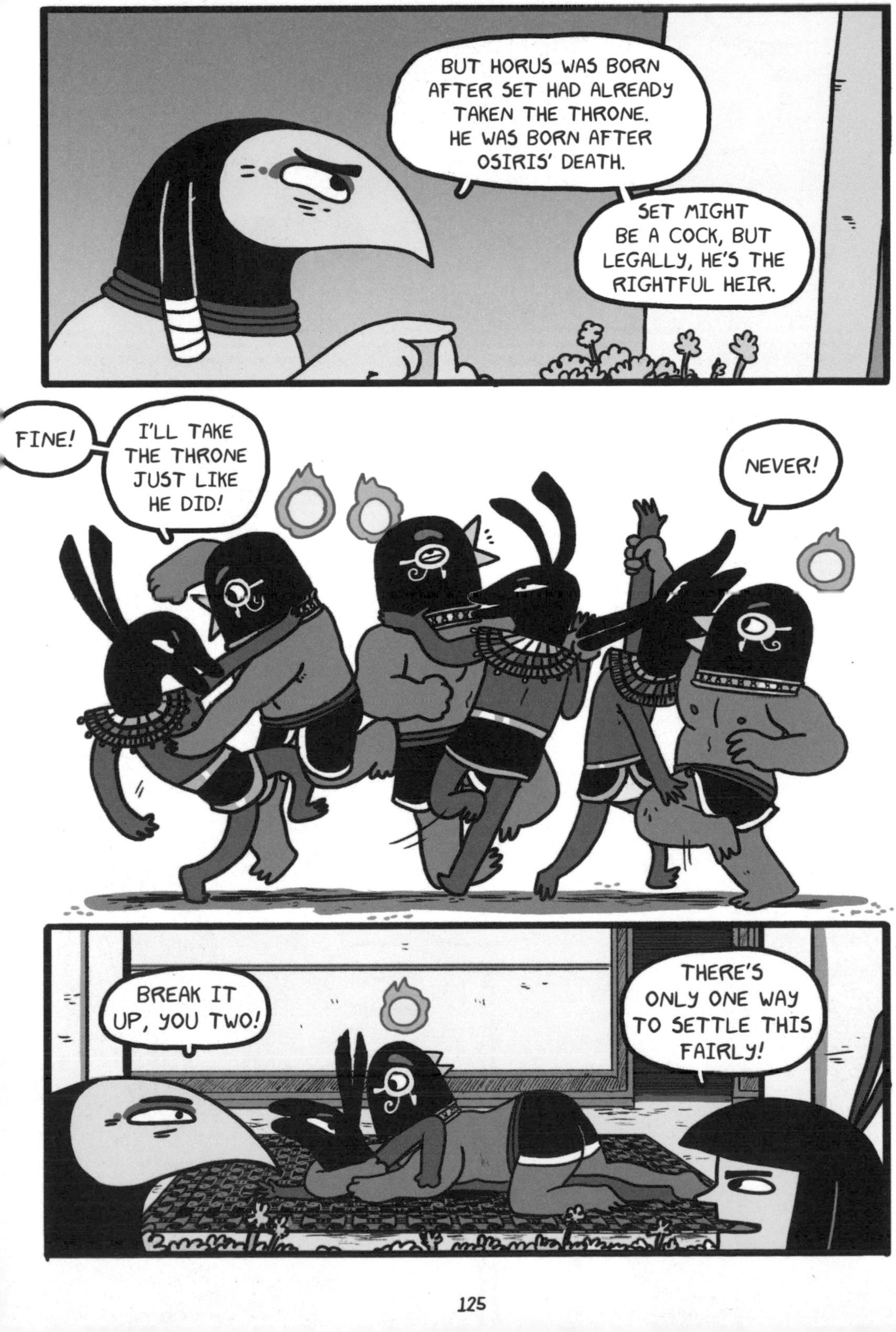
BUT HORUS WAS BORN AFTER SET HAD ALREADY TAKEN THE THRONE. HE WAS BORN AFTER OSIRIS' DEATH.
SET MIGHT BE A COCK, BUT LEGALLY, HE'S THE RIGHTFUL HEIR.
FINE!
I'LL TAKE THE THRONE JUST LIKE HE DID!
NEVER!
BREAK IT UP, YOU TWO!
THERE'S ONLY ONE WAY TO SETTLE THIS FAIRLY!

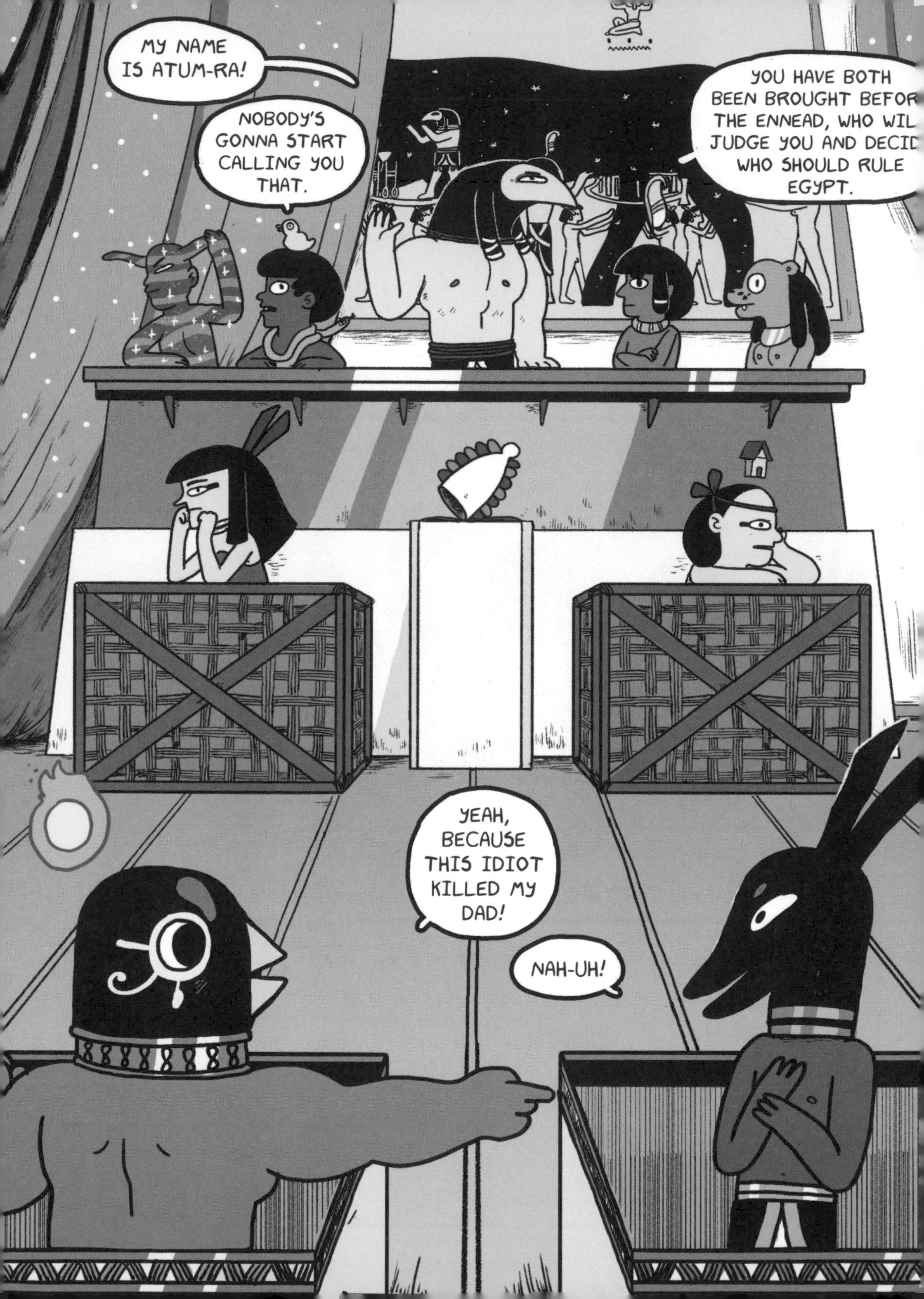
MY NAME IS ATUM-RA!
NOBODY'S GONNA START CALLING YOU THAT.
YOU HAVE BOTH BEEN BROUGHT BEFOR THE ENNEAD, WHO WIL JUDGE YOU AND DECID WHO SHOULD RULE EGYPT.
YEAH, BECAUSE THIS IDIOT KILLED MY DAD!
NAH-UH!

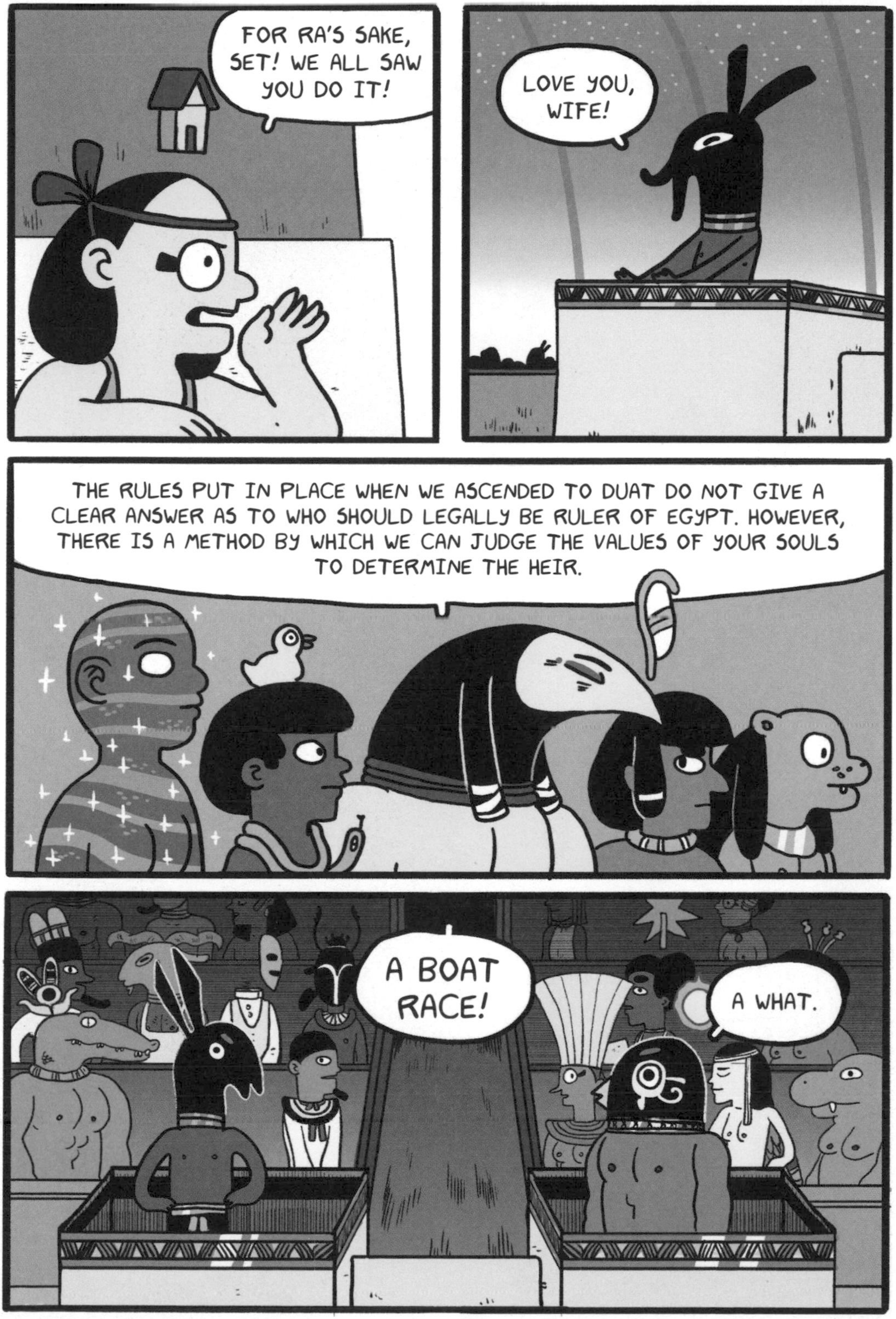
FOR RA'S SAKE, SET! WE ALL SAW YOU DO IT!
LOVE YOU, WIFE!
THE RULES PUT IN PLACE WHEN WE ASCENDED TO DUAT DO NOT GIVE A CLEAR ANSWER AS TO WHO SHOULD LEGALLY BE RULER OF EGYPT. HOWEVER, THERE IS A METHOD BY WHICH WE CAN JUDGE THE VALUES OF YOUR SOULS TO DETERMINE THE HEIR.
A BOAT RACE!
A WHAT.

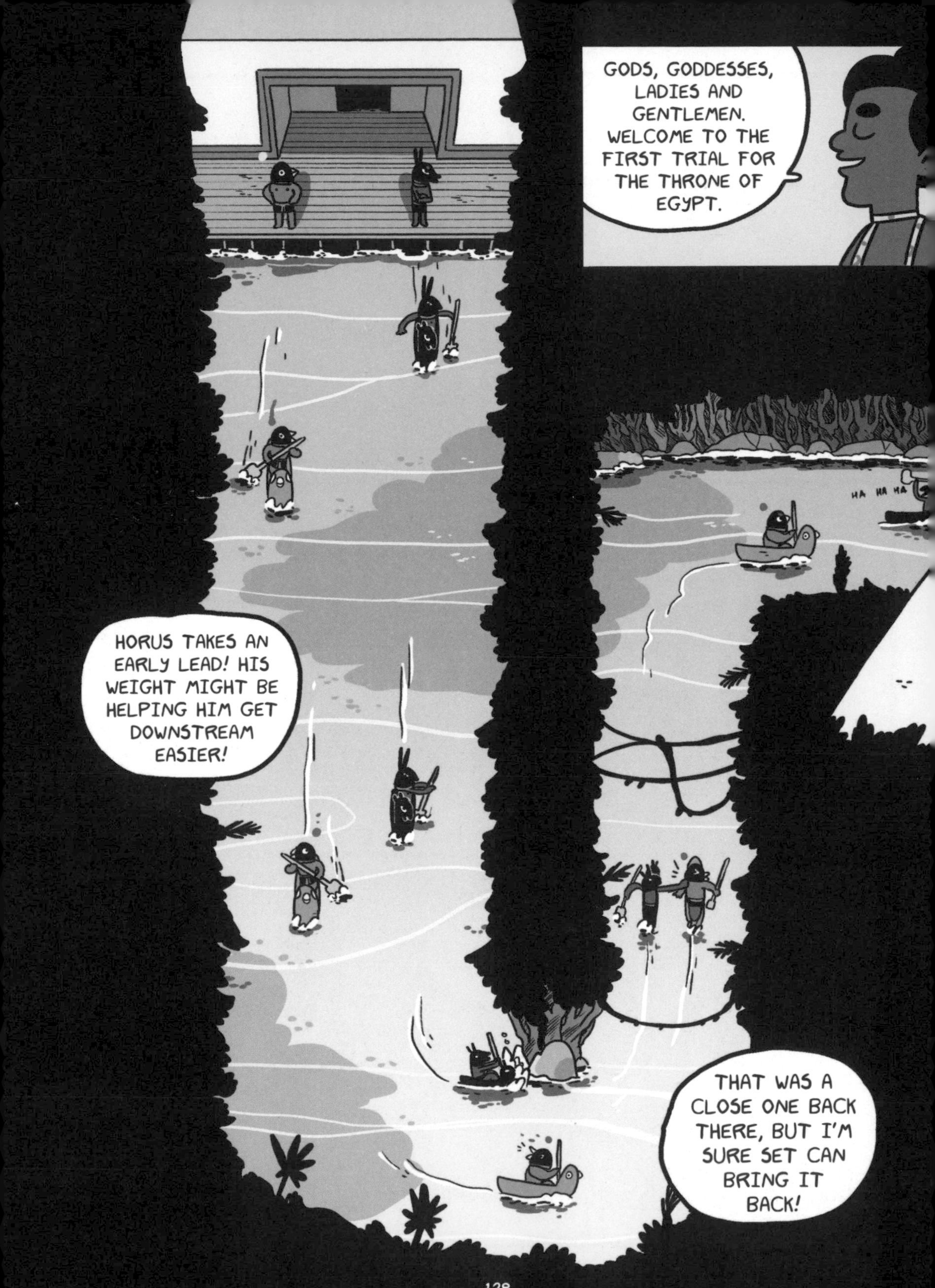
GODS, GODDESSES, LADIES AND GENTLEMEN. WELCOME TO THE FIRST TRIAL FOR THE THRONE OF EGYPT.
HORUS TAKES AN EARLY LEAD! HIS WEIGHT MIGHT BE HELPING HIM GET DOWNSTREAM EASIER!
HA HA HA
THAT WAS A CLOSE ONE BACK THERE, BUT I'M SURE SET CAN BRING IT BACK!

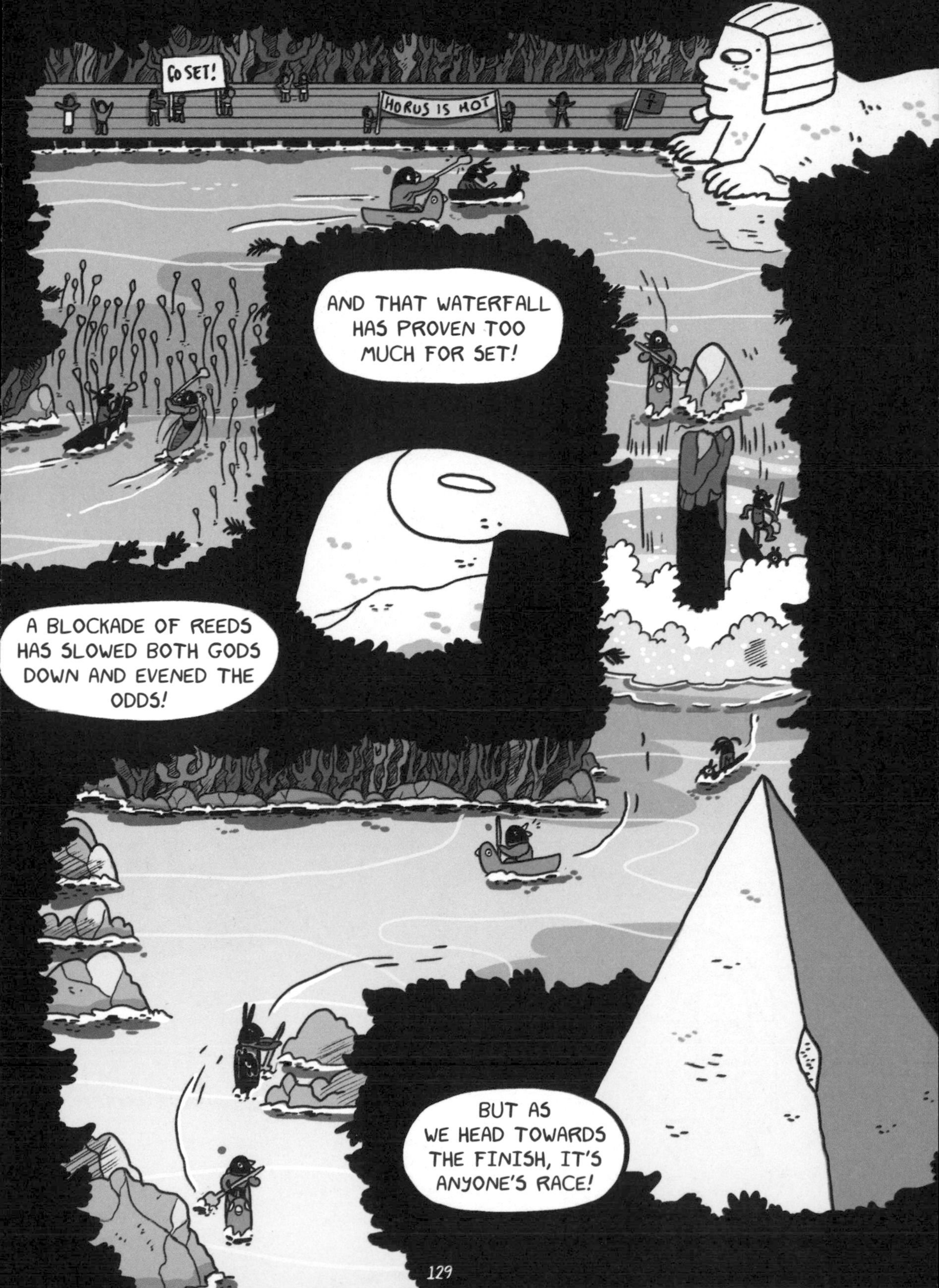
GO SET!
HORUS IS HOT
AND THAT WATERFALL HAS PROVEN TOO MUCH FOR SET!
A BLOCKADE OF REEDS HAS SLOWED BOTH GODS DOWN AND EVENED THE ODDS!
BUT AS WE HEAD TOWARDS THE FINISH, IT'S ANYONE'S RACE!

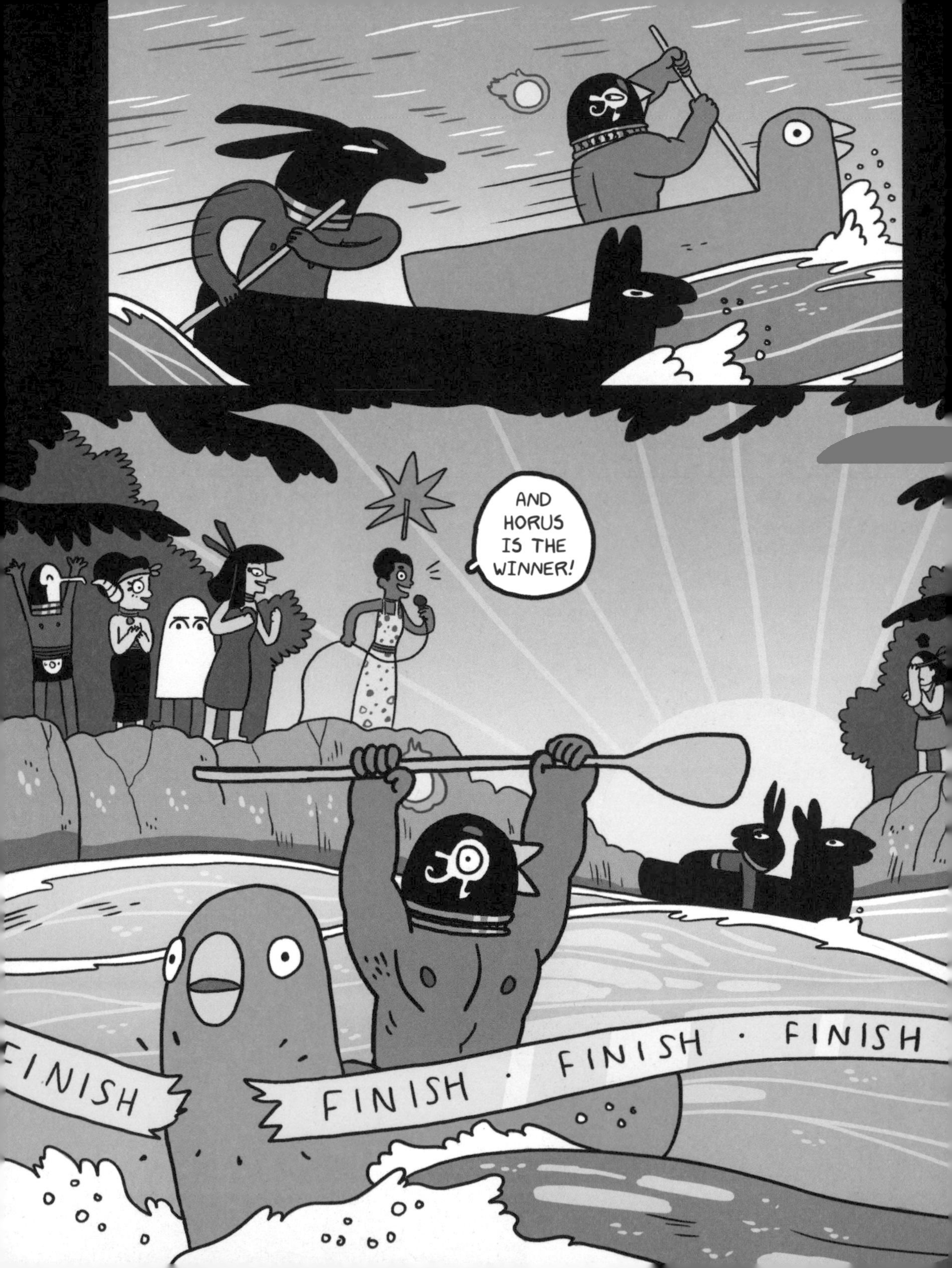
AND HORUS IS THE WINNER!
FINISH · FINISH · FINISH · FINISH

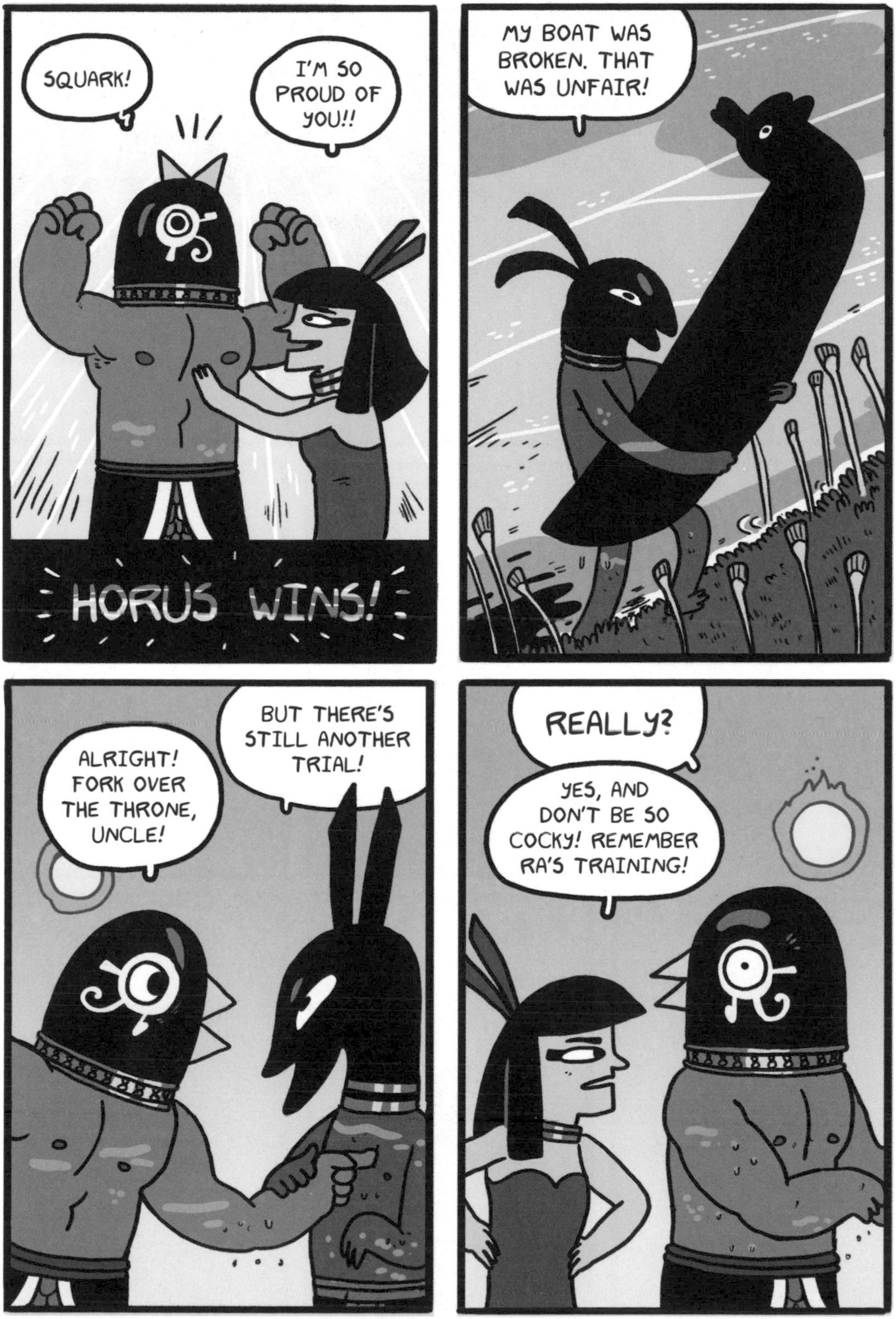
SQUARK!
I'M SO PROUD OF YOU!!
HORUS WINS!
MY BOAT WAS BROKEN. THAT WAS UNFAIR!
ALRIGHT! FORK OVER THE THRONE, UNCLE!
BUT THERE'S STILL ANOTHER TRIAL!
REALLY?
YES, AND DON'T BE SO COCKY! REMEMBER RA'S TRAINING!

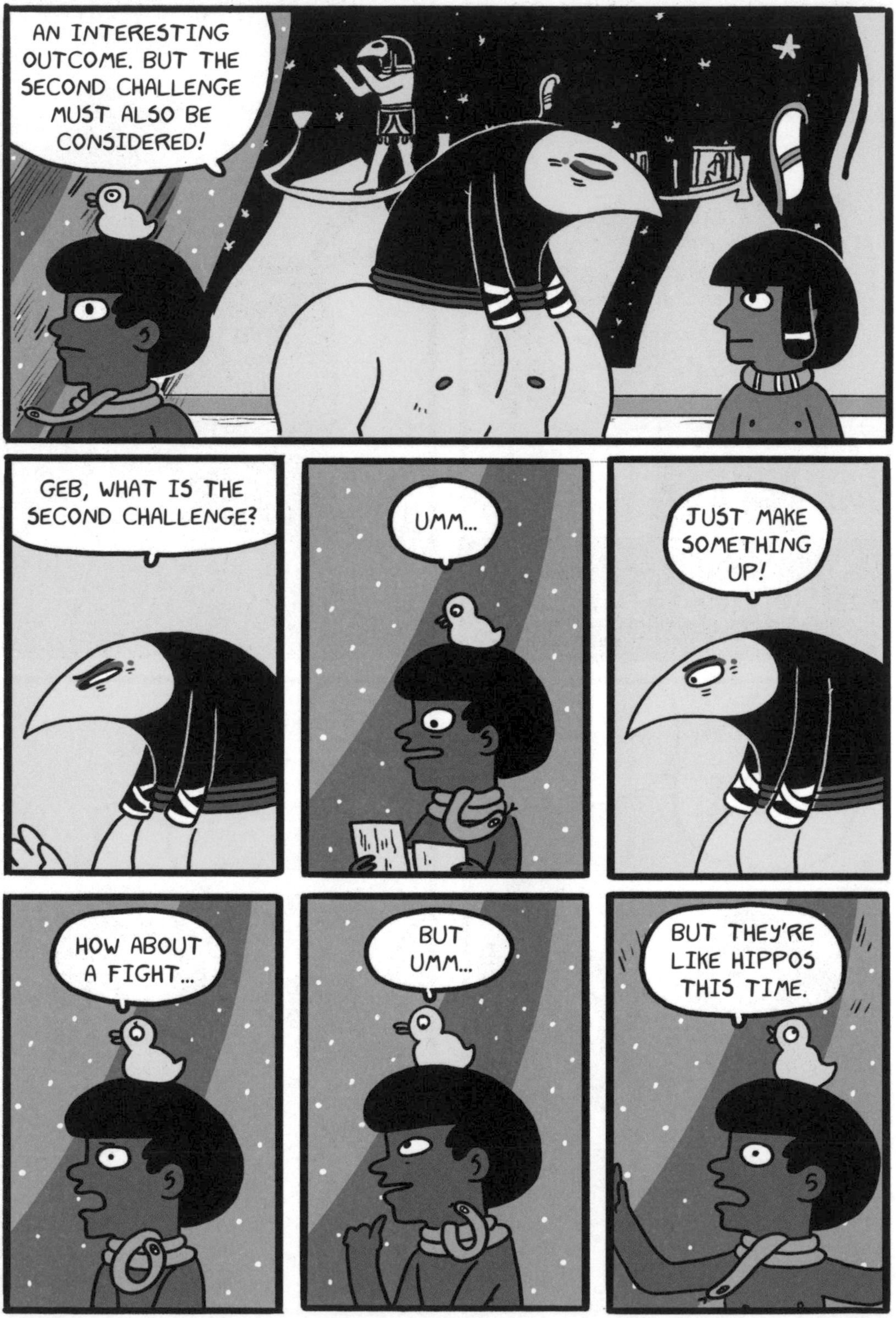
AN INTERESTING OUTCOME. BUT THE SECOND CHALLENGE MUST ALSO BE CONSIDERED!
GEB, WHAT IS THE SECOND CHALLENGE?
UMM...
JUST MAKE SOMETHING UP!
HOW ABOUT A FIGHT...
BUT UMM...
BUT THEY'RE LIKE HIPPOS THIS TIME.

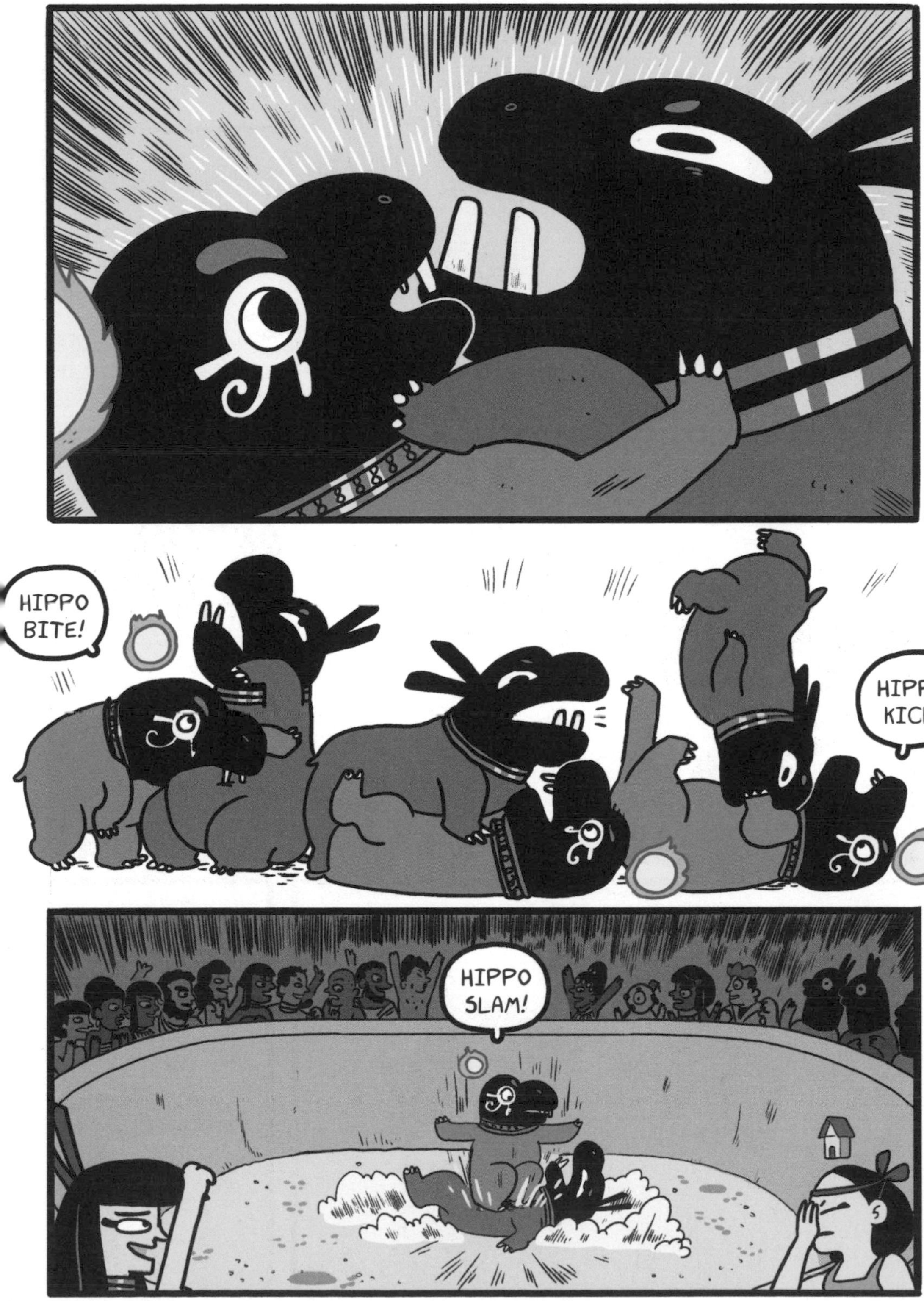
HIPPO BITE!
HIPPO KICK!
HIPPO SLAM!

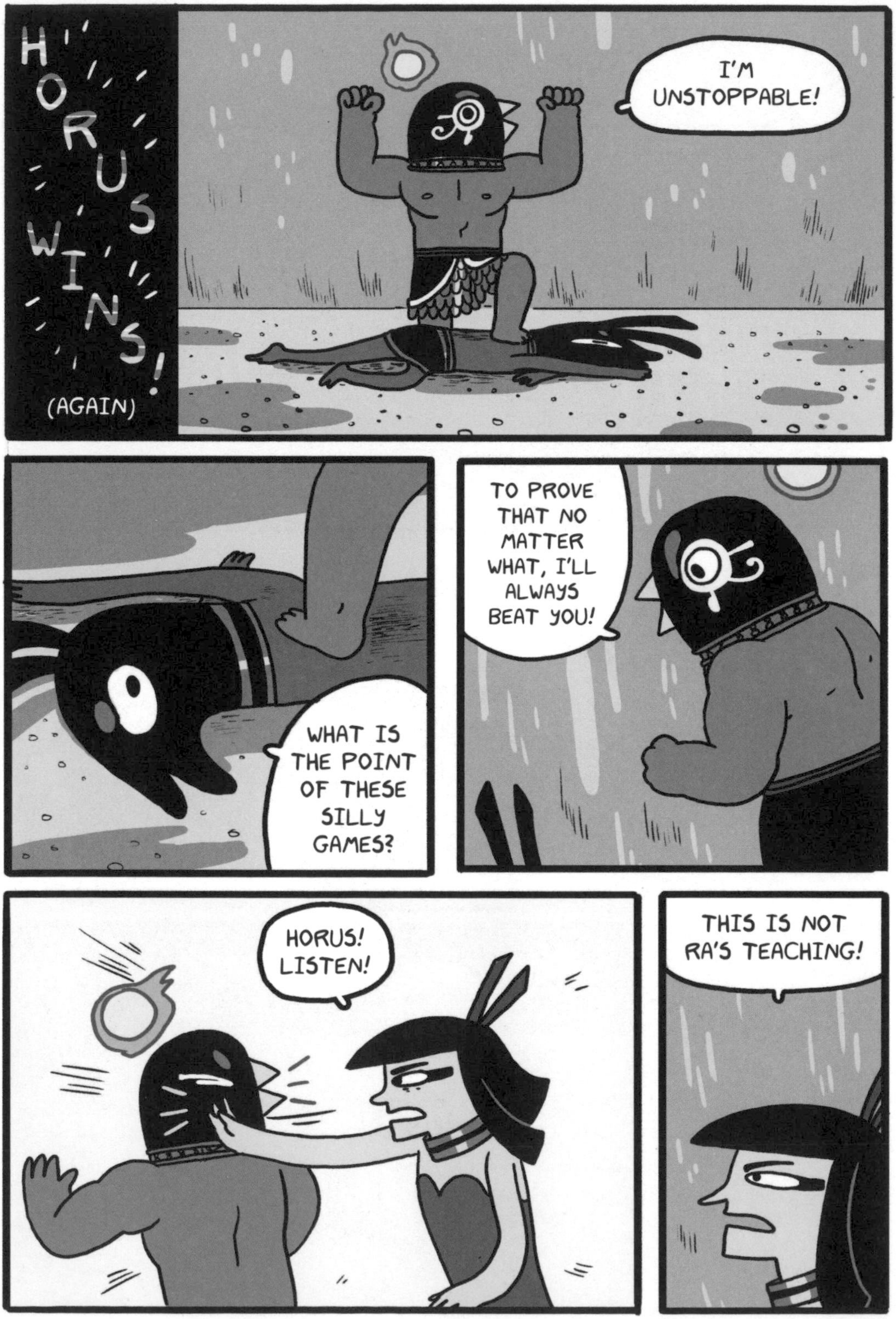
HORUS WINS!
(AGAIN)
I'M UNSTOPPABLE!
WHAT IS THE POINT OF THESE SILLY GAMES?
TO PROVE THAT NO MATTER WHAT, I'LL ALWAYS BEAT YOU!
HORUS! LISTEN!
THIS IS NOT RA'S TEACHING!

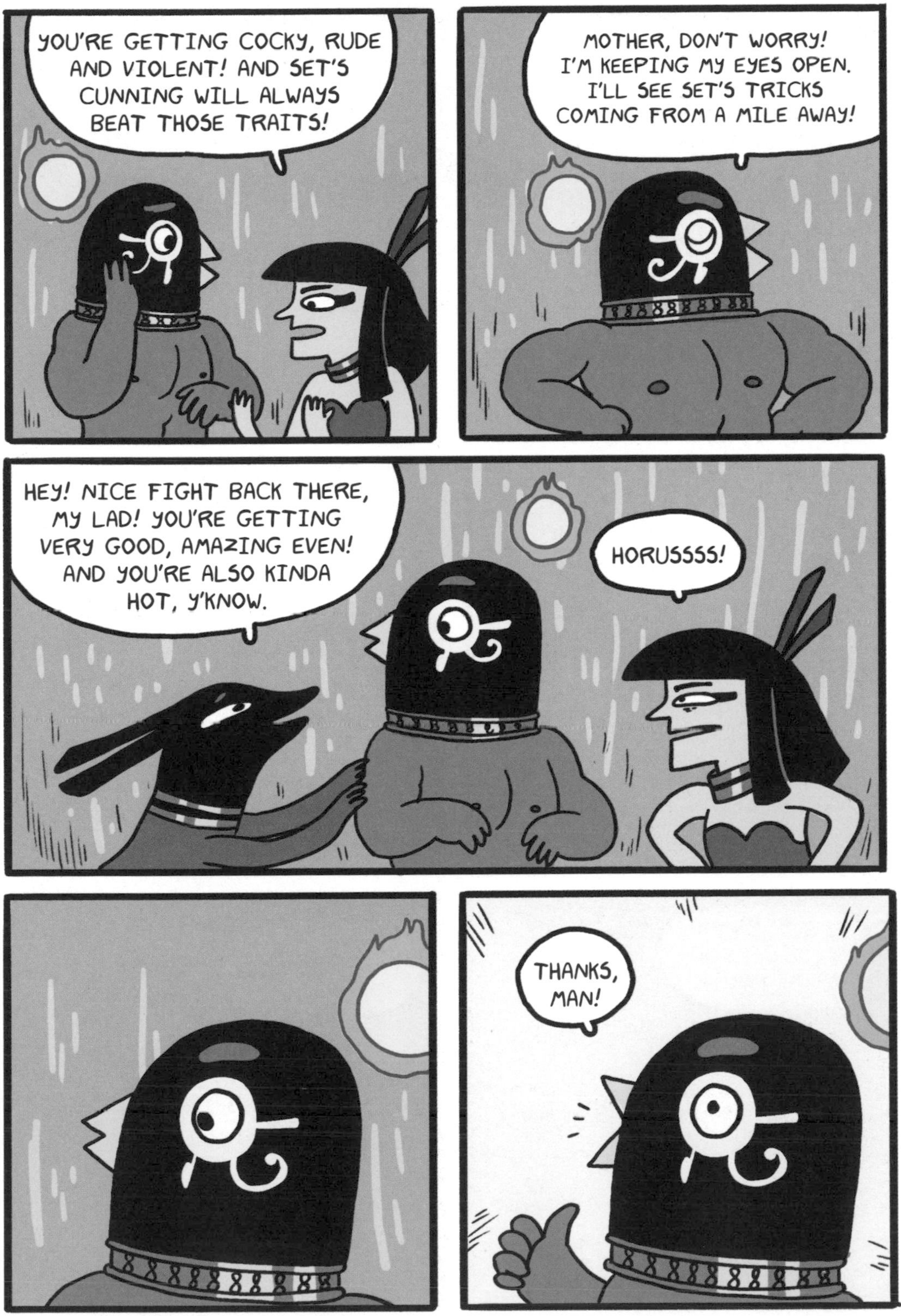
YOU'RE GETTING COCKY, RUDE AND VIOLENT! AND SET'S CUNNING WILL ALWAYS BEAT THOSE TRAITS!
MOTHER, DON'T WORRY! I'M KEEPING MY EYES OPEN. I'LL SEE SET'S TRICKS COMING FROM A MILE AWAY!
HEY! NICE FIGHT BACK THERE, MY LAD! YOU'RE GETTING VERY GOOD, AMAZING EVEN! AND YOU'RE ALSO KINDA HOT, Y'KNOW.
HORUSSSS!
THANKS, MAN!

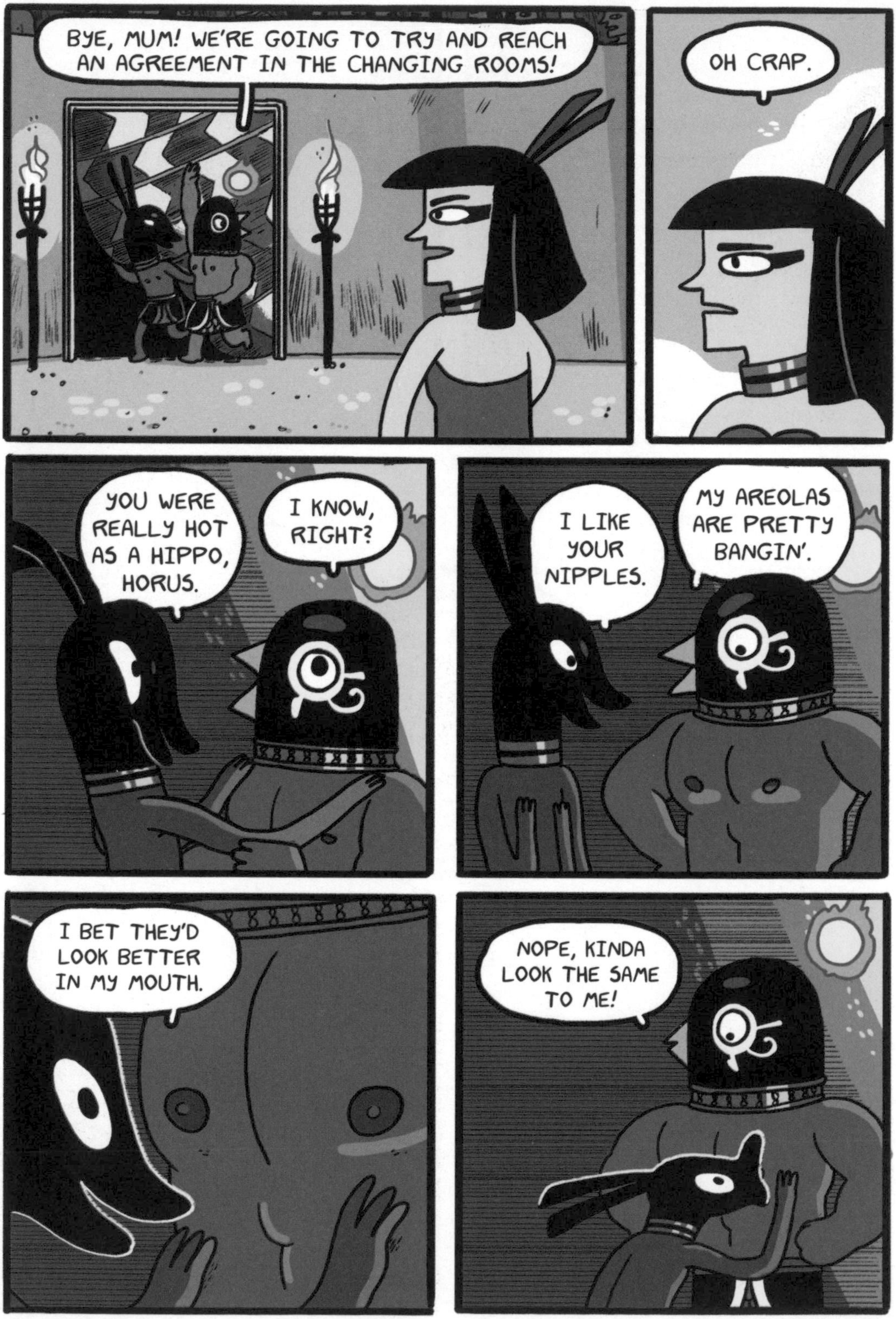
BYE, MUM! WE'RE GOING TO TRY AND REACH AN AGREEMENT IN THE CHANGING ROOMS!
OH CRAP.
YOU WERE REALLY HOT AS A HIPPO, HORUS.
I KNOW, RIGHT?
I LIKE YOUR NIPPLES.
MY AREOLAS ARE PRETTY BANGIN'.
I BET THEY'D LOOK BETTER IN MY MOUTH.
NOPE, KINDA LOOK THE SAME TO ME!

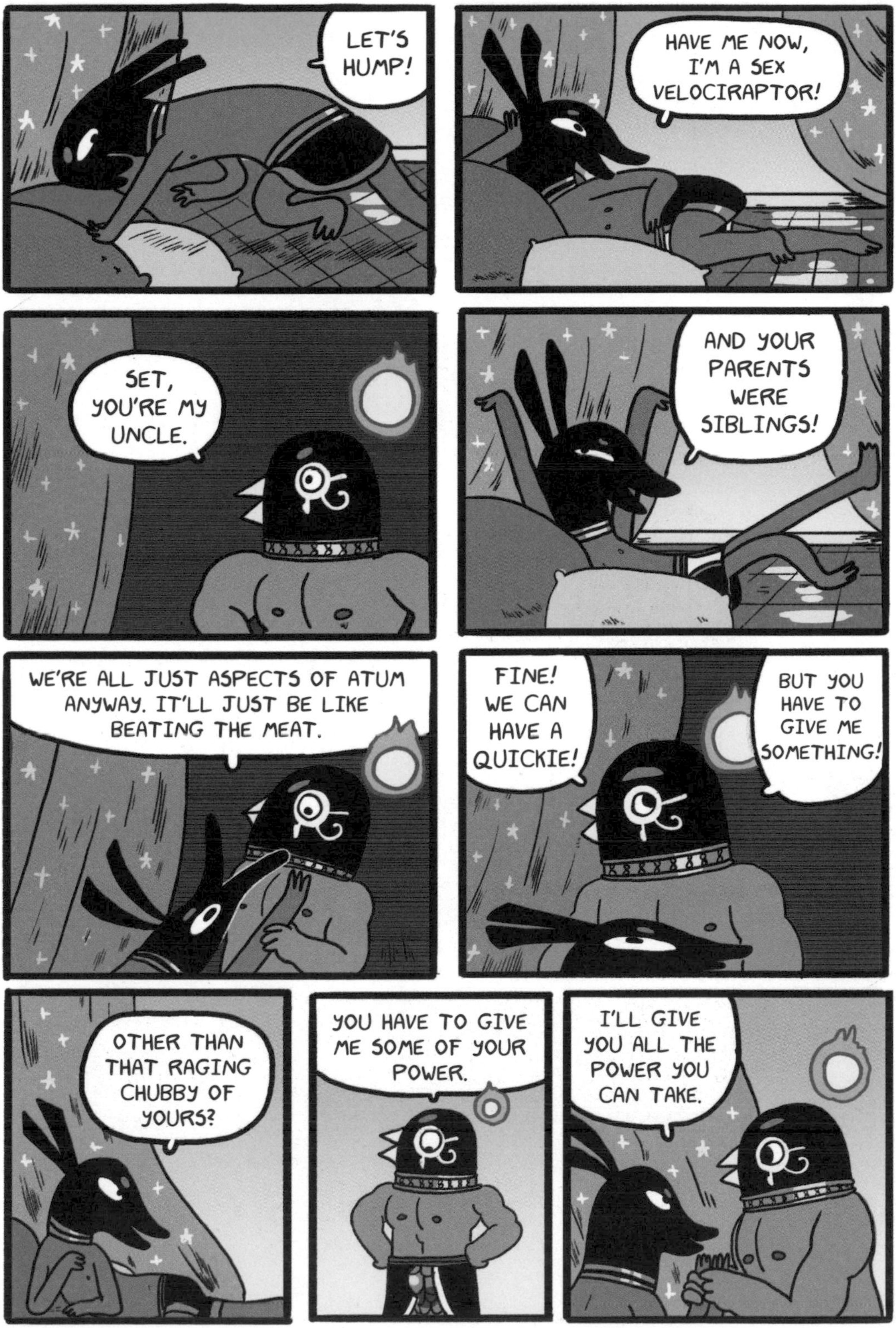

LET'S HUMP!
HAVE ME NOW, I'M A SEX VELOCIRAPTOR!
SET, YOU'RE MY UNCLE.
AND YOUR PARENTS WERE SIBLINGS!
WE'RE ALL JUST ASPECTS OF ATUM ANYWAY. IT'LL JUST BE LIKE BEATING THE MEAT.
FINE! WE CAN HAVE A QUICKIE!
BUT YOU HAVE TO GIVE ME SOMETHING!
OTHER THAN THAT RAGING CHUBBY OF YOURS?
YOU HAVE TO GIVE ME SOME OF YOUR POWER.
I'LL GIVE YOU ALL THE POWER YOU CAN TAKE.

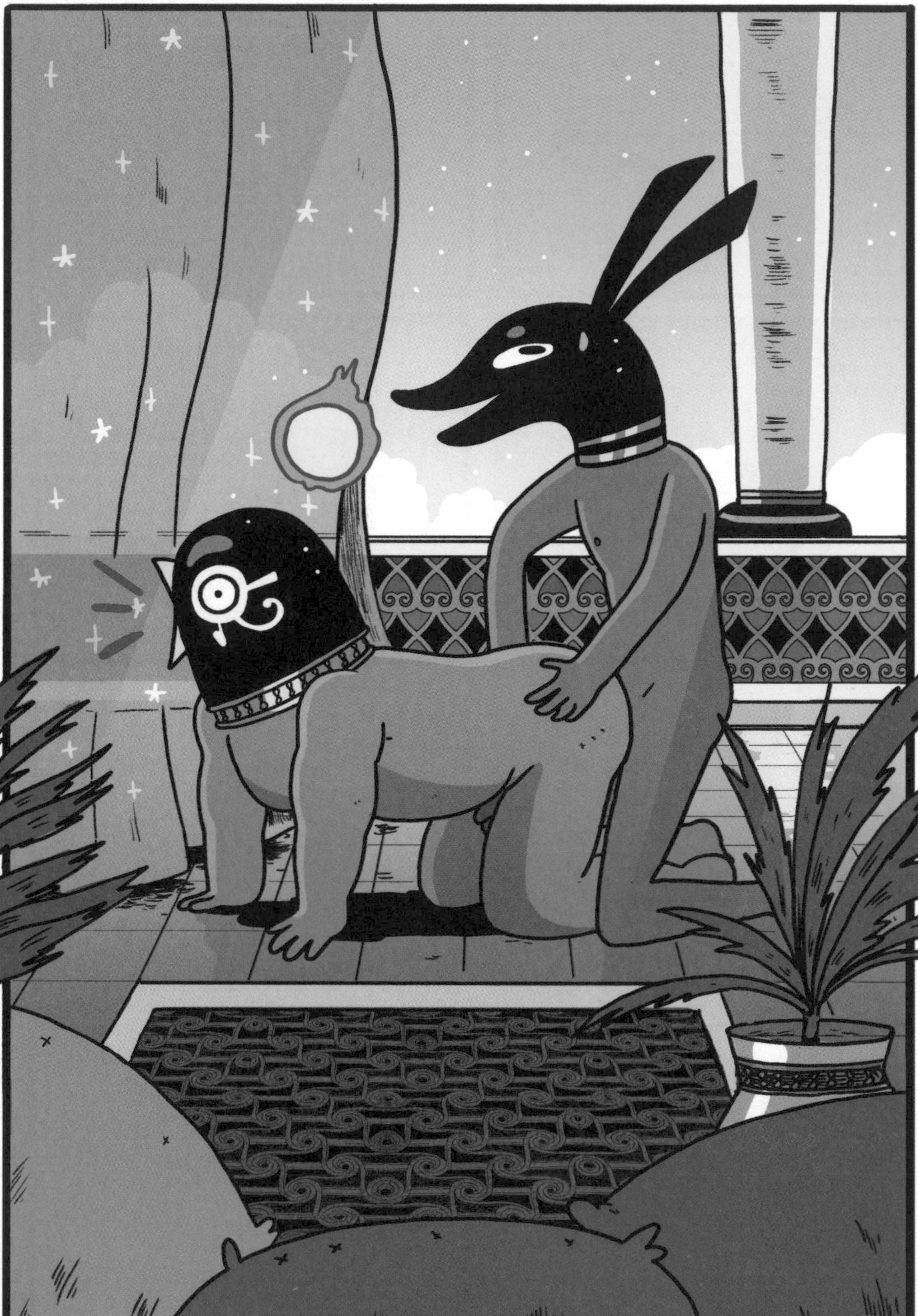

CHAPTER NINE

★★★ DECEPTION ★★★

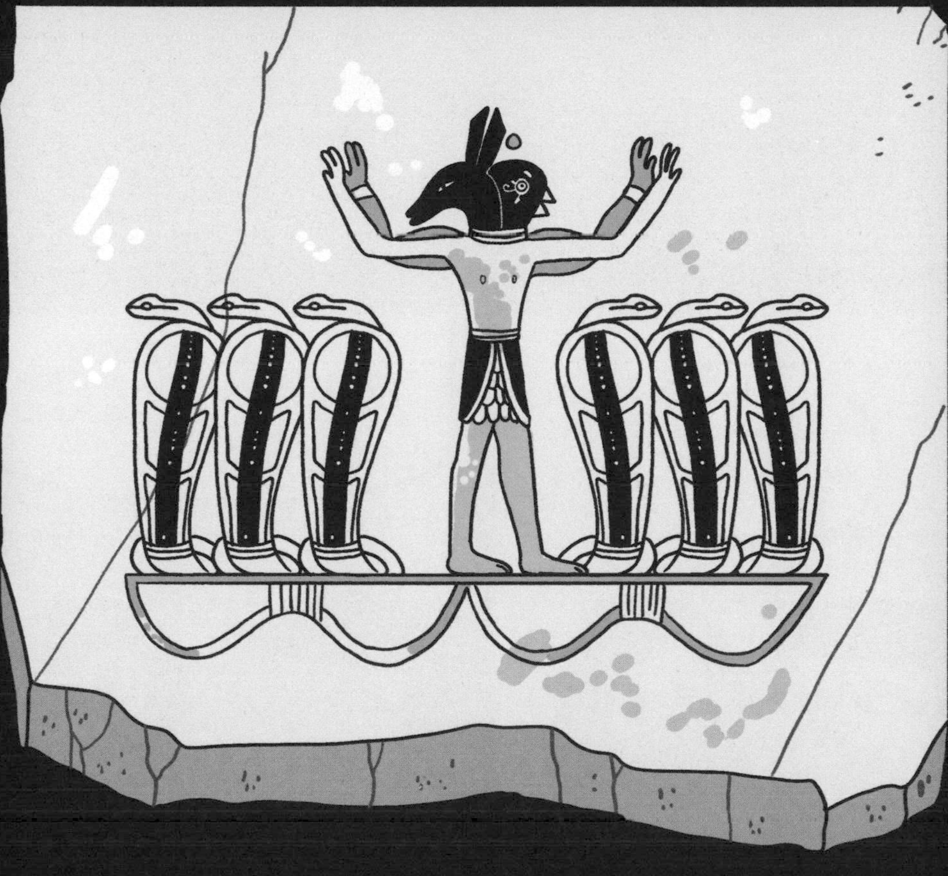

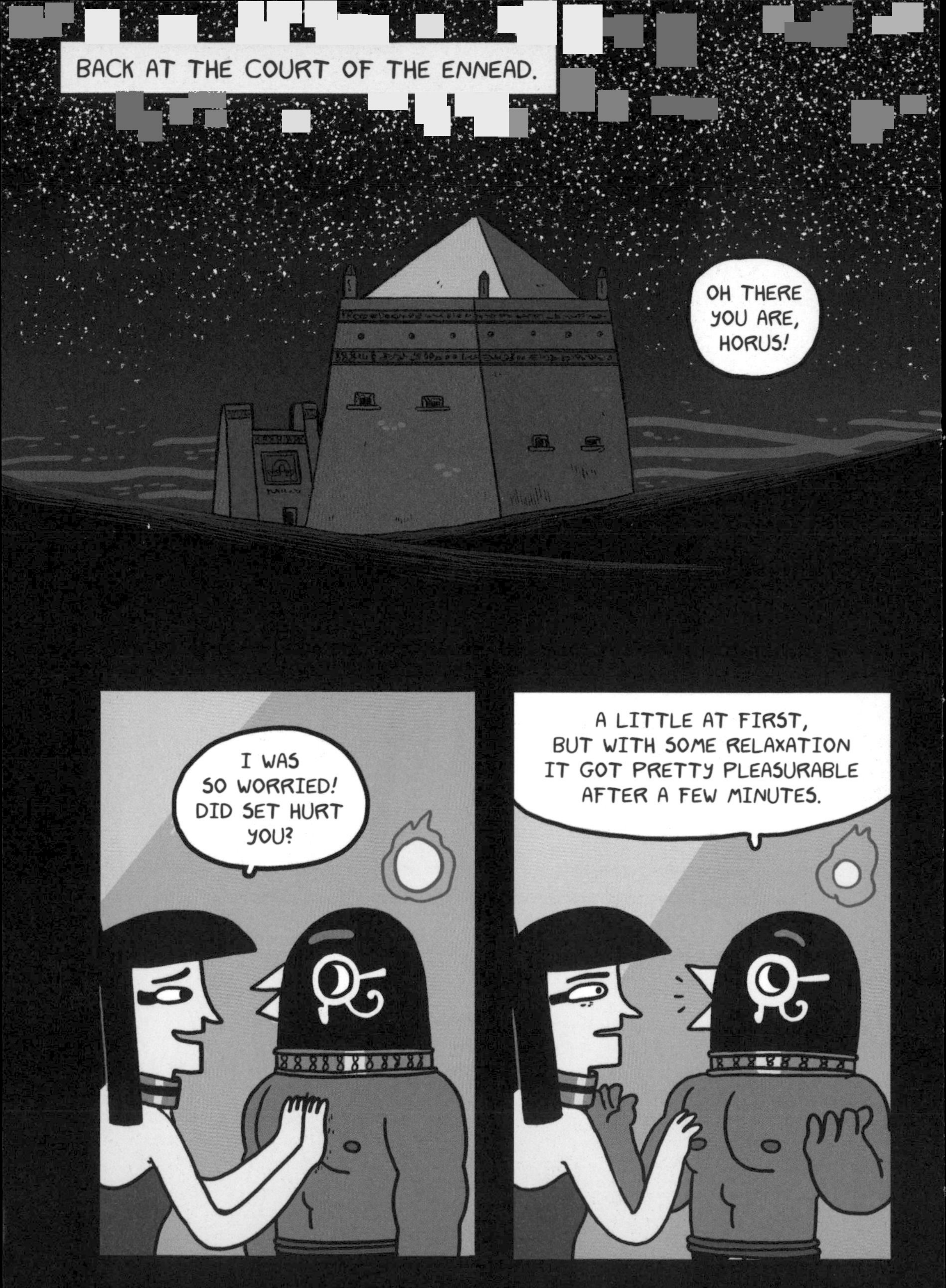
BACK AT THE COURT OF THE ENNEAD.
OH THERE YOU ARE, HORUS!
I WAS SO WORRIED! DID SET HURT YOU?
A LITTLE AT FIRST, BUT WITH SOME RELAXATION IT GOT PRETTY PLEASURABLE AFTER A FEW MINUTES.

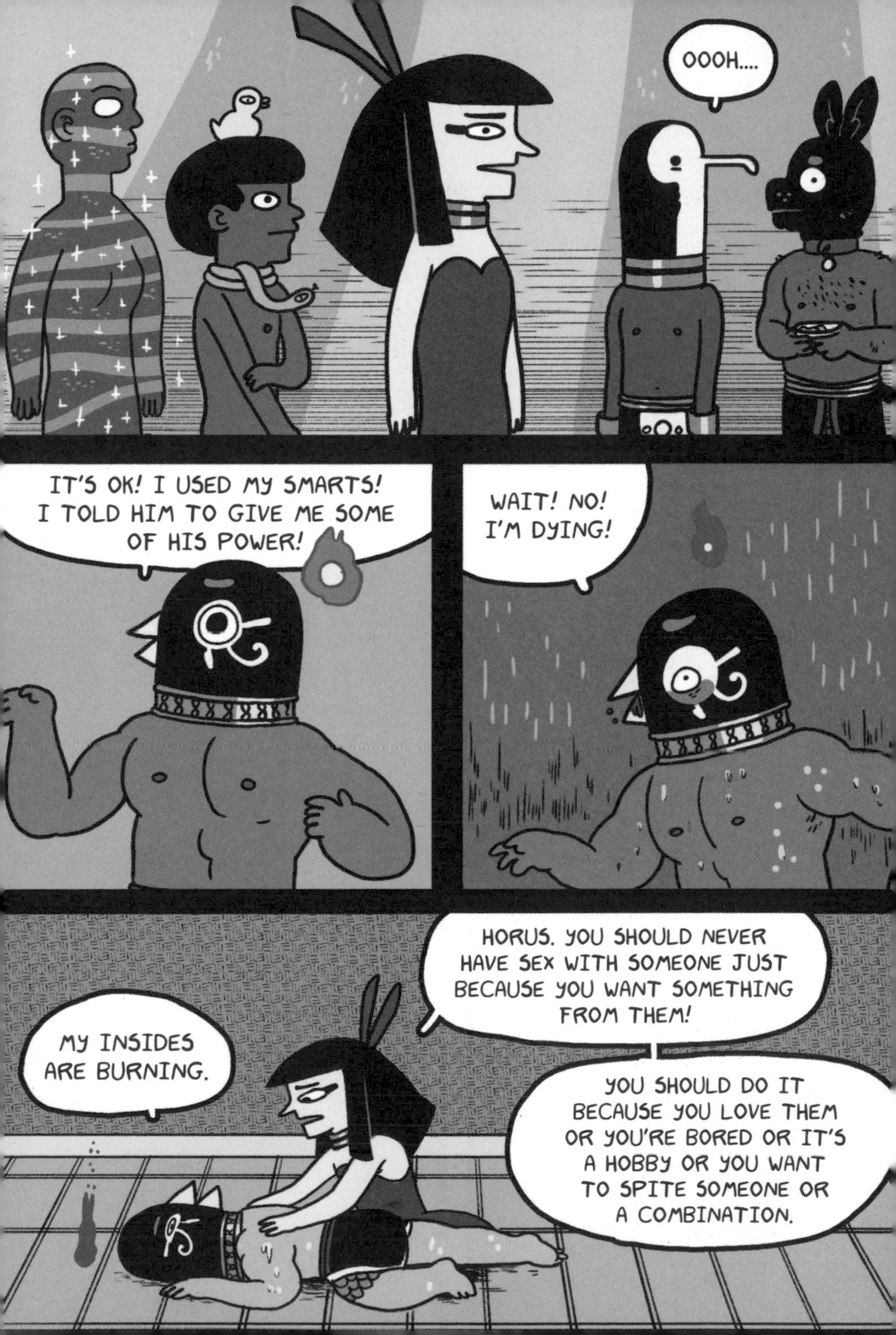
OOOH....
IT'S OK! I USED MY SMARTS! I TOLD HIM TO GIVE ME SOME OF HIS POWER!
WAIT! NO! I'M DYING!
MY INSIDES ARE BURNING.
HORUS. YOU SHOULD NEVER HAVE SEX WITH SOMEONE JUST BECAUSE YOU WANT SOMETHING FROM THEM!
YOU SHOULD DO IT BECAUSE YOU LOVE THEM OR YOU'RE BORED OR IT'S A HOBBY OR YOU WANT TO SPITE SOMEONE OR A COMBINATION.

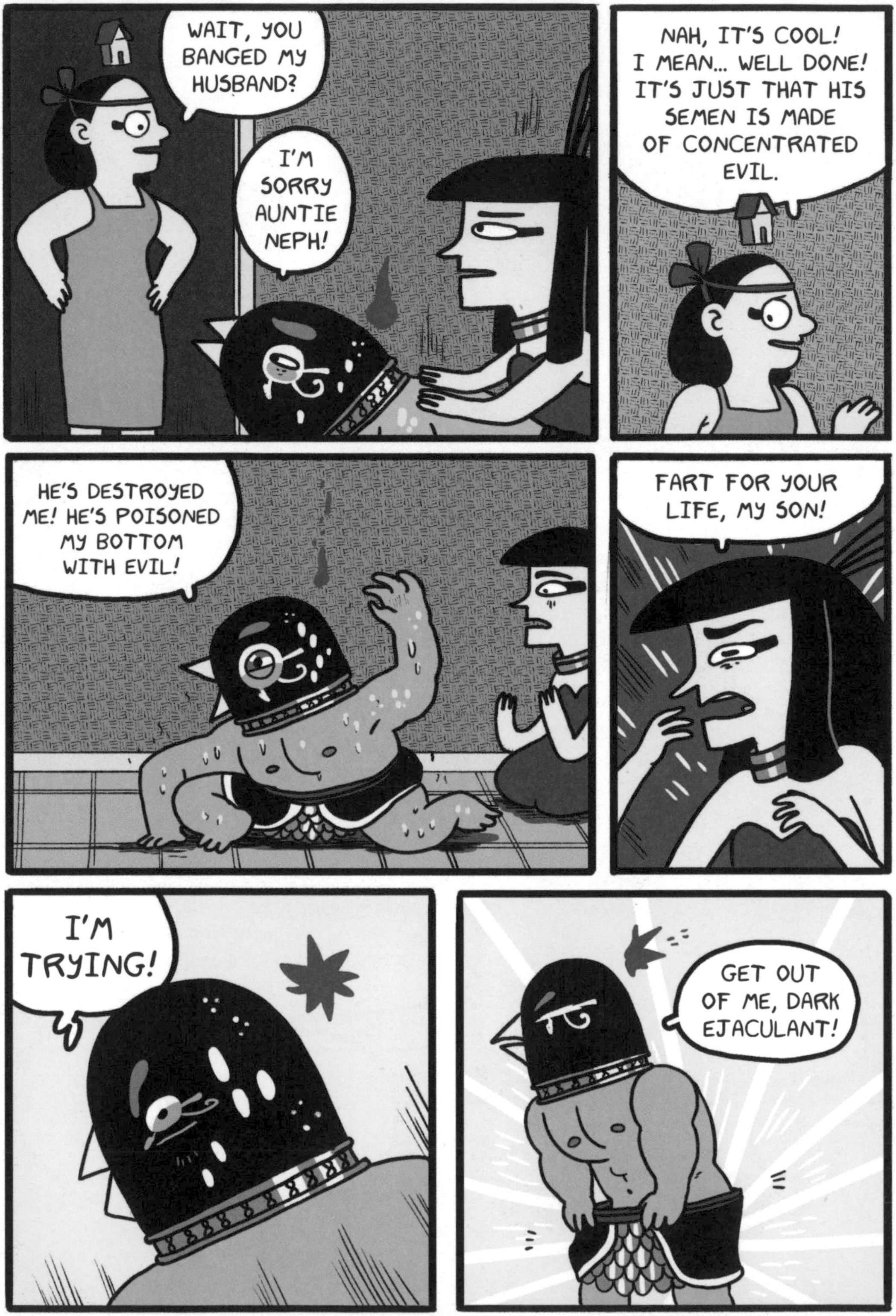
WAIT, YOU BANGED MY HUSBAND?
I'M SORRY AUNTIE NEPH!
NAH, IT'S COOL! I MEAN... WELL DONE! IT'S JUST THAT HIS SEMEN IS MADE OF CONCENTRATED EVIL.
HE'S DESTROYED ME! HE'S POISONED MY BOTTOM WITH EVIL!
FART FOR YOUR LIFE, MY SON!
I'M TRYING!
GET OUT OF ME, DARK EJACULANT!

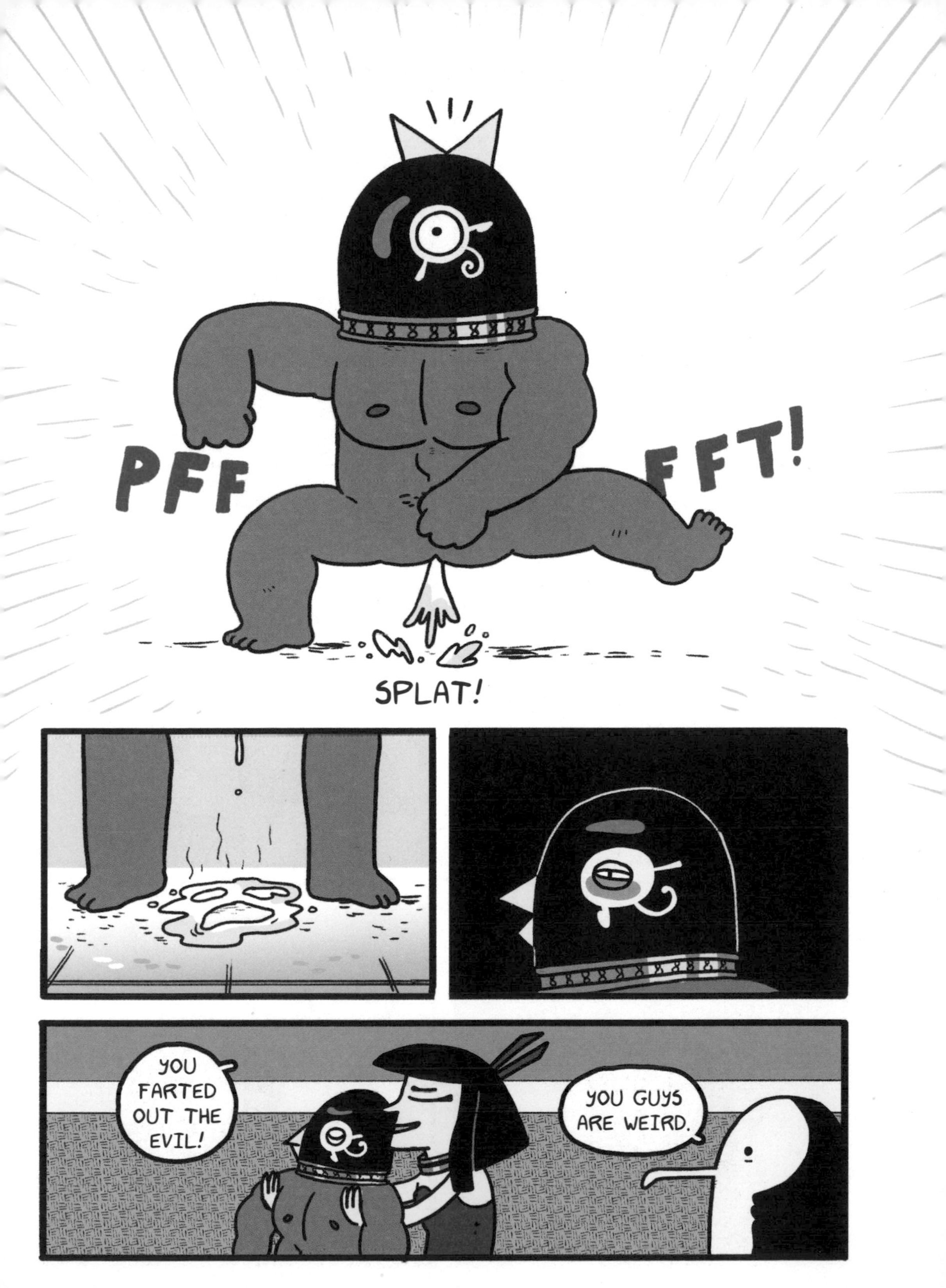

PFF FFT!
SPLAT!
YOU FARTED OUT THE EVIL!
YOU GUYS ARE WEIRD.

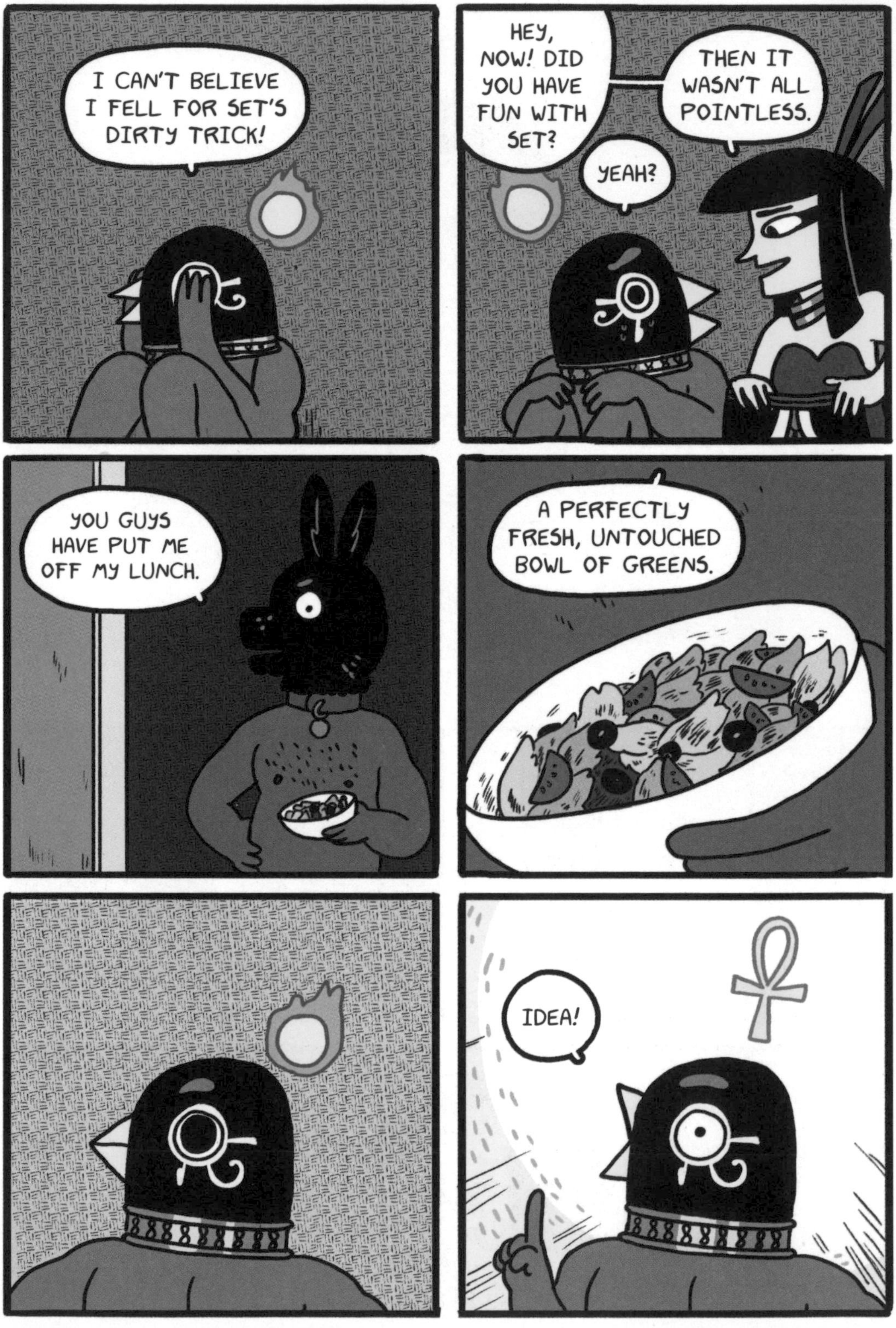
I CAN'T BELIEVE I FELL FOR SET'S DIRTY TRICK!
HEY, NOW! DID YOU HAVE FUN WITH SET?
YEAH?
THEN IT WASN'T ALL POINTLESS.
YOU GUYS HAVE PUT ME OFF MY LUNCH.
A PERFECTLY FRESH, UNTOUCHED BOWL OF GREENS.
IDEA!

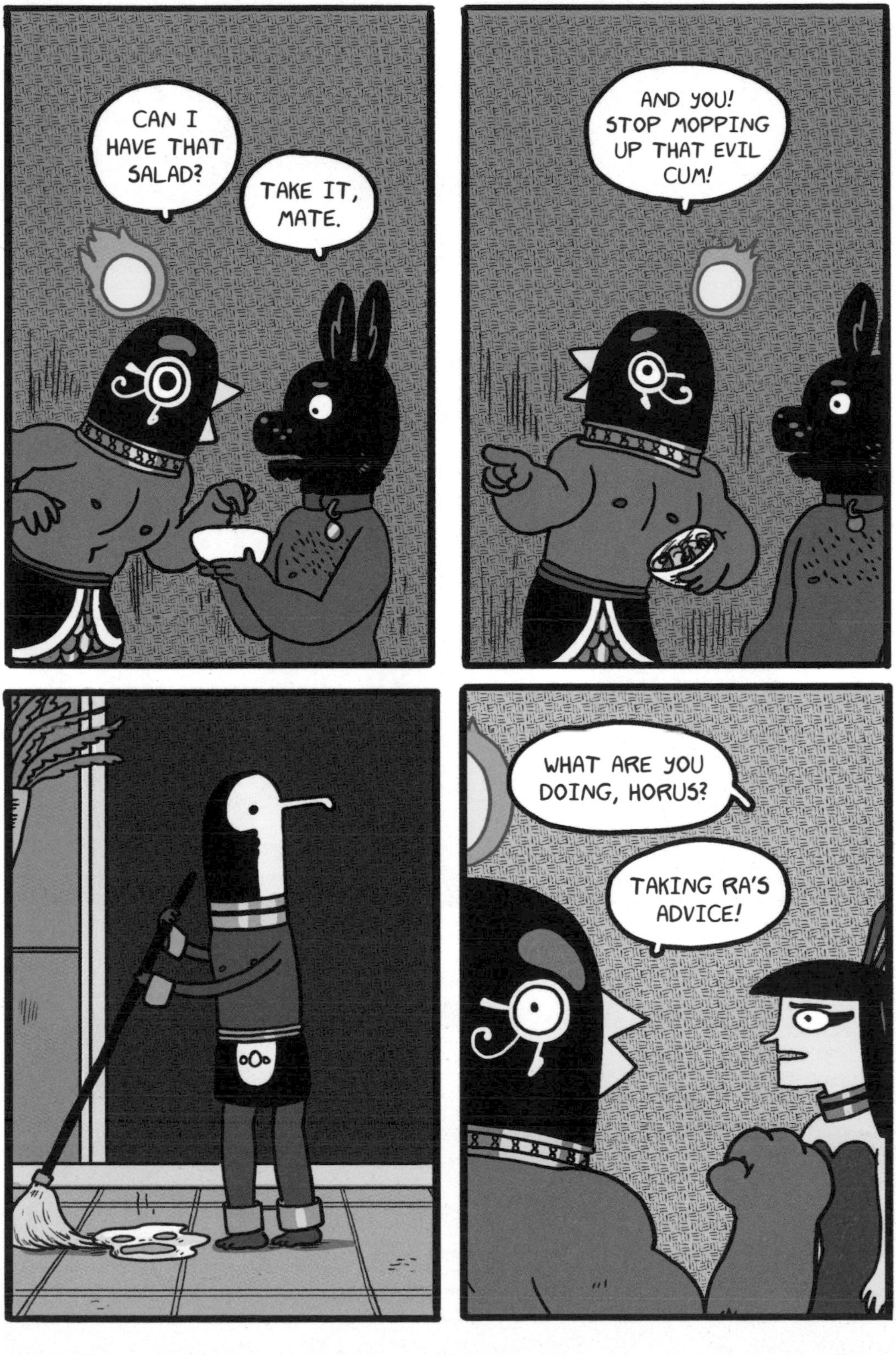
CAN I HAVE THAT SALAD?
TAKE IT, MATE.
AND YOU! STOP MOPPING UP THAT EVIL CUM!
WHAT ARE YOU DOING, HORUS?
TAKING RA'S ADVICE!

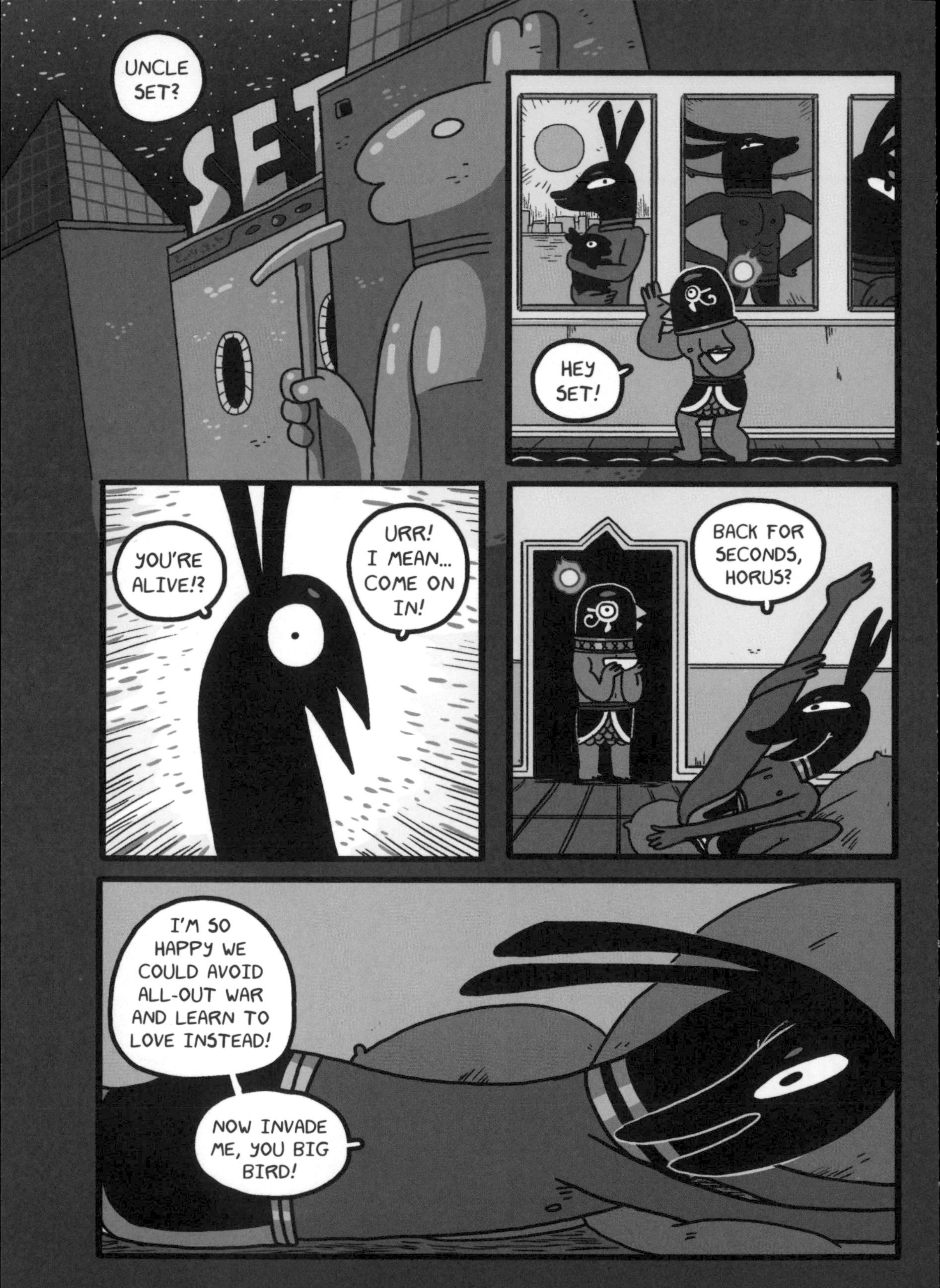
UNCLE SET?
SET
HEY SET!
YOU'RE ALIVE!?
URR! I MEAN... COME ON IN!
BACK FOR SECONDS, HORUS?
I'M SO HAPPY WE COULD AVOID ALL-OUT WAR AND LEARN TO LOVE INSTEAD!
NOW INVADE ME, YOU BIG BIRD!

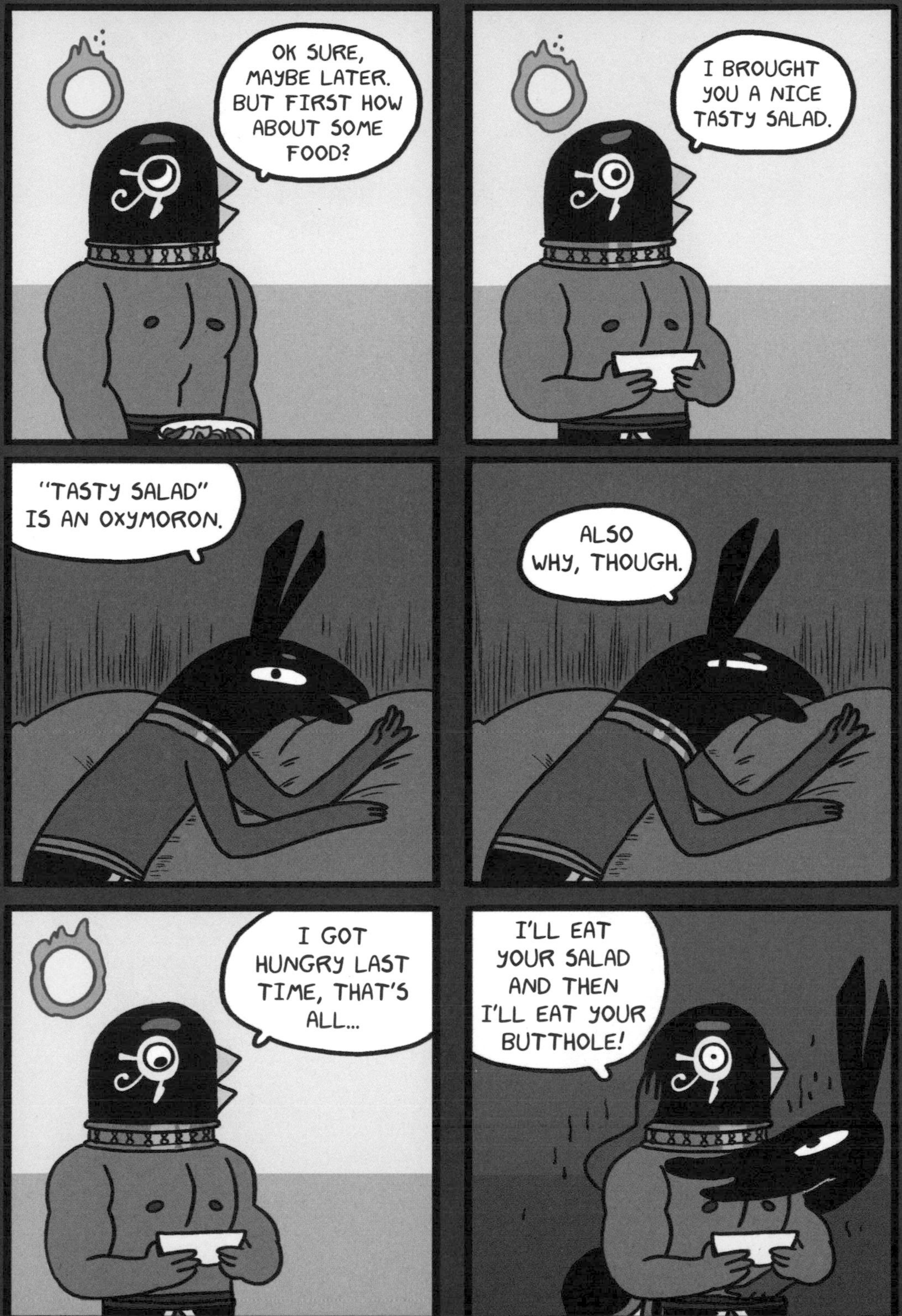
OK SURE, MAYBE LATER. BUT FIRST HOW ABOUT SOME FOOD?
I BROUGHT YOU A NICE TASTY SALAD.
"TASTY SALAD" IS AN OXYMORON.
ALSO WHY, THOUGH.
I GOT HUNGRY LAST TIME, THAT'S ALL...
I'LL EAT YOUR SALAD AND THEN I'LL EAT YOUR BUTTHOLE!

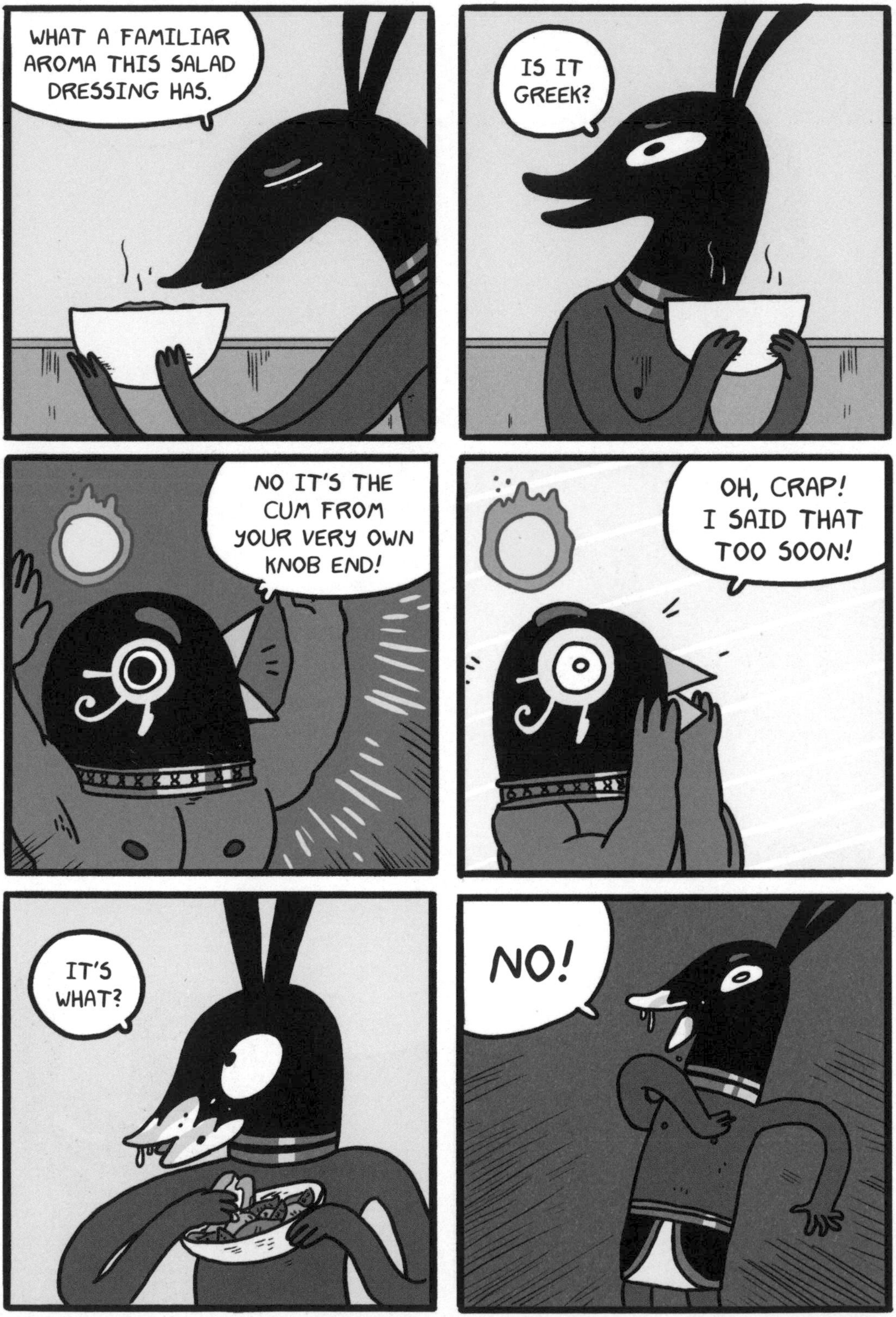
WHAT A FAMILIAR AROMA THIS SALAD DRESSING HAS.
IS IT GREEK?
NO IT'S THE CUM FROM YOUR VERY OWN KNOB END!
OH, CRAP! I SAID THAT TOO SOON!
IT'S WHAT?
NO!

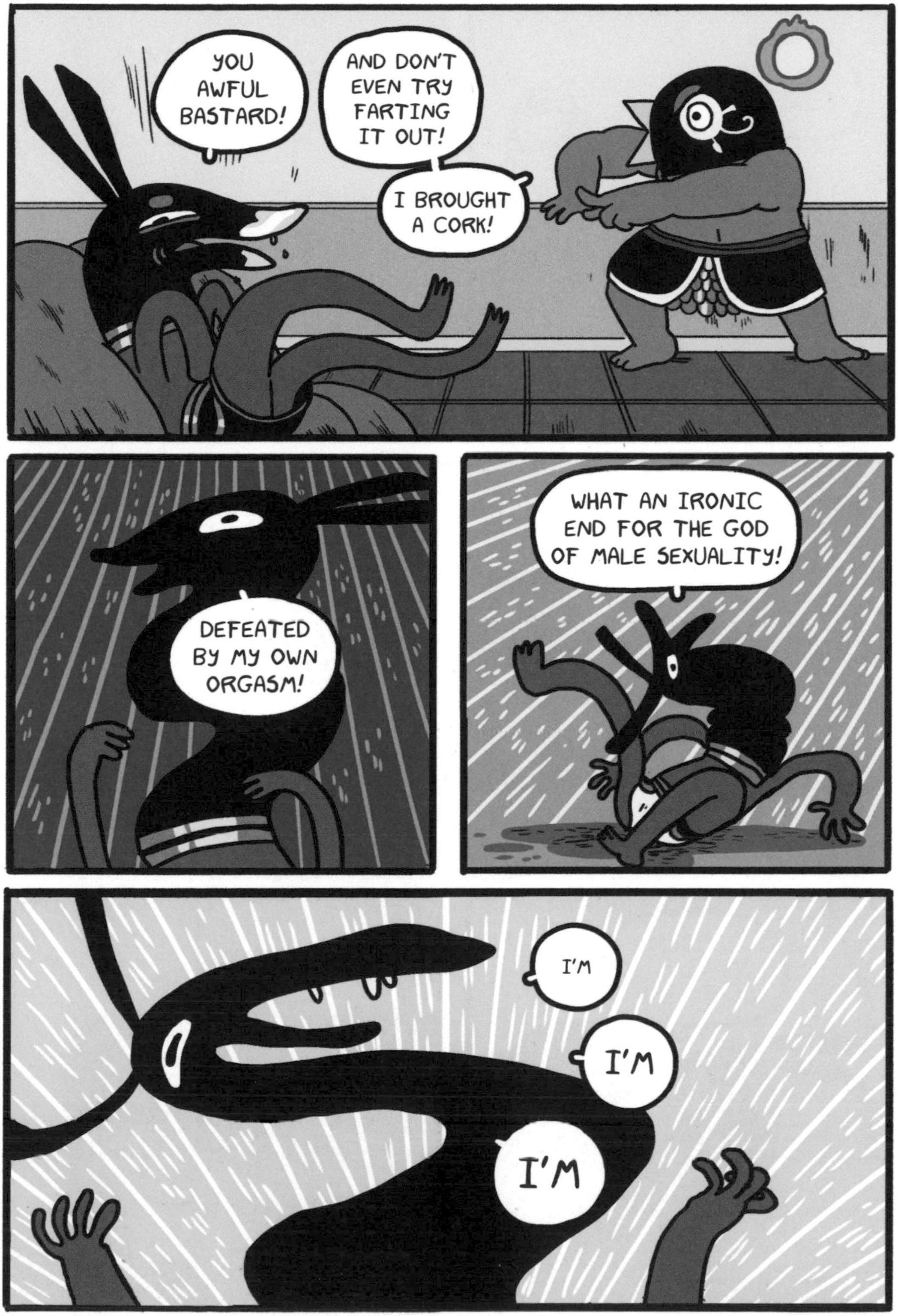
YOU AWFUL BASTARD!
AND DON'T EVEN TRY FARTING IT OUT!
I BROUGHT A CORK!
DEFEATED BY MY OWN ORGASM!
WHAT AN IRONIC END FOR THE GOD OF MALE SEXUALITY!
I'M
I'M
I'M

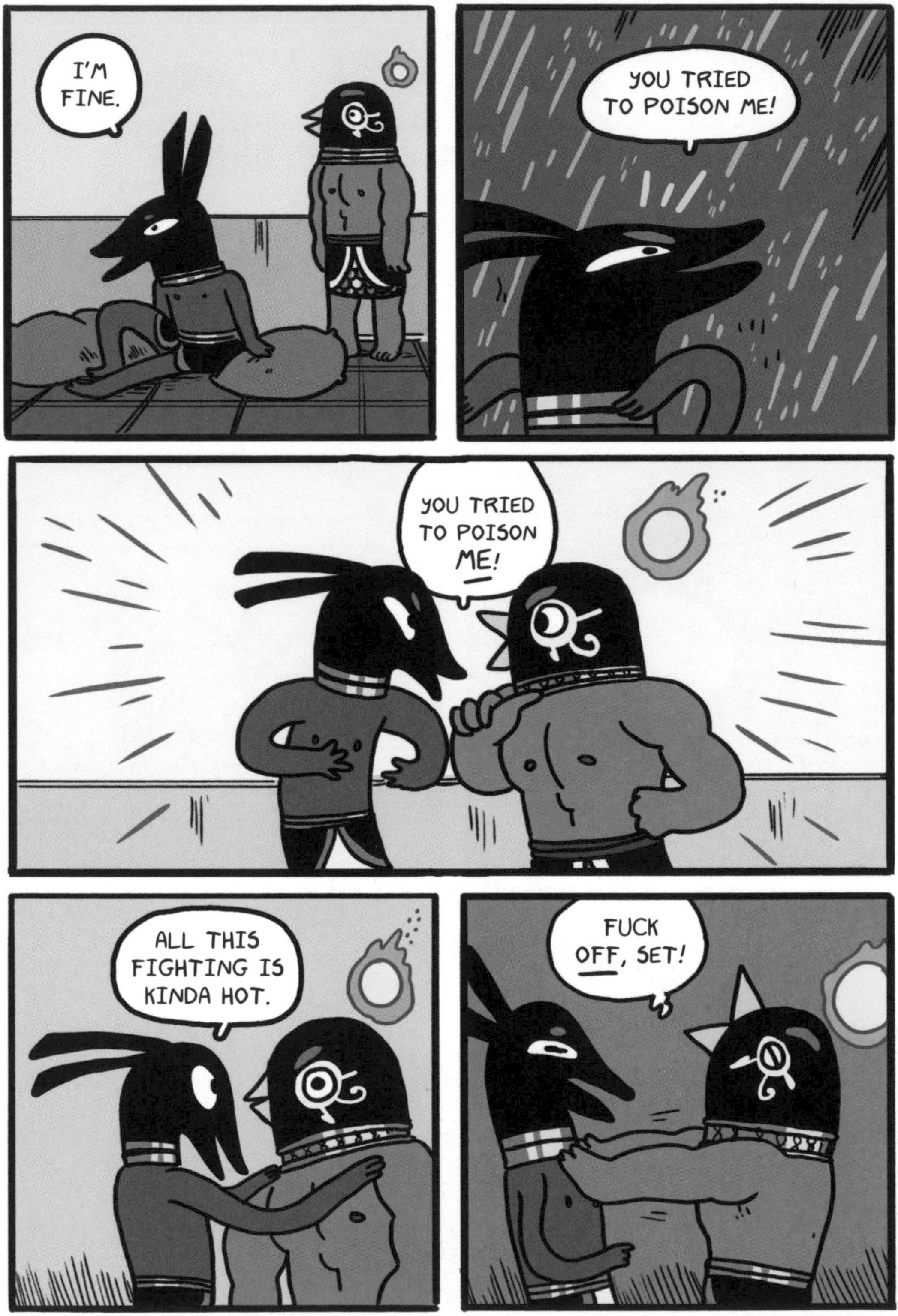
I'M FINE.
YOU TRIED TO POISON ME!
YOU TRIED TO POISON ME!
ALL THIS FIGHTING IS KINDA HOT.
FUCK OFF, SET!

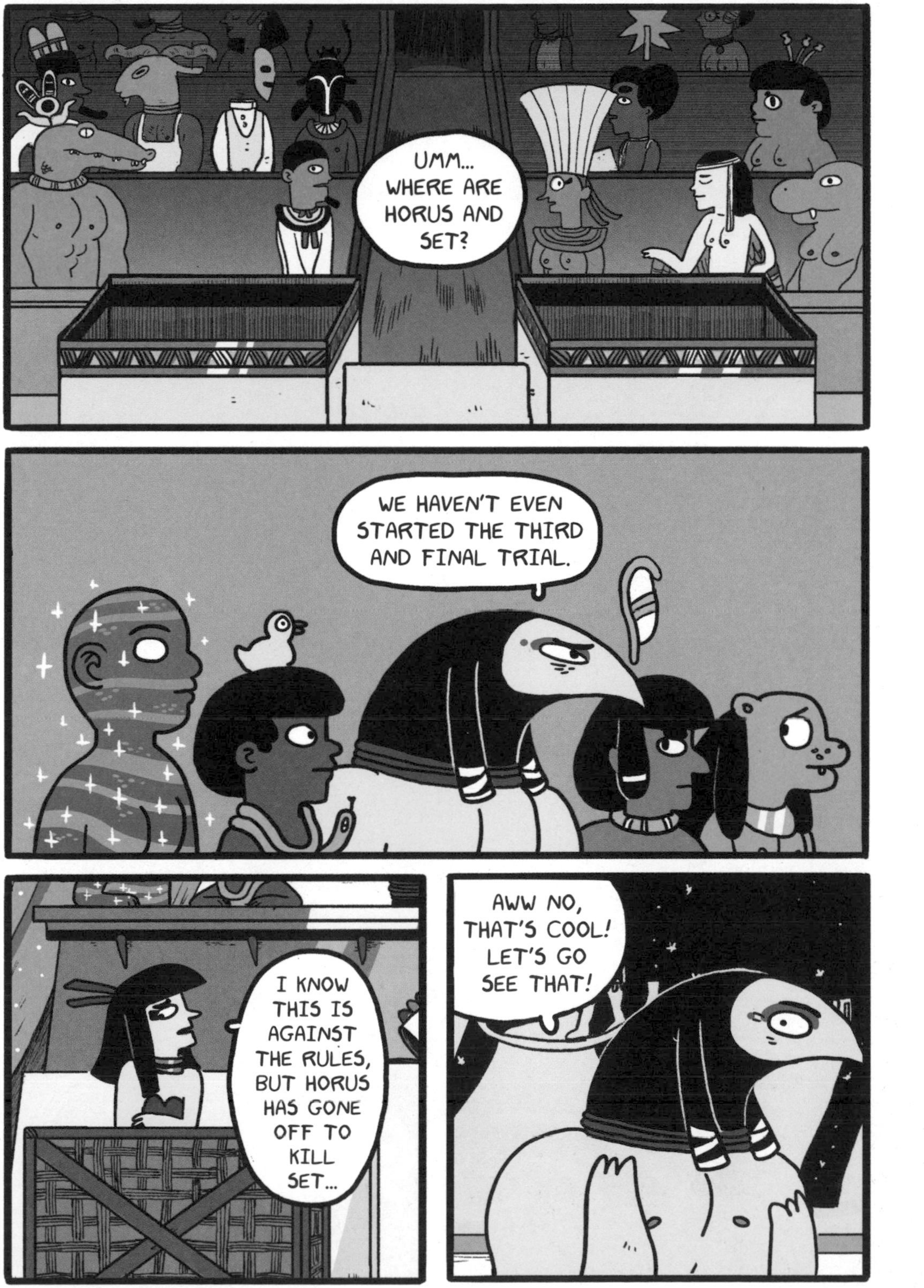
UMM... WHERE ARE HORUS AND SET?
WE HAVEN'T EVEN STARTED THE THIRD AND FINAL TRIAL.
I KNOW THIS IS AGAINST THE RULES, BUT HORUS HAS GONE OFF TO KILL SET...
AWW NO, THAT'S COOL! LET'S GO SEE THAT!

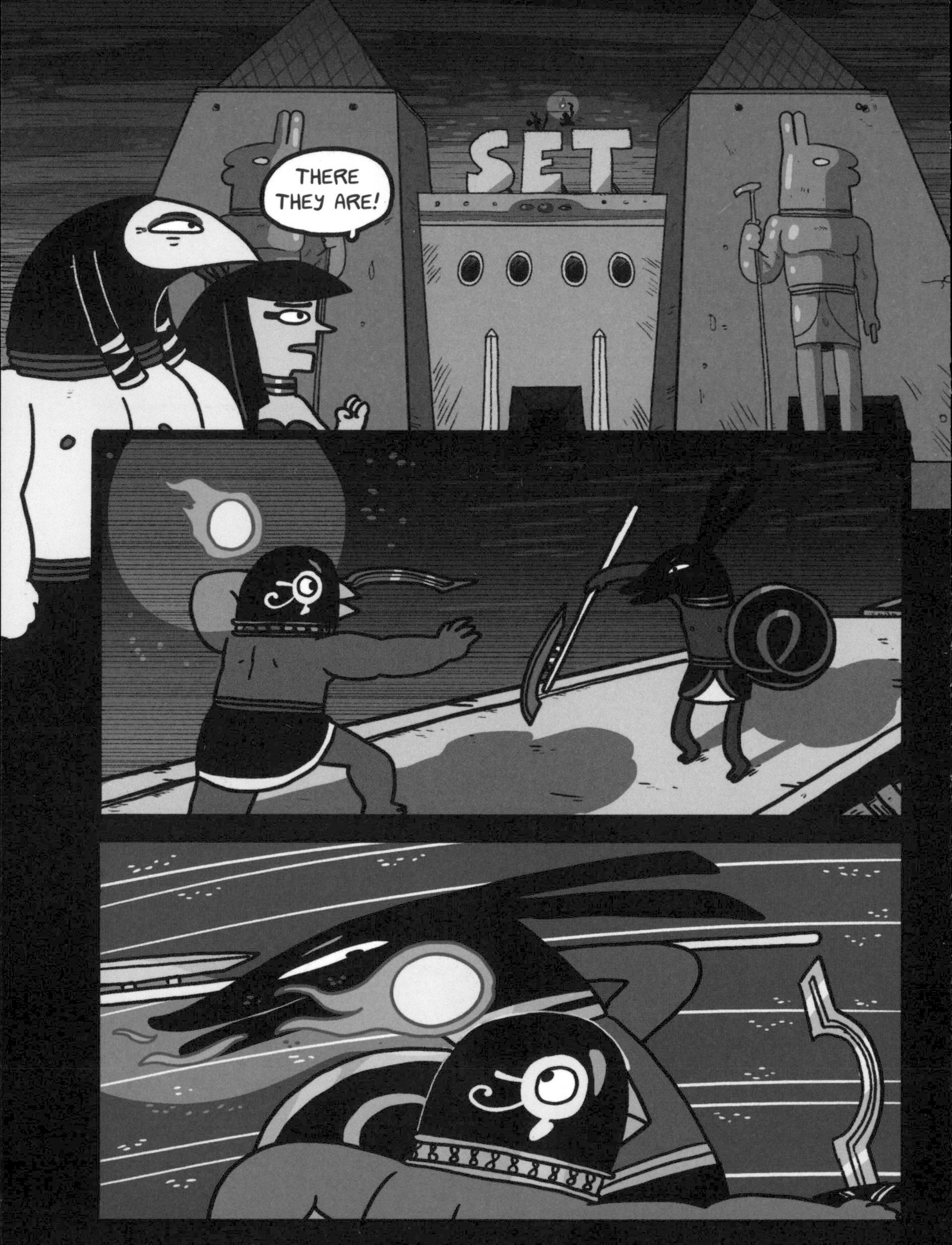
SET
THERE THEY ARE!

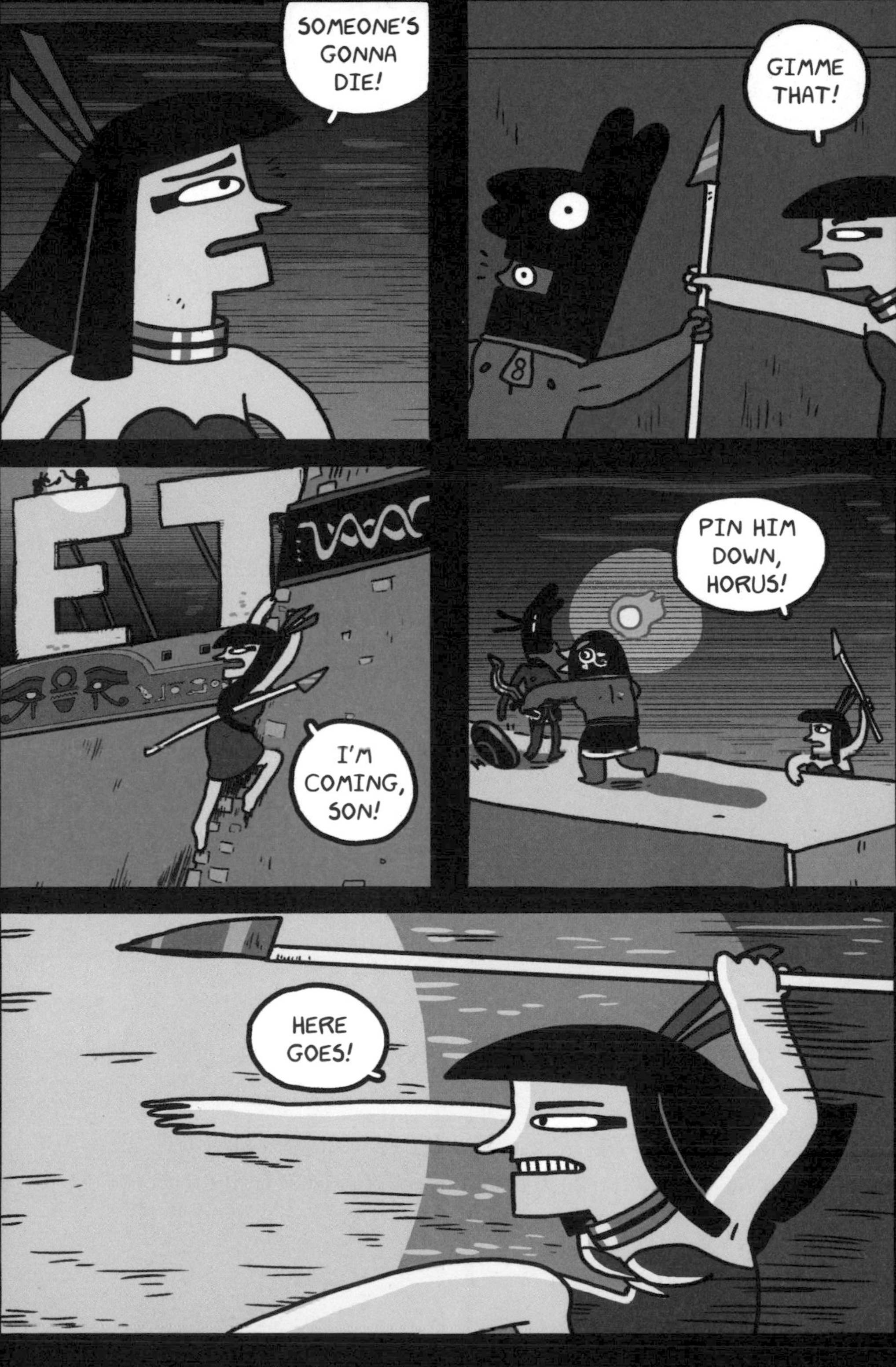
SOMEONE'S GONNA DIE!
GIMME THAT!
I'M COMING, SON!
PIN HIM DOWN, HORUS!
HERE GOES!

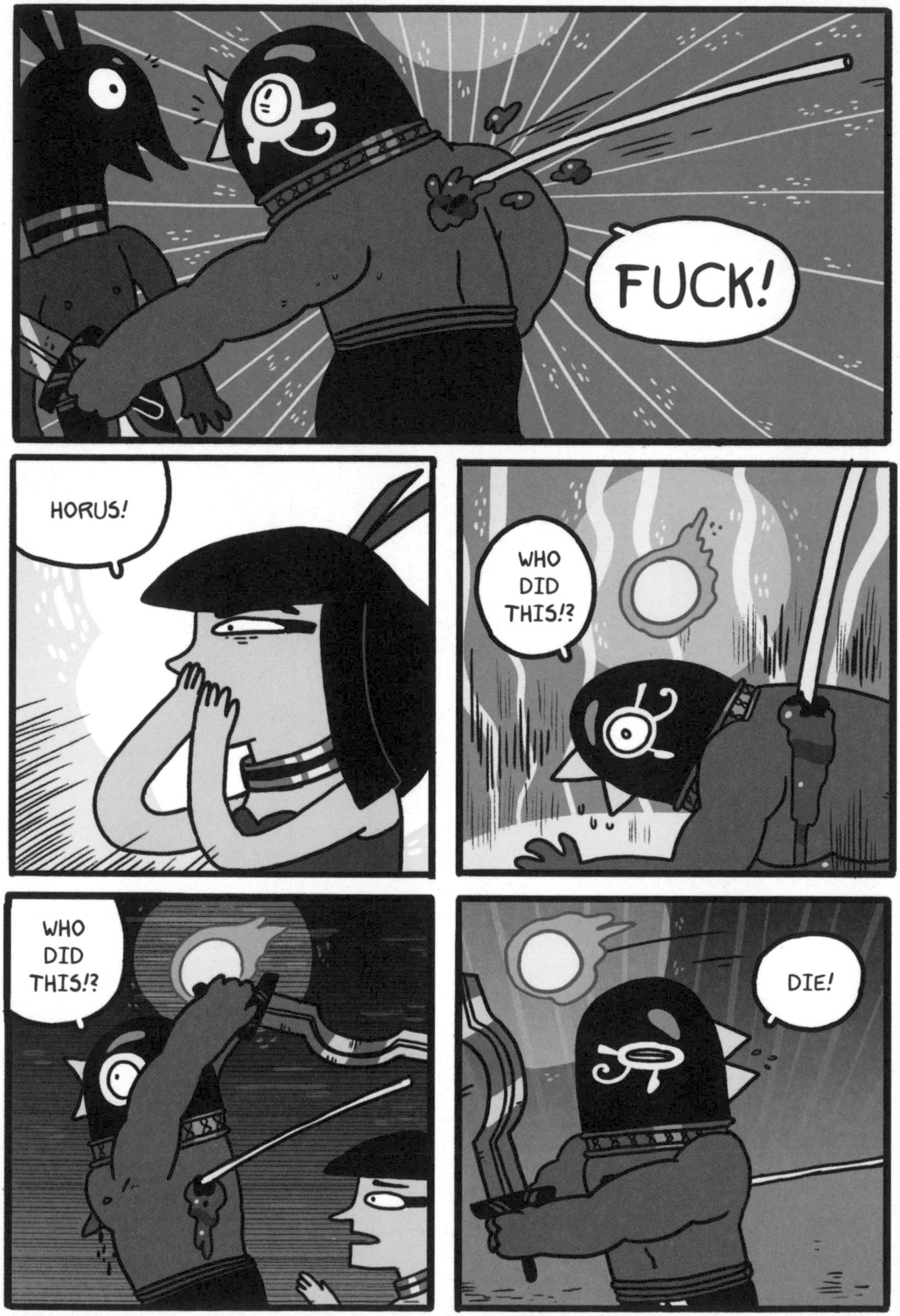
FUCK!
HORUS!
WHO DID THIS!?
WHO DID THIS!?
DIE!

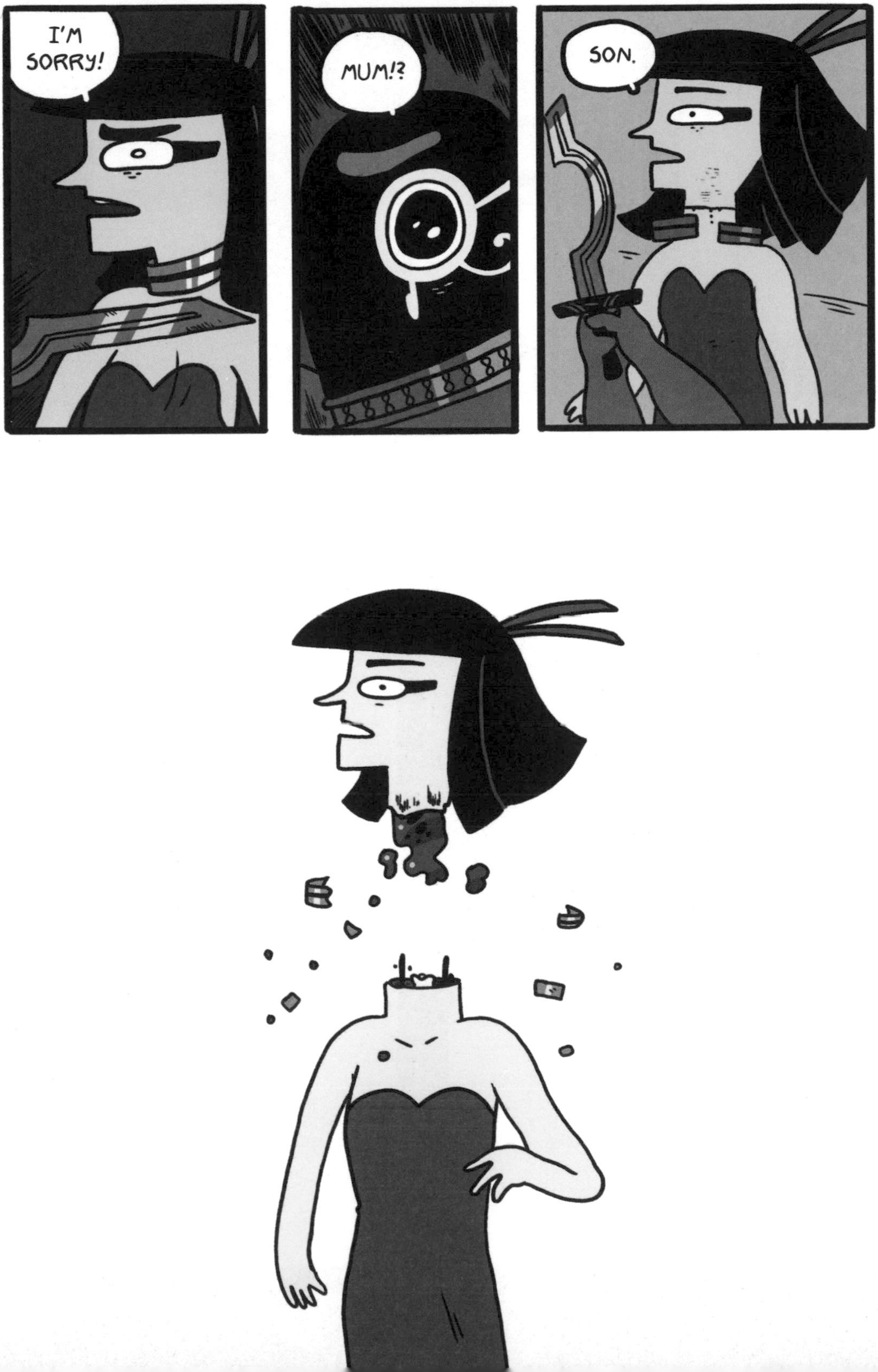
I'M SORRY!
MUM!?
SON.

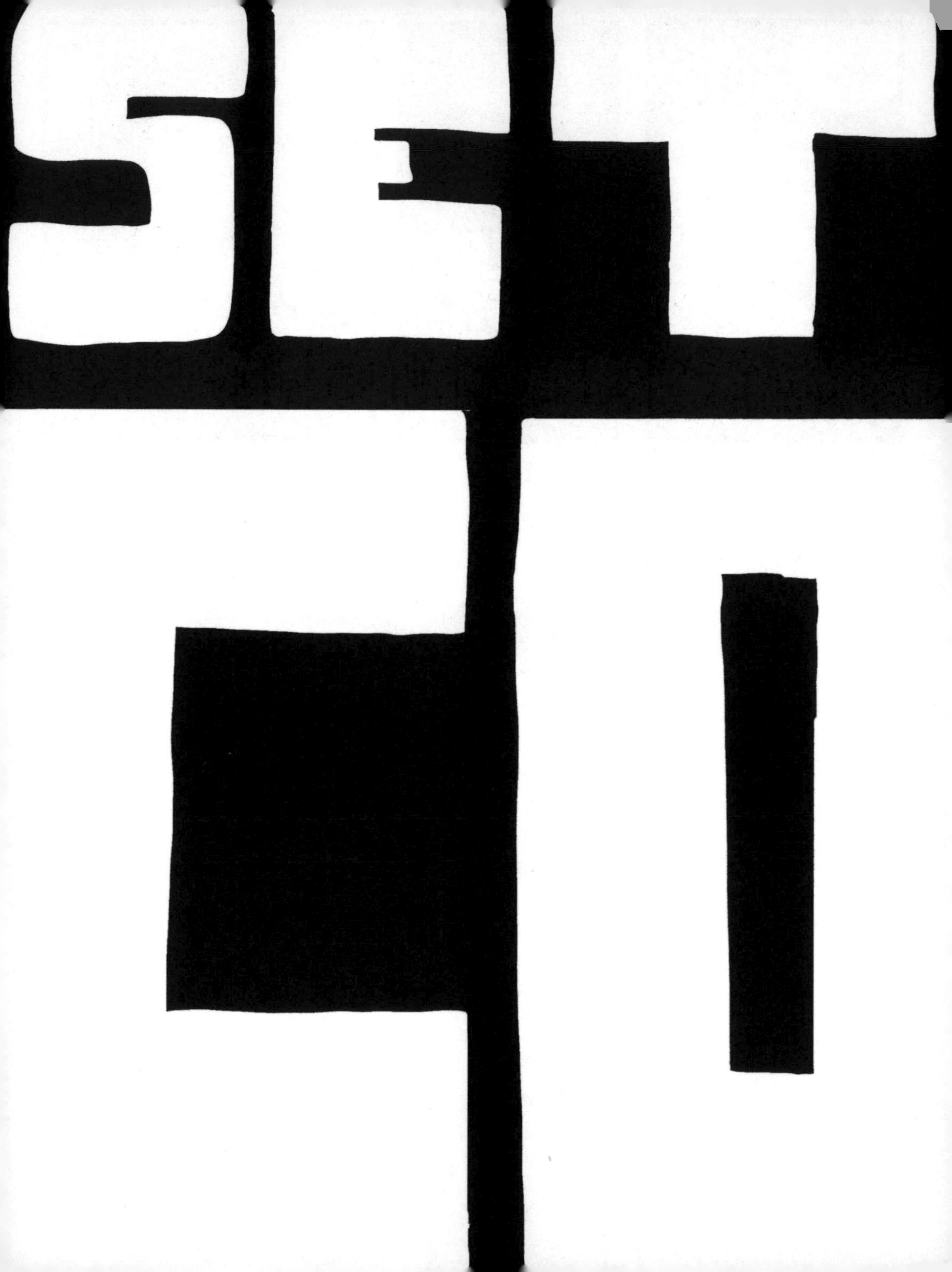

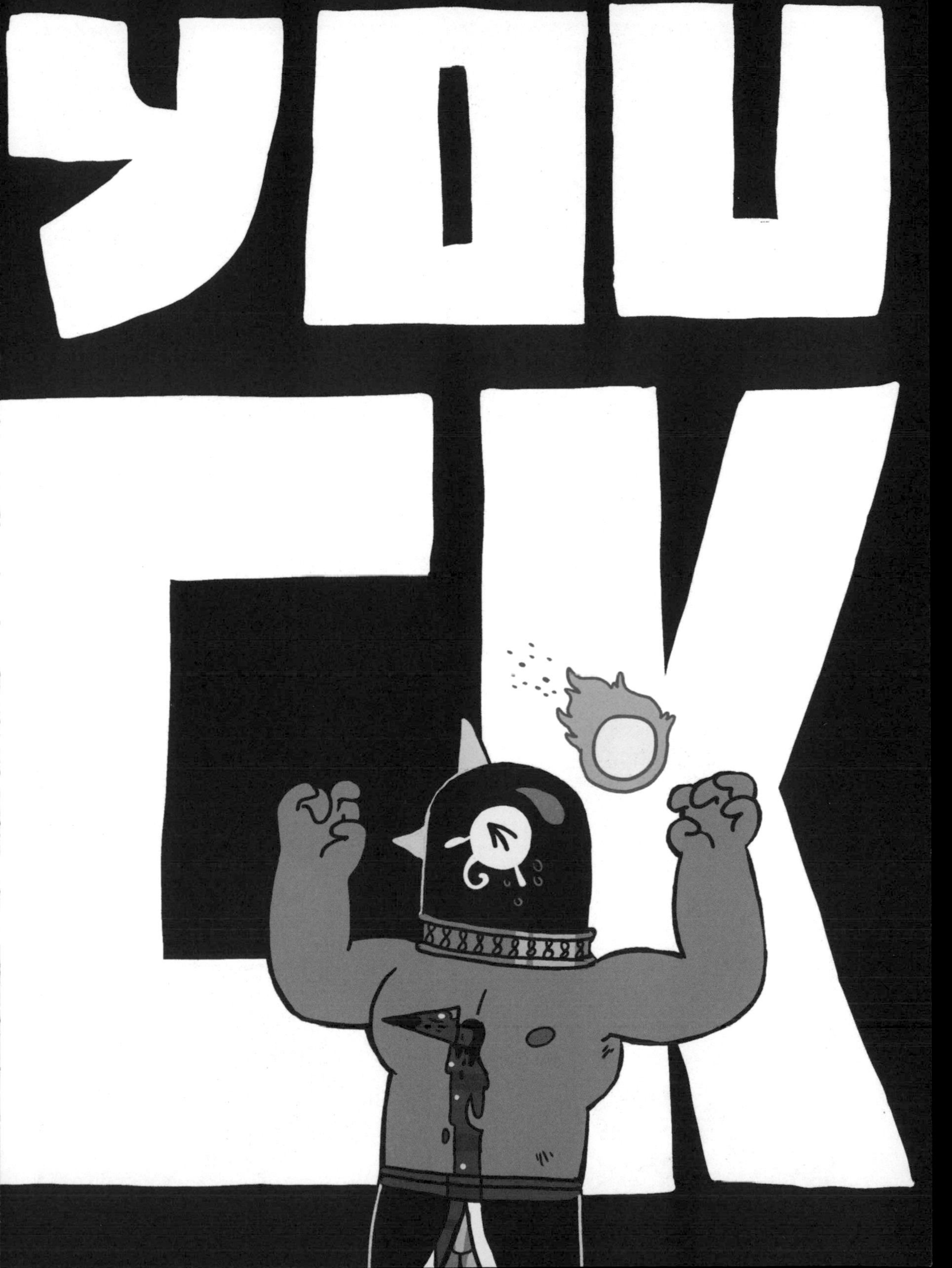
YOU

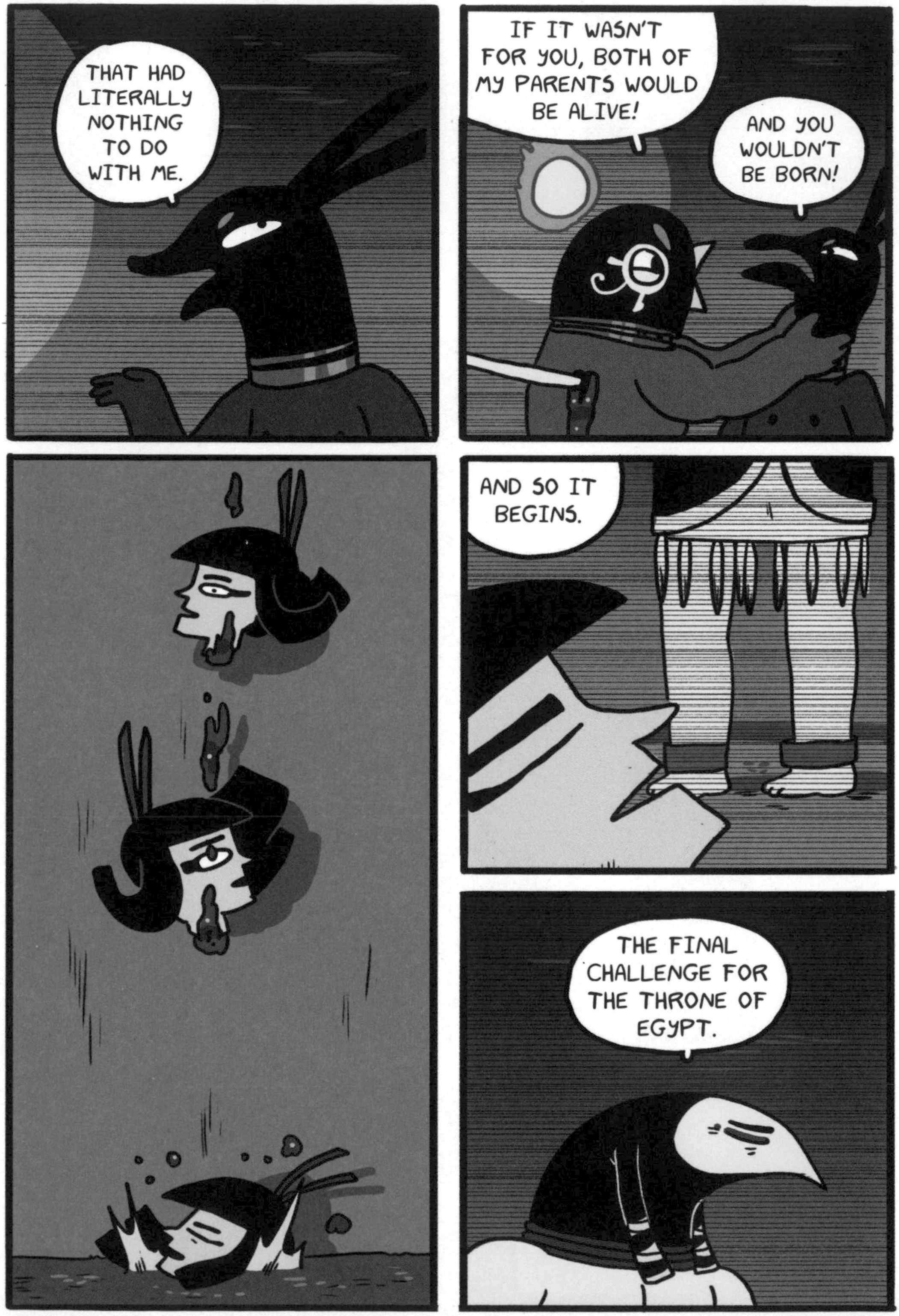
THAT HAD LITERALLY NOTHING TO DO WITH ME.
IF IT WASN'T FOR YOU, BOTH OF MY PARENTS WOULD BE ALIVE!
AND YOU WOULDN'T BE BORN!
AND SO IT BEGINS.
THE FINAL CHALLENGE FOR THE THRONE OF EGYPT.

CHAPTER TEN

★★★ WAR ★★★

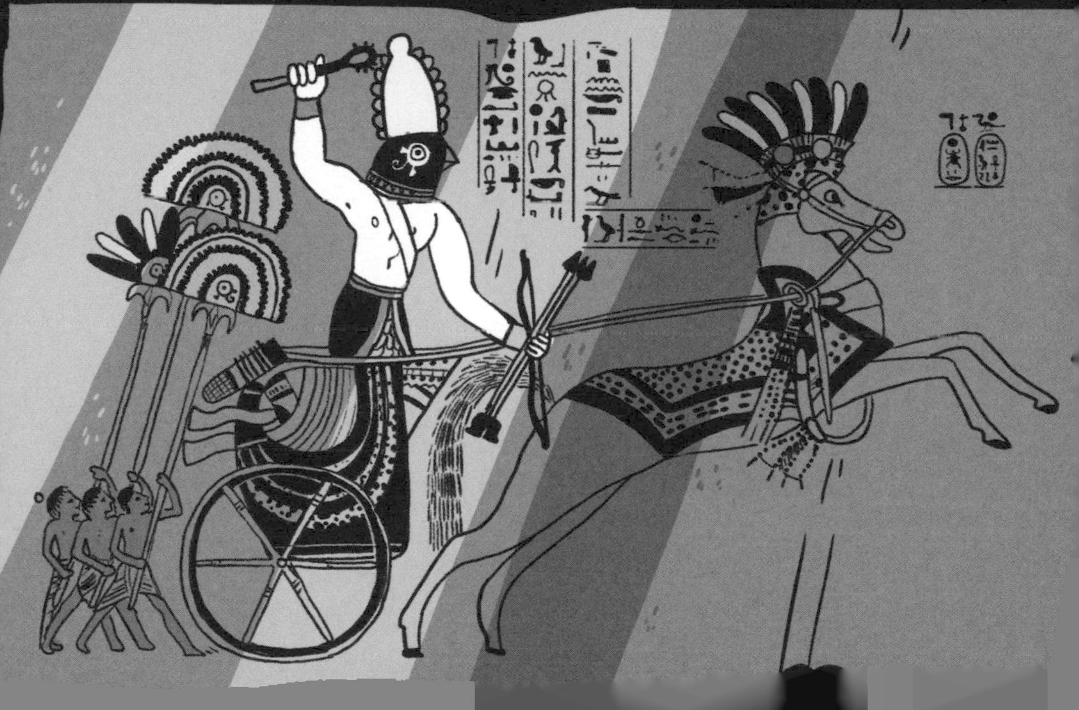

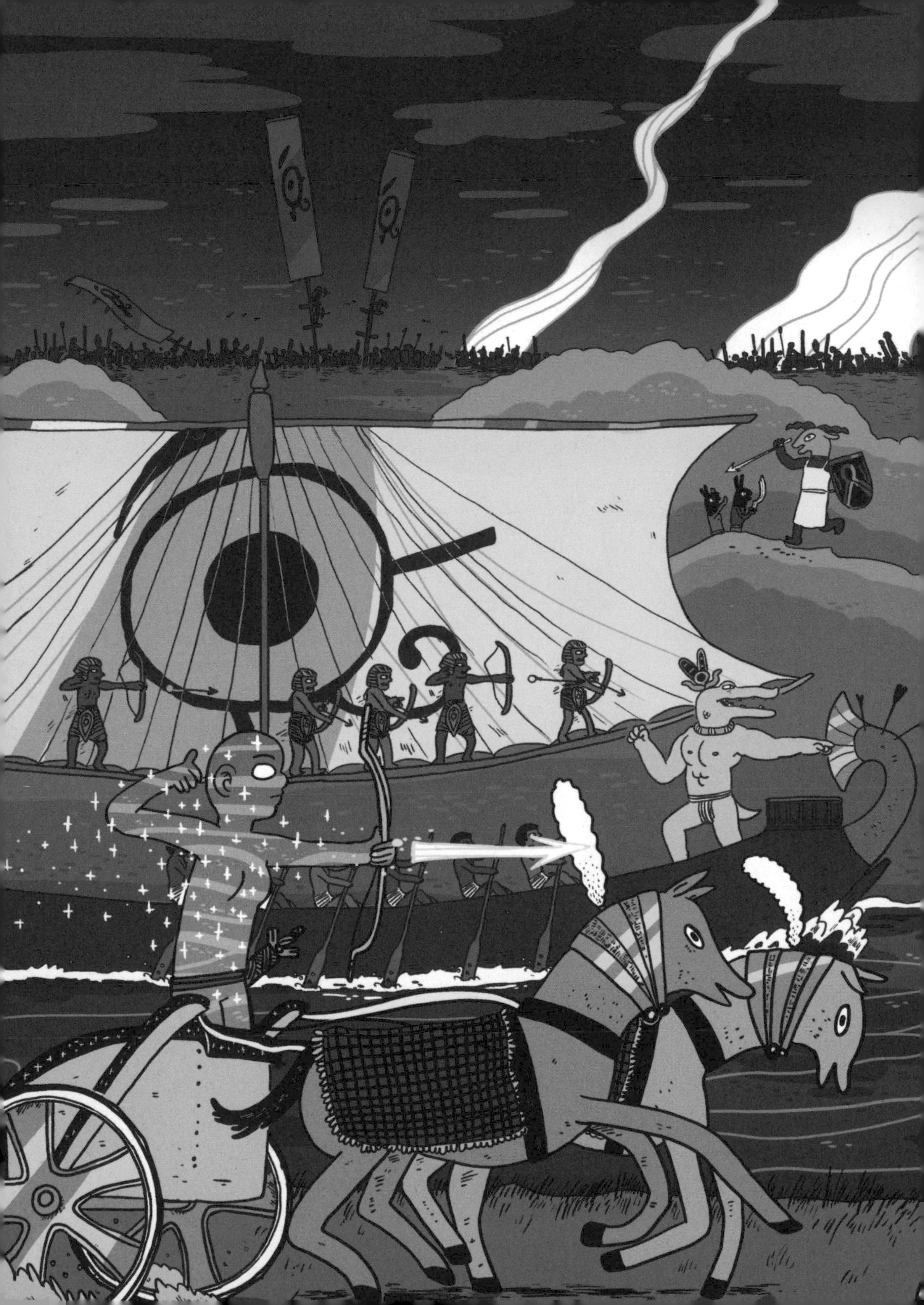

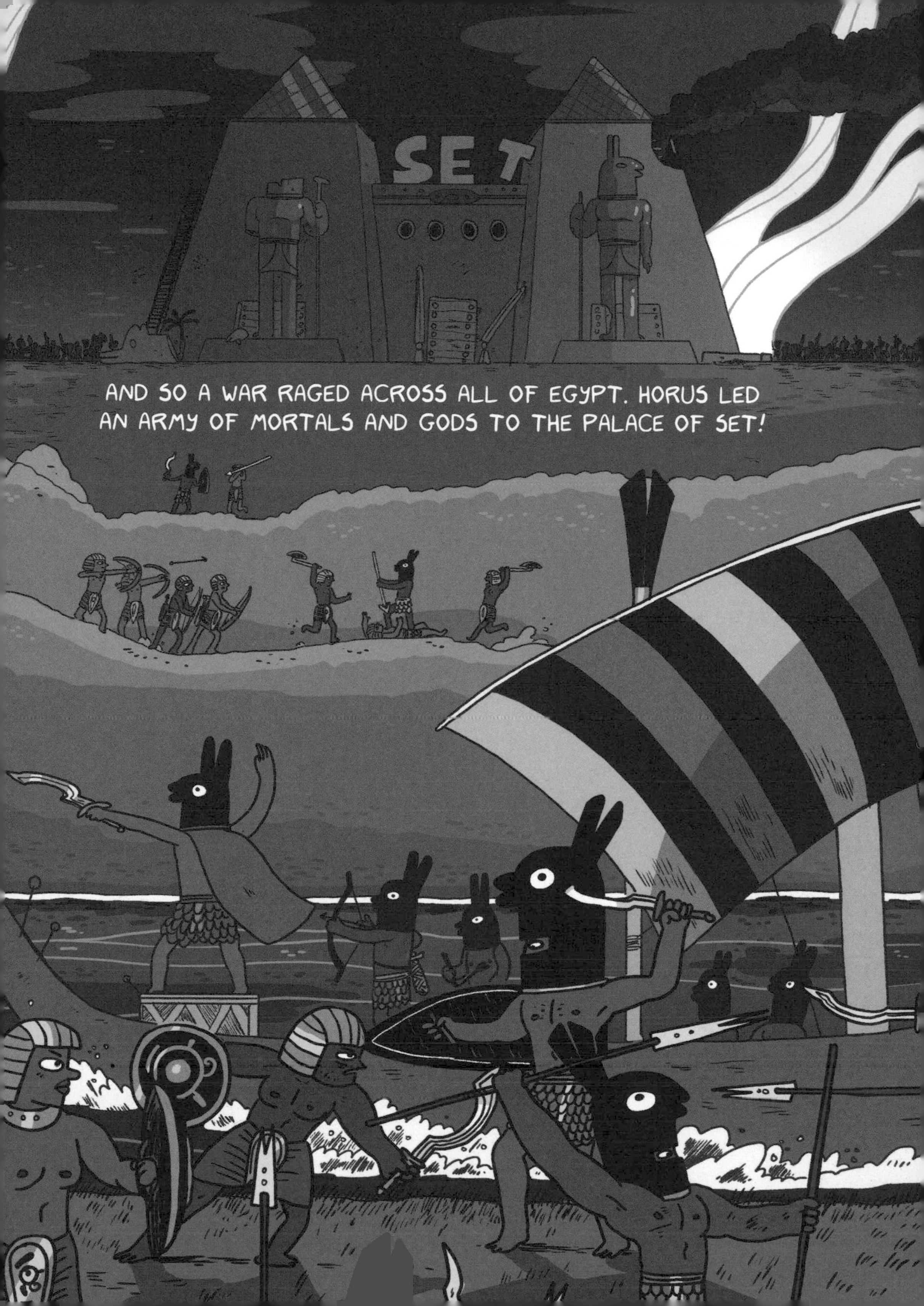
AND SO A WAR RAGED ACROSS ALL OF EGYPT. HORUS LED AN ARMY OF MORTALS AND GODS TO THE PALACE OF SET!
SET

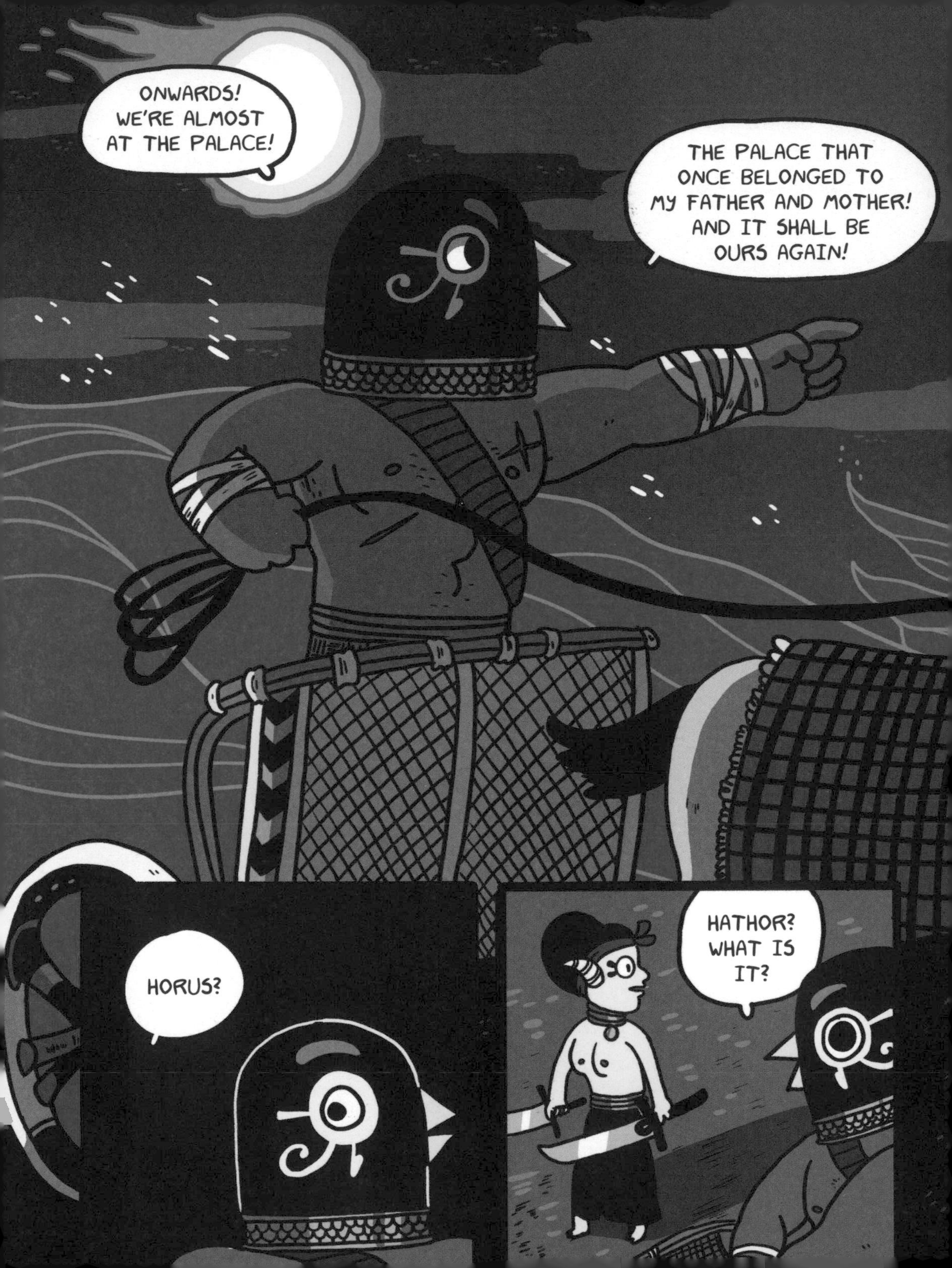
ONWARDS! WE'RE ALMOST AT THE PALACE!
THE PALACE THAT ONCE BELONGED TO MY FATHER AND MOTHER! AND IT SHALL BE OURS AGAIN!
HORUS?
HATHOR? WHAT IS IT?

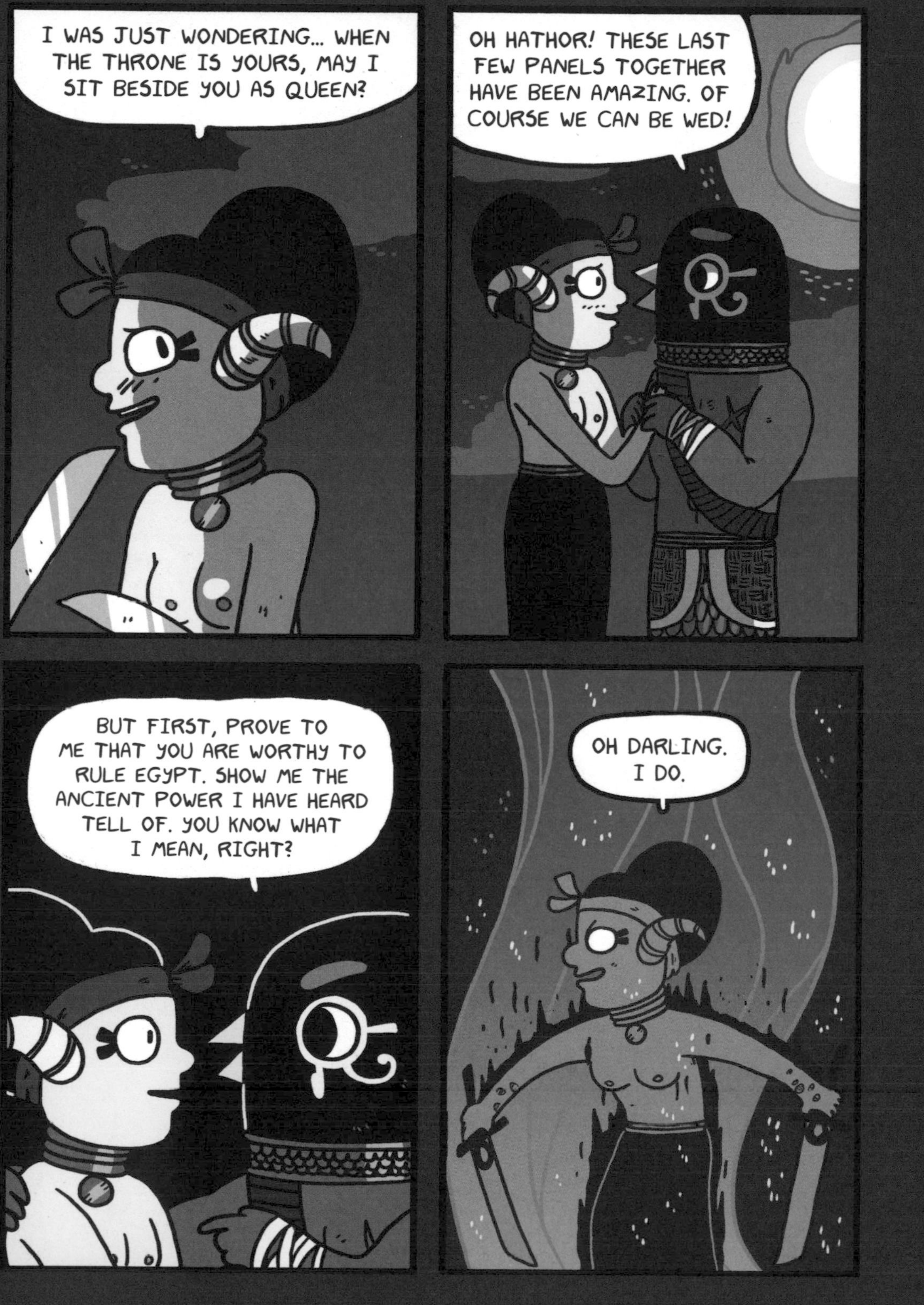
I WAS JUST WONDERING... WHEN THE THRONE IS YOURS, MAY I SIT BESIDE YOU AS QUEEN?
OH HATHOR! THESE LAST FEW PANELS TOGETHER HAVE BEEN AMAZING. OF COURSE WE CAN BE WED!
BUT FIRST, PROVE TO ME THAT YOU ARE WORTHY TO RULE EGYPT. SHOW ME THE ANCIENT POWER I HAVE HEARD TELL OF. YOU KNOW WHAT I MEAN, RIGHT?
OH DARLING. I DO.

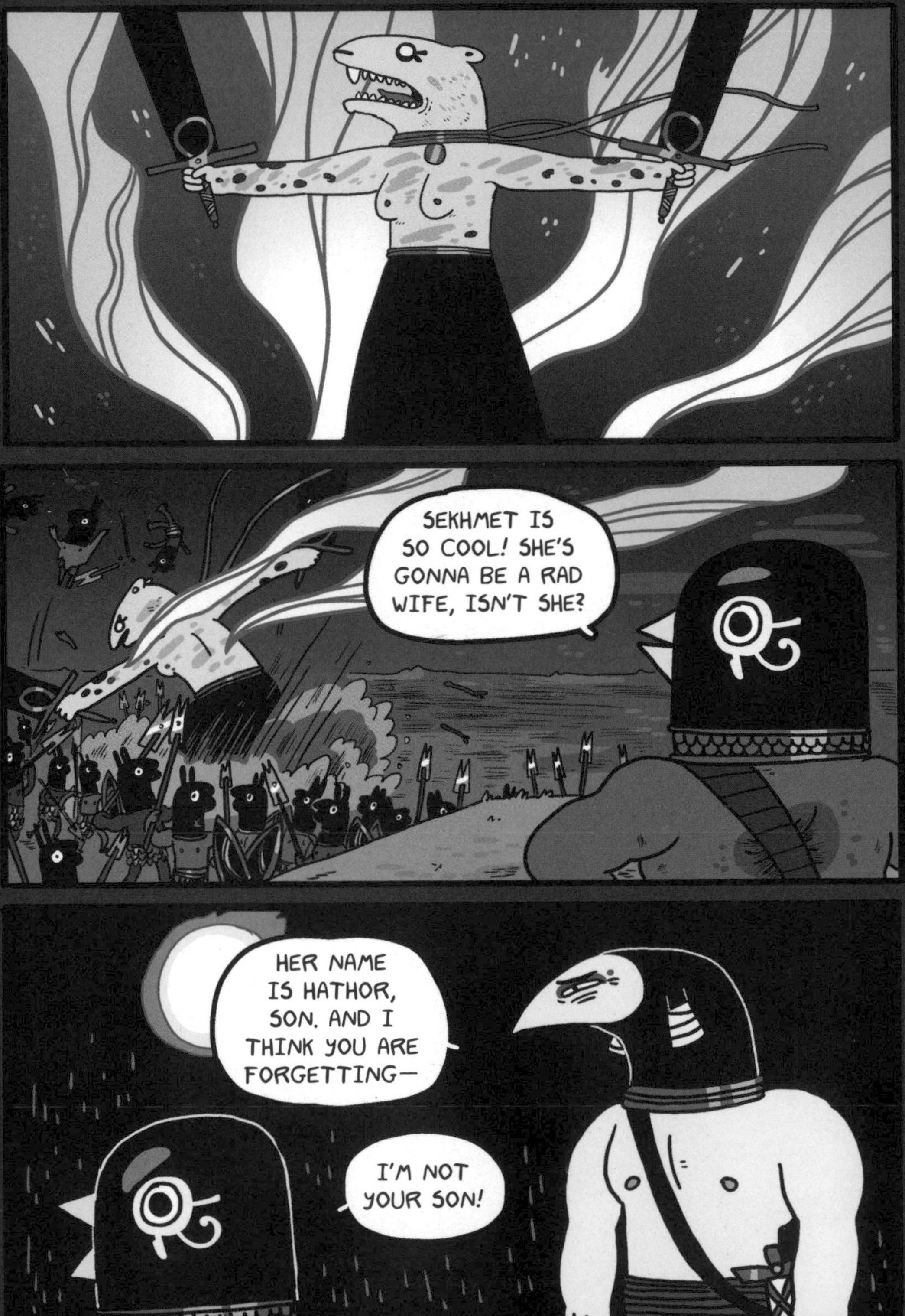
SEKHMET IS SO COOL! SHE'S GONNA BE A RAD WIFE, ISN'T SHE?
HER NAME IS HATHOR, SON. AND I THINK YOU ARE FORGETTING—
I'M NOT YOUR SON!

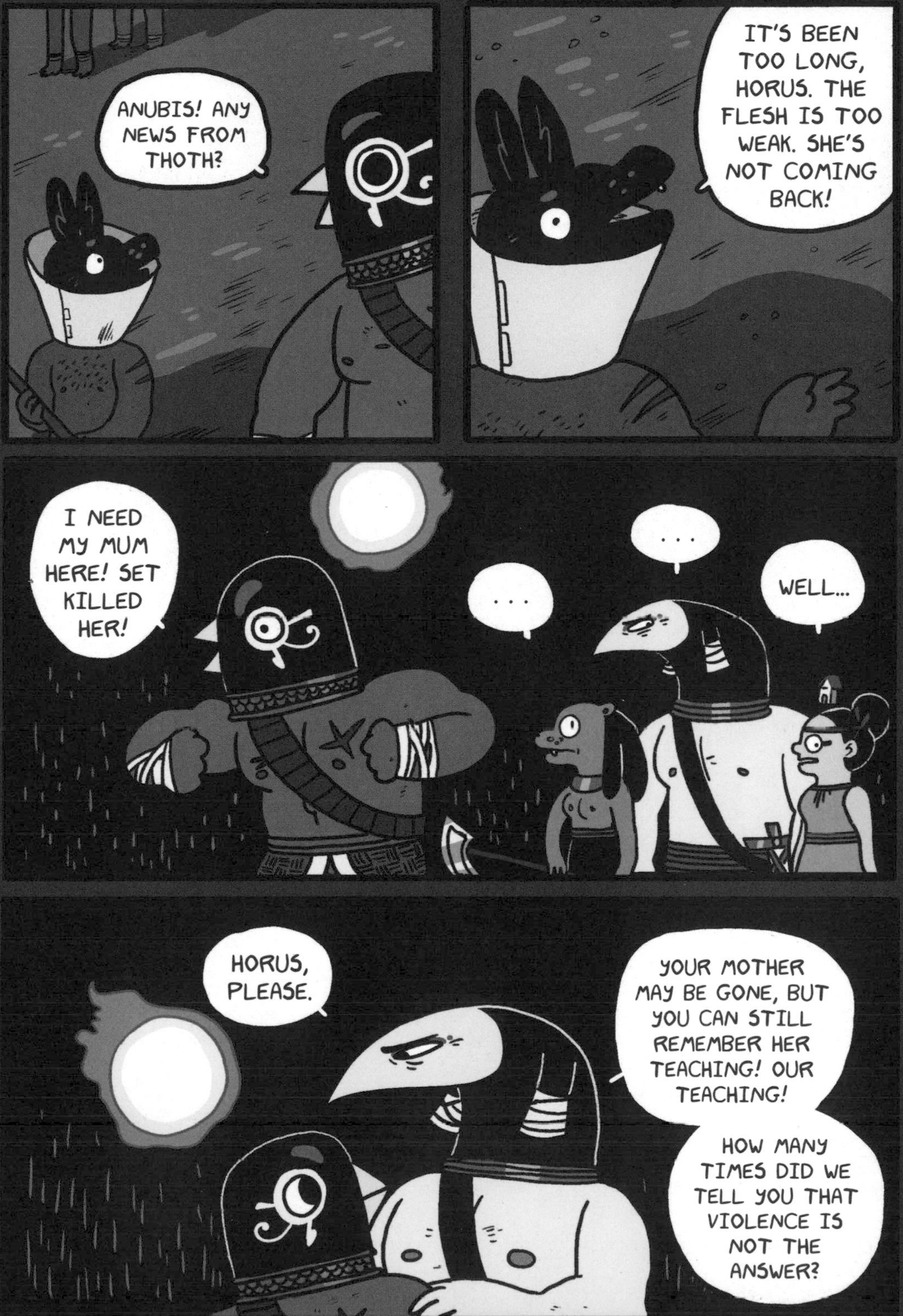
ANUBIS! ANY NEWS FROM THOTH?
IT'S BEEN TOO LONG, HORUS. THE FLESH IS TOO WEAK. SHE'S NOT COMING BACK!
I NEED MY MUM HERE! SET KILLED HER!
. . .
. . .
WELL...
HORUS, PLEASE.
YOUR MOTHER MAY BE GONE, BUT YOU CAN STILL REMEMBER HER TEACHING! OUR TEACHING!
HOW MANY TIMES DID WE TELL YOU THAT VIOLENCE IS NOT THE ANSWER?

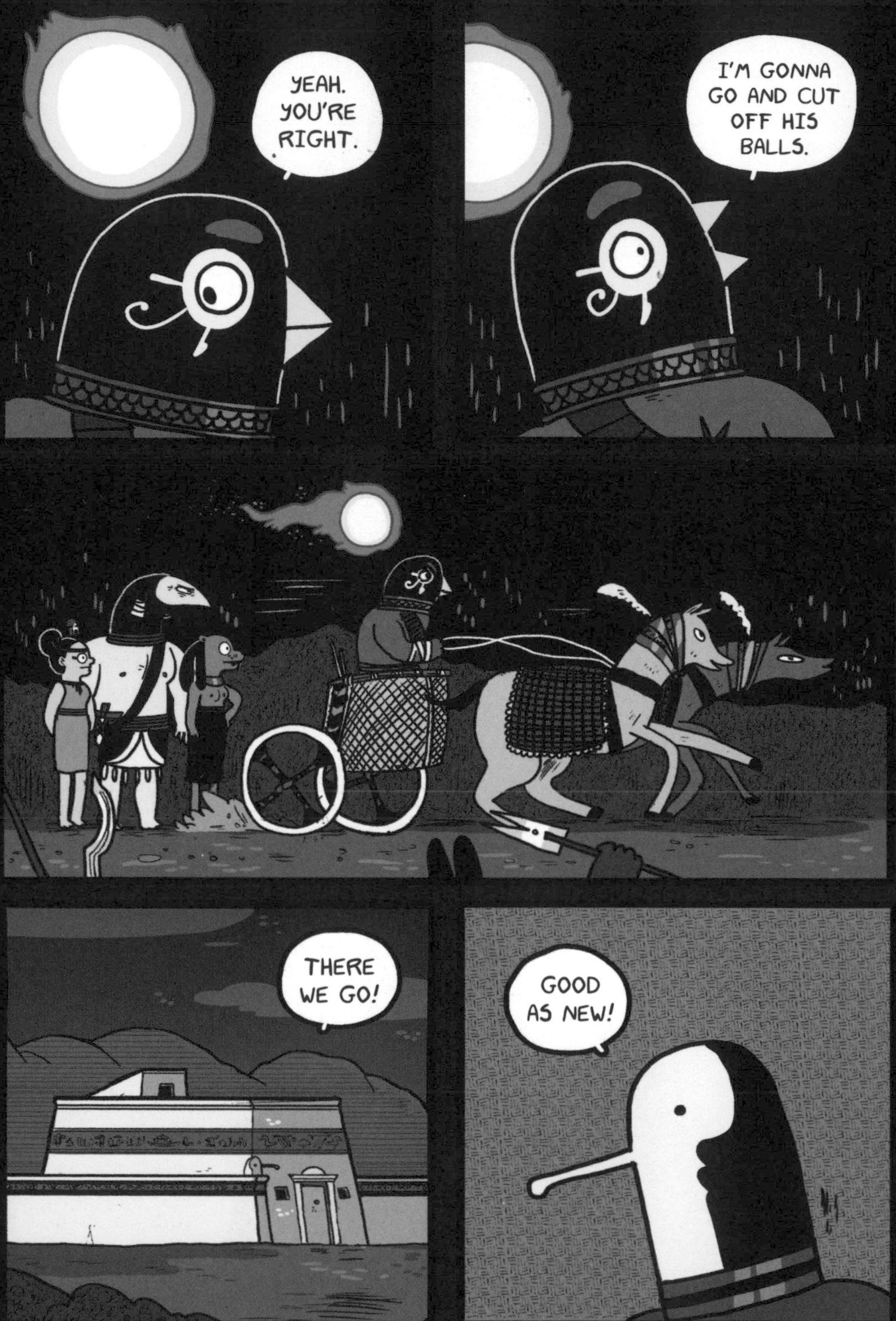
YEAH. YOU'RE RIGHT.
I'M GONNA GO AND CUT OFF HIS BALLS.
THERE WE GO!
GOOD AS NEW!

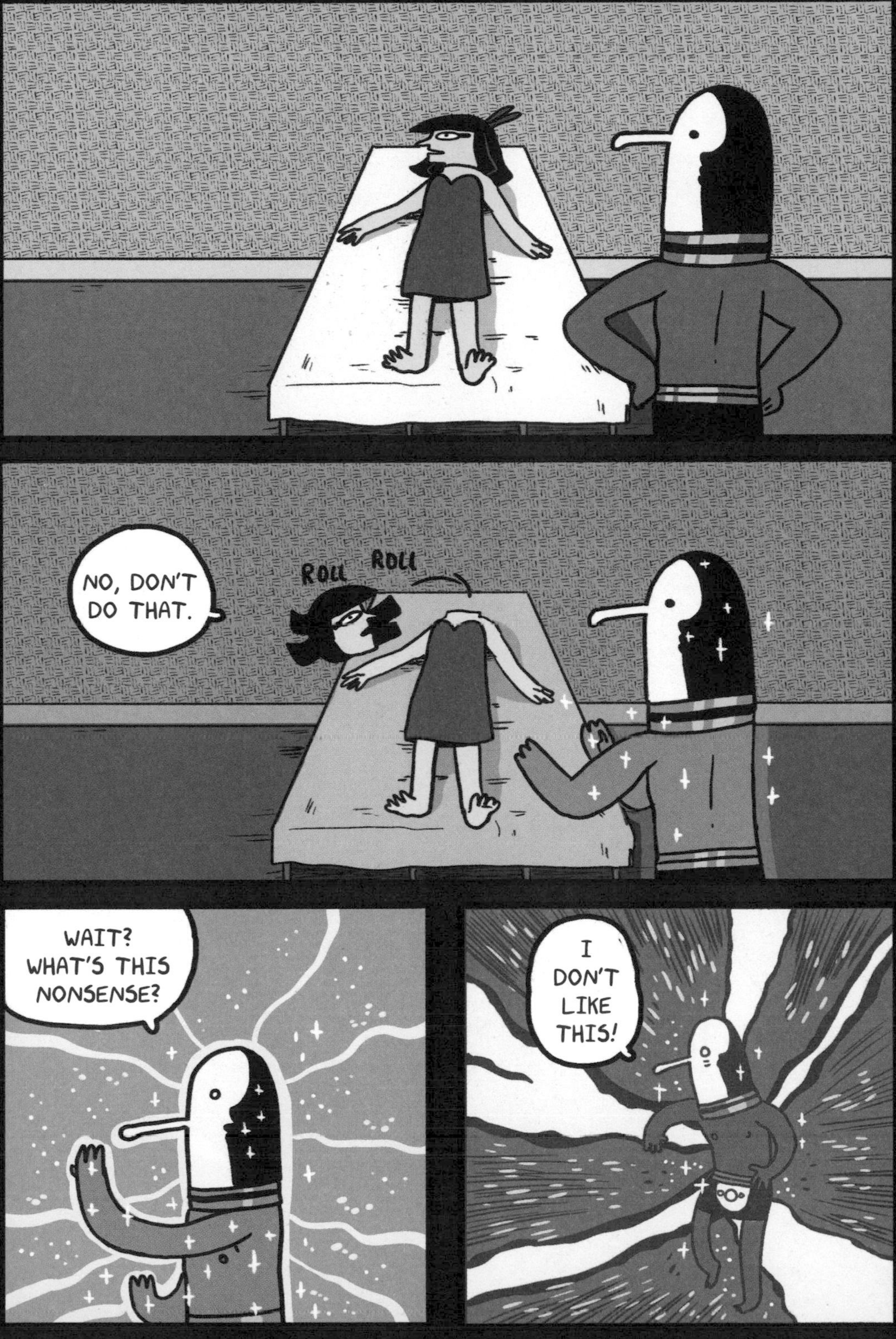
ROLL
ROLL
NO, DON'T DO THAT.
WAIT? WHAT'S THIS NONSENSE?
I DON'T LIKE THIS!

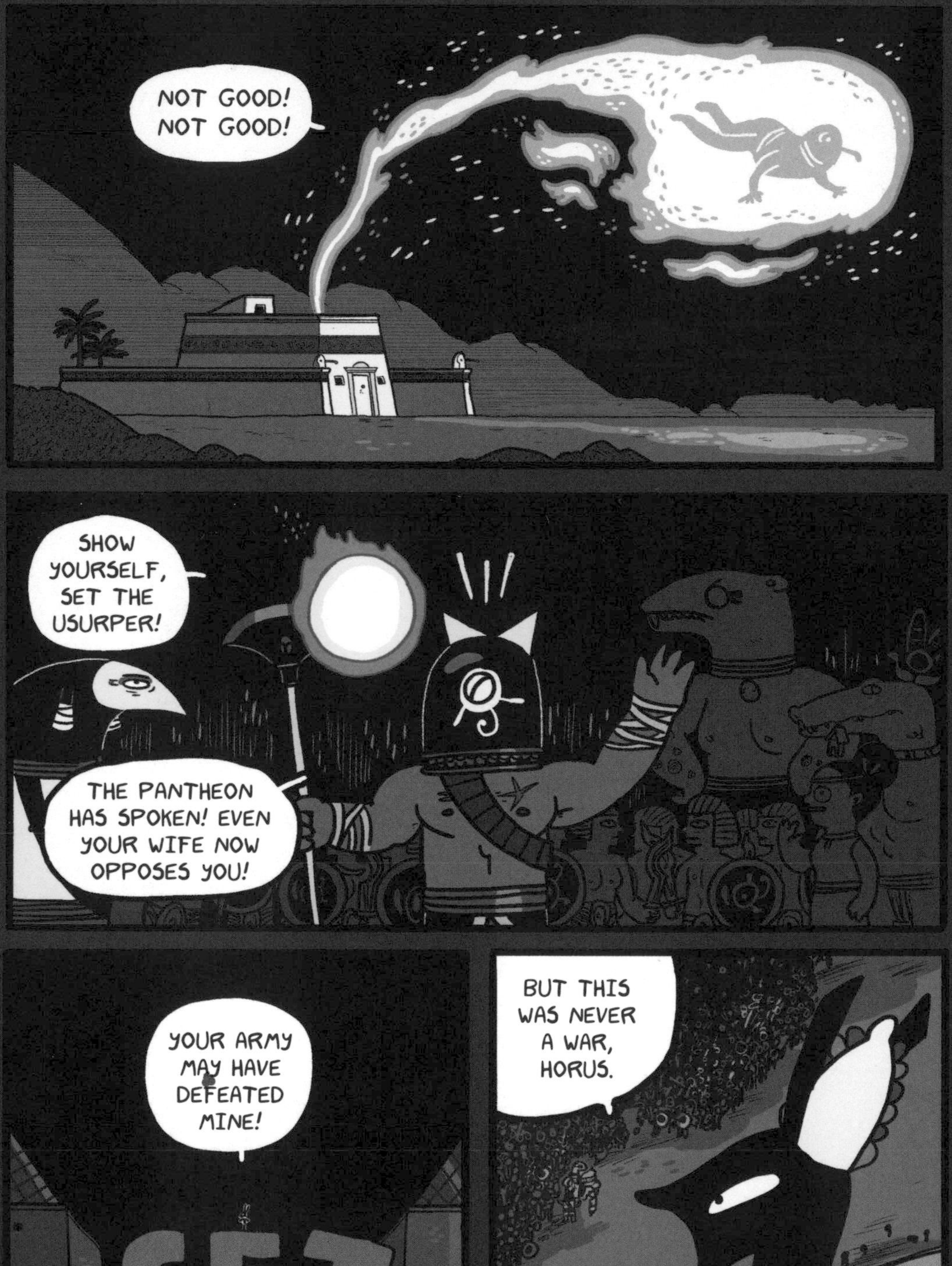
NOT GOOD! NOT GOOD!
SHOW YOURSELF, SET THE USURPER!
THE PANTHEON HAS SPOKEN! EVEN YOUR WIFE NOW OPPOSES YOU!
YOUR ARMY MAY HAVE DEFEATED MINE!
SET
BUT THIS WAS NEVER A WAR, HORUS.

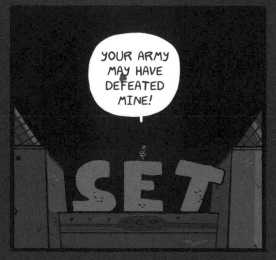

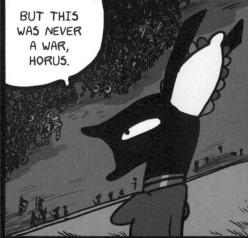

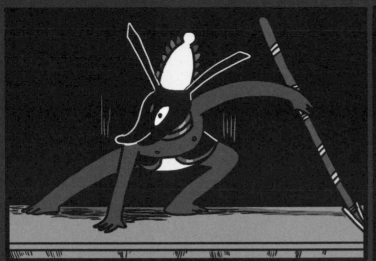

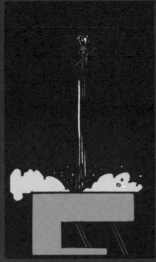

IF THE PANTHEON HAD REALLY SPOKEN, I WOULD HAVE BEEN EASILY DEFEATED!

LET ME DO IT, DARLING!

INDEED! EVEN YOUR GIRLFRIEND COULD KILL ME IN A SINGLE SWING OF HER SWORD!

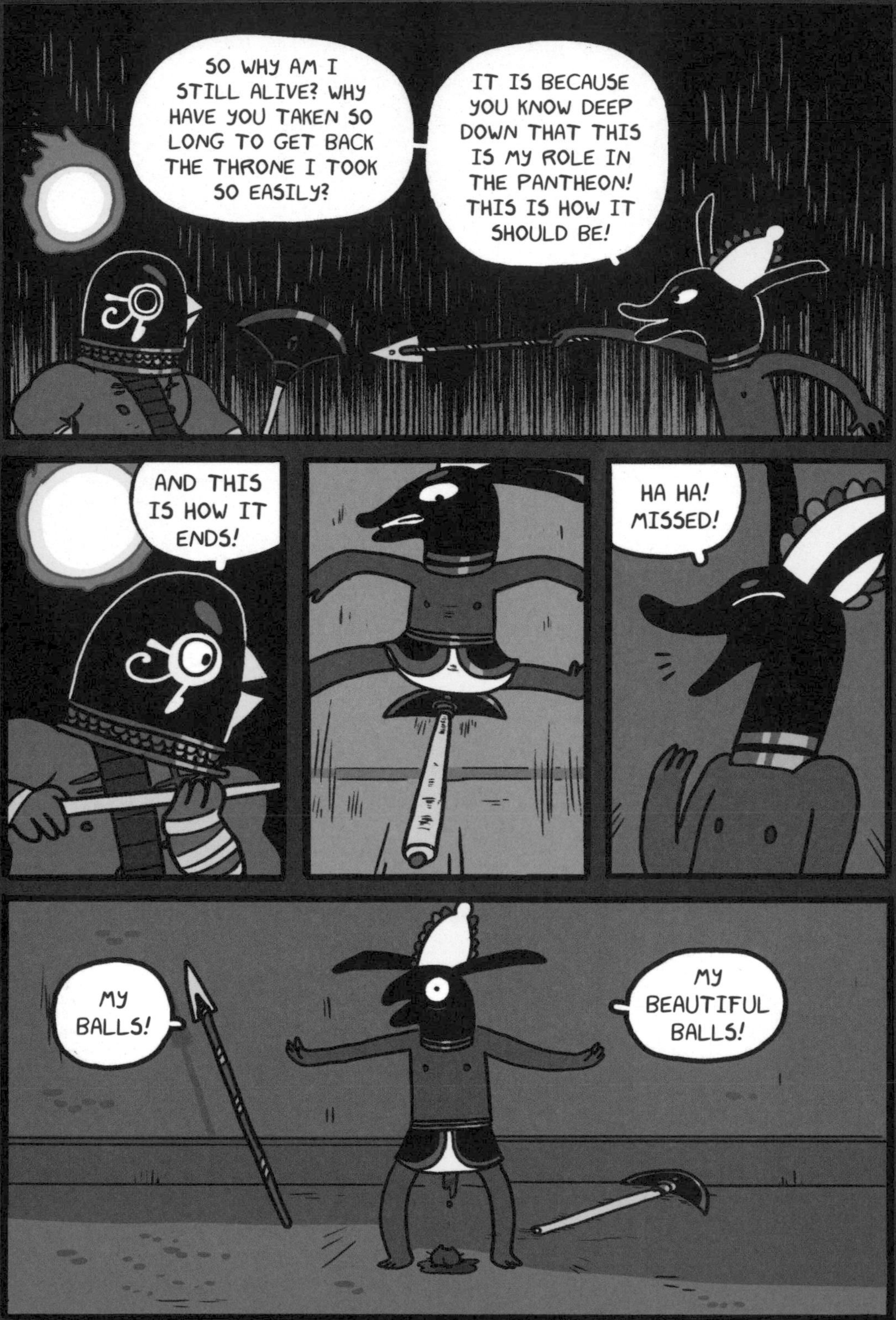
SO WHY AM I STILL ALIVE? WHY HAVE YOU TAKEN SO LONG TO GET BACK THE THRONE I TOOK SO EASILY?
IT IS BECAUSE YOU KNOW DEEP DOWN THAT THIS IS MY ROLE IN THE PANTHEON! THIS IS HOW IT SHOULD BE!
AND THIS IS HOW IT ENDS!
HA HA! MISSED!
MY BALLS!
MY BEAUTIFUL BALLS!

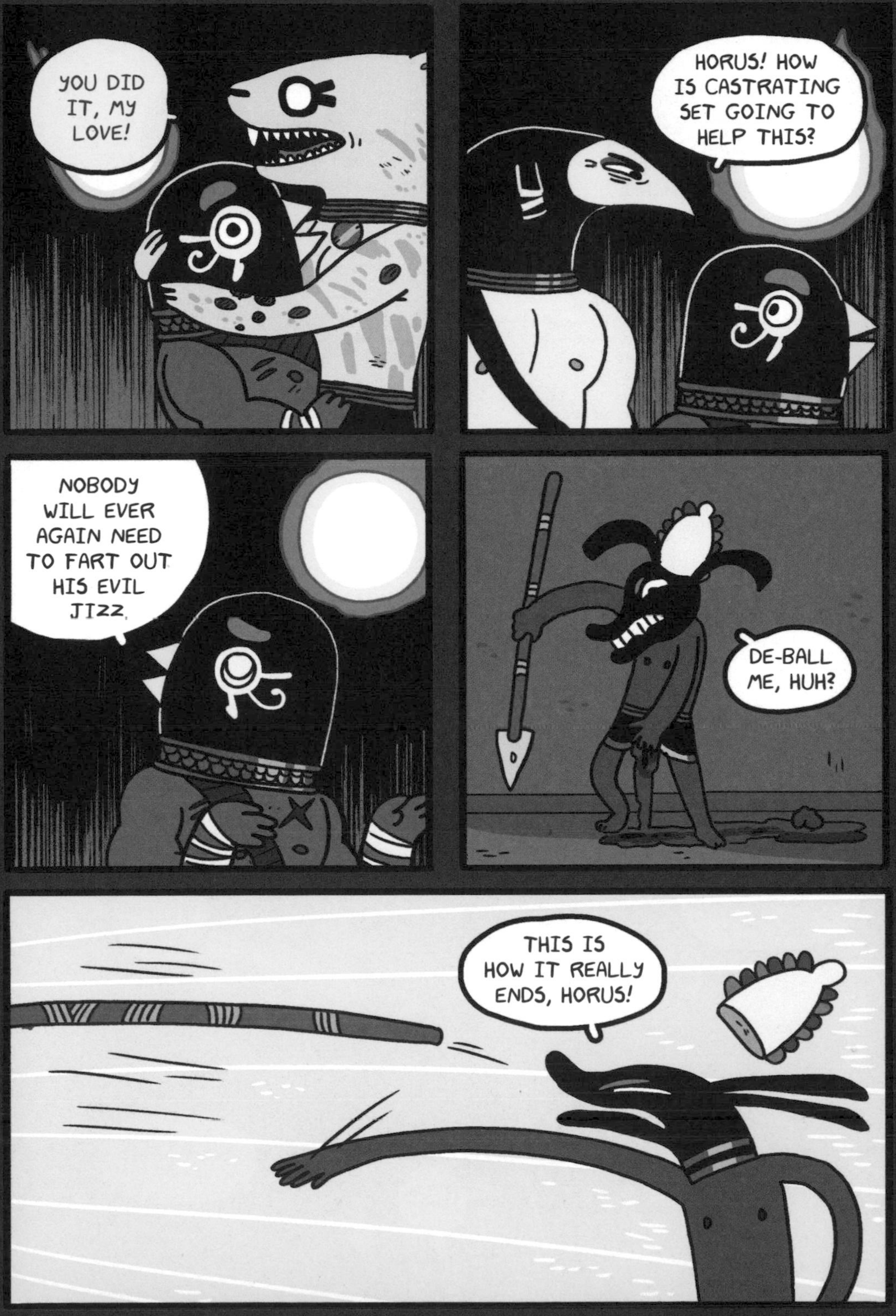
YOU DID IT, MY LOVE!
HORUS! HOW IS CASTRATING SET GOING TO HELP THIS?
NOBODY WILL EVER AGAIN NEED TO FART OUT HIS EVIL JIZZ.
DE-BALL ME, HUH?
THIS IS HOW IT REALLY ENDS, HORUS!

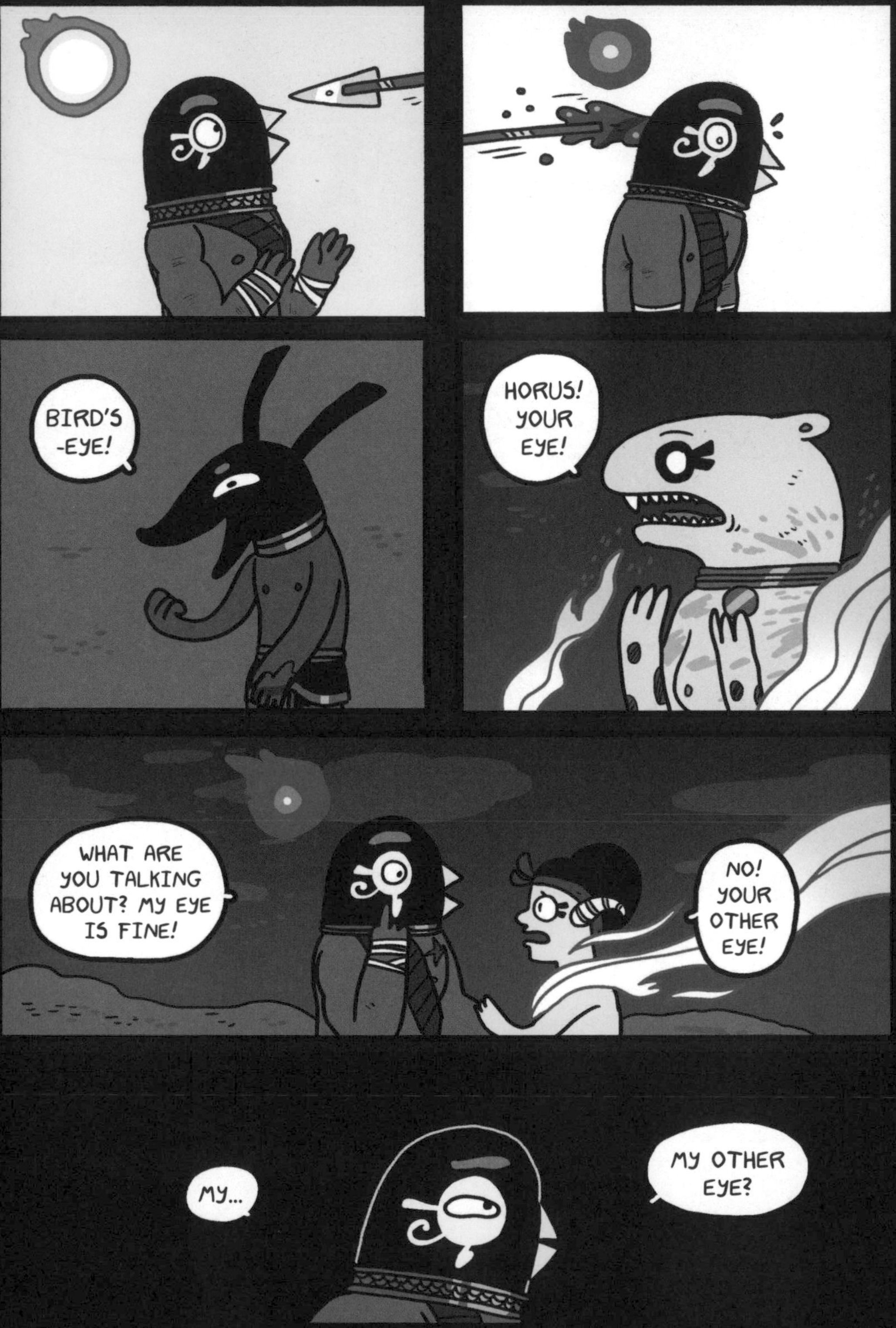
BIRD'S
-EYE!
HORUS!
YOUR
EYE!
WHAT ARE
YOU TALKING
ABOUT? MY EYE
IS FINE!
NO!
YOUR
OTHER
EYE!
MY...
MY OTHER
EYE?

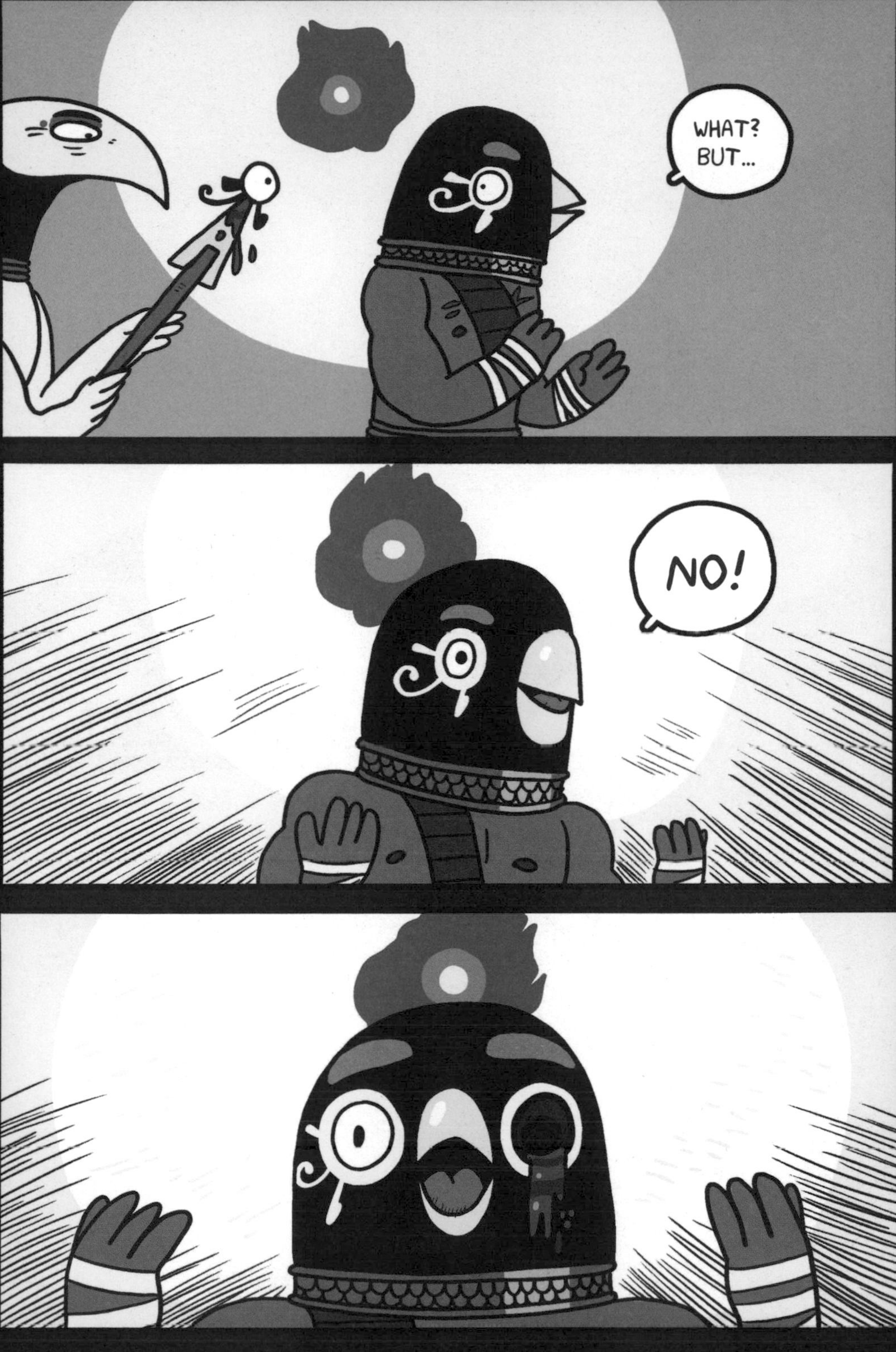
WHAT? BUT...
NO!

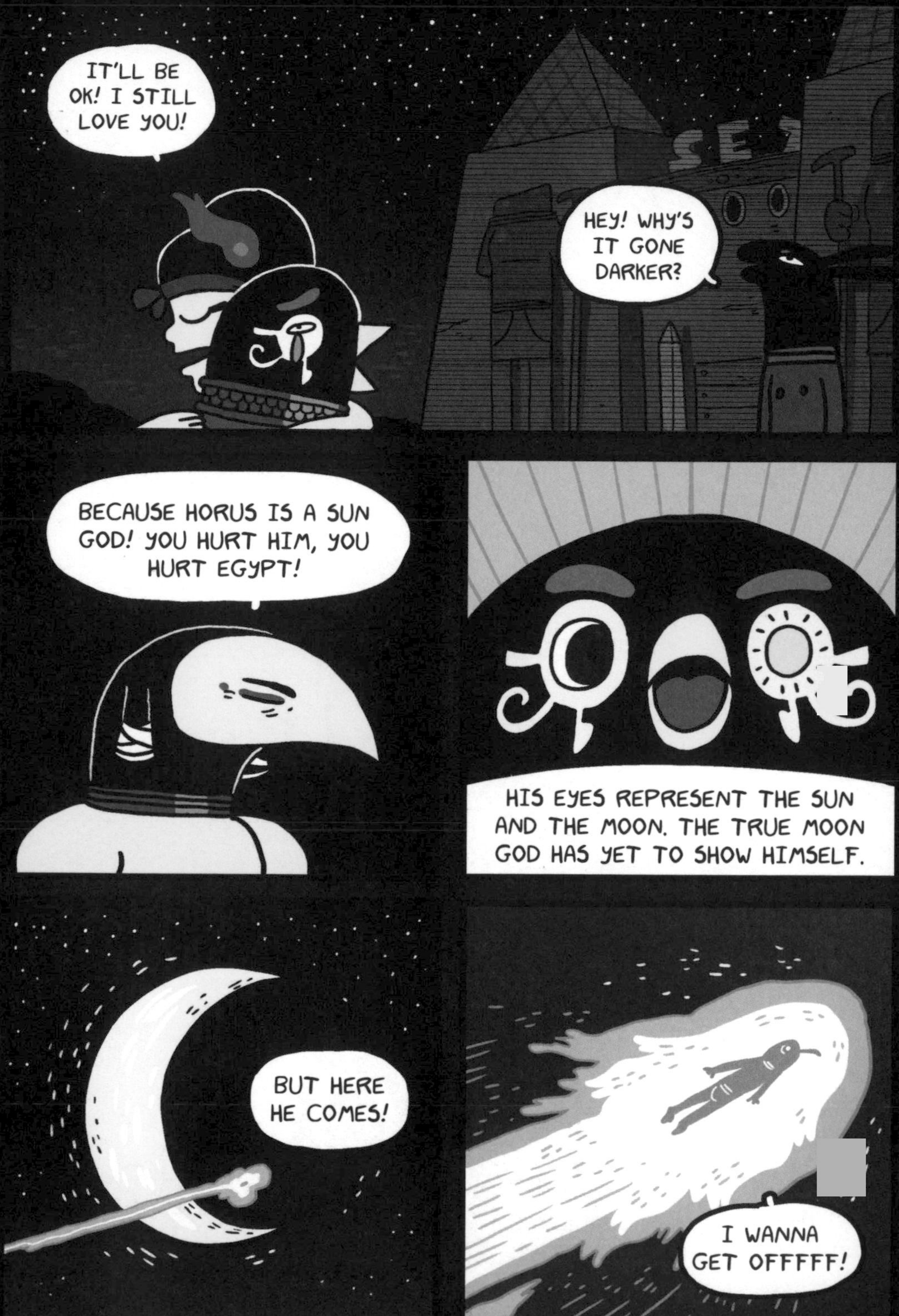
IT'LL BE OK! I STILL LOVE YOU!
HEY! WHY'S IT GONE DARKER?
BECAUSE HORUS IS A SUN GOD! YOU HURT HIM, YOU HURT EGYPT!
HIS EYES REPRESENT THE SUN AND THE MOON. THE TRUE MOON GOD HAS YET TO SHOW HIMSELF.
BUT HERE HE COMES!
I WANNA GET OFFFFF!

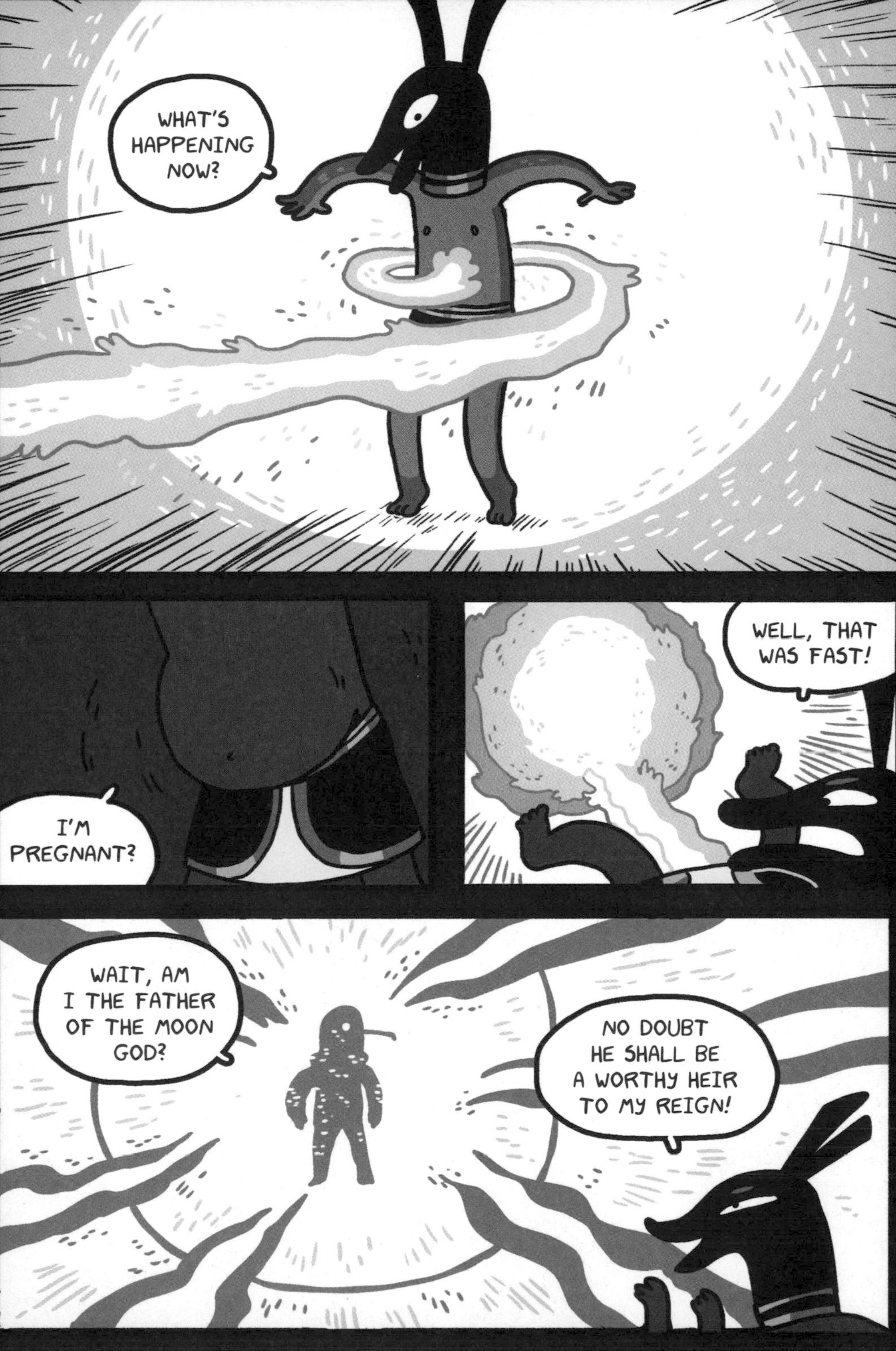
WHAT'S HAPPENING NOW?
I'M PREGNANT?
WELL, THAT WAS FAST!
WAIT, AM I THE FATHER OF THE MOON GOD?
NO DOUBT HE SHALL BE A WORTHY HEIR TO MY REIGN!

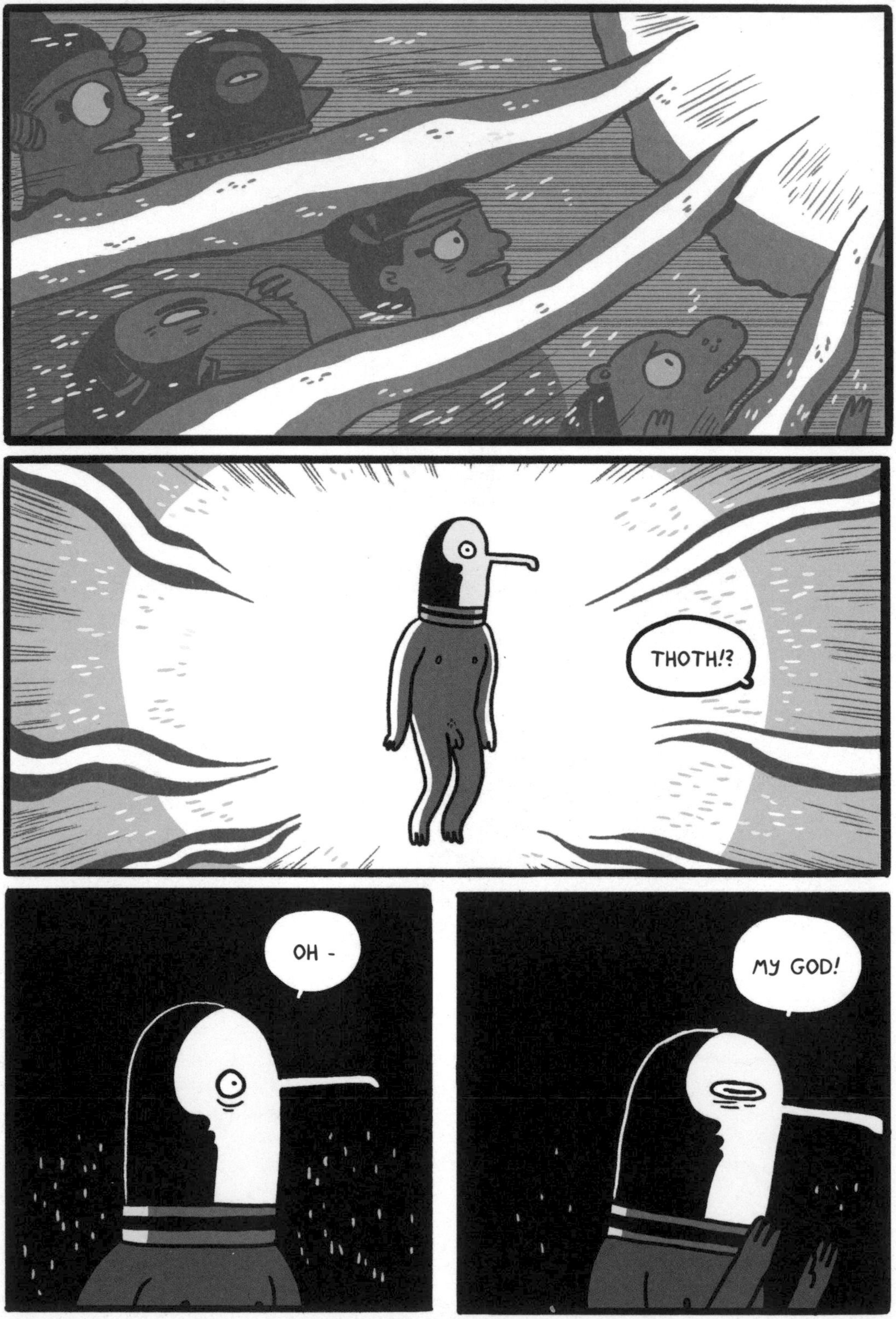
THOTH!?
OH -
MY GOD!

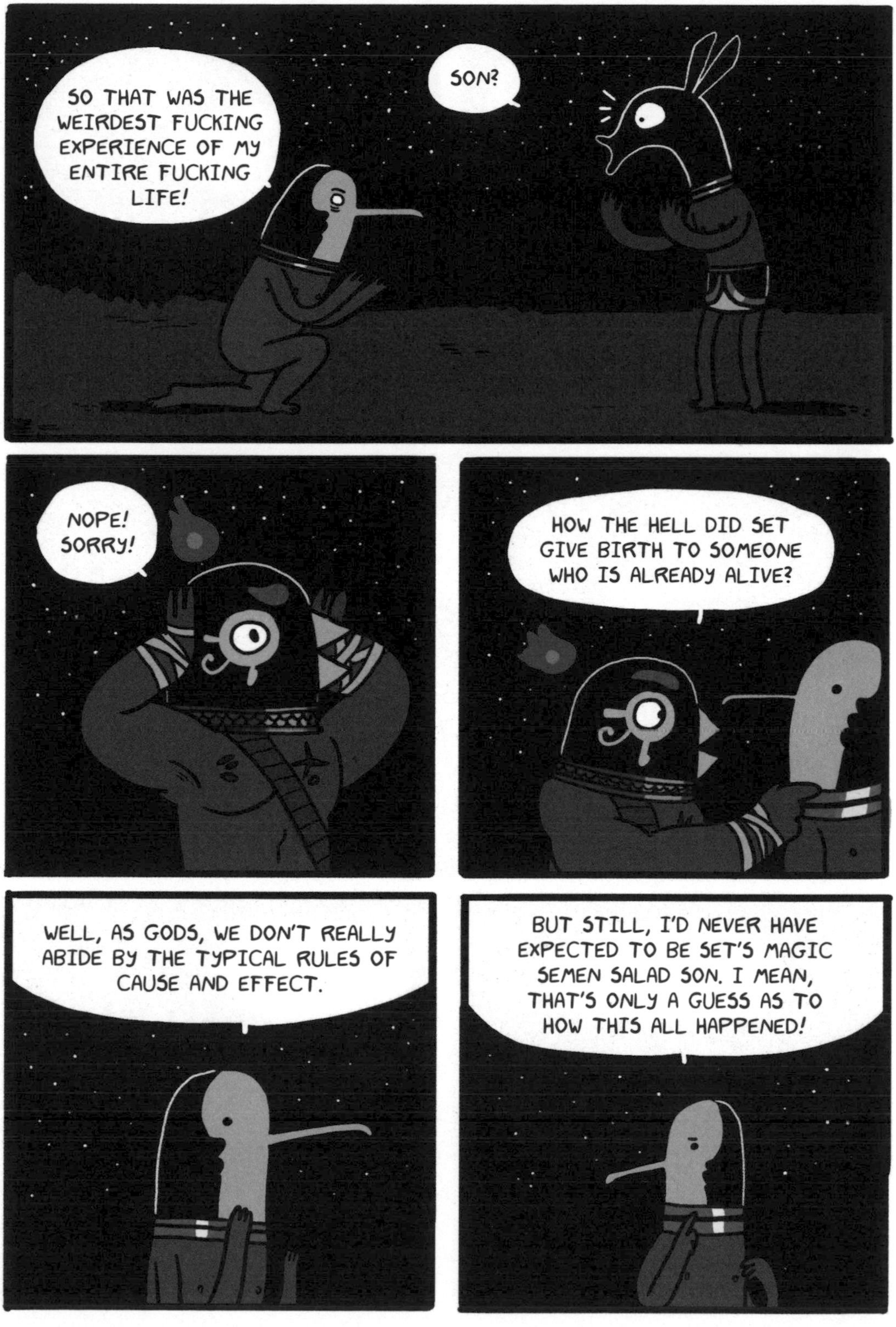
SO THAT WAS THE WEIRDEST FUCKING EXPERIENCE OF MY ENTIRE FUCKING LIFE!
SON?
NOPE! SORRY!
HOW THE HELL DID SET GIVE BIRTH TO SOMEONE WHO IS ALREADY ALIVE?
WELL, AS GODS, WE DON'T REALLY ABIDE BY THE TYPICAL RULES OF CAUSE AND EFFECT.
BUT STILL, I'D NEVER HAVE EXPECTED TO BE SET'S MAGIC SEMEN SALAD SON. I MEAN, THAT'S ONLY A GUESS AS TO HOW THIS ALL HAPPENED!

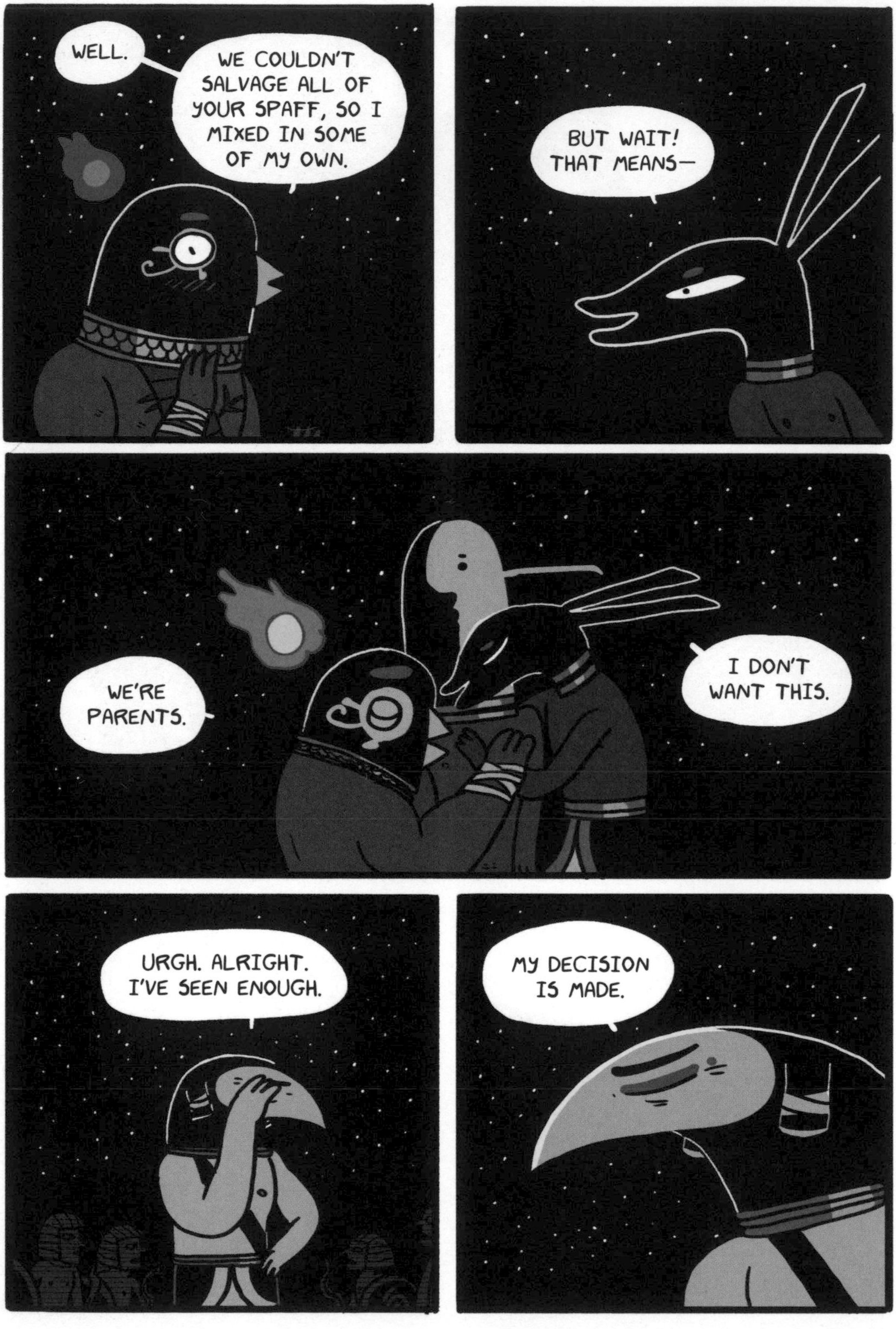
WELL.
WE COULDN'T SALVAGE ALL OF YOUR SPAFF, SO I MIXED IN SOME OF MY OWN.
BUT WAIT! THAT MEANS—
WE'RE PARENTS.
I DON'T WANT THIS.
URGH. ALRIGHT. I'VE SEEN ENOUGH.
MY DECISION IS MADE.

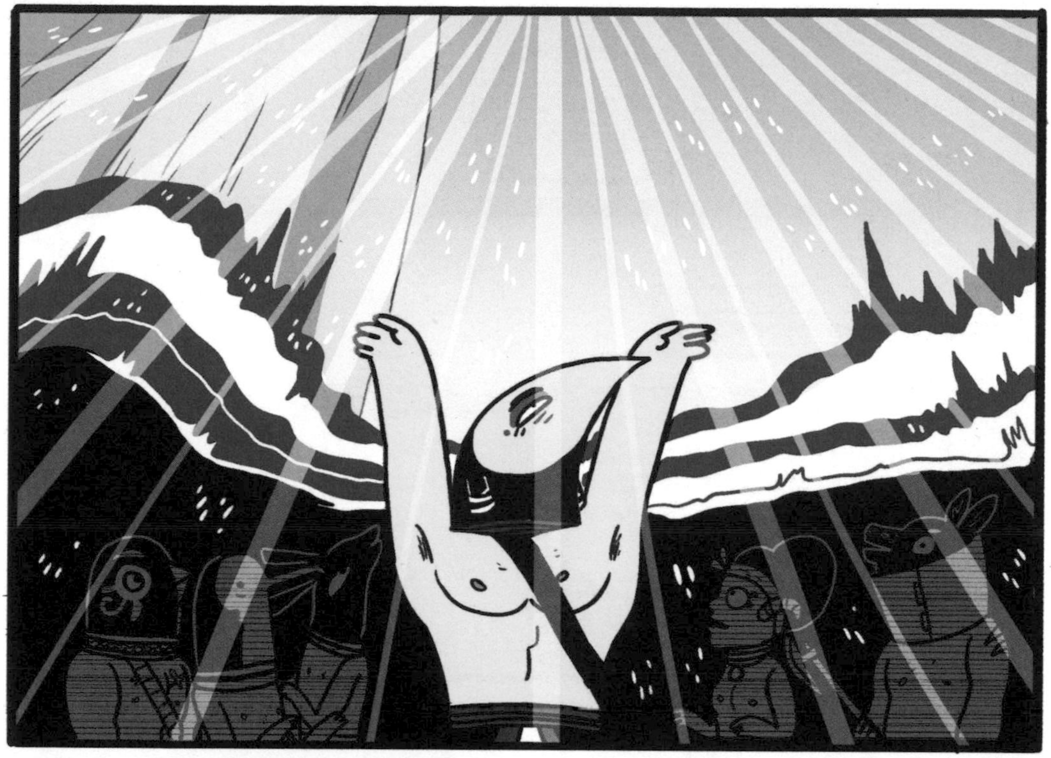

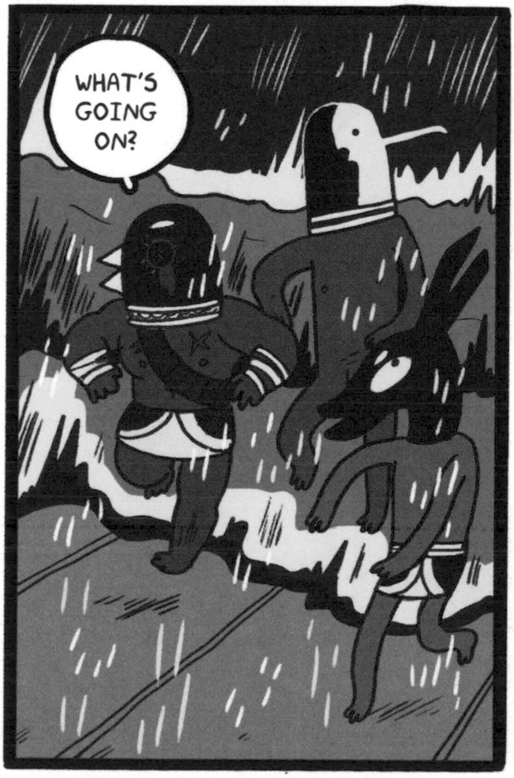
WHAT'S GOING ON?

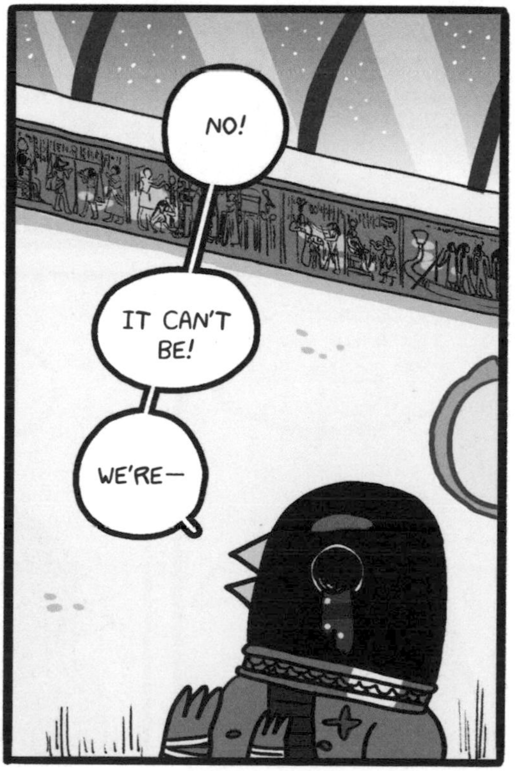
NO!
IT CAN'T BE!
WE'RE—

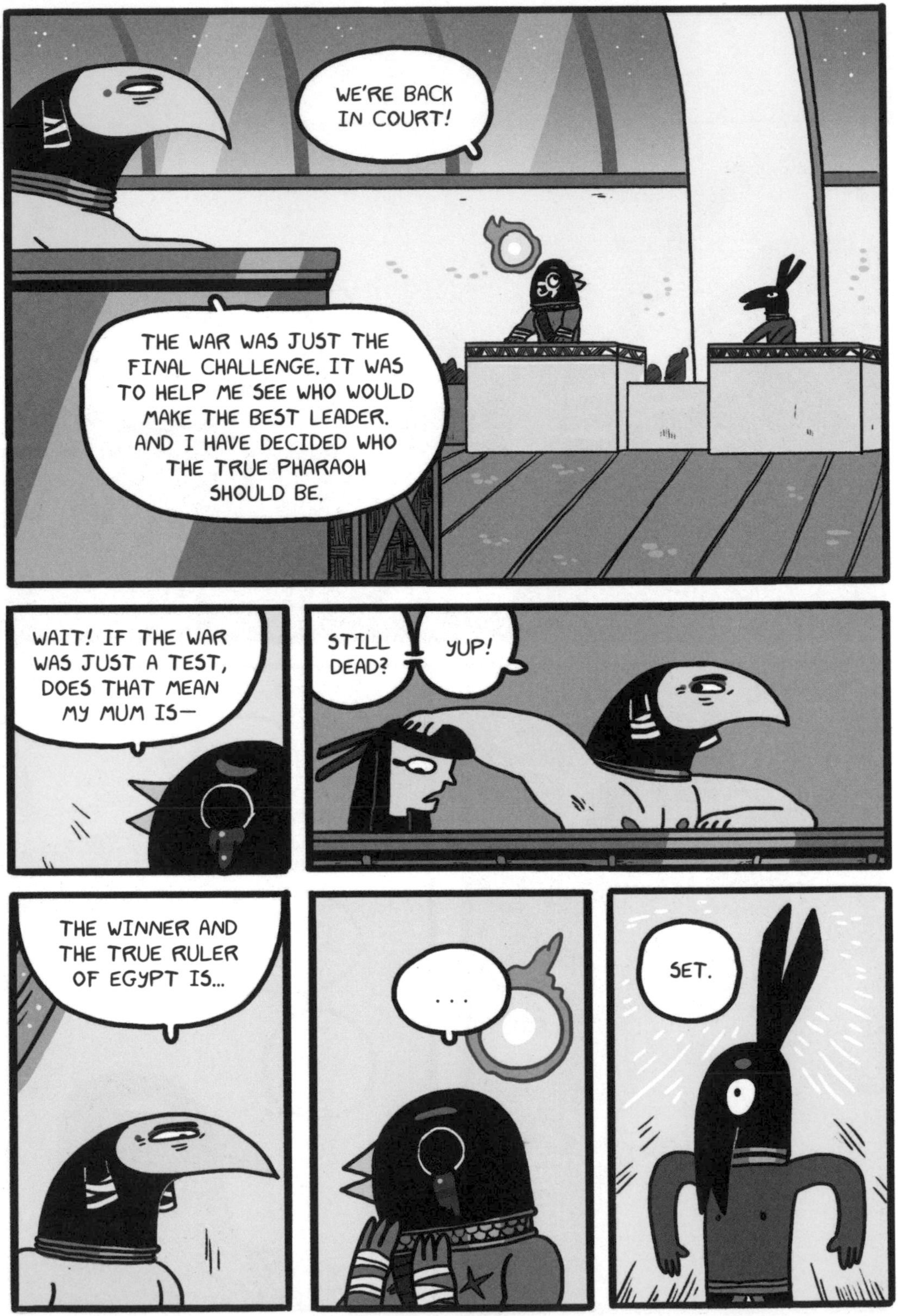
WE'RE BACK IN COURT!
THE WAR WAS JUST THE FINAL CHALLENGE. IT WAS TO HELP ME SEE WHO WOULD MAKE THE BEST LEADER. AND I HAVE DECIDED WHO THE TRUE PHARAOH SHOULD BE.
WAIT! IF THE WAR WAS JUST A TEST, DOES THAT MEAN MY MUM IS—
STILL DEAD?
YUP!
THE WINNER AND THE TRUE RULER OF EGYPT IS...
. . .
SET.

CHAPTER ELEVEN

★★★   BALANCE   ★★★

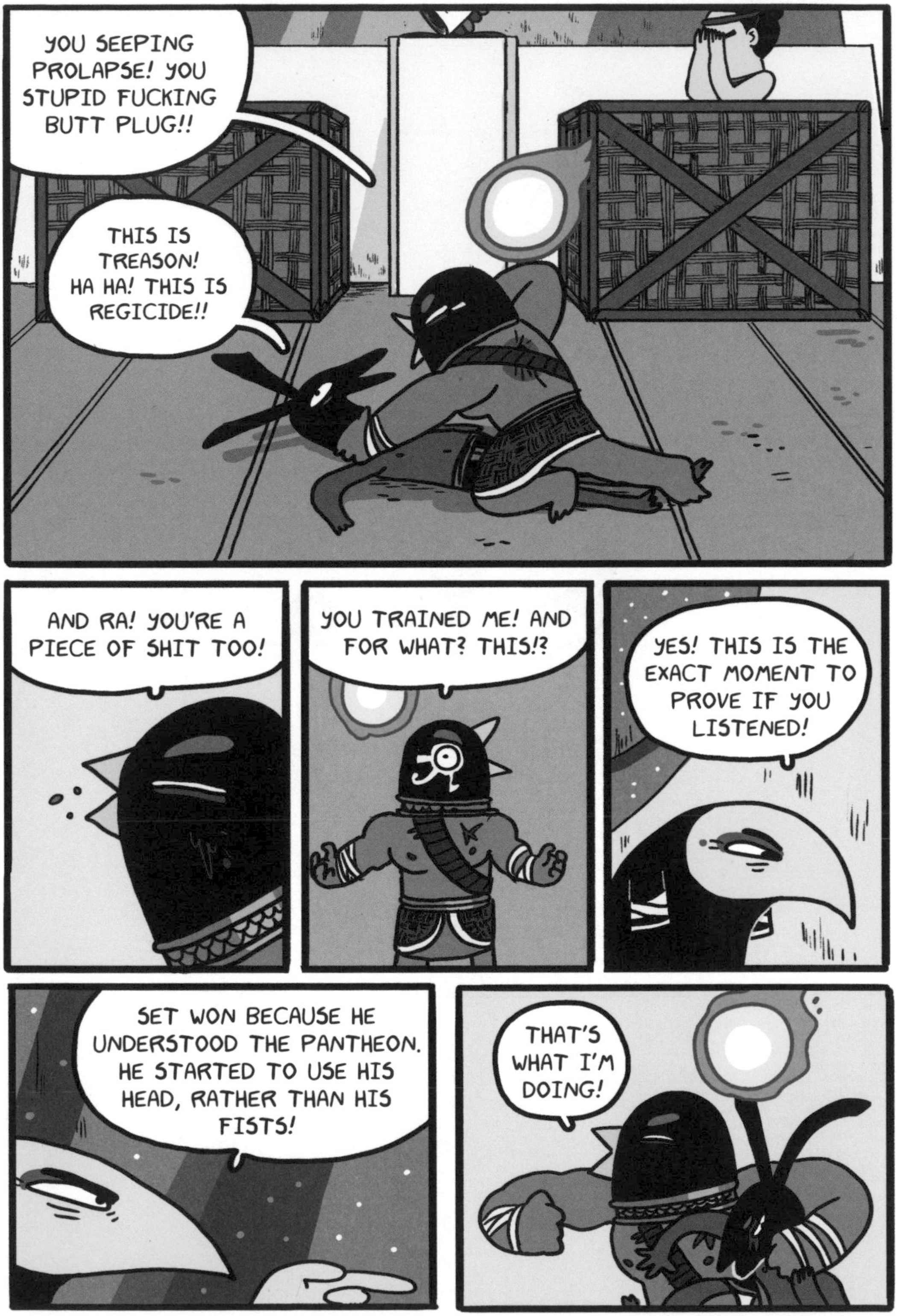
YOU SEEPING PROLAPSE! YOU STUPID FUCKING BUTT PLUG!!
THIS IS TREASON! HA HA! THIS IS REGICIDE!!
AND RA! YOU'RE A PIECE OF SHIT TOO!
YOU TRAINED ME! AND FOR WHAT? THIS!?
YES! THIS IS THE EXACT MOMENT TO PROVE IF YOU LISTENED!
SET WON BECAUSE HE UNDERSTOOD THE PANTHEON. HE STARTED TO USE HIS HEAD, RATHER THAN HIS FISTS!
THAT'S WHAT I'M DOING!

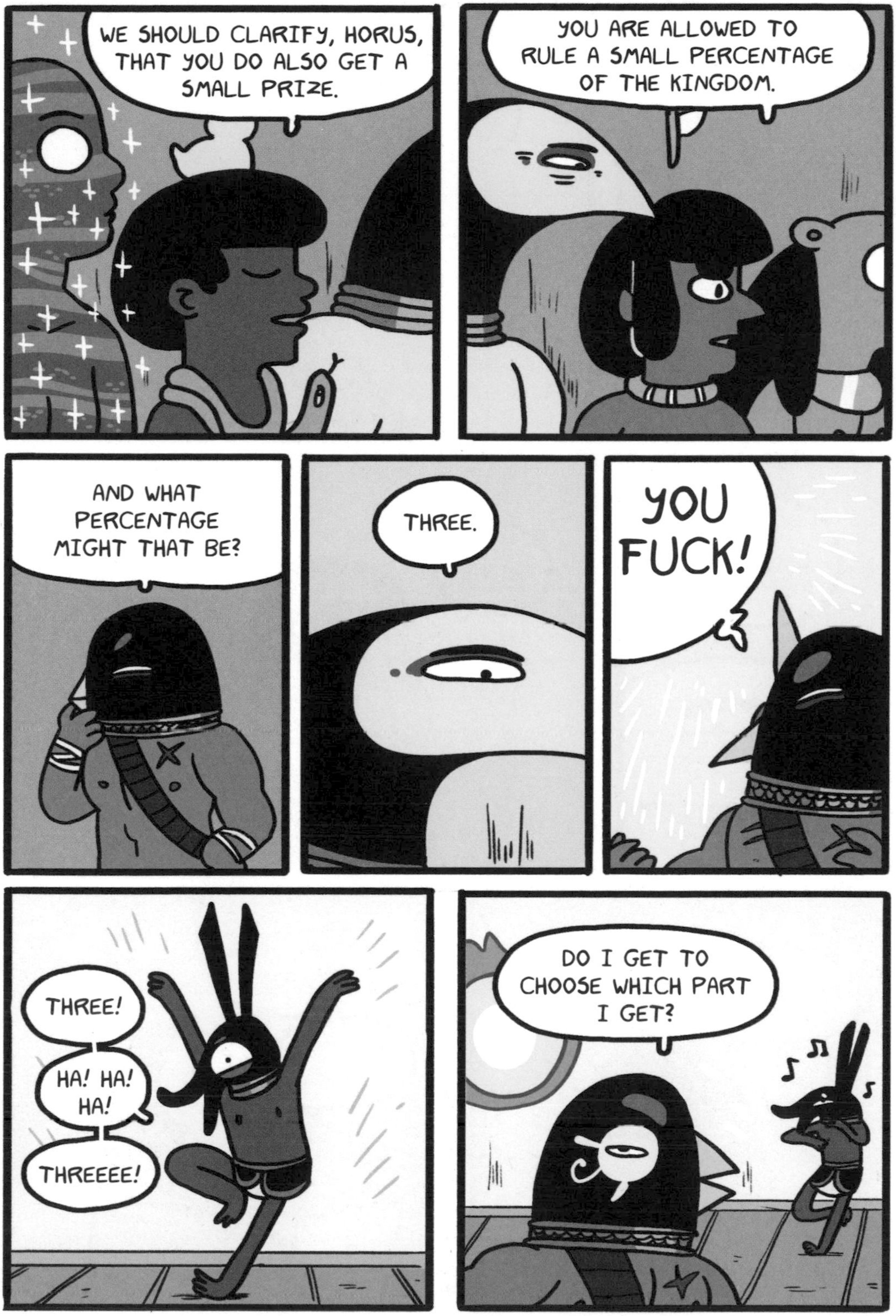
WE SHOULD CLARIFY, HORUS, THAT YOU DO ALSO GET A SMALL PRIZE.
YOU ARE ALLOWED TO RULE A SMALL PERCENTAGE OF THE KINGDOM.
AND WHAT PERCENTAGE MIGHT THAT BE?
THREE.
YOU FUCK!
THREE!
HA! HA! HA!
THREEEE!
DO I GET TO CHOOSE WHICH PART I GET?

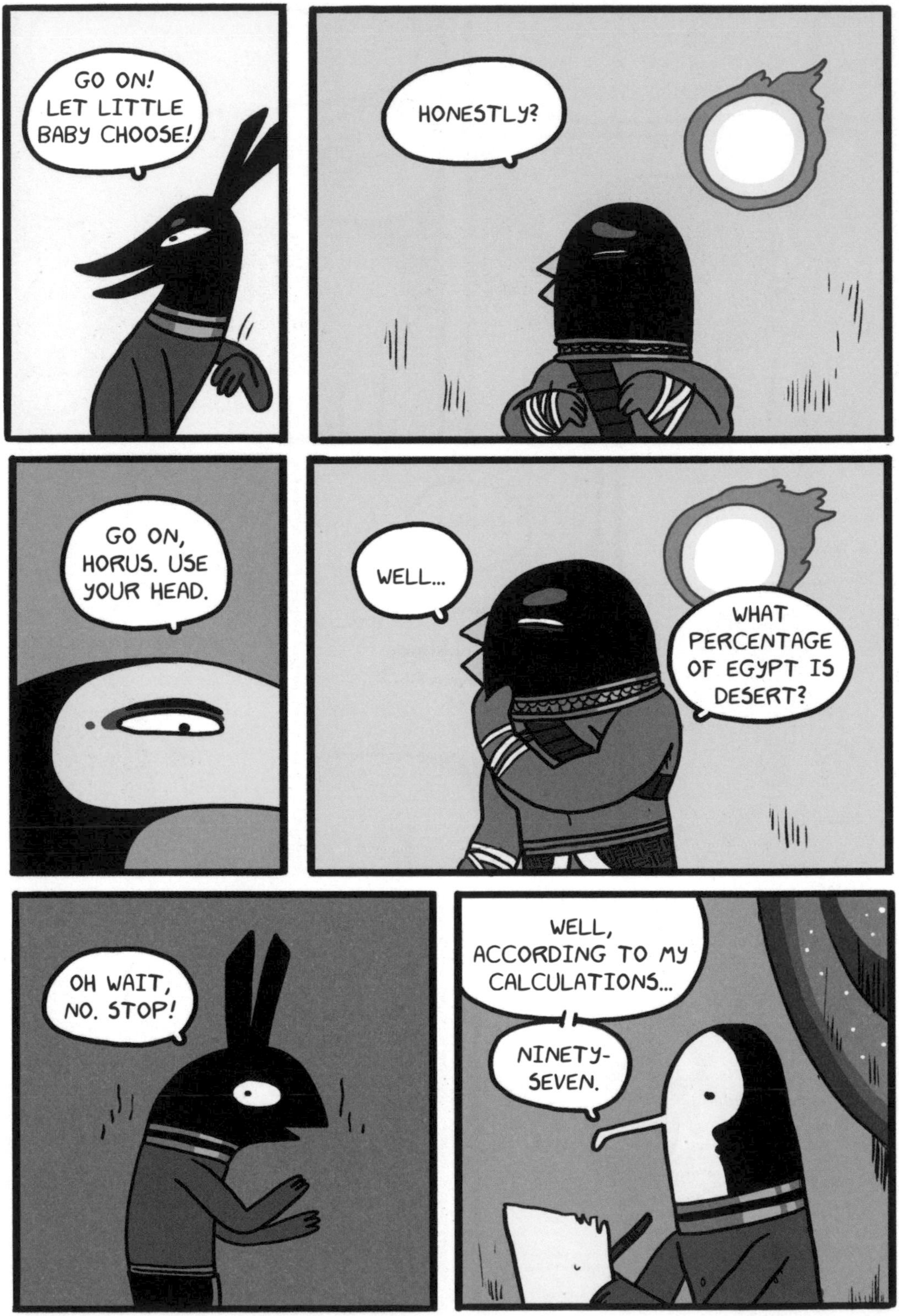
GO ON! LET LITTLE BABY CHOOSE!
HONESTLY?
GO ON, HORUS. USE YOUR HEAD.
WELL...
WHAT PERCENTAGE OF EGYPT IS DESERT?
OH WAIT, NO. STOP!
WELL, ACCORDING TO MY CALCULATIONS...
NINETY-SEVEN.

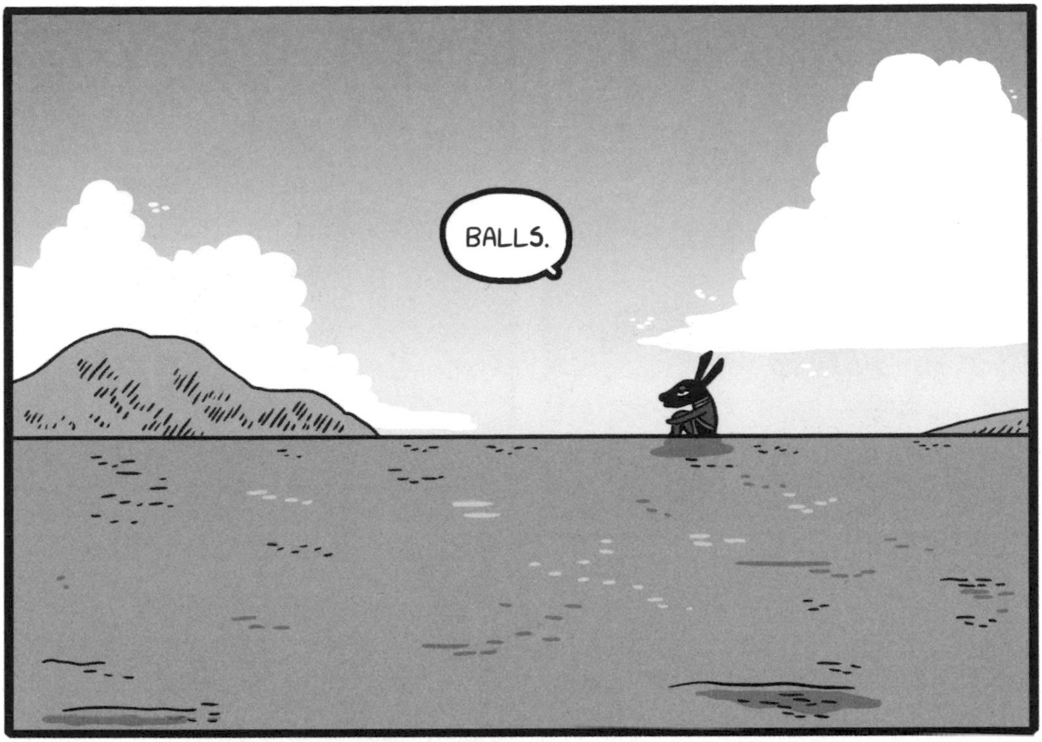
BALLS.

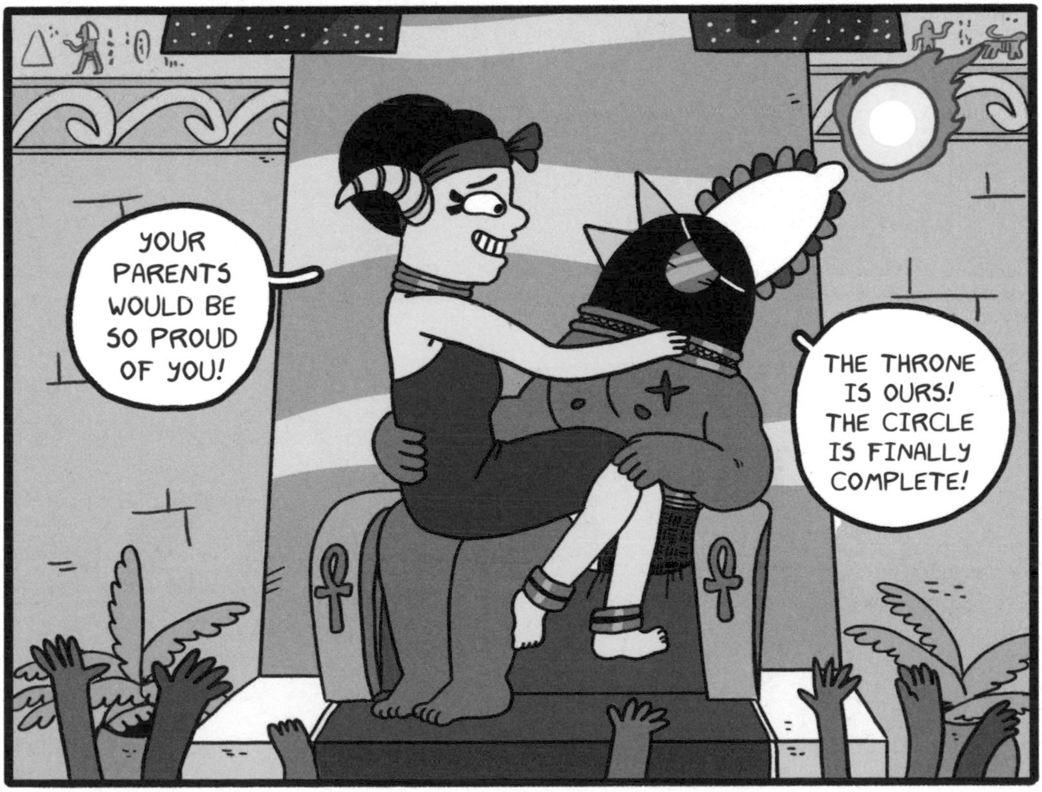
YOUR PARENTS WOULD BE SO PROUD OF YOU!
THE THRONE IS OURS! THE CIRCLE IS FINALLY COMPLETE!

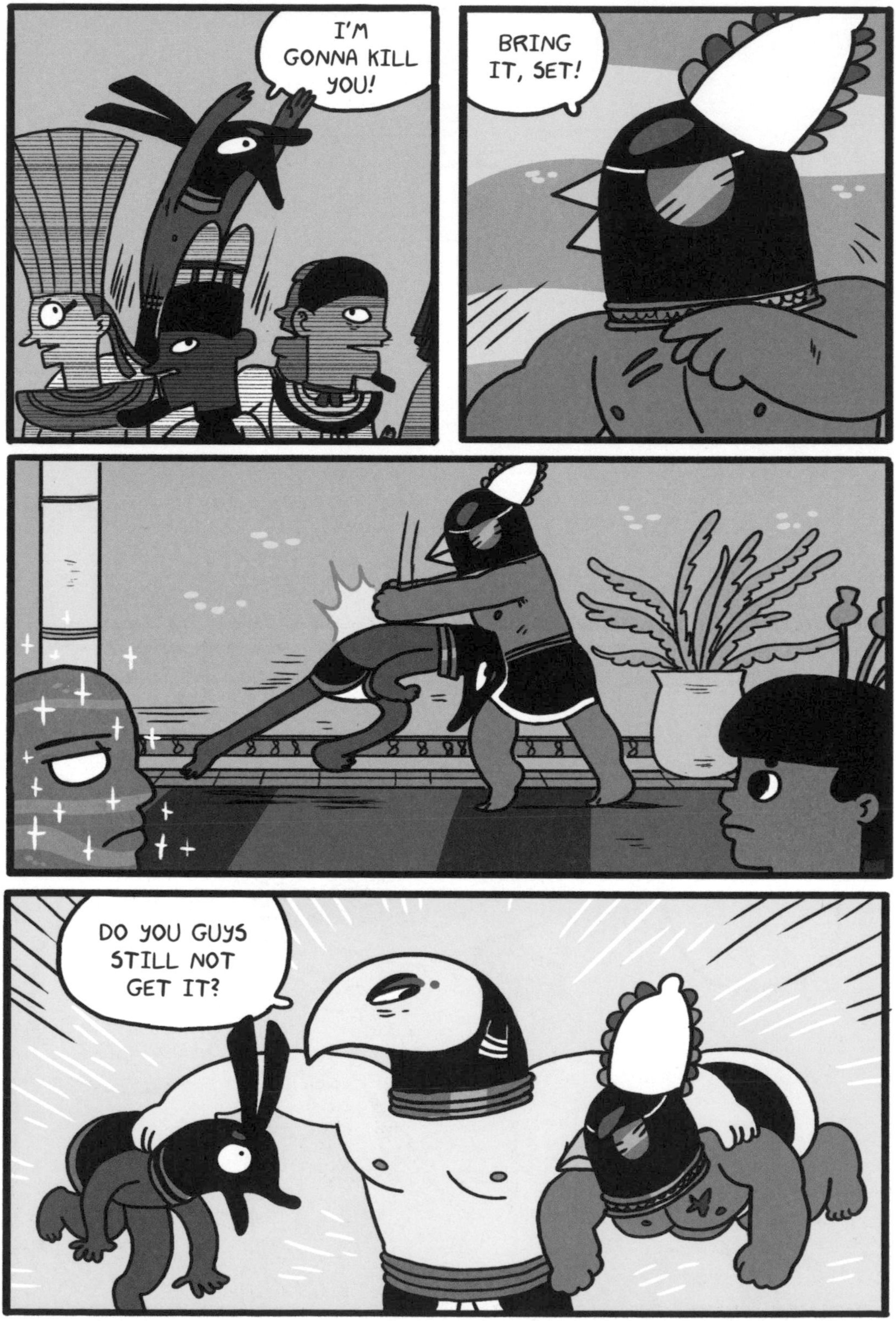
I'M GONNA KILL YOU!
BRING IT, SET!
DO YOU GUYS STILL NOT GET IT?

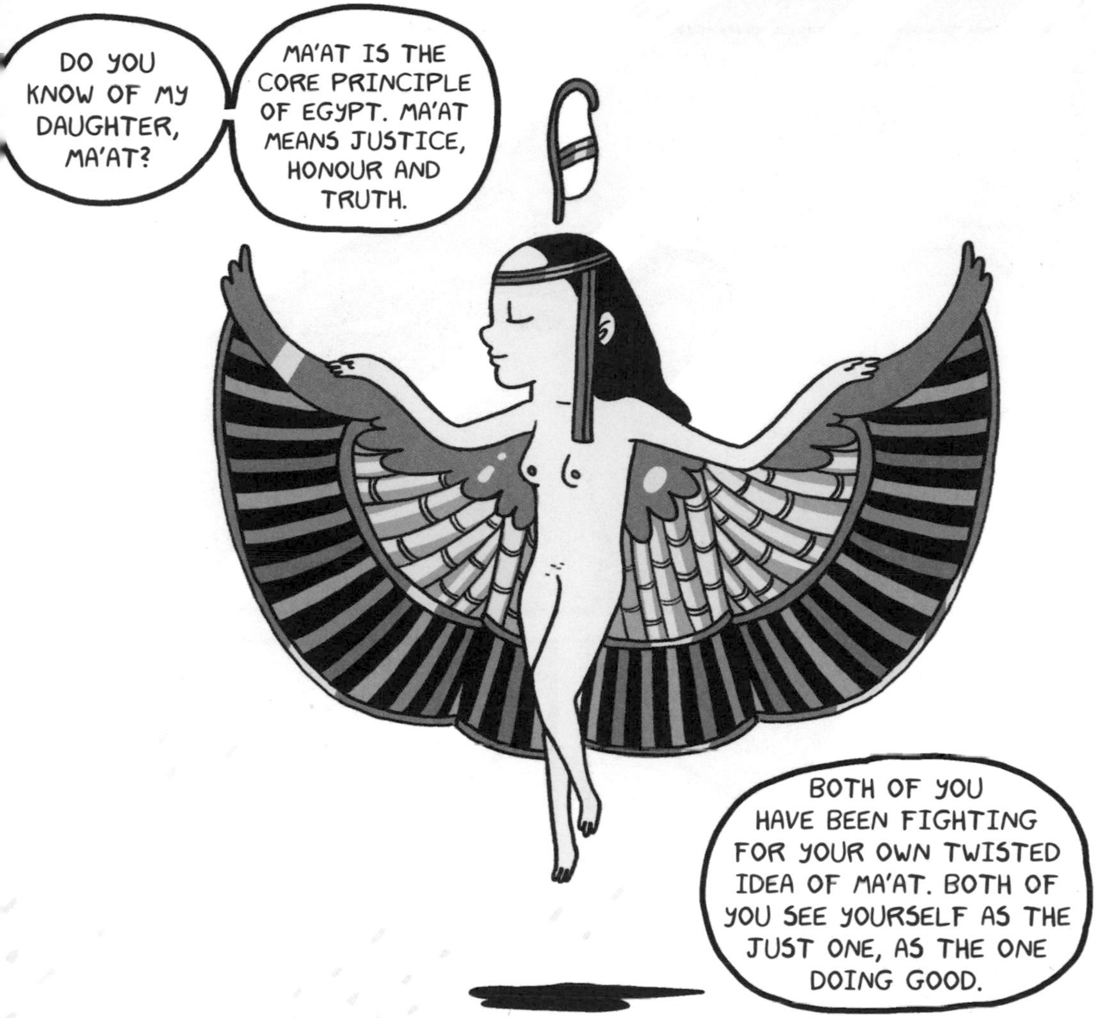
DO YOU KNOW OF MY DAUGHTER, MA'AT?
MA'AT IS THE CORE PRINCIPLE OF EGYPT. MA'AT MEANS JUSTICE, HONOUR AND TRUTH.
BOTH OF YOU HAVE BEEN FIGHTING FOR YOUR OWN TWISTED IDEA OF MA'AT. BOTH OF YOU SEE YOURSELF AS THE JUST ONE, AS THE ONE DOING GOOD.

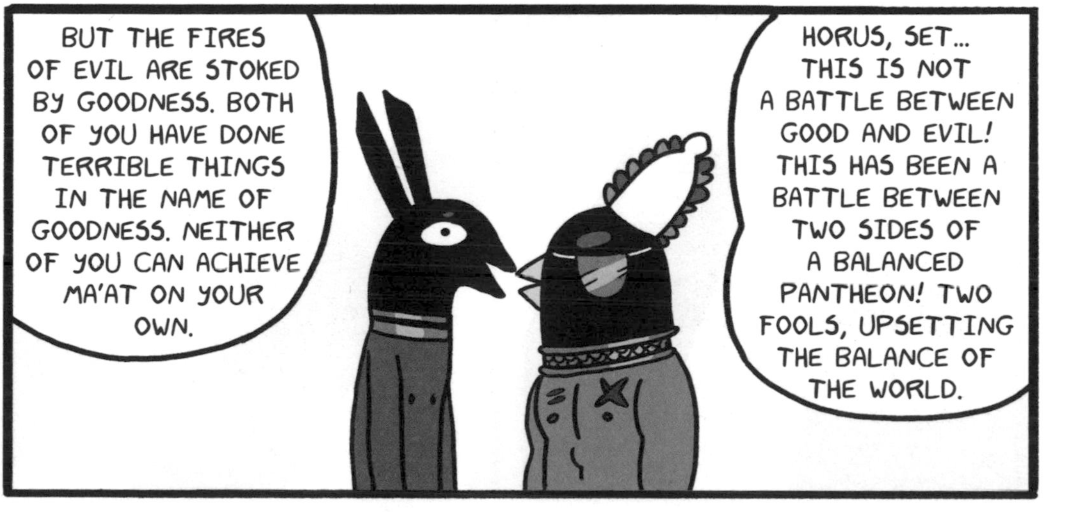
BUT THE FIRES OF EVIL ARE STOKED BY GOODNESS. BOTH OF YOU HAVE DONE TERRIBLE THINGS IN THE NAME OF GOODNESS. NEITHER OF YOU CAN ACHIEVE MA'AT ON YOUR OWN.
HORUS, SET... THIS IS NOT A BATTLE BETWEEN GOOD AND EVIL! THIS HAS BEEN A BATTLE BETWEEN TWO SIDES OF A BALANCED PANTHEON! TWO FOOLS, UPSETTING THE BALANCE OF THE WORLD.

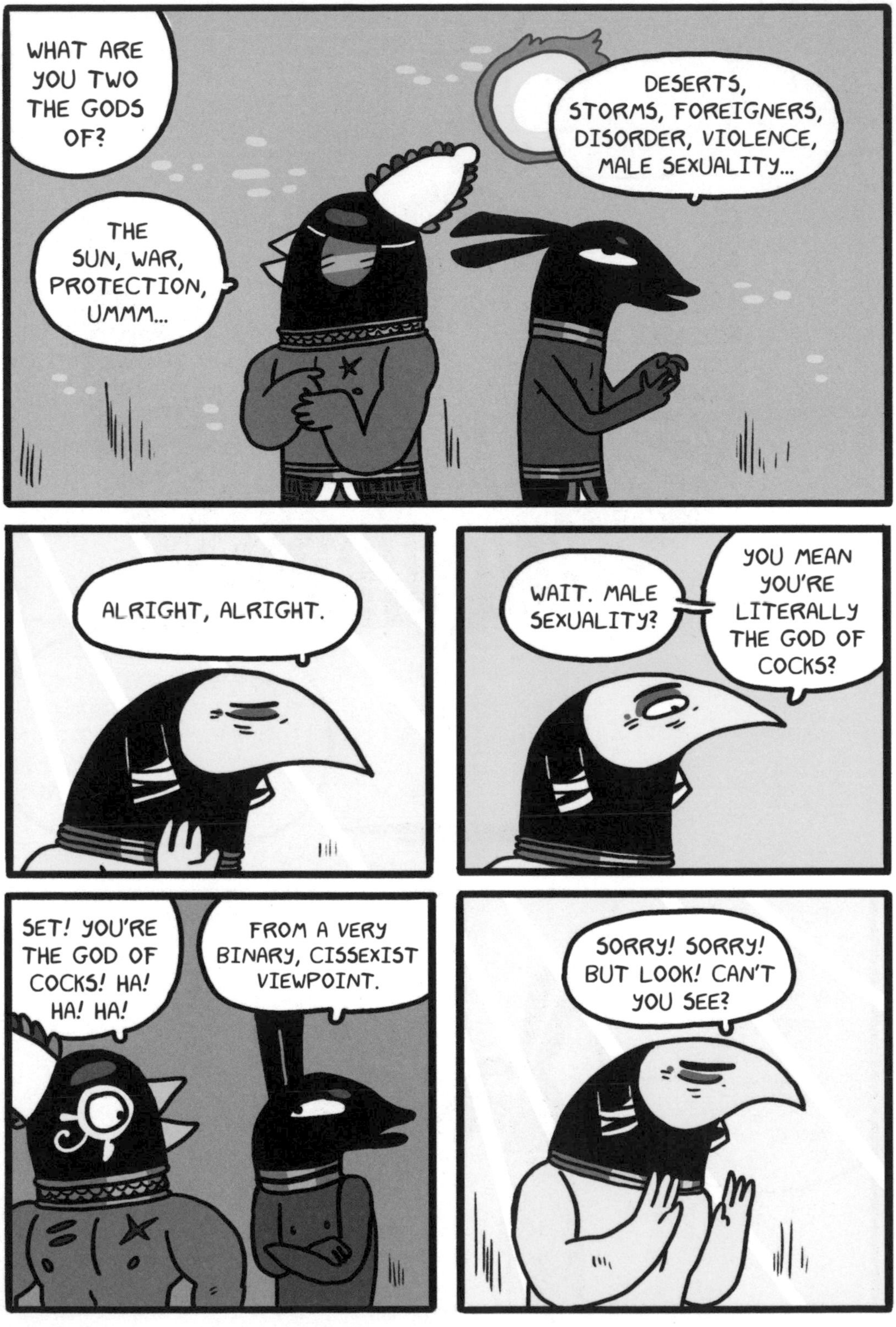
WHAT ARE YOU TWO THE GODS OF?
THE SUN, WAR, PROTECTION, UMMM...
DESERTS, STORMS, FOREIGNERS, DISORDER, VIOLENCE, MALE SEXUALITY...
ALRIGHT, ALRIGHT.
WAIT. MALE SEXUALITY?
YOU MEAN YOU'RE LITERALLY THE GOD OF COCKS?
SET! YOU'RE THE GOD OF COCKS! HA! HA! HA!
FROM A VERY BINARY, CISSEXIST VIEWPOINT.
SORRY! SORRY! BUT LOOK! CAN'T YOU SEE?

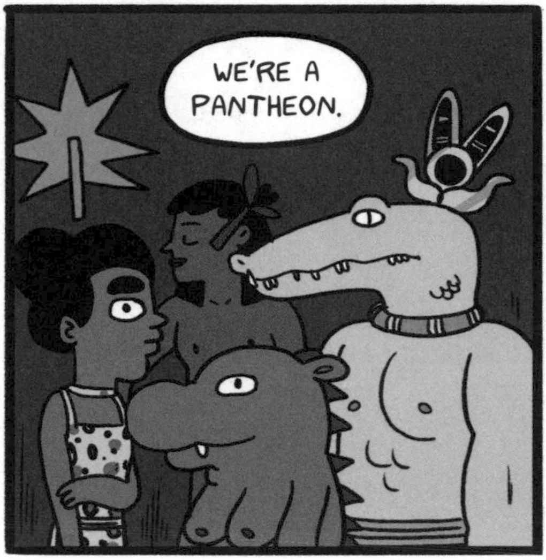
WE'RE A PANTHEON.

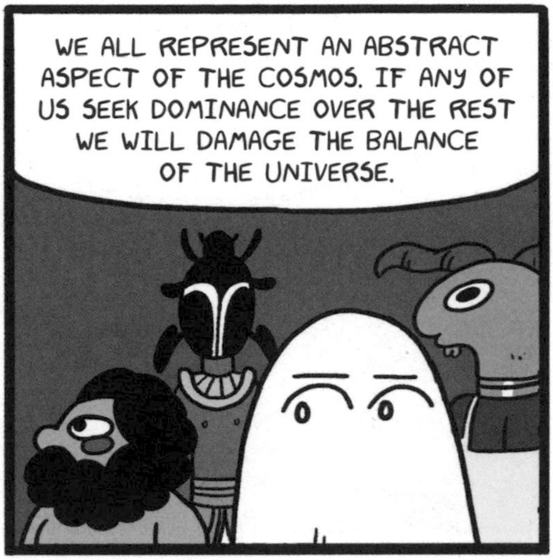
WE ALL REPRESENT AN ABSTRACT ASPECT OF THE COSMOS. IF ANY OF US SEEK DOMINANCE OVER THE REST WE WILL DAMAGE THE BALANCE OF THE UNIVERSE.

BUT HUMANS DON'T REPRESENT ANYTHING. THEY'RE NOT BORN WITH A ROLE TO PLAY. THEY LOOK TO US FOR GUIDANCE, BUT THEY ALL HAVE THEIR OWN UNIQUE, UNPREDICTABLE POTENTIAL. THEY'RE ALL EQUAL, THEY'RE ALL THE SAME AND THEY'RE ALL DIFFERENT.

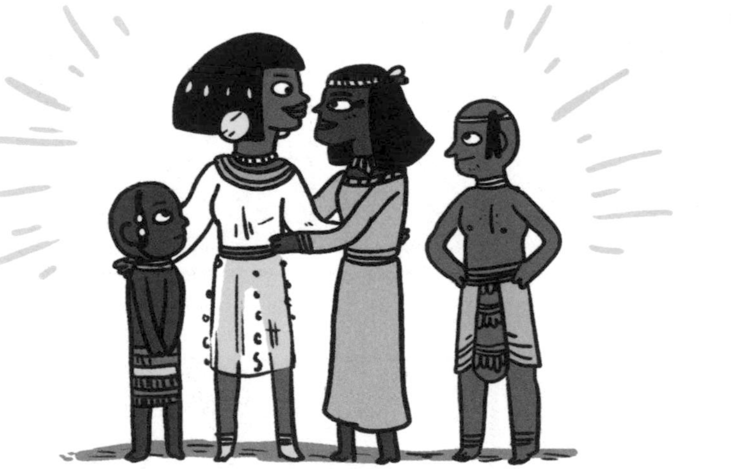

WHEN I FIRST LEFT EGYPT, WHEN THE OLD GODS JOURNEYED TO DUAT ON THE HEAVENLY COW, I THOUGHT HUMANS NEEDED AN INTERMEDIATE BETWEEN GOD AND MAN. I GAVE THEM OSIRIS, HOPING HE COULD BRIDGE THE GAP. BUT AS LONG AS A GOD WALKS AMONG HUMANS, THERE WILL BE NO MA'AT, BECAUSE THERE WILL BE SOMEONE WHO IS NOT EQUAL TO HUMANS.

WE NEED GODS OF DESTRUCTION, AS WELL AS GODS OF PEACE. IT IS NOT OUR JOB TO RULE HUMANS, IT IS OUR JOB TO BE THE WORLD THAT THEY RULE.

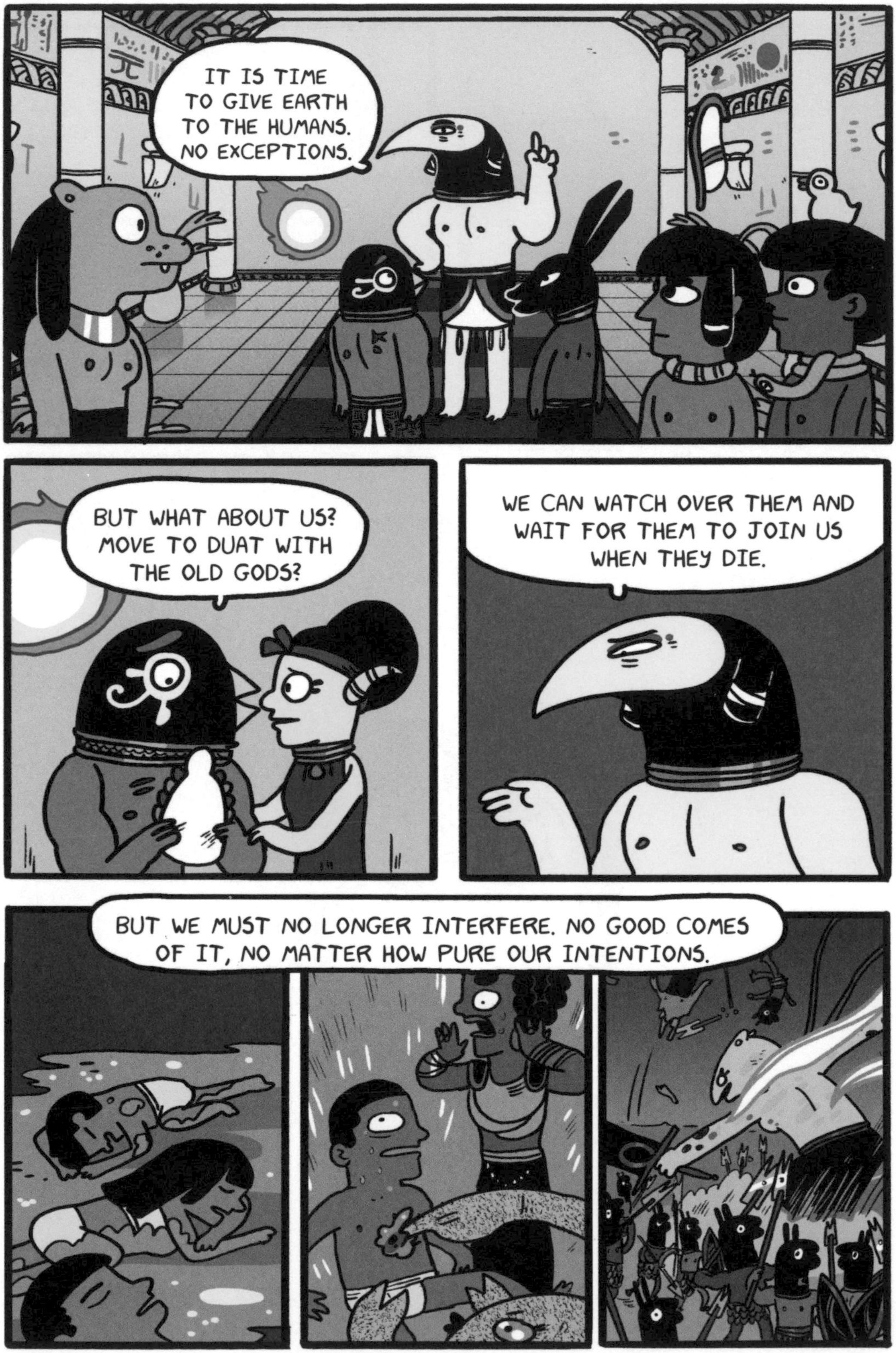
IT IS TIME TO GIVE EARTH TO THE HUMANS. NO EXCEPTIONS.
BUT WHAT ABOUT US? MOVE TO DUAT WITH THE OLD GODS?
WE CAN WATCH OVER THEM AND WAIT FOR THEM TO JOIN US WHEN THEY DIE.
BUT WE MUST NO LONGER INTERFERE. NO GOOD COMES OF IT, NO MATTER HOW PURE OUR INTENTIONS.

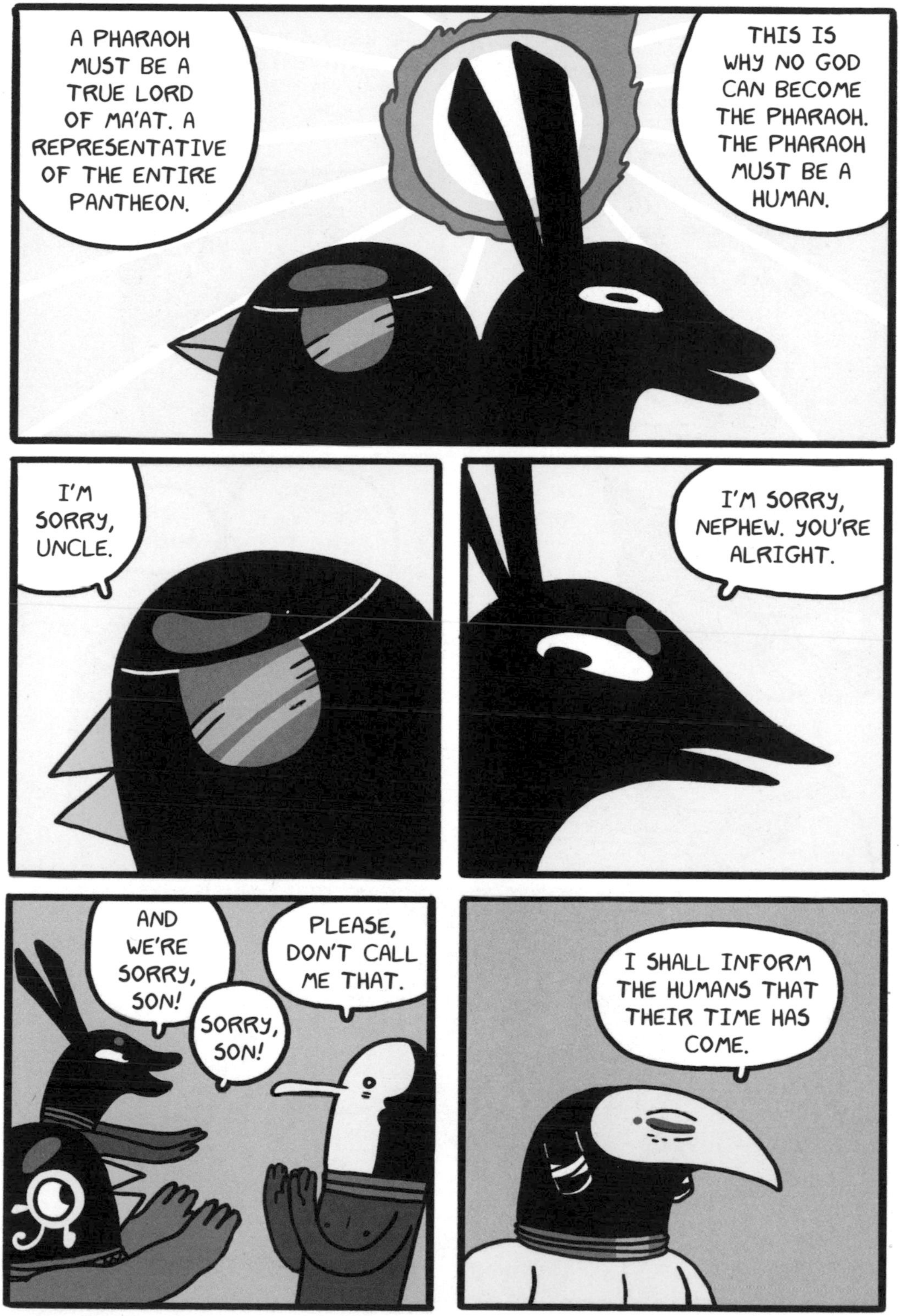
A PHARAOH MUST BE A TRUE LORD OF MA'AT. A REPRESENTATIVE OF THE ENTIRE PANTHEON.
THIS IS WHY NO GOD CAN BECOME THE PHARAOH. THE PHARAOH MUST BE A HUMAN.
I'M SORRY, UNCLE.
I'M SORRY, NEPHEW. YOU'RE ALRIGHT.
AND WE'RE SORRY, SON!
SORRY, SON!
PLEASE, DON'T CALL ME THAT.
I SHALL INFORM THE HUMANS THAT THEIR TIME HAS COME.

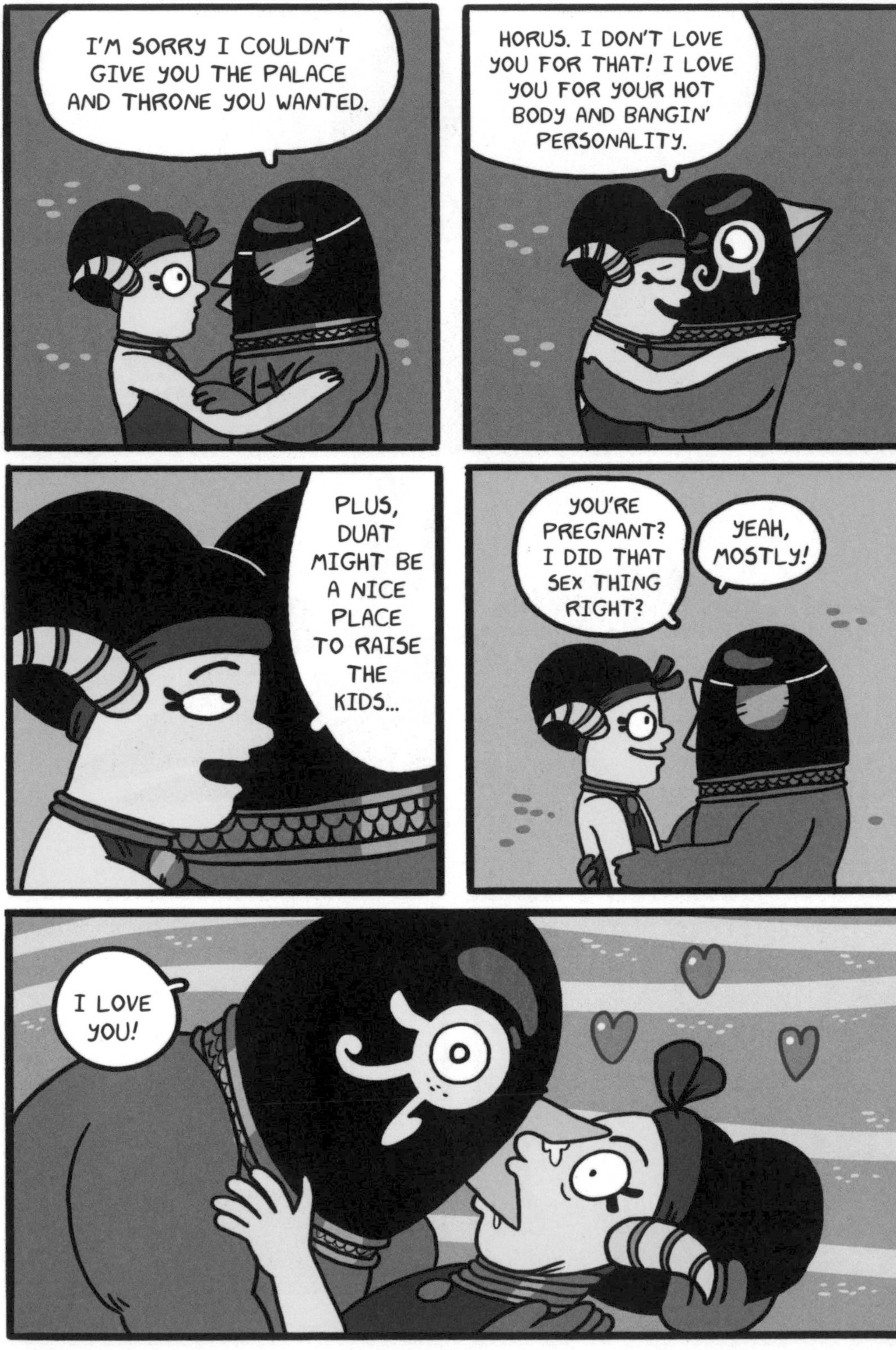
I'M SORRY I COULDN'T GIVE YOU THE PALACE AND THRONE YOU WANTED.
HORUS. I DON'T LOVE YOU FOR THAT! I LOVE YOU FOR YOUR HOT BODY AND BANGIN' PERSONALITY.
PLUS, DUAT MIGHT BE A NICE PLACE TO RAISE THE KIDS...
YOU'RE PREGNANT? I DID THAT SEX THING RIGHT?
YEAH, MOSTLY!
I LOVE YOU!

CHAPTER TWELVE

★ ★ ★ CORONATION ★ ★ ★

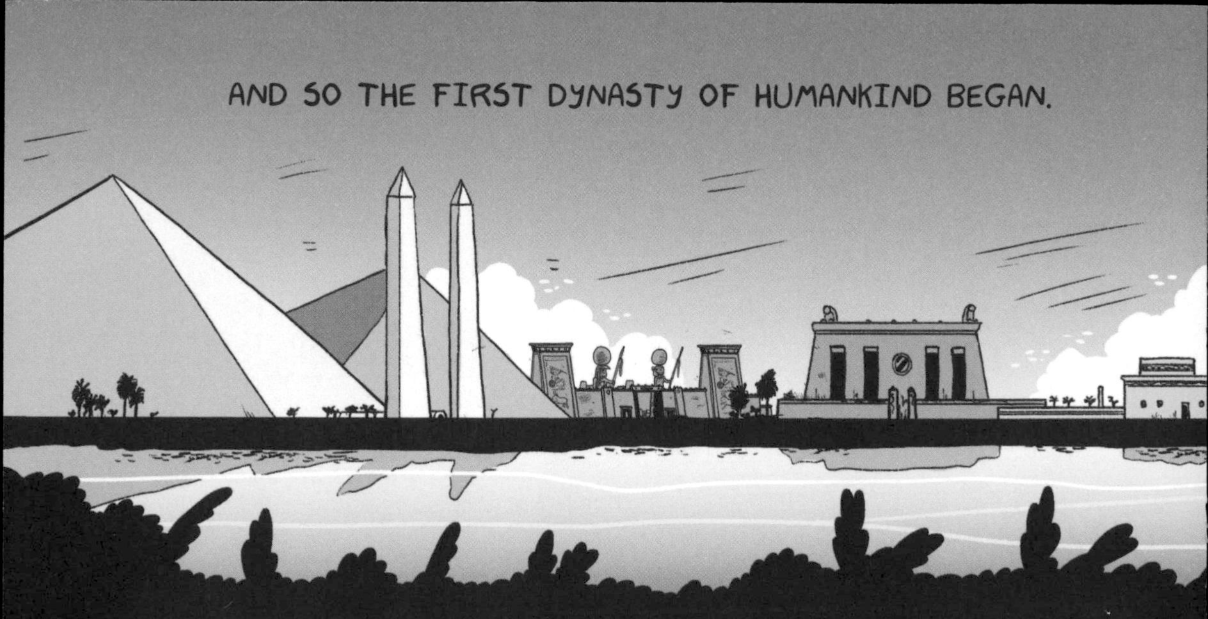
AND SO THE FIRST DYNASTY OF HUMANKIND BEGAN.

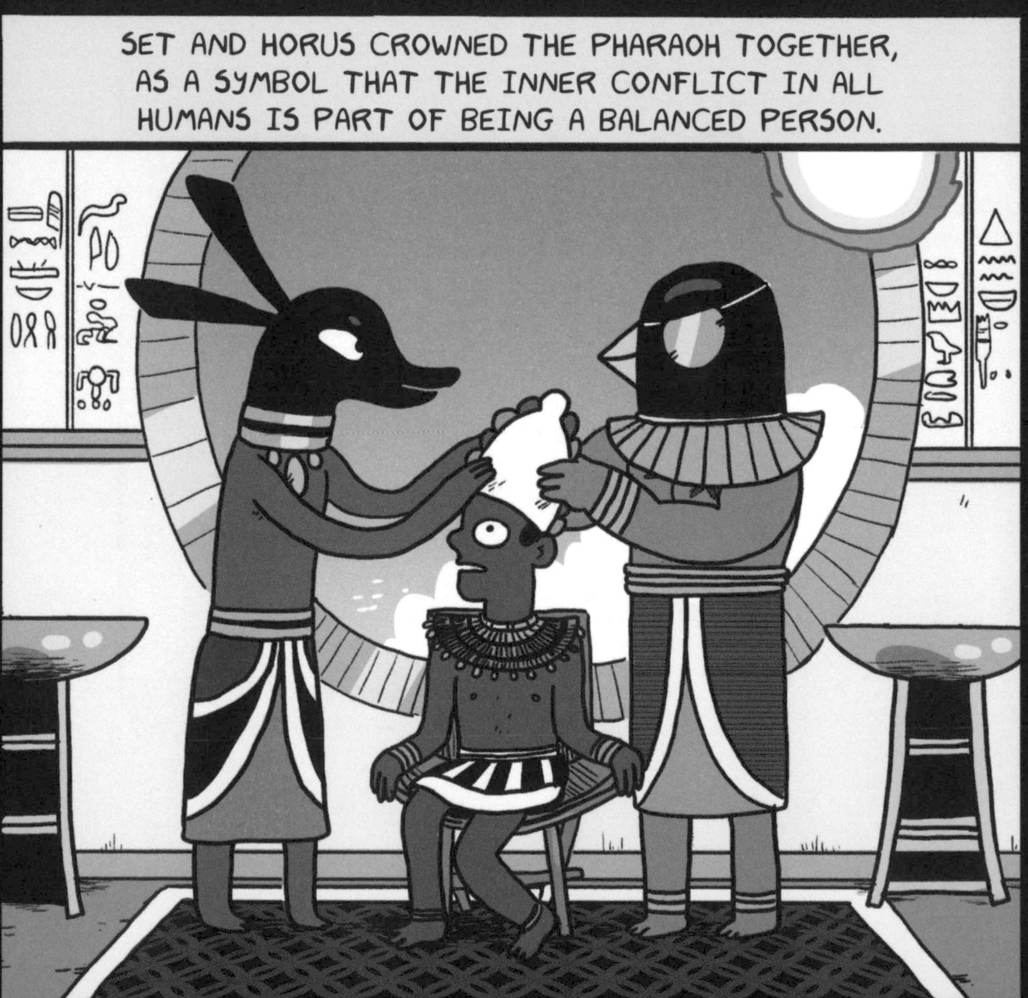
SET AND HORUS CROWNED THE PHARAOH TOGETHER, AS A SYMBOL THAT THE INNER CONFLICT IN ALL HUMANS IS PART OF BEING A BALANCED PERSON.

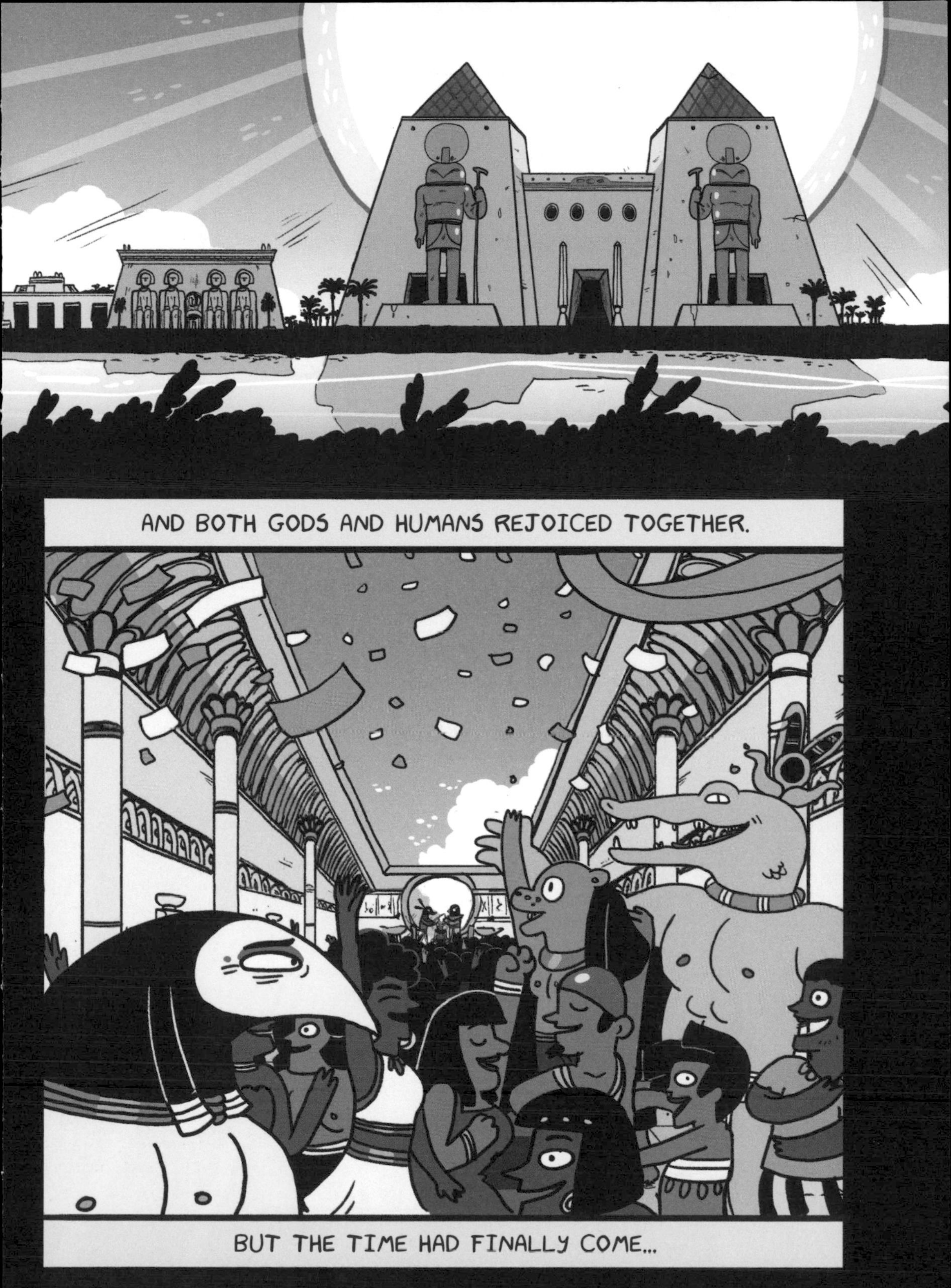
AND BOTH GODS AND HUMANS REJOICED TOGETHER.
BUT THE TIME HAD FINALLY COME...

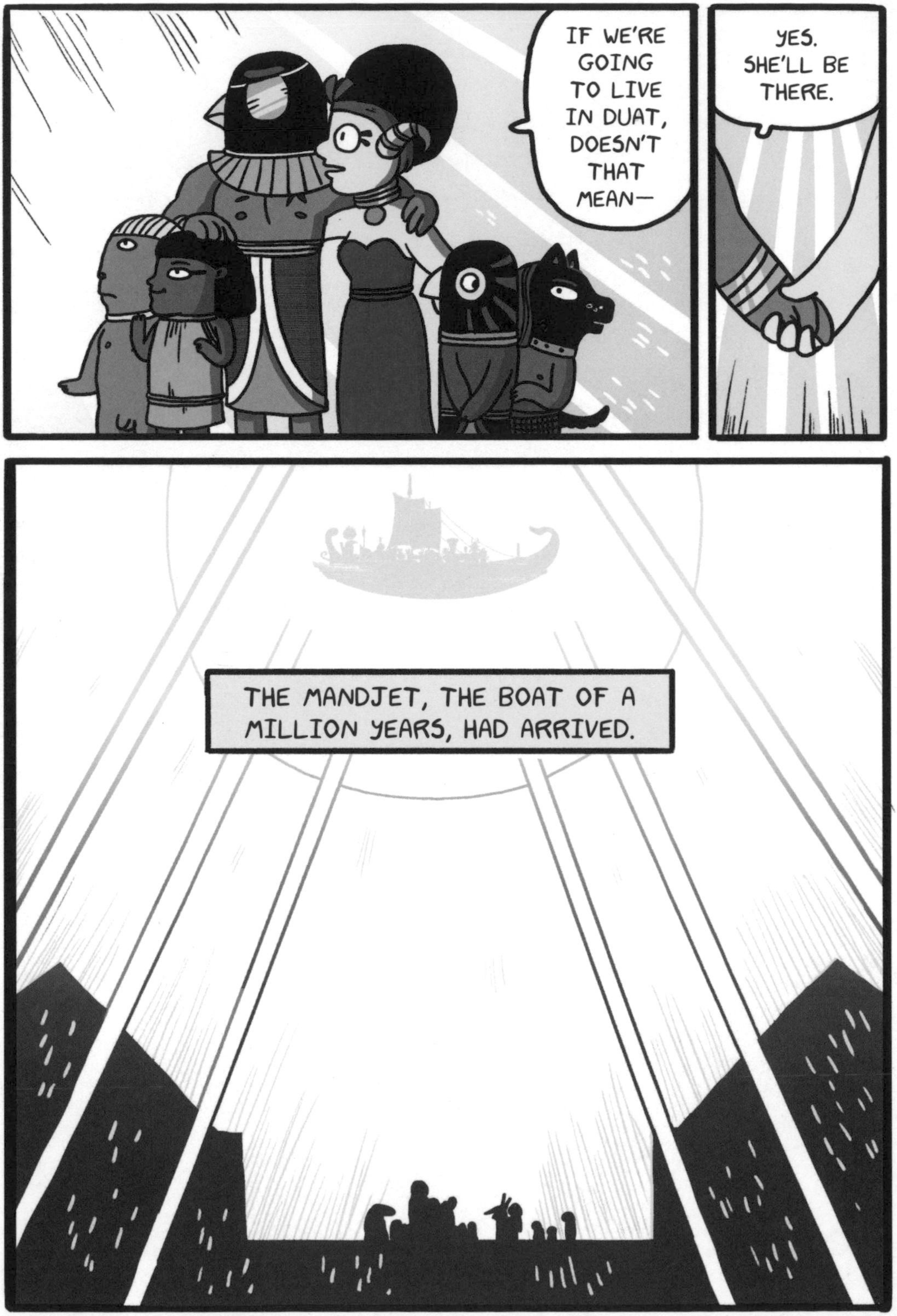
IF WE'RE GOING TO LIVE IN DUAT, DOESN'T THAT MEAN—
YES. SHE'LL BE THERE.
THE MANDJET, THE BOAT OF A MILLION YEARS, HAD ARRIVED.

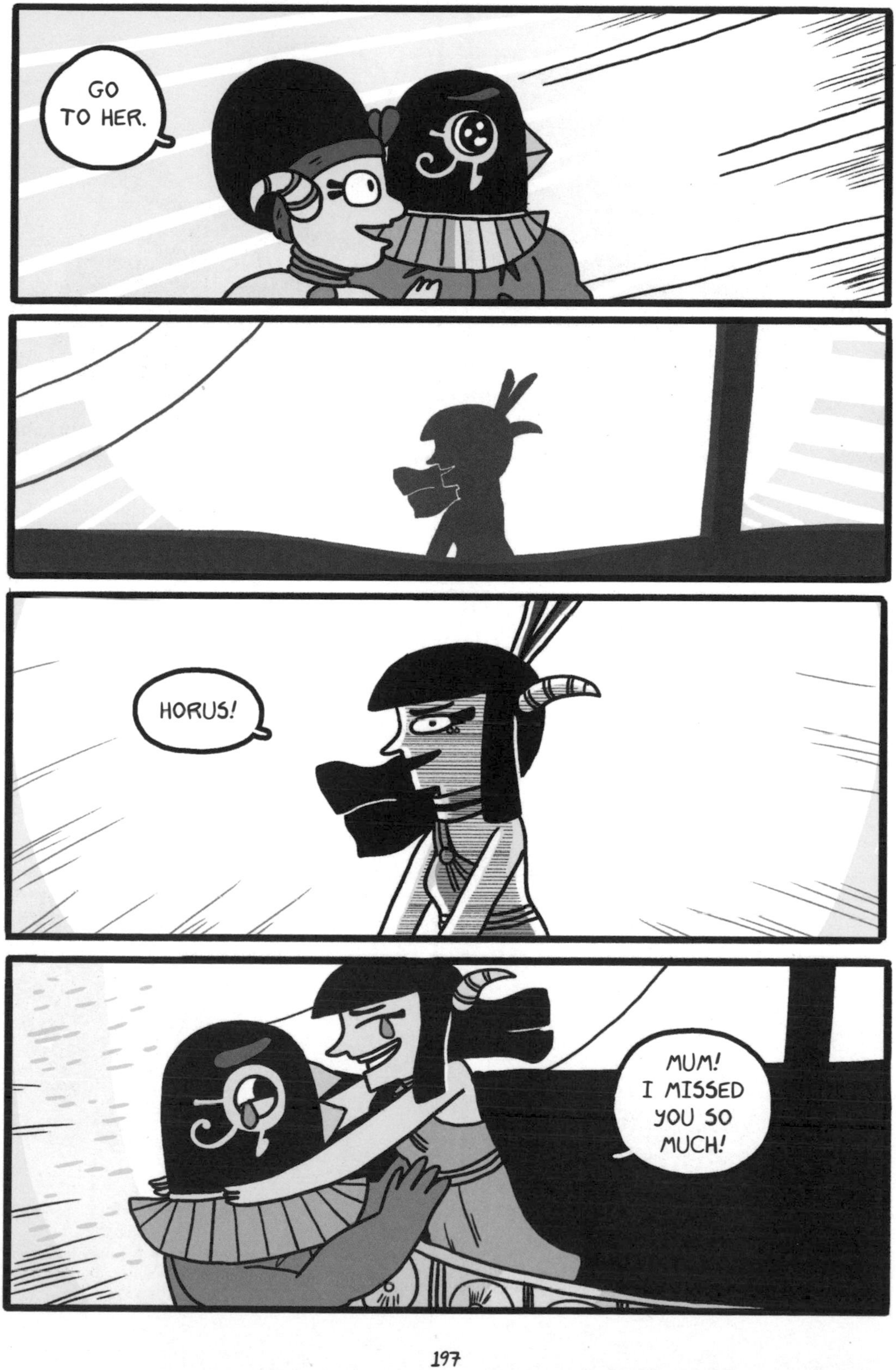
GO TO HER.
HORUS!
MUM! I MISSED YOU SO MUCH!

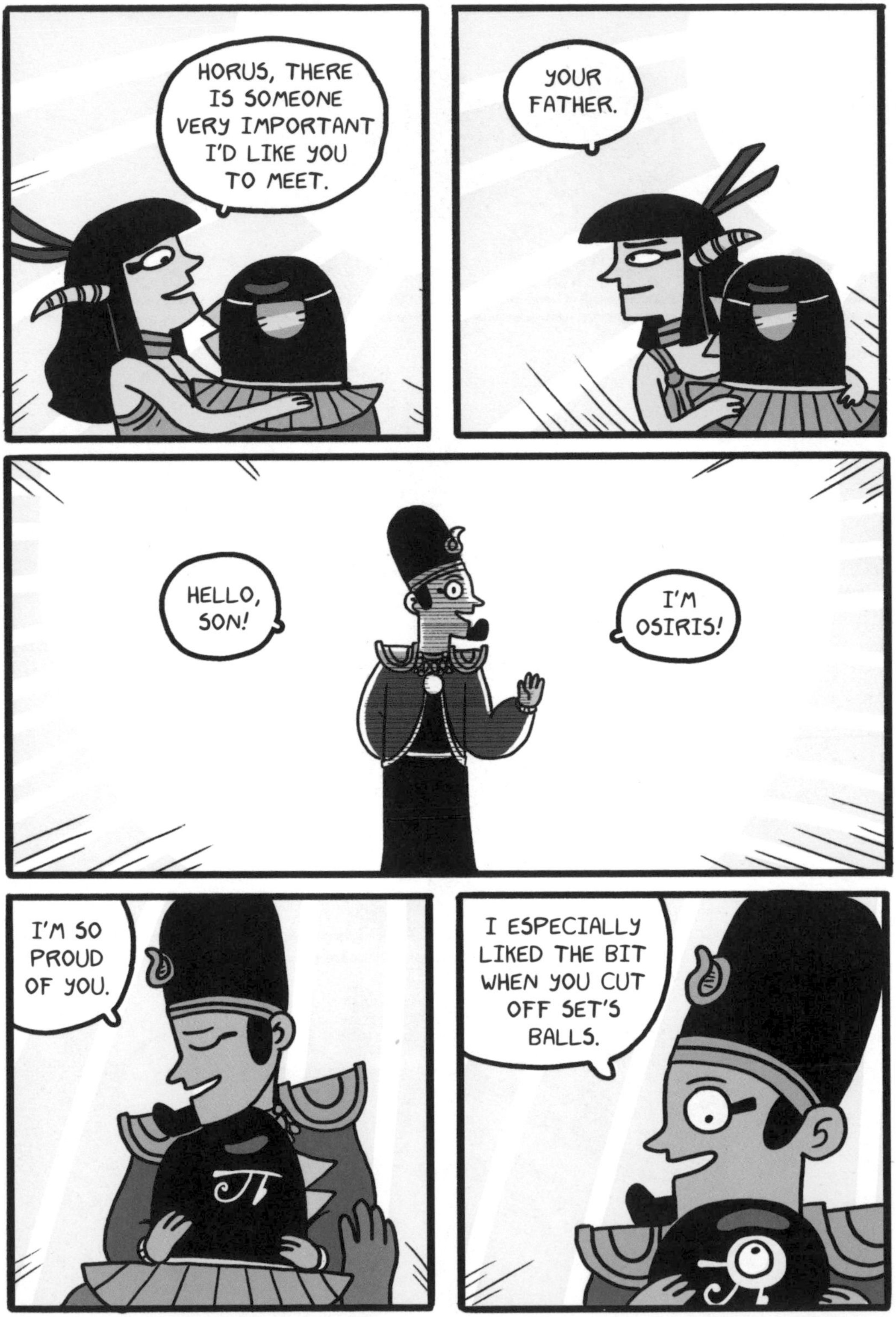
HORUS, THERE IS SOMEONE VERY IMPORTANT I'D LIKE YOU TO MEET.
YOUR FATHER.
HELLO, SON!
I'M OSIRIS!
I'M SO PROUD OF YOU.
I ESPECIALLY LIKED THE BIT WHEN YOU CUT OFF SET'S BALLS.

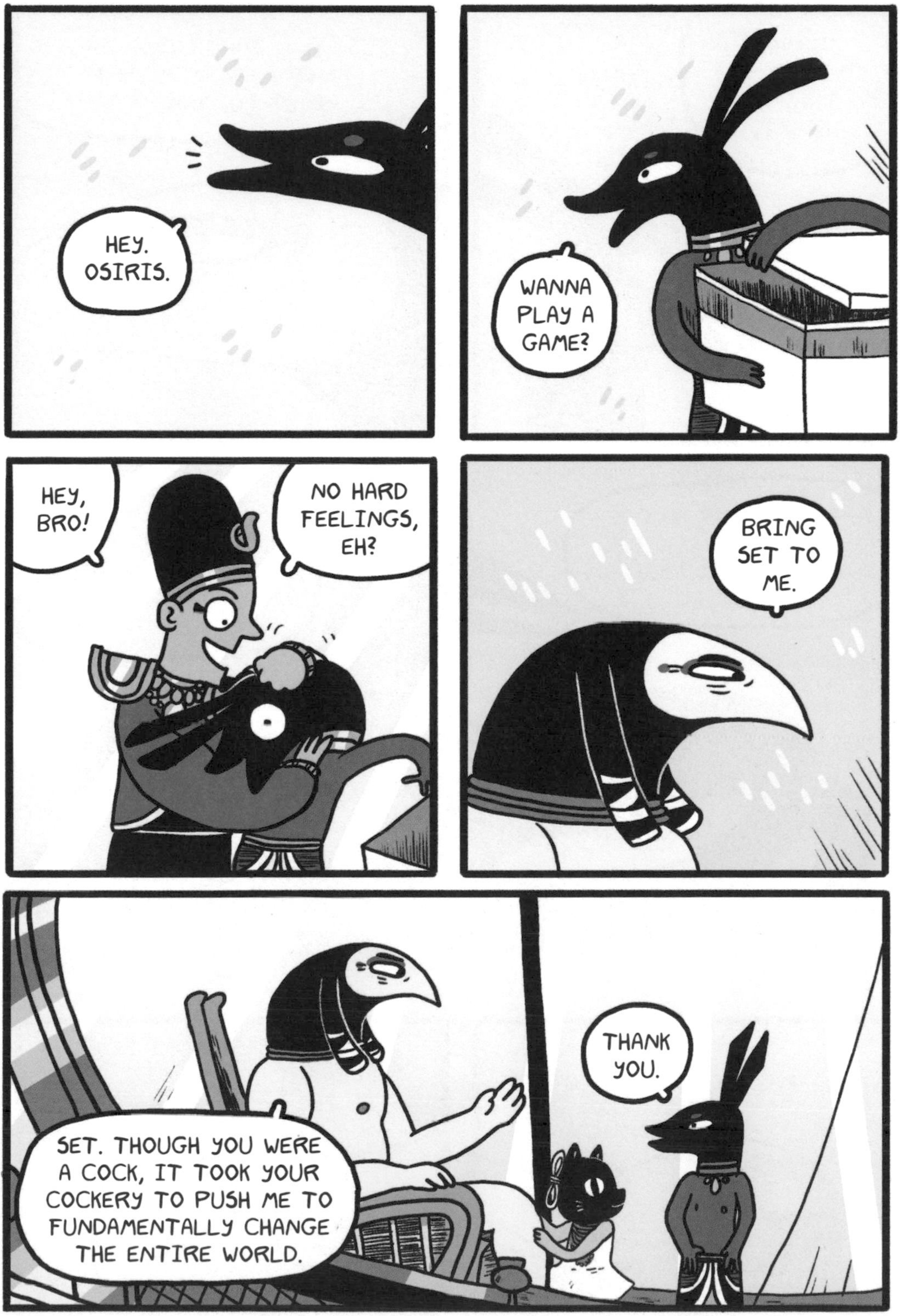
HEY. OSIRIS.
WANNA PLAY A GAME?
HEY, BRO!
NO HARD FEELINGS, EH?
BRING SET TO ME.
SET. THOUGH YOU WERE A COCK, IT TOOK YOUR COCKERY TO PUSH ME TO FUNDAMENTALLY CHANGE THE ENTIRE WORLD.
THANK YOU.

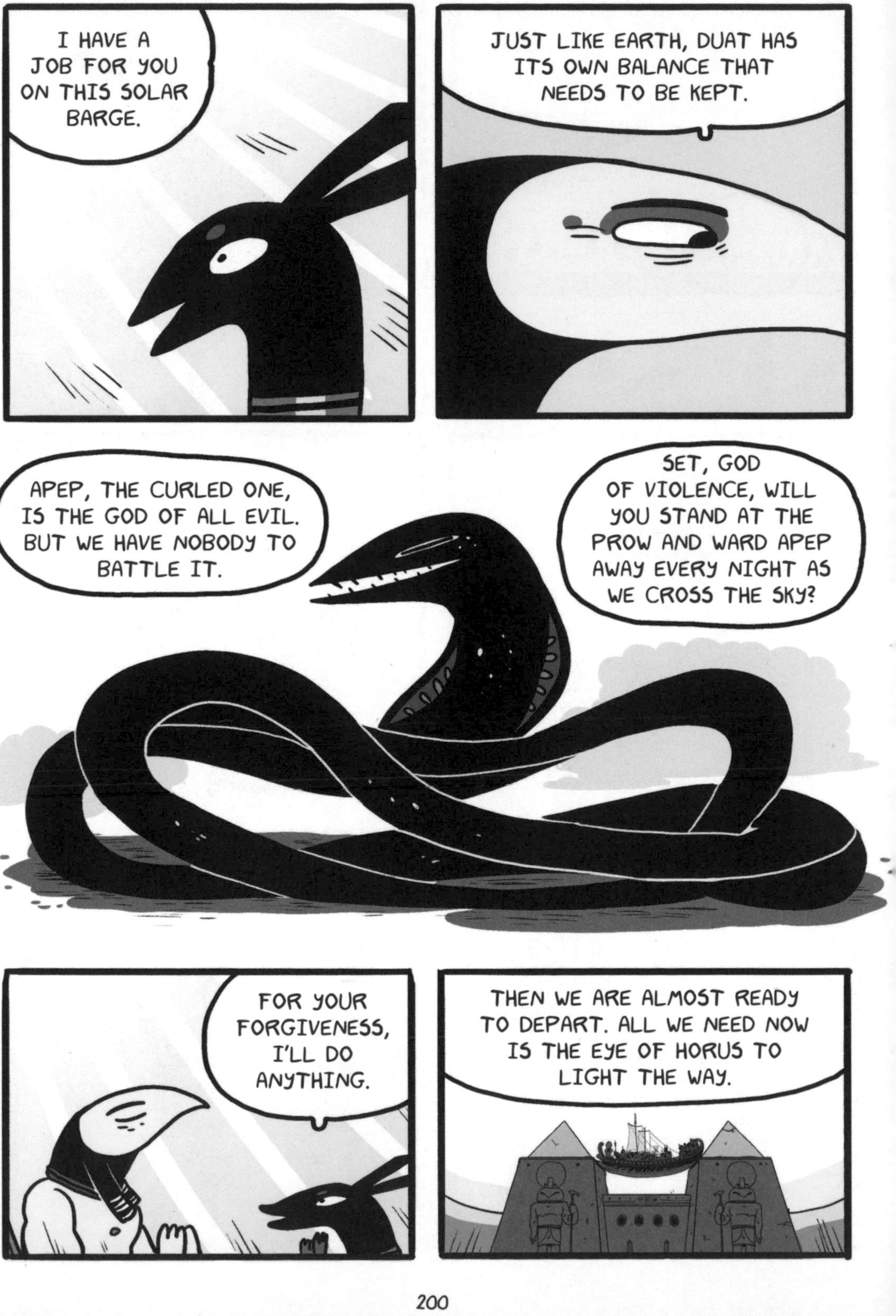
I HAVE A JOB FOR YOU ON THIS SOLAR BARGE.
JUST LIKE EARTH, DUAT HAS ITS OWN BALANCE THAT NEEDS TO BE KEPT.
APEP, THE CURLED ONE, IS THE GOD OF ALL EVIL. BUT WE HAVE NOBODY TO BATTLE IT.
SET, GOD OF VIOLENCE, WILL YOU STAND AT THE PROW AND WARD APEP AWAY EVERY NIGHT AS WE CROSS THE SKY?
FOR YOUR FORGIVENESS, I'LL DO ANYTHING.
THEN WE ARE ALMOST READY TO DEPART. ALL WE NEED NOW IS THE EYE OF HORUS TO LIGHT THE WAY.

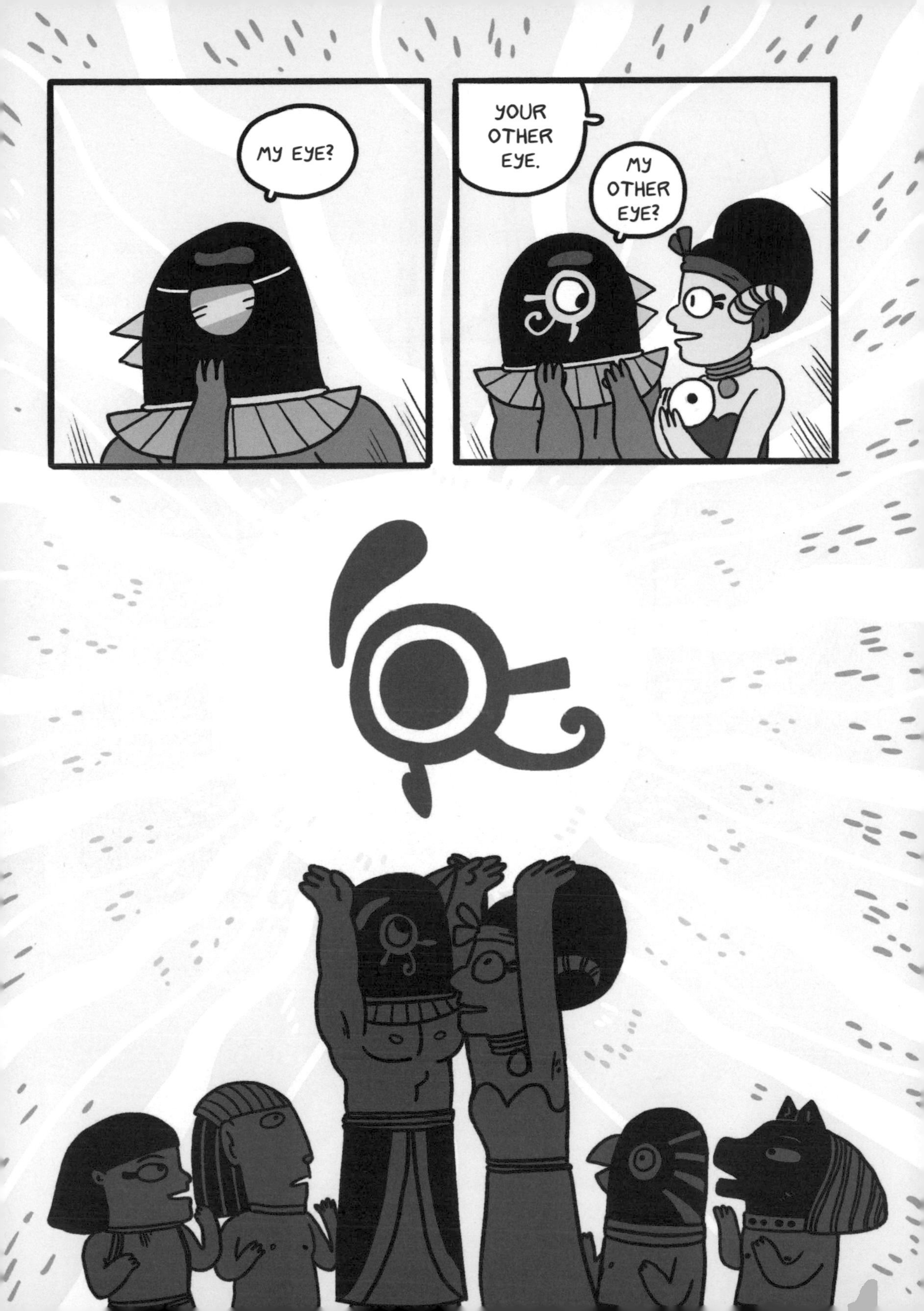
MY EYE?
YOUR OTHER EYE.
MY OTHER EYE?

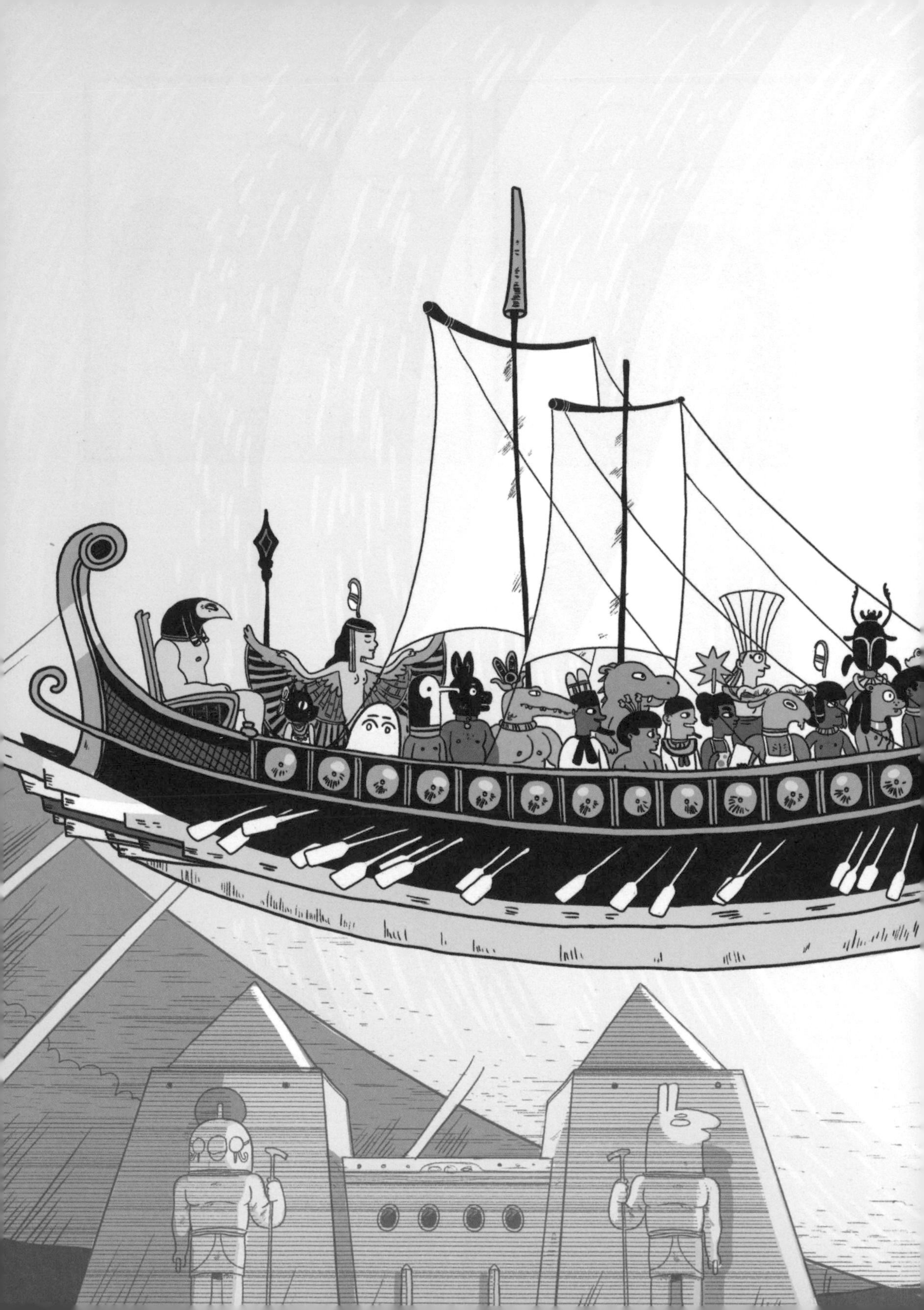

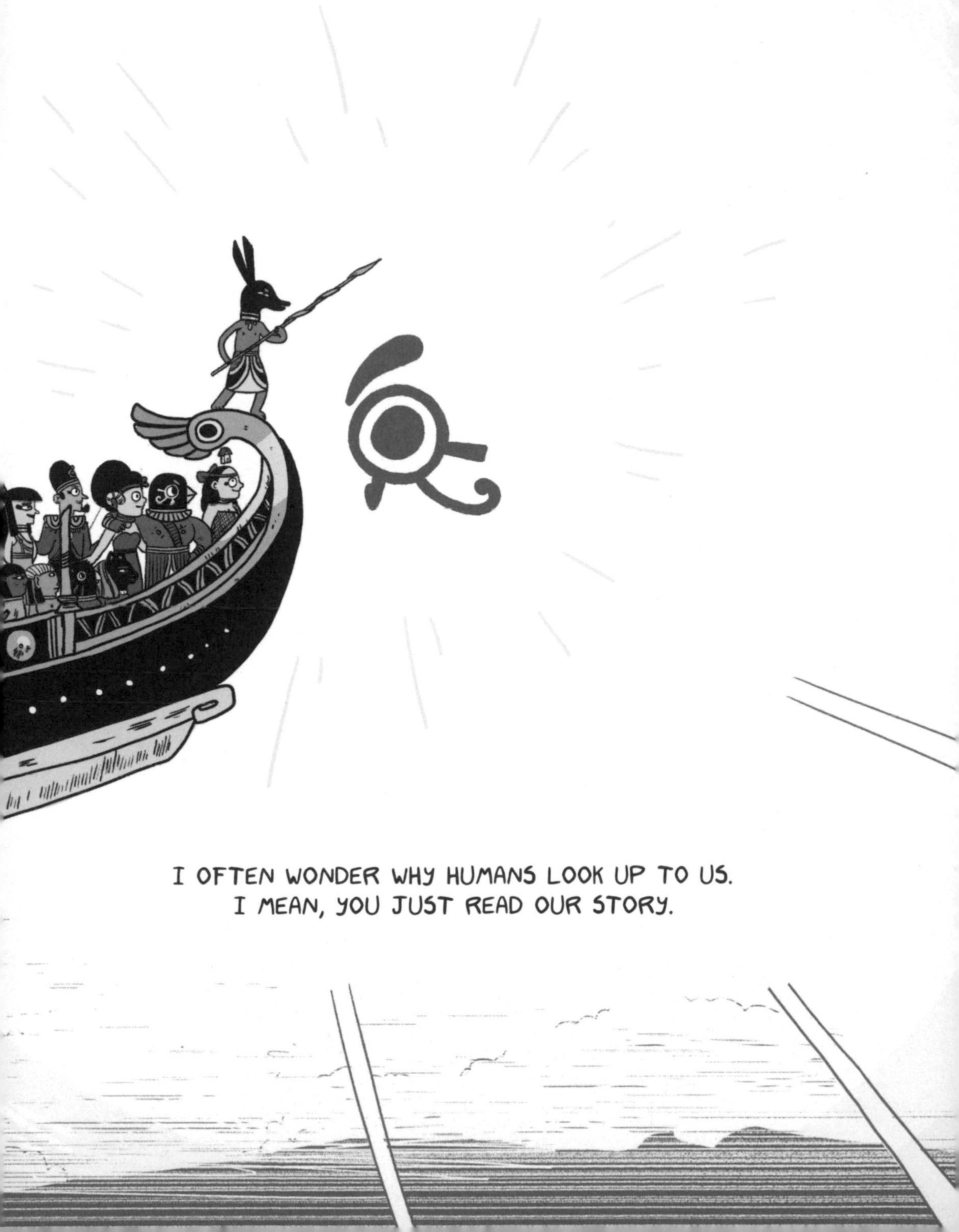
I OFTEN WONDER WHY HUMANS LOOK UP TO US.
I MEAN, YOU JUST READ OUR STORY.

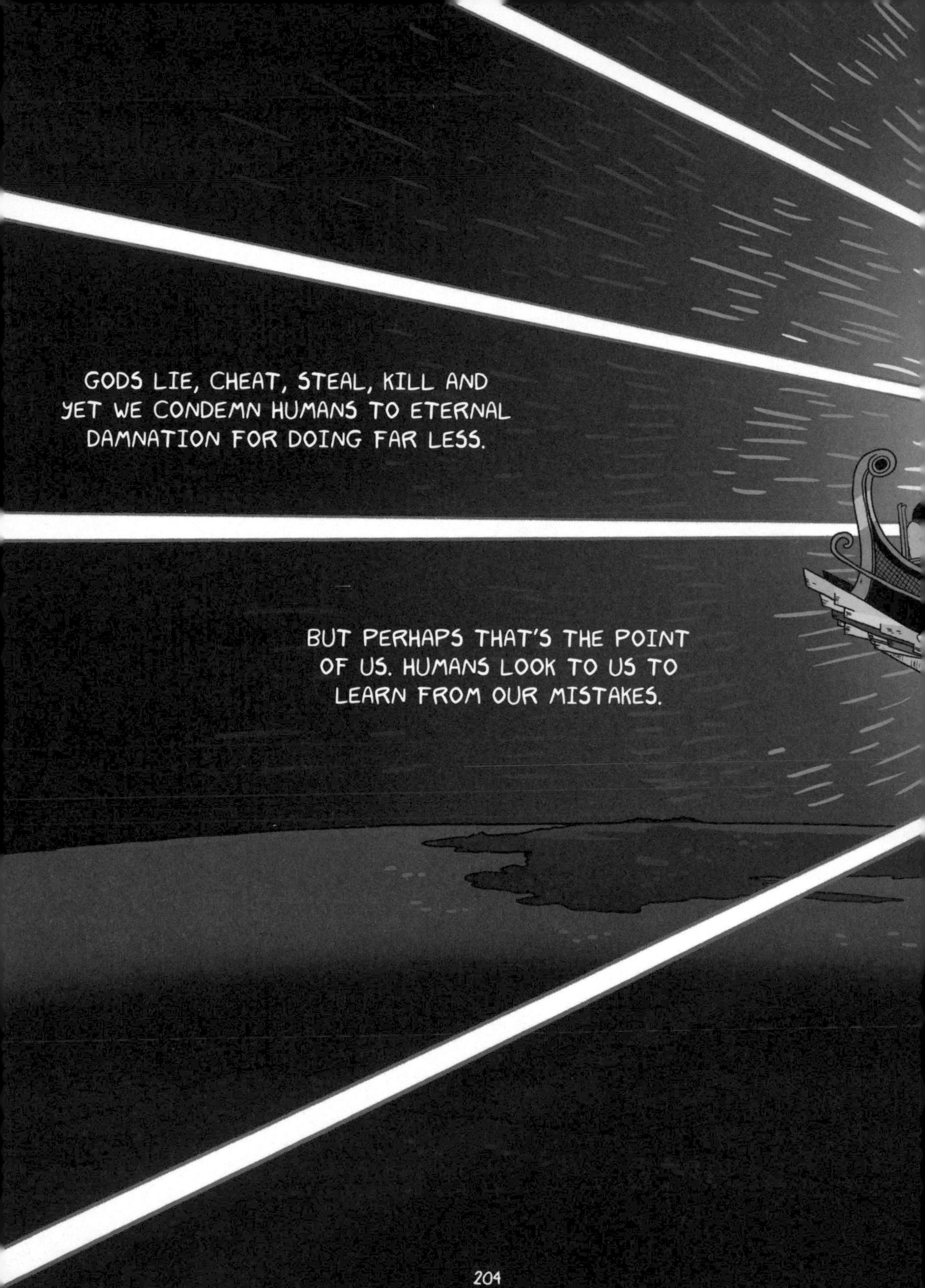
GODS LIE, CHEAT, STEAL, KILL AND YET WE CONDEMN HUMANS TO ETERNAL DAMNATION FOR DOING FAR LESS.
BUT PERHAPS THAT'S THE POINT OF US. HUMANS LOOK TO US TO LEARN FROM OUR MISTAKES.

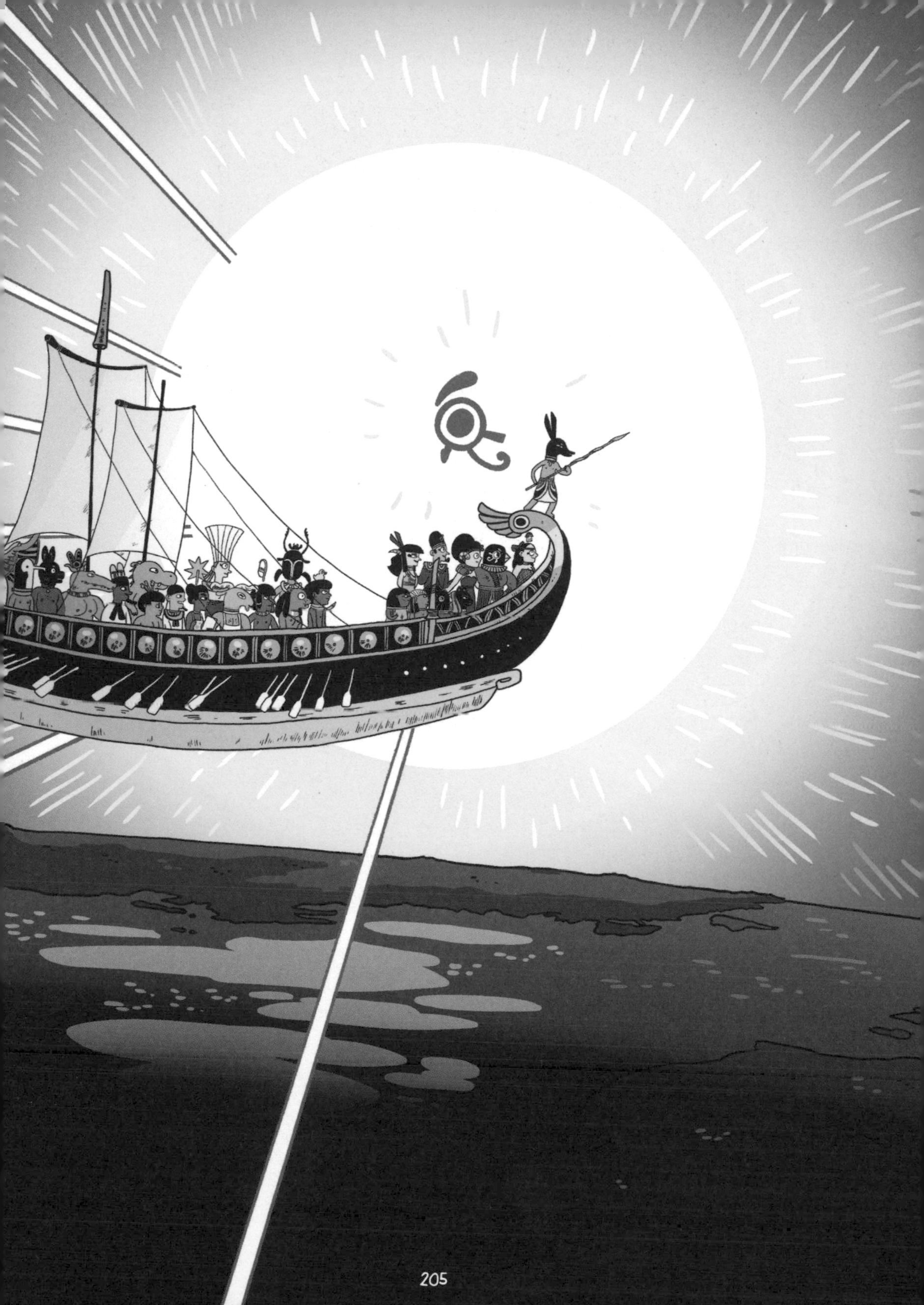

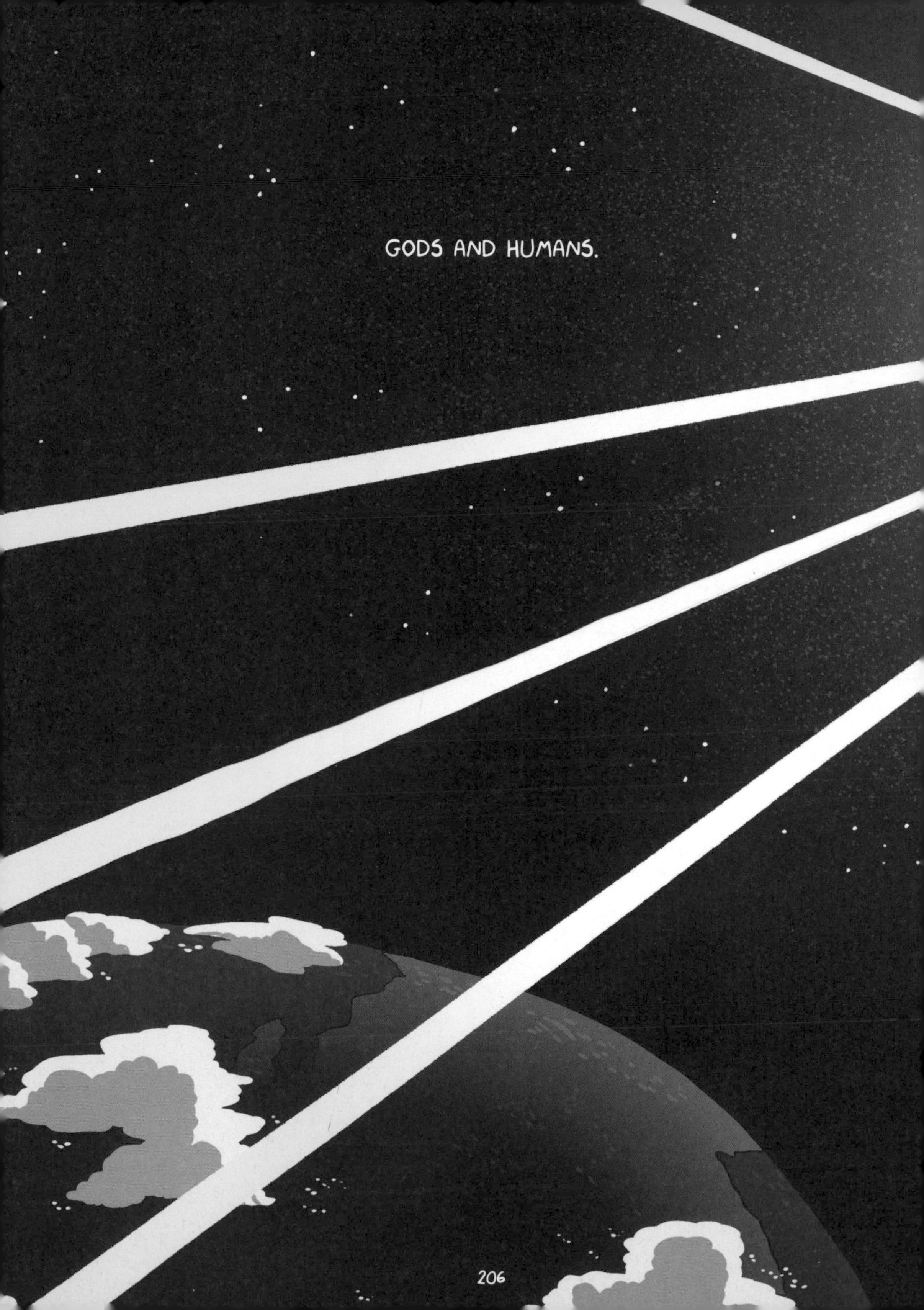
GODS AND HUMANS.

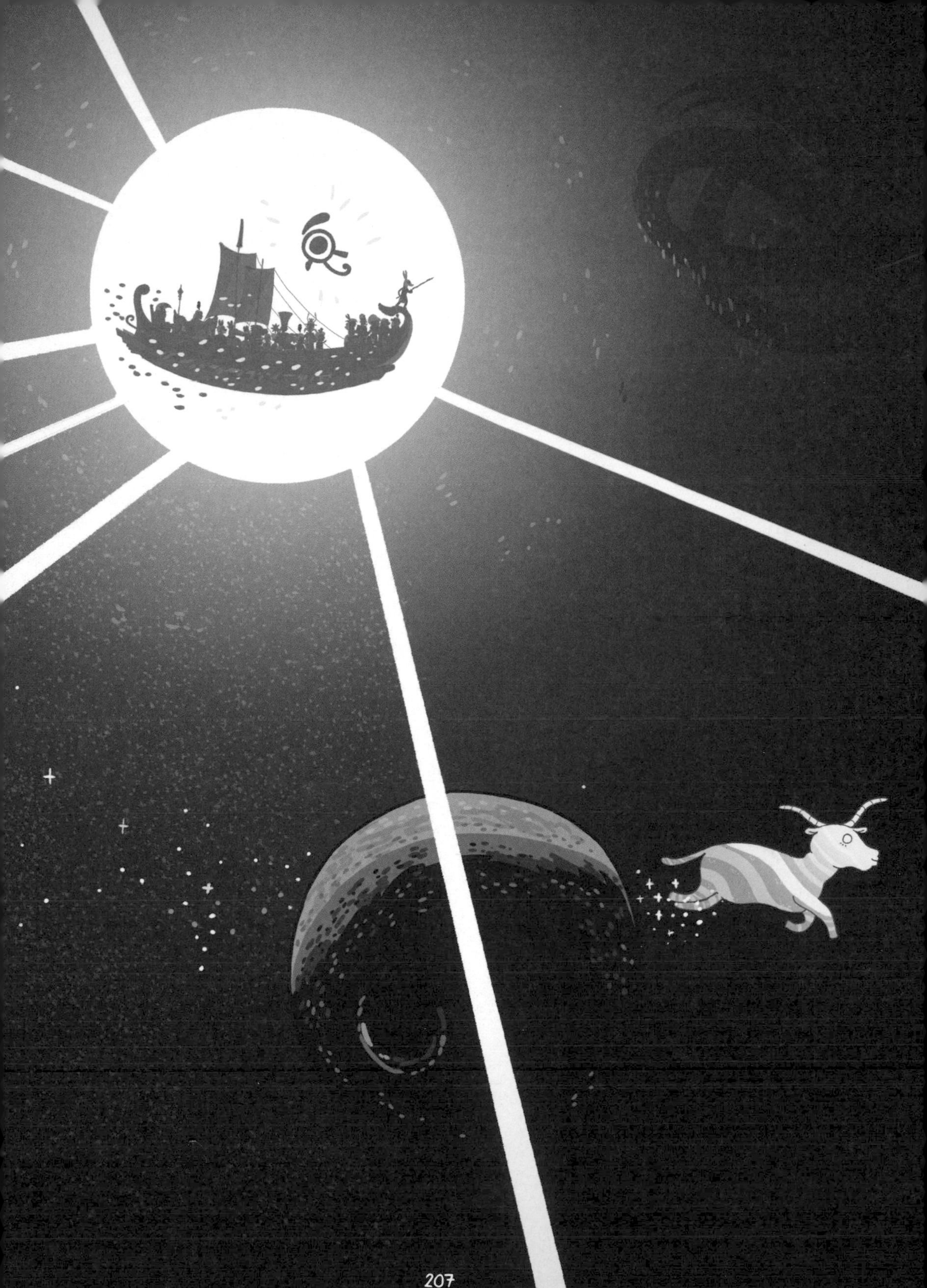

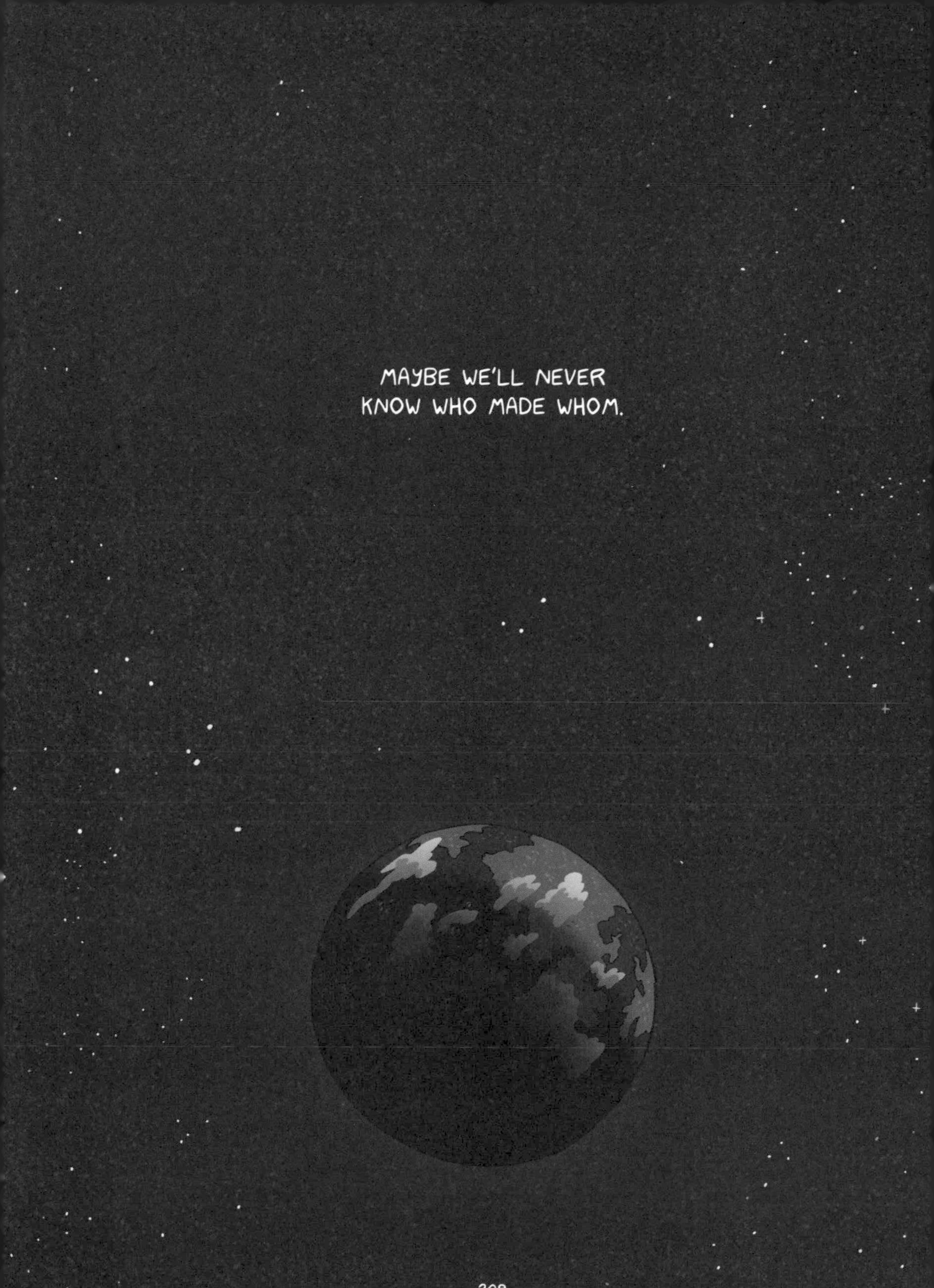
MAYBE WE'LL NEVER KNOW WHO MADE WHOM.

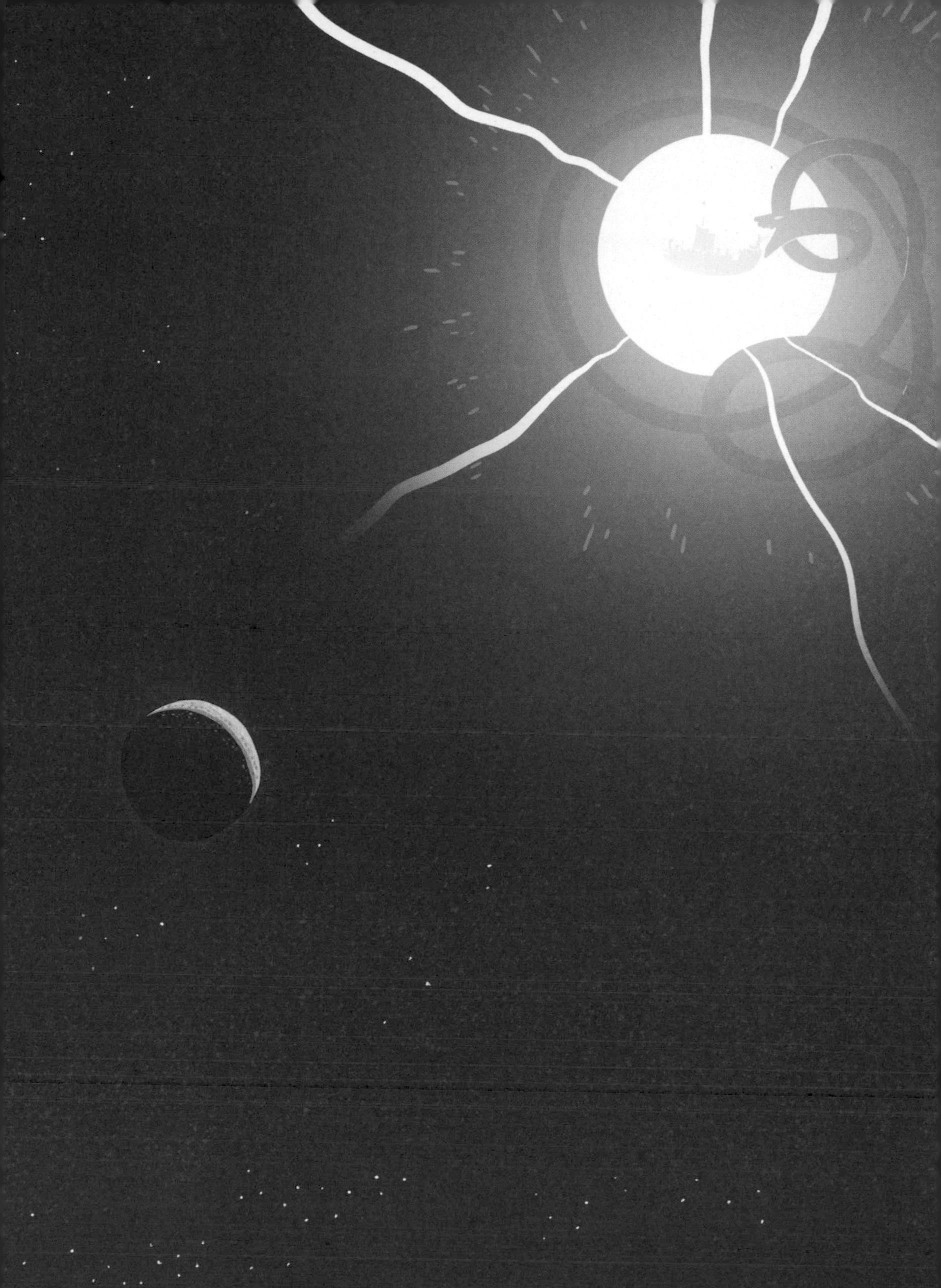

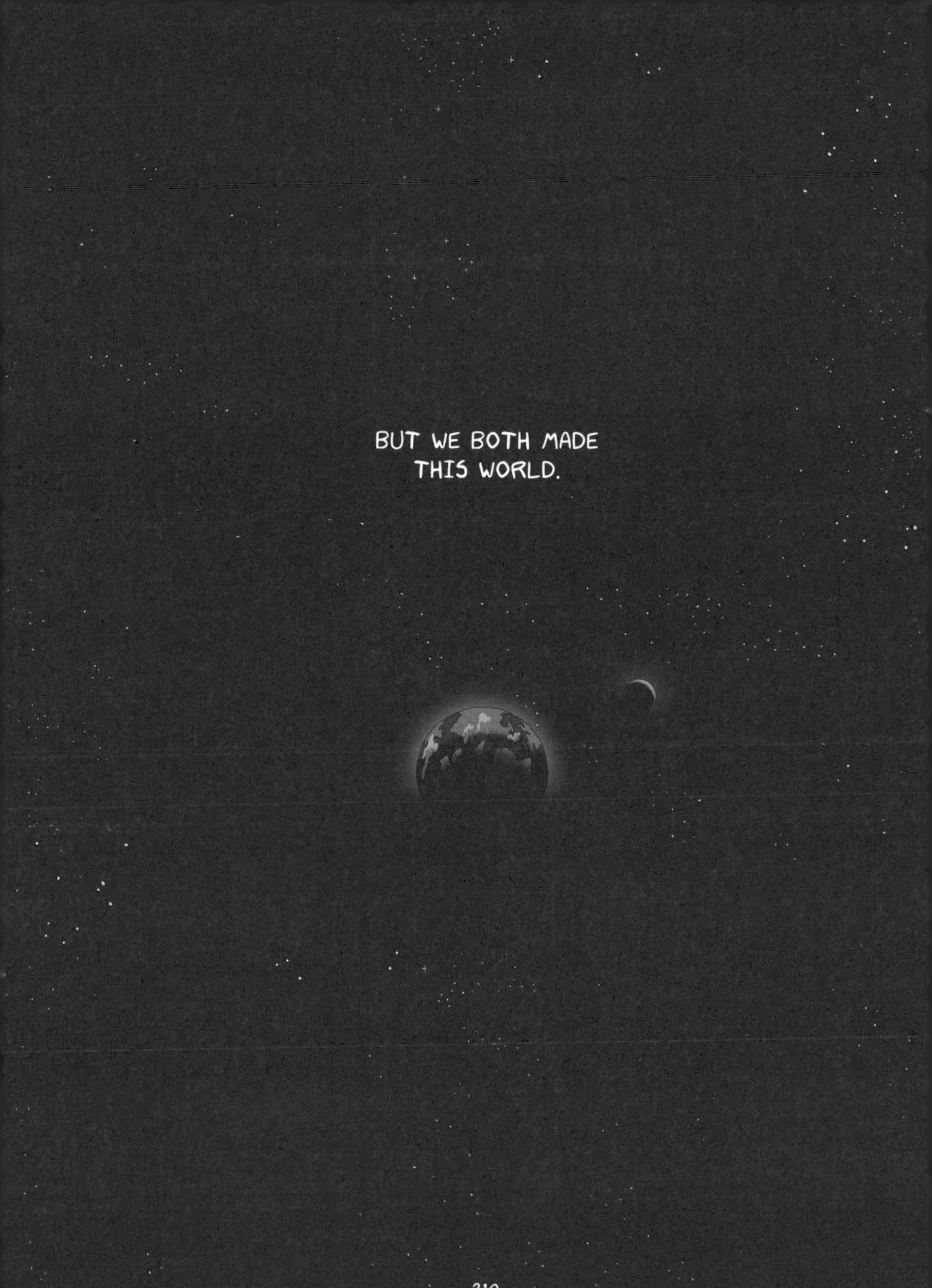
BUT WE BOTH MADE THIS WORLD.

THE END

AUTHOR'S NOTE

* * * * * * *

PANTHEON IS MY ATTEMPT TO TELL THE
MOST FAITHFUL AND ENTERTAINING VERSION
OF THE GREAT EGYPTIAN MYTHS AS POSSIBLE.
HOWEVER, 'FAITHFUL', WHEN IT COMES TO
ANCIENT MYTHOLOGY, IS A TRICKY WORD.

THERE IS NO DEFINITIVE VERSION
OF THIS STORY. IT WAS ASSEMBLED BY
ARCHAEOLOGISTS FROM SOURCES THAT RANGED
GREATLY IN TIME AND PLACE, AND CONTAINS
COMPLEX SYMBOLISM THAT HELD GREAT
IMPORTANCE TO ANCIENT EGYPTIANS. BUT IT
WAS NEVER MEANT TO BE TAKEN COMPLETELY
LITERALLY — IT WAS SUPPOSED TO BE FUNNY
AND ENTERTAINING, AND THAT IS HOW IT IS
PRESENTED HERE. BY INJECTING THE HUMOUR
BACK INTO THE TEXT, I WANTED TO CAPTURE
A MORE AUTHENTIC VERSION OF THE MYTH.

I HOPE YOU ENJOYED MY RESURRECTION
OF THIS FANTASTIC TALE!

— HAMISH

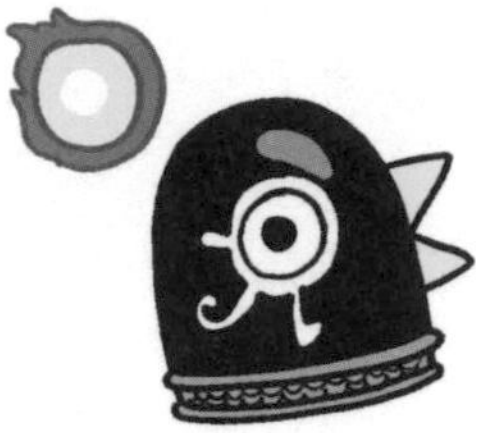

FOR JUSTIN

IF YOUR BROTHER EVER CUT YOU INTO 42 PIECES AND SPREAD YOU ACROSS EGYPT, I WOULD RECOVER YOU, REVIVE YOU, AND THEN CONCEIVE A BIRD-HEADED CHILD WITH YOU WHO WOULD AVENGE YOUR DEATH.

THIS IS A SECOND EDITION.
FIRST EDITION PUBLISHED IN 2017 BY NOBROW LTD.
27 WESTGATE STREET, LONDON E8 3RL.

PUBLISHED IN THE US BY NOBROW (US) INC.
PRINTED IN POLAND ON FSC® CERTIFIED PAPER.

ISBN: 978-1-910620-20-5

MIX
Paper from responsible sources
FSC® C001693

ORDER FROM WWW.NOBROW.NET

* * * * * * *

HAMISH STEELE GREW UP IN GLASTONBURY, SURROUNDED BY MYTHS, FOLKTALES, AND CRYSTAL SHOPS. SINCE GRADUATING IN 2013, HE'S WORKED AS AN ANIMATION DIRECTOR IN LONDON FOR BLINK INDUSTRIES AND IS THE CREATOR OF THE WEBCOMIC DEADENDIA. HAMISH HAS ALWAYS BEEN FASCINATED BY GODS AND HOPES ONE DAY TO BECOME ONE.

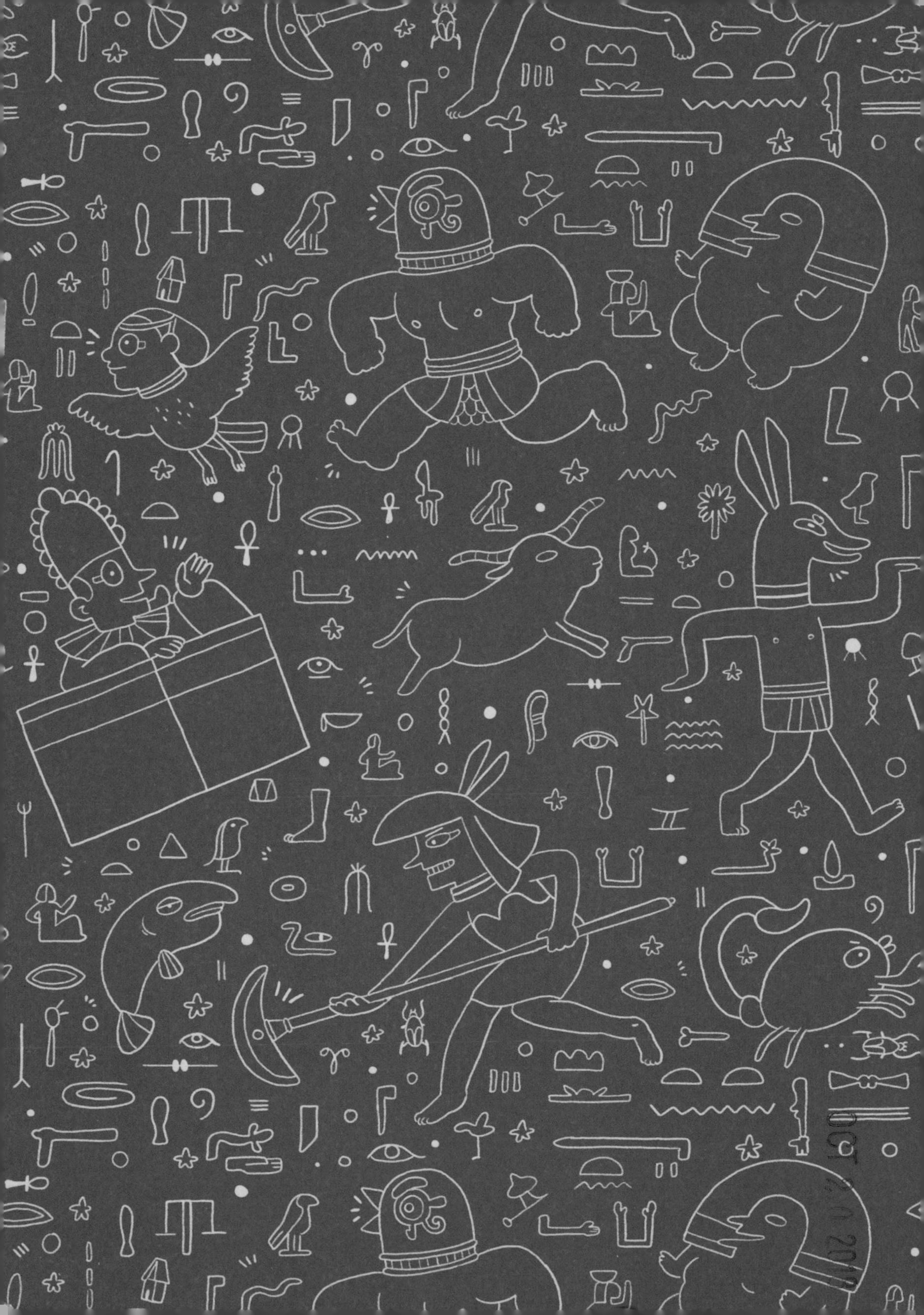